Your
Chinese
Horoscope

for Each and
Every Year

Your
Chinese
Horoscope

for Each and
Every Year

NEIL
SOMERVILLE

Thorsons

Thorsons
An imprint of HarperCollins*Publishers*
1 London Bridge Street
London SE1 9GF

HarperCollins*Publishers*
Macken House, 39/40 Mayor Street Upper,
Dublin 1, D01 C9W8, Ireland

www.harpercollins.co.uk

First published by Thorsons 2017

© Neil Somerville 2017

Neil Somerville asserts the moral right to
be identified as the author of this work

A catalogue record of this book is
available from the British Library

ISBN 978-0-00-819105-4

Printed and bound in the UK using 100% Renewable Electricity at CPI Group (UK) Ltd

About the Author

Neil Somerville is one of the most widely read writers in the West on Chinese horoscopes. His 30-year annual series, *Your Chinese Horoscope*, enjoyed an international following and was translated into many languages. He is also the author of the bestselling books *Chinese Love Signs* (Thorsons, 2000), *Chinese Success Signs* (Thorsons, 2001), *The Answers* (Element, 2004) and *Cat Wisdom* (Thorsons, 2017).

Neil has always felt that much can be learned from the wisdom of the East and, as a hobby, enjoys writing haiku. A keen walker and traveller, he lives with his wife in Berkshire, England, and has a son and a daughter and far too many books.

TO ROS, RICHARD AND EMILY

As we march through life,
we each have our hopes, our ambitions and our dreams.

Sometimes fate and circumstance will assist us,
sometimes we will struggle and despair,
but march we must.

For it is those who keep going,
and who keep their aspirations alive,
who stand the greatest chance of securing what they want.

March determinedly,
and your determination will, in some way, be rewarded.

Neil Somerville

Contents

Acknowledgements

The world of a writer is both wonderful and strange, and I would like to give a special thanks to my family, Ros, Richard and Emily, for their great support and for putting up with the mountain of paperwork I produce and trail of notes I leave in my wake. And thank you too to my parents, Peggy and Don, for all they did.

Thanks too to Carolyn Thorne, my editor at HarperCollins, for her encouragement and support, as well as to Lizzie Henry for all her work over the years. A special mention as well to Barbara Booker for her thoughtfulness and faith, and to Barbara Smith, who has kindly given me an opinion on many an occasion.

I am also grateful to the many who have helped me in my study of Chinese horoscopes, including those who first awakened my interest in the wisdom of the East. And I acknowledge too the work of other writers on Chinese horoscopes, all of whom have added to the subject and shared their insights. Particularly to Derek Walters, Theodora Lau and Suzanne White, all of whose work I recommend, and other luminaries, thank you.

And to you who are now reading these words, thank you for taking the time and for your interest. And wherever you may be reading and at whatever time, I hope that in some way this book will help and encourage you as well as alert you to the specialness and potential that are within you.

Introduction

Whether in indicating portents or highlighting strengths and weaknesses, Chinese horoscopes offer a timeless wisdom from which we can all profit. Although their origins date back to at least 2637 BC, when Emperor Huang Ti introduced the Chinese calendar, it is only recently that the subject has gained prominence in the West. As a result, many are now familiar with their animal sign and look forward to reading what each Chinese year has in store. It is a fascinating subject and a helpful one.

For those new to Chinese horoscopes, the Chinese year is based on the lunar year, which starts in late January or early February. Each of the Chinese years is named after an animal and there is a legend offering an explanation for this. It describes how one Chinese new year, the Buddha invited all the animals in the kingdom to a party. Only 12 showed up – the Rat, Ox, Tiger, Rabbit, Dragon, Snake, Horse, Goat, Monkey, Rooster, Dog and Pig. In gratitude, the Buddha named a year after each of the animals and said that those born in that year would have some of the personality of that animal.

Another legend offers an explanation for the order of the years. According to this, the animals had to race across a river and the order they finished in would be the order of the years. The Rat, very much an opportunist and determined to win, craftily rode on the back of the Ox and, just as the Ox reached the riverbank, leaped off and ran ahead, so winning the race. This is said to be why the Rat starts the cycle of years and the Ox is next, followed by the other 10 animals. The Pig, who is known as a great finisher, aptly came in last.

To discover which animal year you were born in, you will need to look up your year of birth in the table of years that follows. If born in 1988, for example, you were born in the Year of the Dragon – and born under the sign of luck. However, if your birthday falls in January or February, do carefully check the dates to see in which year your birthdate actually falls.

Once you have identified your sign, you can look up the traits of the animal in the relevant chapter. Although there are many variations, which can be studied in more detail by considering elements and ascendants (described in the appendix), it is remarkable how Chinese horoscopes can indicate our true natures. Whether these show the loyalty and sense of duty seen in so many born under the sign of the Dog or the versatility, quick wits and memory skills of those born in the Monkey year, Chinese horoscopes can be illuminating. In addition to the main traits described in each chapter, there are also special tips to help each sign be at their best, together with inspirational quotes from people born under that sign.

The subject of relationships is also a fascinating one and each chapter contains a guide to how each sign relates to the other signs. Some signs are considered to be compatible and others complete opposites, but there are again many exceptions. While, for example, a Chinese proverb decrees, 'The Ox and the Horse cannot share the same stable', I am sure there are some born under these two signs who love each other very much and live happily together.

The main part of this book is, however, devoted to horoscopes, which are based on the trends and influences of each Chinese year. These give an indication of the most propitious years and the most problematic. Forewarned is forearmed, and Chinese horoscopes can help us to make the best of what is to come. This is one of the key values of them (and, I believe, of the *I Ching* too). They speak to us as if to a friend, but it is *we ourselves* who are masters of our destiny and we who must determine how best to direct our lives.

There is a Chinese proverb which reminds us, 'Every moment is precious' and what we do with our lives is precious too.

As you journey through the years, I wish you every good fortune.

The Chinese Years

Horse	11 February	1918	to	31 January	1919
Goat	1 February	1919	to	19 February	1920
Monkey	20 February	1920	to	7 February	1921
Rooster	8 February	1921	to	27 January	1922
Dog	28 January	1922	to	15 February	1923
Pig	16 February	1923	to	4 February	1924
Rat	5 February	1924	to	23 January	1925
Ox	24 January	1925	to	12 February	1926
Tiger	13 February	1926	to	1 February	1927
Rabbit	2 February	1927	to	22 January	1928
Dragon	23 January	1928	to	9 February	1929
Snake	10 February	1929	to	29 January	1930
Horse	30 January	1930	to	16 February	1931
Goat	17 February	1931	to	5 February	1932
Monkey	6 February	1932	to	25 January	1933
Rooster	26 January	1933	to	13 February	1934
Dog	14 February	1934	to	3 February	1935
Pig	4 February	1935	to	23 January	1936
Rat	24 January	1936	to	10 February	1937
Ox	11 February	1937	to	30 January	1938
Tiger	31 January	1938	to	18 February	1939
Rabbit	19 February	1939	to	7 February	1940
Dragon	8 February	1940	to	26 January	1941
Snake	27 January	1941	to	14 February	1942
Horse	15 February	1942	to	4 February	1943

Goat	5 February	1943	to	24 January	1944
Monkey	25 January	1944	to	12 February	1945
Rooster	13 February	1945	to	1 February	1946
Dog	2 February	1946	to	21 January	1947
Pig	22 January	1947	to	9 February	1948
Rat	10 February	1948	to	28 January	1949
Ox	29 January	1949	to	16 February	1950
Tiger	17 February	1950	to	5 February	1951
Rabbit	6 February	1951	to	26 January	1952
Dragon	27 January	1952	to	13 February	1953
Snake	14 February	1953	to	2 February	1954
Horse	3 February	1954	to	23 January	1955
Goat	24 January	1955	to	11 February	1956
Monkey	12 February	1956	to	30 January	1957
Rooster	31 January	1957	to	17 February	1958
Dog	18 February	1958	to	7 February	1959
Pig	8 February	1959	to	27 January	1960
Rat	28 January	1960	to	14 February	1961
Ox	15 February	1961	to	4 February	1962
Tiger	5 February	1962	to	24 January	1963
Rabbit	25 January	1963	to	12 February	1964
Dragon	13 February	1964	to	1 February	1965
Snake	2 February	1965	to	20 January	1966
Horse	21 January	1966	to	8 February	1967
Goat	9 February	1967	to	29 January	1968
Monkey	30 January	1968	to	16 February	1969
Rooster	17 February	1969	to	5 February	1970
Dog	6 February	1970	to	26 January	1971
Pig	27 January	1971	to	14 February	1972
Rat	15 February	1972	to	2 February	1973
Ox	3 February	1973	to	22 January	1974
Tiger	23 January	1974	to	10 February	1975

Rabbit	11 February	1975	to	30 January	1976
Dragon	31 January	1976	to	17 February	1977
Snake	18 February	1977	to	6 February	1978
Horse	7 February	1978	to	27 January	1979
Goat	28 January	1979	to	15 February	1980
Monkey	16 February	1980	to	4 February	1981
Rooster	5 February	1981	to	24 January	1982
Dog	25 January	1982	to	12 February	1983
Pig	13 February	1983	to	1 February	1984
Rat	2 February	1984	to	19 February	1985
Ox	20 February	1985	to	8 February	1986
Tiger	9 February	1986	to	28 January	1987
Rabbit	29 January	1987	to	16 February	1988
Dragon	17 February	1988	to	5 February	1989
Snake	6 February	1989	to	26 January	1990
Horse	27 January	1990	to	14 February	1991
Goat	15 February	1991	to	3 February	1992
Monkey	4 February	1992	to	22 January	1993
Rooster	23 January	1993	to	9 February	1994
Dog	10 February	1994	to	30 January	1995
Pig	31 January	1995	to	18 February	1996
Rat	19 February	1996	to	6 February	1997
Ox	7 February	1997	to	27 January	1998
Tiger	28 January	1998	to	15 February	1999
Rabbit	16 February	1999	to	4 February	2000
Dragon	5 February	2000	to	23 January	2001
Snake	24 January	2001	to	11 February	2002
Horse	12 February	2002	to	31 January	2003
Goat	1 February	2003	to	21 January	2004
Monkey	22 January	2004	to	8 February	2005
Rooster	9 February	2005	to	28 January	2006
Dog	29 January	2006	to	17 February	2007

Pig	18 February	2007	to	6 February	2008
Rat	7 February	2008	to	25 January	2009
Ox	26 January	2009	to	13 February	2010
Tiger	14 February	2010	to	2 February	2011
Rabbit	3 February	2011	to	22 January	2012
Dragon	23 January	2012	to	9 February	2013
Snake	10 February	2013	to	30 January	2014
Horse	31 January	2014	to	18 February	2015
Goat	19 February	2015	to	7 February	2016
Monkey	8 February	2016	to	27 January	2017
Rooster	28 January	2017	to	15 February	2018
Dog	16 February	2018	to	4 February	2019
Pig	5 February	2019	to	24 January	2020
Rat	25 January	2020	to	11 February	2021
Ox	12 February	2021	to	31 January	2022
Tiger	1 February	2022	to	21 January	2023
Rabbit	22 January	2023	to	9 February	2024
Dragon	10 February	2024	to	28 January	2025
Snake	29 January	2025	to	16 February	2026
Horse	17 February	2026	to	5 February	2027
Goat	6 February	2027	to	25 January	2028
Monkey	26 January	2028	to	12 February	2029
Rooster	13 February	2029	to	1 February	2030
Dog	2 February	2030	to	22 January	2031
Pig	23 January	2031	to	10 February	2032
Rat	11 February	2032	to	30 January	2033
Ox	31 January	2033	to	18 February	2034
Tiger	19 February	2034	to	7 February	2035
Rabbit	8 February	2035	to	27 January	2036
Dragon	28 January	2036	to	14 February	2037
Snake	15 February	2037	to	3 February	2038
Horse	4 February	2038	to	23 January	2039

Goat	24 January	2039	to	11 February	2040
Monkey	12 February	2040	to	31 January	2041

Note

The names of the signs in the Chinese zodiac occasionally differ, although the characteristics of the signs remain the same. In some books the Ox is referred to as the Buffalo or Bull, the Rabbit as the Hare or Cat, the Goat as the Sheep or Ram, the Rooster as the Cock and the Pig as the Boar.

24 January 1936–10 February 1937 — *Fire Rat*

10 February 1948–28 January 1949 — *Earth Rat*

28 January 1960–14 February 1961 — *Metal Rat*

15 February 1972–2 February 1973 — *Water Rat*

2 February 1984–19 February 1985 — *Wood Rat*

19 February 1996–6 February 1997 — *Fire Rat*

7 February 2008–25 January 2009 — *Earth Rat*

25 January 2020–11 February 2021 — *Metal Rat*

11 February 2032–30 January 2033 — *Water Rat*

The Rat

The Personality of the Rat

According to legend, when the Buddha invited the animals of the kingdom to a party, the Rat was the first to show. And Rats certainly like to be at the forefront. Active, sociable and born under the sign of charm, they make popular company.

They are also quick to latch onto opportunity. Wherever they are, they like to make the most of their situation. In conversation they engage with others, find out information and invariably make an impression. If a member of a group, club or indeed workplace, they like to be involved and play their part. They also have a good way with words, including persuasive skills. Their observant nature allows them to appraise situations and they are worth seeking out for an honest and unbiased opinion. They also make superb critics.

However, while seemingly outgoing, Rats can be guarded. While they may not be averse to learning about the plans and secrets of others, they keep their own very much to themselves. And while they may offer advice, they rarely ask for it themselves. It would be to their advantage to share their true feelings (and concerns) more often.

It has been said that the more people you know, the more opportunities come your way. And this is certainly true for Rats. Their active lifestyle brings them into contact with many people and they are able to garner good support. In addition, they are often helped by their versatility. Their interests are many and skills wide-ranging. They are also alert, keen and ambitious, and if they sense an opportunity, they will be quick to pursue it. Little gets past them. However, because they involve themselves in so much – Rats never like to miss out – they can be restless and can abandon activities if they think there are better rewards elsewhere. This lack of persistence can sometimes work against them and they may not always reap the full rewards of their efforts. At times, greater discipline and persistence would help.

This also applies to money matters. Rats value money and like to protect and preserve their assets. However, having saved so hard, they may then succumb to lavish and indulgent spending sprees. They find bargains and sales irresistible! They are also very generous to their loved ones.

Although many Rat homes are tidy, the cupboards and storage spaces are likely to be crammed with items accumulated over the years. Rats can be notorious hoarders and rarely throw anything away lest it should have some future use.

With their versatile and personable nature, Rats can enjoy success in many lines of work. Being observant and interested in what is going on around them, they are often skilled communicators and make good writers, commentators and teachers. They also excel in professions calling for persuasive skills, including politics and the law. Banking, accountancy or one of the sciences may also appeal to their sharp, analytical mind. Ambitious, resourceful and capable, they have skills that can take them far.

Another of their abilities is problem-solving and if a way out of a tricky situation is needed, they will be sure to have an idea. Rats are masters of self-preservation.

They like to be busy and when not working will be usefully occupied pursuing their own interests and/or enjoying the company of others, usually both. Keen socializers, they like to party and go to shows and other forms of entertainment as well as take an interest in events happening locally.

Rats are also romantic and very much enjoy the thrill, passion and excitement of love. Tender, caring and attentive, they have much to offer and will very much treasure the love and affection of a partner. Family life is very important to them and they often have a large family. If they are parents, their diverse interests and fertile imagination will inspire and encourage many a young mind, and they often have a great love of their own parents and a desire to emulate them.

For female Rats, their family and home are their first priority. Caring, well organized and interested in others, they keep tabs on all that is going on and will often have a lot revolving around them. They are also incredibly versatile and use their talents in many different ways. They present themselves well and choose stylish and fashionable clothes. At work, they are ambitious, but will always try to ensure their commitments do not impact adversely on those who are important to them. Again, family and home are their priority.

With energy, enthusiasm, wit and charm, Rats are irrepressible. They just like to get on and do things, and will fill their days in many ways. Admittedly, they can be restless and impulsive and sometimes spread their energies too widely, but they are, above all, resourceful and energetic. And, being so companionable, they are also good to be with.

Top Tips for Rats

- You may like to make the most of your situation and be very adept at spotting opportunities, but don't always be looking over your shoulder and wondering if there are better prospects elsewhere. With persistence and staying power, you will often be able to achieve far more rewarding results.
- You have a creative and inventive mind and a strong intuitive nature. But sometimes you may underestimate what you are capable of and not promote your ideas and special talents as fully as you should. In some instances this may be down to a fear of failure. Take note and believe in yourself!

- Despite being so outgoing, you can be a private and guarded individual. Although you will gladly dispense advice, you will rarely ask for it, or even share what is on your mind. If you were to open up more, you would be able to benefit from the assistance and support others can give. In some cases, extra help could make an appreciable difference.
- Time management! You tend to spread your energies widely and sometimes prioritizing and greater focus would make you more effective. Also, a longer-term strategy would help you to direct your energies in specific ways and often result in you achieving substantially more.

Relations with Others

With another Rat

Two Rats understand each other, have similar values and get on well together.

In work, their drive and enterprise can reward them well, although both need to focus and resist spreading their energies too widely.

In love, Rat couples are loving and devoted and enjoy many shared interests. Home life is especially important. A good match.

With an Ox

Although these two signs are very different in personality, they complement each other well and relations between them are mutually beneficial.

In work, the Rat has great respect for the conscientious and methodical Ox. The signs can quickly establish trust and, by drawing on each other's strengths, enjoy an excellent working relationship.

In love, each gains from the other, with the Rat valuing the Ox's strength of character and dependability. With both striving for a settled and stable home life, they can make an often excellent match.

With a Tiger

Lively, sociable and enterprising, Rats and Tigers like and respect each other and enjoy good relations.

In work, when these two join forces and have a common aim, their combined energy and inventiveness make them a formidable team.

In love, there can be passion and much attraction between these two, with the Rat valuing the Tiger's confident and ebullient manner. Although both can be candid and different attitudes to money will need addressing (with the Tiger sometimes spending more than the Rat may like!), with goodwill and understanding, this can be a rewarding match.

With a Rabbit

Although both signs are sociable and enjoy conversation, their general chemistry does not always make for easy relations.

In work, the Rat may recognize the Rabbit's acumen and attention to detail, but to be successful these two need to build trust and rapport, which they may not find easy.

In love, both may be passionate and sensual, but the Rat's liking for a busy lifestyle and sometimes forthright manner will not sit comfortably with the Rabbit. Although both are home-loving, adjustments will be called for if the relationship is to endure.

With a Dragon

The Rat finds the Dragon stimulating company and these two signs like and respect each other.

In work, the Rat values the Dragon's enterprising and enthusiastic manner, and as both are hard-working signs, they could enjoy considerable success.

In love, their shared interests, outlooks and devotion to each other make for an excellent match. The Rat will particularly value the Dragon's confident and determined ways, and together they can find much happiness.

With a Snake

The Rat and Snake may not always understand each other, especially as both can, when the mood takes them, be guarded and secretive, but nevertheless there will be warmth and goodwill between them.

In work, both are ambitious and their different strengths will often be complementary. The Rat will have a high regard for the Snake's planning skills.

In love, there can be a powerful sexual chemistry between the two, with the Rat often captivated by the Snake's quiet, seductive charm. With both appreciating material comforts and loving their home, theirs can be a strong and mutually beneficial relationship.

With a Horse

Outgoing and sociable the Rat and Horse may be, but they are both forthright and opinionated too, and sooner or later differences of opinion will be aired!

In work, each will be keen to take the lead and, with the Rat having misgivings about the Horse's self-willed and impulsive nature, relations could be difficult.

In love, they could be attracted by each other's lively manner and, being keen socializers, have a lot of fun. But their strong wills and candid natures could lead to difficulty, as could their differing attitudes to money. A challenging match.

With a Goat

These two have a fondness for the good things in life, but their different natures and attitudes will present problems.

In work, the Rat could feel the Goat lacks drive and ambition and the portents are not good.

In love, both are sociable and fun-loving, but in time the Rat will despair over the Goat's capriciousness and inclination to spend, while the sensitive Goat will be uncomfortable with the Rat's candour. A difficult match.

With a Monkey

There is mutual liking and respect between these two vivacious signs and they get on well.

In work, both are determined and enterprising and each is capable of bringing out the best in the other. By pursuing specific goals, they can enjoy considerable success.

In love, these two are well matched. Sharing many interests and enjoying active lifestyles, they live life to the full, and the Rat will be reassured by having such a positive, enterprising and understanding partner. An excellent match.

With a Rooster

These two signs are certainly lively, active and outgoing but, as both are also candid, relations can be tricky.

In work the Rat likes to seize the moment, while the Rooster likes to plan and proceed cautiously. With their general approaches being so different and their characters being strong-minded and candid, these two do not work well together.

In love, both value their home life as well as enjoy many interests, but each likes to have their own way and they will be liable to clash. A challenging match.

With a Dog

Although their personalities and outlooks are very different, there is mutual appreciation and respect between these two, especially on a personal level.

In work, though, relations could be muted. The go-getting Rat likes to make the most of opportunities and could find the Dog's more disciplined approach inhibiting.

In love, each will admire the qualities and strengths of the other and the Rat will especially value the Dog's loyal and dependable nature. With both signs being romantic and passionate and having a love of their home, they can make a good and lasting match.

With a Pig

With the Rat's charm and Pig's geniality, these two signs enjoy each other's company and have much in common. Relations between them are good.

In work, their shared enterprise and zeal can work well, with the Rat valuing the Pig's commercial acumen. Together they can make an effective and successful team.

In love, there can be a great bond between them. Both are family-oriented and will work hard to enjoy a good lifestyle. The Rat will particularly value having such a supportive, loving and good-natured partner. A successful match.

Horoscopes for Each of the Chinese Years

RAT FORTUNES IN THE YEAR OF THE RAT

This not only marks the start of a new cycle of animal years, but is a special one for Rats. Who better to understand the ways and workings of the year than Rats themselves?

This is very much a year for making and carrying out plans. 'There is no time like the present', as the saying reminds us, and for Rats who have been nurturing certain hopes or plans, *now* is the time. Their energy and resourcefulness will help them to do well.

At work, the Rat year can bring some excellent possibilities, but Rats need to actively follow up openings. Many will find that positions of greater responsibility will become available in their present place of work and the depth of their knowledge will make them strong candidates. As a result, many can make important progress this year and take their career to new levels.

If currently dissatisfied or seeking a position, they will find this is a good year to explore possibilities and consider other ways in which they use their strengths. Rats are resourceful and in their own year their wide-ranging abilities can lead to some worthy results.

Rat years also encourage personal development, and whether in their work or their own interests, Rats themselves should look to further their knowledge. This is an excellent year for starting projects, setting challenges and developing skills. However, while the aspects are encouraging, Rats do need to be disciplined. Although they may start activities with enthusiasm, sometimes this can wane as fresh temptations come along. Rats, take note and keep in mind the benefits that *concerted* effort can bring. And what you undertake in your own year can often leave a far-reaching legacy.

The successes of the year can also help financially and the income of many Rats is set to increase. There can be an element of good fortune, too, with some Rats benefiting from the receipt of additional funds or from making some shrewd and timely purchases. Rats have an eye for a good deal. However, while a favourable year financially, it could be useful for Rats to give some thought to the longer term, including perhaps setting funds aside for future requirements or adding to a savings or pension policy. With good management, the situation of many can improve this year.

Rats are by nature sociable and will again enjoy positive relations with many of those around them this year. In their home life they will be keen to carry out domestic improvements as well as be active in supporting and advising loved ones. Their ability to keep tabs on a great many things at once will often amaze others, but such are the talents of Rats! Also, for any Rats who have thoughts of moving, this is a year to explore possibilities. Once ideas are acted upon, developments can quickly assist the process and serendipity can prove a useful friend over the year. With good support and family members all playing their part, many plans and projects can be successfully advanced over the course of the Rat year.

On a social level, Rats will also value their close friendships as well as their various chances to go out. They will often be on sparkling form and can look forward to extending their social network.

For the unattached and those who have experienced recent personal disappointment, their own year can mark the start of a new and sometimes life-changing romance. For some, the sound of wedding bells may be heard. These can be personally special times for Rats and the year is rich in possibility.

With resolve, energy and enterprise, Rats can accomplish a great deal in their own year and their achievements can be of long-term consequence.

Tips for the Year
Seize the initiative and set plans in motion. This is a year for action. However, do remain disciplined and use your time well. Giving up, giving less than your best or getting distracted could all undermine your efforts. Also, preserve time for your interests and to enjoy with others. Your personal relations can make this year even more special.

RAT FORTUNES IN THE YEAR OF THE OX

Rats are by nature hard-working and are set to do well in the Ox year. The gains made in the previous year can now be built on and continued headway made.

In work, many Rats will find their area of responsibility increasing and employers keen to use and develop their strengths. These can be encouraging times, with many Rats advancing their career. However, while good progress can be made, pressures will increase and some Rats will be daunted by the demands being placed on them. At such times, it will be a case of knuckling down, focusing on what needs to be done and learning about the different aspects of any new role. The Ox, who governs the year, can be a hard taskmaster, but by rising to the challenge, many Rats will prove themselves in a new capacity.

For Rats who are keen to move from where they are or are seeking work, the Ox year can open up interesting possibilities. By considering different ways in which they can use their strengths and keeping alert for openings, many Rats can secure a position they can build upon in the future. Effort and application will be needed, but what many Rats take on now will broaden their skills and be to their future benefit.

The income of many Rats will increase this year, but all Rats will need to be disciplined in their spending. While money may flow into their accounts, it may all too easily flow out again. Financial paperwork and legal documents also need to be checked and filed away carefully. Lapses could prove problematic. Rats, take note.

In view of their busy and often demanding lifestyle, it is also important that Rats give some thought to their well-being this year, including their diet and level of exercise, and allow themselves some time for rest and recreation. If not, some could experience fatigue or lack their usual sparkle. In the Ox year some 'me time' can make a real difference.

They should also preserve some time for their own interests. Projects they have been working on and ideas they have been developing can enjoy some success this year, and particular skills and talents will be encouraged. The Ox year favours focus, application and using strengths to advantage. A further (and often unforeseen) advantage of pursuing their interests will be the social element some of them have. Many Rats will extend their social network this year.

They will also value the support of those around them. There could be notable family achievements to mark and many Rats will be proud of the accomplishments of someone close to them. During the year they will find themselves encouraging others and dispensing advice as well as ensuring their household runs well. Their skills and attentiveness will be greatly appreciated and their domestic life busy and a source of considerable pleasure. A carefully planned holiday could also be greatly enjoyed.

In addition, Rats will value the mix of social occasions the Ox year brings as well as the chance to catch up with friends. Some of these could be especially helpful when Rats are facing pressures or decisions. Rats do a lot for others and, in this busy year, should allow others to reciprocate. They are set to widen their social circle this year and, with their charm and personable nature, will impress many. For the unattached, romantic prospects are good and someone met this year may quickly become very special.

Overall, the Ox year will be busy and demanding, but also constructive and rewarding. Throughout, it is important that Rats attend to their own well-being and give themselves the chance to appreciate the rewards they work so hard for as well as enjoy the company of those who are special to them.

Tips for the Year
Make the most of your skills and opportunities. With purpose and effort, you can accomplish a great deal. Also, keep your lifestyle in balance and value those around you. Their support can help in many ways.

RAT FORTUNES IN THE YEAR OF THE TIGER

Rats like security and to feel in control of their situation and they could feel ill at ease with the pace and changes of the Tiger year. This can be a demanding time and to do well Rats need to stay alert and be nimble-footed. However, they are, above all, resourceful and will often be able to turn situations to their advantage and emerge from the year with a lot to their credit.

At work, change will be in the air and, whether through restructuring, the introduction of new systems or the arrival of new personnel and/or management, will have an impact on the role of many Rats. They will not welcome either the uncertainty or the pressure. However, difficult though parts of the year may be, with new duties and roles to be filled, there will often be the chance for Rats to take advantage of the new developments. Despite their misgivings, this is no year to be intransigent.

Similarly, Rats who decide to look for positions elsewhere or are seeking work should not be too restrictive in what they are prepared to consider. By being open to possibility and taking advice, they could be alerted to something that is different but perfectly suited to them. This is a year to be receptive to change and to adapt accordingly. However, with developments happening quickly, speed will be of the essence, and Rats should not delay or prevaricate if they are to benefit. However, while the Tiger year can be an exacting one, Rats are resourceful and, as they have proved many times, able to prevail in all sorts of conditions, and they will do so again this year.

They will, however, need to exercise care in money matters. If taking on a new commitment or making a large purchase, they should check the terms and implications. And should they have misgivings over a financial matter, caution is advised. Haste, risk or a misjudgement could be to their disadvantage. Spending, too, needs to be watched. Rats, take note and be disciplined.

Travel can, though, feature on the agenda, and when possible, Rats should make provision for a holiday as well as take up any invitations to go away. A change of scene and the chance to explore new areas can do them a lot of good.

Although they will often have many commitments, it is also important they allow time for their own interests and recreational pursuits. New ideas and activities often come to the fore in Tiger years, so if something appeals to them, they should find out more. By embracing the spirit of the time, they can broaden their interests and extend their knowledge.

They should also make sure their social life does not suffer. Tiger years offer some lively and sometimes surprising times. Lonely and unattached Rats can make some important friends, although with romance it could be best to proceed steadily rather than rush into a commitment. That way, the relationship can develop in a meaningful and significant way.

While the Tiger year will bring some special times, some Rats could, however, be called upon to help a loved one or close friend in a difficult situation. While this may be worrying, their support and ability to empathize can make an important difference. Rats have wonderful people skills and should not underestimate the good they can do.

Domestically, a lot is set to happen and there will need to be good cooperation and communication between everyone in the Rat household. Here the Rat's attentiveness and inclusive nature can be of considerable value. Sharing activities and concerns will help, as will spreading out practical projects over the year rather than rushing them or concentrating them all in a short space of time. Tiger years require a certain flexibility.

In general, the Tiger year will be active and challenging, and Rats may be uncomfortable with some of the fast-moving developments. But there are chances to be grasped, lessons to be learned, opportunities to be developed and travel and shared activities to be enjoyed. Determined and ever-resourceful, Rats have the ability to turn a lot to their advantage.

Tips for the Year
Engage, adapt and make the most of unfolding situations. Be careful in money matters, but if you can, take advantage of travel opportunities and seize any chances to extend your skills and your personal interests.

RAT FORTUNES IN THE YEAR OF THE RABBIT

This can be a reasonable year for Rats, but there is a 'but'. Rats like to involve themselves in many activities and in the Rabbit year they could feel constrained. This year is conducted at a steadier pace and along structured lines, and Rats will have to adapt accordingly. This is not a time to rock the boat or forge ahead regardless.

However, while the Rabbit year's slower pace may not suit the Rat's style, there is still much to be gained from it. In particular, it can be an excellent time for Rats to evaluate their lifestyle and undertake some personal development. Particularly for those who lead busy and pressured existences, this will be a good year to strive for a better lifestyle balance. Rats should not feel they have to be on the go all the time. Occasionally they deserve a respite. And the Rabbit year encourages this.

Rabbit years also favour learning and personal growth, and Rats should consider ways in which they could further their interests as well as try out any new recreational pursuits that appeal to them, including any that have a keep-fit element. Rats who enjoy creative activities could see their ideas developing in particularly encouraging ways.

At work, rather than looking too far ahead, Rats should focus on their current duties and make the most of where they are. By working closely with their colleagues, networking and using their experience to advantage, they can considerably enhance their reputation. They can also benefit from training opportunities. Those seeking work will find that highlighting their willingness to learn may prove significant. Work-wise, Rats can impress this year, but do need to demonstrate their strengths. Progress may not be swift or necessarily substantial, but the Rabbit year does reward commitment and will prepare Rats for future opportunities.

In money matters, this is a year for care. At times, spending levels could creep up and outgoings be greater than anticipated. During the year Rats should keep track of their outgoings as well as carefully check the terms of any new agreements and commitments they enter into. Financially, it is a time to remain vigilant and thorough.

On a personal level, however, the Rabbit year can bring some memorable times. In many Rat homes there could be celebrations in store as the family increases in numbers, whether through birth or marriage. As always, Rats will be keen to support those dear to them and be proud of their achievements. Many Rats will make a deliberate effort to spend more time with those close to them this year. And their home life will benefit from this improved lifestyle balance.

Rats will also appreciate the social opportunities of the year and, with their personable nature, will add to their network of friends and contacts. As has been found, the more people you know, the more you benefit, and this is very true for Rats. This year some of the people they meet can not only offer friendship but also be of help with both current and future activities. However, while good times can be had, Rats do need to be attentive to the needs of others and, if in a potentially difficult or fraught situation, watch their words. An ill-timed comment or criticism could prove awkward. At times, despite their forthright tendencies (Rats do like to say what they think), they will find that greater tact will not go amiss.

Overall, Rats need to keep alert, join with others and consider their actions and responses carefully. This is no year for rushing or being too independent-minded, but one for making the most of current opportunities and building on experience. On a personal level, all Rats will benefit from a more balanced lifestyle and there could be some memorable (and celebratory) occasions to enjoy as well.

Tips for the Year
Be patient. Rather than try to rush ahead, enjoy the present. Spend time on your interests, develop your skills and value those around you. It is a year to appreciate what you have and strive for a better lifestyle balance.

RAT FORTUNES IN THE YEAR OF THE DRAGON

Dragon years have energy and a certain vibrancy, which appeals to Rats. And they are set to do well this year and be helped along the way by a certain amount of good fortune. Indeed, once they decide on a course of action, serendipity will often kick in and assist them. For any Rats who are nursing disappointment or feel they have been languishing of late (the previous Rabbit year will not have been the easiest), this is a time to draw a line under what has gone before and concentrate on the present. Important corners can be turned and, for some, the Dragon year can mark the start of an exciting new phase.

Rats attach much importance to their relations with others and can benefit from the support and encouragement of many this year. When considering plans or taking decisions, they can often be assisted in significant ways by talking to those they trust. Knowing they have this backing can be an encouraging factor and give impetus to certain endeavours. However, while Rats can profit from support and goodwill, they do need to ensure others don't take advantage of their willing nature or place excessive demands on them. This is a risk this year. If they do feel too much is being asked of them, they should stand their ground and resist being imposed upon.

They will, though, appreciate the many social opportunities of the year. Dragon years can be lively and offer a lot to do. Any Rats who are lonely or have had recent adversity will find that new friends and activities can help brighten their prospects. Romantic prospects are excellent and Cupid's arrow will be aimed in the direction of many Rats who start the year unattached.

Home life can be busy and eventful, especially as many Rats will enthusiastically start on improvement projects as well as assist loved ones in ambitious undertakings. However, with so much happening, they will need to liaise well with others. Making assumptions or rushing activities could lead to some awkward moments. Rats, take note and allow time for your projects rather than moving along at a heady pace.

The Dragon year can also bring some good travel opportunities, and holidays and breaks, including some arranged at short notice and/or with a spontaneous element, can be among the year's highlights.

Work prospects are also encouraging and Rats will often be well placed to benefit from openings and promotion opportunities. Their experience and reputation will stand them in excellent stead and their prospects can be helped by the backing they receive from senior colleagues and other influential contacts. This is a year when their abilities can come into their own.

In this favourable year, Rats desiring change or seeking a position should actively explore possibilities. This is a time when initiative, enterprise and determination will make a difference –

all qualities that are very much part of the Rat make-up. Such are the aspects that those who take on new responsibilities early in the Dragon year could find these giving rise to other opportunities later on in the year.

Progress made at work will also help financially. However, while many Rats will welcome an increase in earnings, rather than spend too freely (or over-indulge!), they should set funds aside for specific plans and purchases. This is a year for good financial management.

In general, Dragon years have great potential for Rats and if they seize their opportunities, they can make some well-deserved progress. And, pleasingly, some of the Dragon's luck can rub off on them too.

Tips for the Year

This is a year to act with determination and make the most of your strengths. Also, enjoy your good relations with those around you and value their support. With resolve and self-belief, you can make this a highly successful year.

RAT FORTUNES IN THE YEAR OF THE SNAKE

A year for patience and care. Rats need to appreciate that Snakes do not like haste and prefer to proceed in measured ways. In the Snake year, they need to temper their zealous natures and let situations develop in their own time. Although this may be frustrating, they can still learn a lot from the year and their prospects will gradually improve as it wears on. Indeed, some of their efforts in the first part of the Snake year can come to fruition in the later months.

At work, rather than regarding this as a time for substantial progress, Rats should concentrate on establishing themselves in their current area of work. By learning more about their industry and familiarizing themselves with ongoing developments, as well as seizing any chances to network and add to their skills, they can help both their present situation and their future prospects. Indeed, what they can do 'behind the scenes' this year, be it gaining extra knowledge, showing initiative or building contacts, can be to their subsequent advantage.

Many Rats will remain with their present employer this year and for those who feel their prospects could be improved by a move elsewhere or who are seeking work, developments can be slow. These can be frustrating times. However, Rats are above all tenacious, and with persistence and self-belief, many will succeed in securing a positon which is a considerable change (and opportunity) for them. Snake years encourage Rats to broaden their capabilities and an important legacy of the year can be the knowledge and skills they now acquire.

They will need to be thorough in financial matters, however, and be wary of risk and haste. To hurry decisions or make rushed purchases could lead to regret. Also, they should exercise careful control over the purse-strings. It could be easy to overspend this year. Financial paperwork and forms also need to be attended to carefully and the terms of any agreement checked. This is a year for vigilance and good control.

More encouragingly, personal interests can prove satisfying and recreational pursuits can be a valuable outlet in this often demanding year. For creative Rats, especially those who enjoy writing, Snake years can be inspirational, and some Rats will be enthused by projects started now.

Throughout the year Rats will also be grateful for the support and advice of their loved ones. However, to benefit, they do need to be forthcoming rather than keep their thoughts or anxieties to themselves. Also, they should consult others about any domestic projects and purchases they have in mind. This is a year for combining talents and sharing ideas. Even though some decisions and plans may take longer than envisaged, the improvements that result will be much appreciated, as will some of the year's family occasions, including the celebration of individual successes.

When possible, Rats should also aim to take a holiday over the year, as they will benefit from the rest and change of scene this brings. There could be additional travel opportunities in the closing weeks of the Snake year.

They will enjoy the year's social opportunities as well, particularly any special events they attend. However, they do need to remain aware of what is going on around them. Another person may let them down or they may find themselves concerned by rumour or gossip. For the unattached, the path of true love could also be bumpy. The patience and personal skills of many Rats will be tested over the year. Rats are adept and can successfully overcome or avert many a difficulty, but this is a time to be alert and attentive to others.

This may not be the easiest of years for Rats, but it is often by being challenged that skills can be gained and strengths highlighted, and so it will be for them this year. By showing patience, they can not only see the results of their efforts but also gain important new insights into their capabilities. Overall a constructive year, even though results may sometimes be slow in coming through.

Tips for the Year
Be vigilant and thorough. Question anything that is unclear and liaise well with those around you. Also make the most of any chances to extend your knowledge as well as to enjoy your personal interests. You can make this a useful and instructive year.

RAT FORTUNES IN THE YEAR OF THE HORSE

Rats have commendable energy and drive. They like to be at the forefront and involved in what is going on. Unfortunately, this year their best endeavours may not get the results they desire. Horse years can be tricky and Rats will need to remain alert and on their guard. However, this is one of the values of Chinese horoscopes. By being forewarned, Rats may be able to avoid the more negative aspects of the year and emerge with gains they can build on in the future.

One area requiring particular care is finance. Throughout the year Rats will need to monitor spending, otherwise outgoings could be greater than allowed for and economies have to be made later. When making sizeable purchases, Rats should also take the time to check that their requirements are being met and that they are conversant with the terms involved. The more care they take, the better their choices will be. They should also be cautious if lending to another person and careful when dealing with financial paperwork. This is no year to be lax or trust to luck. Rats, take note and be vigilant.

Work could also be demanding, especially as some Rats may feel they are not receiving the credit they are due or have misgivings over certain developments. However, frustrating though some situations may be, they could work to their advantage over the longer term. In the meantime, it would be politic for Rats to keep a low profile and focus on what they have to do. As the year proceeds, they are likely to have the chance to further their experience and prove themselves in an often different capacity, perhaps through training, taking on additional duties or applying for a sudden vacancy.

This also applies to those currently seeking work. By keeping alert for openings and remaining determined, they may be able to secure a position with future potential. In work matters, results may be more modest or muted this year, but what is accomplished can have great value at a later stage, when more substantial opportunities arise.

A key feature of the Horse year will be the way that Rats can add to their working knowledge. This also applies to their interests. Despite the pressures of the year, they should allow time for recreational pursuits and look to build on their skills. Some activities can prove immensely satisfying this year and be a good outlet for their talents and ideas. Also, for those lacking regular exercise, some attention to their own well-being could be helpful.

In their personal relations, although Rats have great people skills and are born under the sign of charm, in the Horse year they will need to proceed carefully. In both work situations or when out socializing, they should take note of the sensitivities of others and any potentially awkward undercurrents. To be too candid, outspoken or obtuse could cause problems and possible upset. However, by being forewarned, many Rats can successfully avoid some of the year's pitfalls. And tricky though the aspects may be, the Horse year can still provide a good mix of social opportunities and some lively occasions to enjoy.

Rats enjoying romance, or who find it this year, will need to remain aware of the feelings of others, however. Inattention and preoccupation could lead to problems. As with so much this year, greater awareness and extra care can make an important difference.

With the busyness of the year, Rats will especially appreciate their home life and the activities they can share with their loved ones. They will value the support they are shown during times of pressure, and towards the end of the year there could be some pleasing family news.

Overall, the Horse year will be demanding and sometimes exasperating. Rats like to get on with things, but conditions will not always allow this. However, Rats are survivors and, by seizing their chances to further their knowledge and experience, they can invest in themselves *and* their future. Developing interests and enjoying time with loved ones can also be of great value, especially in view of the year's pressures.

Tips for the Year
Be wary. Think situations through, be tactful and avoid rush or risk. Also use any chances to add to your skills. Knowledge gained now can be put to good use this year *and* be an investment in your future.

RAT FORTUNES IN THE YEAR OF THE GOAT

A welcome upturn in fortunes. And also luck! Having worked hard for recent results and experienced some frustrating times, Rats will find the Goat year bringing a welcome change. To benefit fully, though, they should set about their activities with renewed vigour and go after their goals with a positive 'can do' approach. Their actions can bear fruit now and on a personal level there will be good times to be had.

A key feature of Goat years is that they encourage creativity and trying the new. And for Rats, who are so skilled at seeking out opportunities, these can be interesting and successful times. Particularly in work, the skills and experience they have built up can now deliver. For Rats on a particular career path, positions they have been preparing for could now become available and many Rats will be moving forward and finding a greater level of fulfilment over the year.

Rats who are frustrated in their present position or seeking work should actively pursue openings as well as consider other ways in which they could use their skills. Some interesting openings can be found this year. This is no time to hold back or stand still, and the drive and energy of many Rats will see them reinvigorating their career and prospects.

For those whose work involves communication or has an element of self-expression, this can be a particularly successful year, and these Rats should make the most of their ideas and opportunities. Goat years favour innovation and professional development.

Rats who enjoy creative pursuits should also look to develop their skills and possibly promote what they do. This can be an exciting and stimulating time. Projects and activities started now can prove satisfying and often offer additional benefits, including a greater lifestyle balance. Goat years are encouraging and inspiring ones and Rats can benefit from them.

Financially, progress made at work may bring additional earnings and some Rats will also find ways of supplementing their income through their ideas and interests. However, while any increase will be welcome, with Rats' active lifestyles and ambitious plans, outgoings will be high, and they should keep careful control over their budget and ideally make advance provision for larger outgoings.

They will welcome the increased social opportunities of the year, and if they are alone or have had some recent personal upset, they will find the Goat year heralds a brighter time. Chance too can play a big part and a fortuitous meeting could lead to a potentially significant friendship, or for the unattached, be capable of transforming their life.

Rats should also make the most of what is happening in their locality. With Goat years favouring culture, there could be a good mix of events and special occasions taking place. Rats like to be involved and there will be opportunities aplenty.

They will also value their home life. The Goat year favours a coming together and the addressing of any difficulties or concerns, and this will be particularly appreciated by Rats who have experienced strains in some relationships of late (possibly not helped by tiredness and preoccupation). With good communication, understanding and a more balanced lifestyle, their home life this year can be much improved. By sharing ideas and projects, they can see exciting plans take shape and enjoy many special occasions with their loved ones. In addition, there could be several personal achievements to mark. Domestically, it is a year favouring togetherness and cooperative effort.

With Rats often doing a great deal this year, it could also be to their advantage to consider their own well-being. Some attention to their diet and level of exercise could help them give of their best.

Resourceful and keen to make the most of opportunities, Rats can do well this year. Whether through improved work prospects, a new position, rewarding personal interests or good relations with others, they have a lot in their favour and can accomplish a great deal.

Tips for the Year
Make good use of your ideas and creative strengths. Also, be willing to venture forward. Good progress can be made this year. Sharing time with others can also bring both pleasure and increased support.

Rat Fortunes in the Year of the Monkey

With openings to pursue and ideas aplenty, Rats will feel inspired and motivated in this encouraging year. For those nurturing particular aims or wanting to start new projects, this is an excellent time to do so. A great deal is possible.

At work, the Monkey year can see much activity. Many workplaces will be implementing change as well as be affected by internal reorganization and reviews. As a result, opportunities will arise and Rats will often be well placed to benefit. When they sense an opening, they should be quick to signify interest. Initiative and speed count for a lot this year and much of it will be conducted at a fast pace.

Rats who are unfulfilled in their work or seeking a position should not be too restrictive in what they consider. By widening their search, many will secure a position which not only suits their abilities but also offers future potential. Work-wise, Monkey years are encouraging and the versatile Rat can fare well.

Travel too can feature prominently over the year, whether work-related, connected with personal interests or purely for pleasure. There could be the chance of some short breaks – often organized quickly – and their spontaneity will add to their appeal. Monkey years have the capacity to surprise.

This is also an excellent year for personal and career development and if Rats feel that another skill or qualification could be to their advantage, they should see what can be arranged. What they do now can be an investment in both themselves and their future. Those currently studying or embarking on courses will find that commitment can lead to some impressive results. The Monkey year is an encouraging one for Rats.

This also applies to their personal interests. Over the year they should allow themselves time to develop their ideas and skills, as a lot can be gained from them.

While many Rats will enjoy an increase in income over the year, spending does need to be watched, however, and large projects or purchases, especially for home, carefully considered and budgeted for. It is a time for good financial management.

Socially, Rats will delight in the considerable opportunities the Monkey year will bring and revel in the chance to extend their network of friends and contacts. As is the way, some existing friends and acquaintances will fall away as circumstances change, but new interests and situations will bring Rats into contact with others, and their charm and conviviality will make them popular company.

Affairs of the heart can be special and existing romances will often become more significant, while some Rats who start the year unattached will find new romance.

Domestically, too, this can be an active year and see Rats on inspired form and keen to make home improvements. However, projects could easily become more extensive and time-consuming than envisaged. Rats, be warned, and ideally tackle practical undertakings in stages, while drawing on the help and expertise of others. Amid all the activity there will, though, be personal highlights, family successes and travel to enjoy.

Monkey years offer considerable scope for Rats and if they take their opportunities and look to improve on their position, they can make this a constructive time.

Tips for the Year
Monkey years favour action and initiative. There will be progress to be made, interests to pursue and relationships and travel to enjoy. Seize the moment in this full and often special year.

Rat Fortunes in the Year of the Rooster

Rats like to lead a busy lifestyle and the Rooster year will not disappoint them! A lot is set to happen during its 12 months, but while a lot can be gained, there can be some awkward moments too. Rats cannot afford to slack or relax their guard in Rooster years.

On a personal level, this can be an especially busy time, and throughout the year Rats will need to remain mindful of those around them and show some flexibility. With support, however, much can be accomplished, and synergy will be an important factor.

Socially, in particular, there will be an increase in activity. Rats will have a good range of occasions to enjoy and their personable nature will help them build new friendships and make some potentially important connections.

For the unattached, there will be good romantic possibilities, and if time is allowed for relationships to develop, they may truly blossom. Even for Rats who find a certain romance is not to be, there will be valuable lessons to learn and the chance to move on. Much happens for a reason in Rooster years and often what happens will be to the Rat's ultimate advantage.

This will also be a busy year domestically and cooperation will be required. Domestic and work-related decisions need to be talked through and help offered at pressured times. As always, though, Rats will delight in assisting their loved ones. Some ambitious practical projects will also go ahead in many Rat homes. While sometimes these will involve more time and cost than initially envisaged, the eventual benefits will often delight both the Rats themselves and their loved ones.

Rats do, though, need to follow the correct procedures if undertaking anything hazardous as well as give some thought to their general well-being over the year, including their diet and level of exercise.

Similarly, busy as they may be, they should allow themselves some 'me time'. Developing their interests could open up some interesting possibilities, and creative Rats in particular will feel on inspired form in this encouraging year.

Travel, too, could appeal. Not only do Rats need a break in this active year, but a carefully chosen destination could give rise to some memorable times.

At work, the Rooster year can be demanding. Some weeks are likely to be frenetic as new pressures arise, targets are revised and staff shortages or other problems occur. Many Rats will feel challenged by what is required of them, but what occurs will give them the chance to both use *and* widen their skills and many will enhance their reputation. As a consequence, they will often be well placed when opportunities arise. After much effort, good headway is possible.

Similarly, for Rats who are seeking work or keen to move on from what they currently do, there may be surprising developments in store. In some cases, these Rats will take on something very different from what they have previously been doing and will delight in the fresh start. Rooster years may be challenging, but are not without opportunity.

In money matters, Rats will, though, need to be vigilant. They should be thorough when attending to paperwork or taking on a new commitment and seek professional advice if unsure. This is not a year for risk. Also, in view of some of the expensive plans and undertakings of the year, they should keep careful control over their budget.

Overall, Rats will often be astonished by the great deal they manage to do in these very full and fast-paced 12 months. However, they need to be mindful of developments and respond accordingly. Also, throughout the year, they would do well to listen to their feelings and their inner voice. When faced with difficulties, they will know in their heart what to do, and they should not go against their instincts. Though this is a demanding year, it can, however, also be a rewarding one. Relations with others can be of great value and, with support and joint effort, much can be accomplished.

Tips for the Year

Remember that things happen for a reason. So, make the most of opportunities to build on your skills and experience. With commitment, what you achieve now can lead on to other possibilities. Also, in view of the general busyness of the year, aim for a balanced lifestyle and give time to those who are special to you.

RAT FORTUNES IN THE YEAR OF THE DOG

A reasonable year which also calls for a certain care. While Rats can make good progress, they will need to be alert, attentive and aware of potentially troubling areas, especially in their relations with others. Fortunately, their canny nature will serve them well.

At work, the Dog year will see much activity and many Rats will be able to profit from their considerable experience. As developments occur and workloads become greater, there will be the chance for many to take on further responsibilities and make encouraging headway. They can help their position by working closely with their colleagues and getting themselves better known. Those who work in a creative environment in particular may find themselves winning plaudits for their work. With commitment and their typical enthusiasm, they can enjoy this promising and productive time.

Rats seeking work or keen to take on something different should not only explore possibilities but also speak to contacts and employment advisers. By keeping alert and taking note of any suggestions offered, many could secure an important opening which offers the chance of further progress in the near future. Perseverance and some patience may be needed, but Dog years invariably deliver.

Another important factor of the year is the way it encourages personal development. This is a time for Rats to build on their skills and capabilities and further personal interests. Some may choose to enrol on courses of study, while others develop in other ways, but efforts made now can not only be personally satisfying but also have far-reaching value.

Progress made at work can help income and some Rats may also find ways to put a skill or interest to profitable use over the year. The enterprising talents of some could really pay off. However, while financially an improved year, it may also be one in which outgoings are high, especially as many Rats will proceed with costly plans and purchases for their home as well as take on new financial commitments. As a result, they will need to watch their outgoings as well as check the terms of any new agreement. A risk, oversight or hasty decision could lead to regret. Rats, take note and be thorough.

Another area where care is required is relations with others. With busy lifestyles and often demanding work situations, Rats could feel under pressure or be preoccupied with certain matters. At such times, they do need to share what is on their mind. If they bottle up their feelings, there is a risk that difficulties could arise. Also, throughout the year, they should ensure that, where possible, quality time with others does not suffer. Shared activities, interests and home projects can ease tensions and lead to some enjoyable times.

Similarly, regular contact with friends and time set aside for recreational pursuits can do Rats a lot of good this year.

For those enjoying romance, again care and attention will be very necessary if relationships are to strengthen. With the aspects as they are, this is no time for Rats to take the feelings of others for granted or be too reticent or guarded.

Overall, however, they can fare well this year and build on their achievements, especially in their work. It is a good year for developing their knowledge and skills and raising their profile. However, Dog years can be demanding and Rats do need to make sure that their busy life is also a balanced one. Giving time and attention to others is so very important this year.

Tips for the Year
Consult others and listen to what they have to say. The better your communication, the better you will fare. In addition, with such a lot happening, stay well organized and concentrate on priorities.

RAT FORTUNES IN THE YEAR OF THE PIG

The Pig year offers interesting prospects for the Rat and will see the successful culmination of many plans, projects and activities. But it is also a year for treading carefully and Rats will face many demands on their time as well as a few anxious moments.

At work, their resourcefulness will be valuable and they should aim to contribute, particularly if there are situations requiring new ideas or creative input. This is a year to be proactive and many of the ideas that Rats put forward during it will find favour and enhance their reputation. This is a time when their proven skills can bear fruit, and when positions offering greater responsibility fall vacant, they should be quick to follow them up, as there is the potential to make important headway.

For Rats currently unfulfilled or seeking work, this can be an ideal year to reappraise their situation and consider what it is they actually want to do. In some cases, training or refresher courses could be worth considering. Important opportunities can be identified, and although some of what these Rats take on could come with a steep learning curve, they will often have the chance to establish themselves in a new capacity.

Although progress at work can lead to an increase in income, money matters do need care and attention, however. In particular, Rats should be wary of making hurried decisions or taking on anything potentially risky. When entering into any important agreement, they should check the terms and obligations, and seek clarification if they have any concerns. They should also take care of their possessions, as a loss could be upsetting. Rats, take note and be thorough and vigilant.

More positively, travel will tempt and some exciting plans can take shape. In addition to the possible benefits of a holiday, Rats should allow themselves the chance to relax and unwind from time to time. In this busy year they need an occasional respite. Also, if feeling tired or listless or having any particular health concerns, they would benefit from seeking medical advice. A good lifestyle balance and some self-care are especially advised this year.

If there have been strains in a relationship or friendship of late, this is also an excellent year to address concerns and heal any rift or disagreement. The Rat's personable nature will help in this. And for Rats who are alone and perhaps have experienced some personal hurt, this is a time to draw a line under the past and regard this year as a new start. Pig years reward a positive 'can do' approach and many active and earnest Rats will benefit from their actions during it. Some important new friendships can be formed this year and romantic prospects are potentially significant.

Domestically, too, Pig years favour shared activities, and by drawing on the help of their loved ones, Rats will often be pleased with the domestic plans they carry out as well as see the completion of some longer-term projects. What is achieved this year can be especially gratifying. However, with all the activity going on, some relaxation and quality time should be factored in, as well as, if possible, a holiday. Pig years favour togetherness. Also Rats need to be careful not to let their enthusiasm run away with them and to overcommit themselves or accede to too many requests. Some discipline is needed.

In general, Pig years can be significant for Rats. They reward commitment as well as encourage opportunity and growth. There will be a lot for Rats to do and enjoy, but, because of their involvement in so many activities, they need to look after themselves and take the time to savour the rewards of their efforts.

Tips for the Year
Develop your strengths and make the most of your opportunities. The Pig year's legacy is often significant. Also, enjoy spending time with others and set aside some 'me time' as well. With your busy lifestyle, you need to use your time and energies effectively.

Thoughts and Words of Rats

I want to be all that I am capable of becoming.

KATHERINE MANSFIELD

Cherish your visions, your ideals, the music that stirs in your heart. If you remain true to them, your world will at last be built.

JAMES ALLEN

Life is a great big canvas, and you should throw all the paint you can on it.

DANNY KAYE

Our doubts are traitors,
And make us lose the good we oft might win
By fearing to attempt.

WILLIAM SHAKESPEARE

An enterprise, when fairly once begun
Should not be left till all that ought is won.

WILLIAM SHAKESPEARE

Flaming enthusiasm, backed by horse sense and persistence, is the quality that most frequently makes for success.

DALE CARNEGIE

Believe that you will succeed, and you will.

DALE CARNEGIE

Every individual has a place to fill in the world and is important in some respect, whether he chooses to be so or not.

NATHANIEL HAWTHORNE

There are no gains without pains.

ADLAI STEVENSON

I have brought myself by long meditation to the conviction that a human being with a settled purpose must accomplish it, and that nothing can resist a will which will stake even existence upon its fulfilment.

BENJAMIN DISRAELI

The secret of success in life is for a man to be ready for his opportunity when it comes.

BENJAMIN DISRAELI

11 February 1937–30 January 1938 — *Fire Ox*

29 January 1949–16 February 1950 — *Earth Ox*

15 February 1961–4 February 1962 — *Metal Ox*

3 February 1973–22 January 1974 — *Water Ox*

20 February 1985–8 February 1986 — *Wood Ox*

7 February 1997–27 January 1998 — *Fire Ox*

26 January 2009–13 February 2010 — *Earth Ox*

12 February 2021–31 January 2022 — *Metal Ox*

31 January 2033–18 February 2034 — *Water Ox*

The Ox

The Personality of the Ox

For thousands of years mankind has valued the strength of Oxen. Reliable and hard-working, they can be depended upon and many of their sterling qualities are also found in those born under the Ox sign.

True to their word, Oxen are redoubtable figures. Never half-hearted, when they commit themselves to something, they like to see it through. They are also no-nonsense sorts and, favouring tradition, stick to the tried and tested. New methods, gimmicks and constantly changing from one thing to another are not for them. Instead, they are practical, methodical and thorough. They aim to do things well. However, being self-willed, they can also be stubborn, and changing an Ox's mind once it has been made up is no easy task.

Oxen are also very thoughtful and consider their words and actions carefully. Indeed, when in company, they tend to be reserved and do not open up easily. They have a small but close circle of trusted friends and these friendships will have formed over a long time, with some dating back to childhood. Similarly, in matters of the heart, Oxen like to be sure before they commit themselves and their romances are often long and protracted. Here again they take their responsibilities seriously and are very loyal to and protective of those who are dear to them. In the home, though, they do like to make most of the decisions and will strive to run a well-ordered and efficient household. If anyone slacks off or annoys them in some way, they will be sure to let them know. When rankled (which is rare), they can have a formidable temper.

Oxen like to proceed steadily and surely in most areas of life and when they have chosen a career, they are likely to remain with it, becoming ever more proficient as the years go by. While not outwardly ambitious or materialistic, they like to establish themselves in a certain field of work and take pride in what they do. In many a workplace, their solid nature, know-how and work ethic are greatly valued by their colleagues, with many taking on a more managerial role in later life. They can make good leaders and, with their high standards, also be hard taskmasters. They can find fulfilment in specialist areas where mastery of detail is important. Engineering, design, education and the law could appeal, and with their ability to use their hands, they can also make skilled technicians, surgeons and dentists. Oxen have an affinity with the outdoors, and farming and horticulture could also appeal to them. Another gift and passion can be music – some Oxen are to be found enjoying distinguished careers as musicians or composers.

In matters of finance, Oxen are cautious and manage their situation well. They like to consider their purchases carefully. They do not tend to overindulge and are good providers, making sure their own needs and those of their loved ones are well met. When saving or investing, Oxen prefer more traditional routes, including those offering a set return, rather than speculating. However, should situations ever go against them (financial or otherwise), they can feel it deeply. They are poor losers and regard failure as a personal affront. But in time, they are sure to make good. Resolute, persevering and objective, Oxen are doers and survivors.

They are also very much 'take me as you find me' sorts and do not tend to be flamboyant or showy in nature. It is because they are down to earth and unpretentious that so many hold them in high regard. You know where you stand with them. The female Ox tends to be more outgoing than the male, but, like him, she has a mind of her own, knows what – and who – she likes and sets about her activities in an efficient and organized way. She has a practical disposition and could also have a deep interest in the arts and be talented in certain areas. Both male and female Oxen value family life and regard their home as a private sanctuary for them and their loved ones, as well as a buffer from the sometimes crazy world outside. As parents, Oxen are caring and encouraging as well as inspirational teachers, but are also strong on discipline.

The patient and measured ways of Oxen mean they sometimes hold back and may appear distant and aloof. They certainly do not lower their guard easily and take time before they feel at ease in the company of other people. However, they are loyal, sincere and dependable, and it is because of these qualities, together with their commitment and hard work, that they often do well in life. Napoleon Bonaparte, himself an Ox, once declared, 'Victory belongs to the persevering,' and Oxen are certainly persevering. Slowly, steadily and patiently, they are capable of achieving a great deal – and doing so in their own way and often on their own terms.

Top Tips for Oxen
- You are a private individual and like to keep your thoughts and feelings to yourself. You do not readily engage in idle chatter. However, your reserved nature can sometimes deny others the chance of seeing the depth and warmth of your true personality. Try to open up more, for you could gain so much from interacting with those around you on a deeper level and from networking and allowing others to get to know you. Aim to be more visible so you can be appreciated more.
- You take your responsibilities seriously and work long and hard. But it is important that you give yourself the chance to

enjoy the fruits of your endeavours. Quality time with your loved ones and time spent relaxing and on pleasurable pursuits can do you a lot of good as well as help you to be at your best.

- You may favour tradition and have set views and interests, but, rather than distrust change, do consider the advantages it can bring. Adapting, learning and exploring new areas can open up a whole new world. Venture out from time to time!

- You do not like to fail, so set about your activities cautiously and carefully. This may mean you don't always make the most of chances or fully explore your talents and ideas. Have faith in yourself and be bold. Oliver Wendell Holmes, an Ox, wrote, 'Many people die with their music still in them.' You have so much to give that you do need to make sure you use your gifts and talents fully. Life can be all the more fulfilling (and potentially successful) as a result.

Relations with Others

With a Rat

The Ox likes the Rat's warm and personable nature and relations between them are generally good.

In work, each will recognize and value the strengths of the other and together they will make an effective team. The Ox will especially appreciate the Rat's drive and inventive streak.

In love, these two are well suited. Both value their home life and the Ox will find the Rat supportive and encouraging and value the colour they bring into their life. A close and often successful match.

With another Ox

There may be respect and understanding between these two, but both are independent-minded and like to have their own way. Relations could at times be problematic.

In work, both are cautious, favour tradition and are also very hard-working. If they can unite in a common aim, their tenacity and sense of purpose can deliver some good results.

In love, two Oxen will seek security and stability, but, as both are strong-willed and forthright, differences of opinion could prove awkward. Also, there is a risk they could become set in their ways. With care, however, these two can unite and make their relationship work.

With a Tiger

The Ox, who values stability and keeping things on an even keel, will feel ill at ease with the irrepressible Tiger and relations between the two will be difficult.

In work, the cautious Ox could consider the Tiger colleague rash and impulsive. Sooner or later their styles will clash.

In love, their very different natures may at first be intriguing to both, but, as they live life at different speeds and have many different views (including on how to manage the household budget), there will be issues to address. A challenging match.

With a Rabbit

With many shared interests and a fondness for the quieter things in life, these two signs relate well to each other.

In work, they can combine their strengths to good effect, and the Ox will value the Rabbit's careful approach and sound business sense.

In love, both yearn for a settled existence and attach much importance to their home life. The Ox will appreciate having such a thoughtful and affectionate partner and together they can enjoy much happiness. An ideal match.

With a Dragon

Each recognizes the strengths of the other and in some situations this can work to their advantage while in others can pose problems.

In work, both are ambitious and diligent, and when united in a common aim, they can harness their different strengths to good effect, with the Ox valuing the enthusiasm and enterprise of the Dragon.

In love, again the Ox can enjoy the warmth and zest of the Dragon, but, as both are strong-willed and the Ox prefers a quiet existence and the Dragon a livelier one, there will be differences to reconcile. A tricky match.

With a Snake

Quiet, reserved and thoughtful, these two feel comfortable in each other's company and relations between them are good.

In work, there will be mutual trust and respect and the Ox will value the Snake's patient resolve and thoughtful approach.

In love, they can find considerable contentment together, with each admiring and encouraging the other. Both have cultured tastes and they will share many interests. The Ox will appreciate the Snake's considerate and affectionate ways and gentle humour. A good match.

With a Horse

With both being strong-willed and strong-minded, sooner or later these two will clash. And it will most likely be sooner.

In work, they are both industrious and redoubtable, but the Ox favours a steadier and more cautious approach than the Horse. These two will prefer to stick to their own ways and methods.

In love, these two live their lives at different speeds – the Ox prefers slow and steady, while the Horse favours rushing about – and neither will be disposed to compromise. A difficult match.

With a Goat

The practical and dutiful Ox finds it hard to relate to the imaginative and carefree Goat. Relations between them will often be poor.

In work, the approach and style of the Ox and Goat are so very different that there will be a lack of accord between them.

In love, the Ox, who is so careful and orderly, could soon despair over the Goat's more easy-going and 'live for the moment' ways. A challenging match.

With a Monkey

Their personalities are very different, but there is good respect and accord between these two and relations will often be mutually beneficial.

In work, both have drive and ambition and the Ox will recognize the Monkey's resourceful and enterprising spirit. They can often combine their different strengths to good effect.

In love a positive, optimistic Monkey partner can be good for the Ox and these two complement each other well. Together they can find much contentment and can gain a lot from their relationship.

With a Rooster

The Ox has great admiration for the orderly and efficient Rooster. They have similar interests and relations between them will be good.

In work, both are methodical, conscientious and keen planners, and the Ox will hold the Rooster's abilities and commitment in high regard. Together they make an effective combination.

In love, their similar outlooks and values combine well, as do their shared interests, including a liking for the outdoors. These two can have great understanding and love for each other.

With a Dog

Both are dutiful and dependable, but can be forthright and stubborn. Relations can sometimes be tricky.

In work, the Ox likes to get on with things and could feel hindered by the Dog's deliberations, worrying and idealistic tendencies. Not an effective combination.

In love, these two share a major quality: loyalty. In addition, the Ox will value the Dog's affectionate and well-meaning nature, but they are both redoubtable characters and much effort will be needed if their relationship is to endure.

With a Pig

The Ox likes and admires the genial and principled Pig and relations between the two will be good.

In work, both are scrupulous in their dealings and work hard and well together. The Ox has great respect for the Pig's commercial acumen and enterprise.

In love, both value a calm and harmonious home life and, with interests in common (including a love of the outdoors), can find much happiness together. The Ox can also benefit from the Pig's more outgoing ways.

Horoscopes for Each of the Chinese Years

Ox Fortunes in the Year of the Rat

One of the key characteristics of Oxen is that they like to proceed in measured ways and this is exactly what many will do this year. Rat years are encouraging for them and they will be able to make good headway.

At work, many will find their commitment well rewarded this year and, especially for those who have been with their current employer for some time, their experience and in-house knowledge can make them excellent candidates for greater responsibilities. For Oxen on a particular career path, this is a year when they can progress to new levels and extend their knowledge and experience in the process. Oxen like to advance slowly and steadily and in the Rat year their potential will be recognized and encouraged.

For those looking to broaden their experience by a move elsewhere, or seeking work, determined effort will be required. With openings sometimes limited, it could take time and tenacity to secure a suitable position. Progress needs to be worked for this year, but when it comes, it will give many Oxen a good platform to build on.

What is achieved now can often have long-term value and Oxen should take advantage of any work-related training courses available to them. Similarly, if they have personal interests they are keen to advance, this is an ideal year to do so. Oxen in education will also find their commitment rewarded and their results (and qualifications) helping their prospects. Indeed, the Rat year can leave a valuable legacy that can be built on in the future, especially in the following Ox year.

Progress made now can lead to a rise in income and some Oxen will be able to supplement their earnings through putting an interest, skill or idea to profitable use. Their diligence can be well rewarded this year. However, to make the most of any financial upturn, they should manage their budget well. If able to reduce borrowings and/or make savings, they could help their overall position.

With the long hours many Oxen work, it is important recreational matters do not fall by the wayside this year and that Oxen allow themselves time to rest and unwind. They cannot expect to drive themselves on without respite. Many will find interests that have a social element or allow them to do some exercise can do them a lot of good. Also, in view of their busy lifestyle, they should aim to take a holiday during the year. Again a rest and change of routine can benefit them greatly.

Although Rat years are generally positive, increased mindfulness is advised in relations with others. Oxen have a strong will, but to prevent possible discord this year they do need to pay close attention to the views of others and, in some instances, be more accommodating. To remain intransigent could lead to problems and undermine rapport. Oxen, *do* take note.

Over the year all Oxen should, however, make the most of the social invitations they receive as well as go to special events and other occasions that appeal to them. Going out can add balance to their lifestyle as well as give them the chance to relax, unwind and get to meet people who could become helpful contacts.

Oxen who find love or are in the early stages of a relationship should let the romance develop in its own way rather than make commitments before they feel ready. This way they will be more certain of their feelings. Also taking time, rather than rushing, suits the Ox psyche.

Domestically, this promises to be an active year, with many Oxen being especially proud of the achievements of a loved one or reaching a personal milestone. There could be good reason for a family celebration in many an Ox household. Oxen will also be keen to embark on some practical projects about the home. They should, however, be realistic in what is doable at any one time. Short-term projects that can be broken down and tackled in stages will be easier and more satisfying than overambitious undertakings. To help, Oxen should consult those around them, be mindful of their views and involve them in their plans. This will not only lead to more happening but also more being appreciated.

Overall, Oxen will find their commitment and efforts rewarded this year. Progress can be made and experience gained. Relations with others will need care, attention and good communication. However, if Oxen make the effort, they can gain a lot from the Rat year and emerge from it with knowledge to build upon and opportunities to develop.

Tips for the Year

Be receptive to the possibilities that open up for you this year. You may need to be adaptable, but the skills you gain can not only help your present situation but also the longer term. Value your relations with others and take especial note of their views and feelings. Extra care and attention can enhance this good year.

Ox Fortunes in the Year of the Ox

Oxen are set to fare well in their own year and enjoy some steady growth and pleasing personal developments. Even so, the year will not be without its obstacles and delays. Results can sometimes be slow in coming through and this is more a time of gradual accumulation than spectacular breakthrough.

However, one important factor will be the chance Oxen will have to consider their overall situation, think ahead and introduce some changes. If there is some aspect of their life they are not currently satisfied with, now is the time to act. Oxen like to take responsibility, and this is a year for taking responsibility for their present position *and* future direction. Decisions made now can have far-reaching effects. Oxen can be their own architects this year, designing their life and considering what it is *they* want to see happen.

A particularly positive area concerns their relations with others, and for many there will be personal celebrations in store. Affairs of the heart are favourably aspected and some Oxen who start the year unattached will meet someone who is destined to become very special. For those who are alone and perhaps feeling dispirited, this is a year to reach out, to engage in what is happening around them and to meet new people. Positive effort can lead to a change in personal fortunes. For Oxen who are enjoying romance, marriage and/or settling down with someone are possibilities this year. Some Oxen could start a family or see their family increase in numbers. Domestically, these can be fine and often special times.

Shared interests and family occasions can also bring memorable moments. There may be personal and family news to celebrate as well as the realization of some much-anticipated plans. As ever, Oxen will advise certain family members over key decisions and their wise counsel and solid nature will be much valued.

With travel well aspected, they should also take advantage of any chances to go away with their loved ones. A holiday and trips to certain attractions can be much appreciated.

Socially, the Ox year can bring an increase in activity, with Oxen themselves enjoying spending time with their friends and meeting new people. Such is the nature of the year that some new contacts could be especially helpful with certain undertakings. Indeed, throughout the year, Oxen will have many people rooting for them and encouraging them on.

At work, many will be content to focus on their existing role and use their current skills. Work-wise, Ox years are not always straightforward, though, and certain duties and objectives may be problematic. With support and skill, however, Oxen can still accomplish a great deal and some will have the chance to move to a more specialist role. Steady progress can be made this year.

Oxen who are unfulfilled where they are or are seeking work should give careful thought to how they see themselves developing. By obtaining advice and following it, many will be successful in securing the chance to establish themselves in a new role. This may require time, but Ox years reward commitment.

Progress made at work will help financially and many Oxen will be able to go ahead with plans and purchases they have long considered, including travel.

Personal interests can also be satisfying and Oxen who would welcome new challenges should set time aside to pursue something different. This is an excellent year to follow through ideas, make some changes and enjoy some new interests. Also, Oxen deserve some treats and some 'me time'.

In general, the Ox year holds considerable potential for Oxen. On a personal level, there could be celebrations, special times and new love to enjoy. New activities could add interest to the present time, while at work there will be opportunities for Oxen to demonstrate their skills and move ahead, albeit steadily. A full and fulfilling year and on a personal level an often special one too.

Tips for the Year

Much can change this year and you can be firmly in the driving seat, but you need to decide on your route and set forth. This may require effort, but can offer substantial benefits too. And there will be support, goodwill and good personal times along the way.

Ox Fortunes in the Year of the Tiger

There will be many times during the Tiger year when Oxen will look askance at developments and despair of the pace with which they are happening. Tiger years are fast-moving and lack the stability that Oxen favour. But, while this is not an easy year for them, Oxen are made of stern stuff and, with care, can still benefit.

With the aspects as they are, they should, however, proceed cautiously and, when situations call for it, keep a low profile. Although Oxen are usually forthright, in volatile situations they should consider their responses carefully. 'A word once spoken cannot be retrieved', as the Chinese proverb tells us, and Oxen would do well to bear this in mind this year. In addition, while they may have doubts over certain developments, sometimes their initial fears could be misplaced and patience will often be the best approach.

A feature of Tiger years is that they give rise to ideas and initiatives, and this is particularly evident in the workplace. Often new systems and ways of working will be introduced and Oxen, who favour tradition, could feel uneasy about the changes and the inevitable teething problems they bring. To compound situations, new colleagues and/or the unhelpful attitude of some could be of concern, but amid the challenges, there are important gains to be had. Sometimes training will be available which will not only further the skills of Oxen but also be helpful in their subsequent progress. Also, as workloads increase and staff change, openings can arise. Tiger years can be demanding – and exasperating – but, by being prepared to adapt, learn and make the most of situations, Oxen can make headway.

With the Tiger year being one of change, some Oxen will seek a position elsewhere and some will decide to take their career in an entirely new direction. For these Oxen, as well as those seeking work, obtaining a new position will require great effort, but with persistence and initiative, they can succeed. Many redoubtable Oxen can triumph this year in spite of often difficult conditions.

Financially, too, this is a need for care. Not only could there be increased accommodation (and commuting) costs, but equipment could fail, necessitating repair or replacement. With many outgoings likely, Oxen need to manage their situation carefully as well as make advance provision for forthcoming expenses and more substantial purchases.

A more positive area is personal interests. With all the activity of the year, Oxen will often be glad to spend time on their own pursuits. Sometimes new ideas or equipment will enable them to further what they do. Also, if they would like to introduce a new element into their lifestyle, they should consider taking up different activities. Busy they may be, but recreational interests offer real benefit. For the more creative, Tiger years can be stimulating and inspiring times.

Oxen will appreciate their home life this year – indeed, some will regard their home as a sanctuary from outside pressures. All will enjoy sharing interests with their loved ones as well as deciding on key plans and purchases, including travel. This is a year favouring collective effort and input.

Also, in view of the pressures and changes Oxen face this year, it is important they speak of their concerns, so that others can better understand and help. If tired or tense, they should also be careful not to take irritations out on others. Here again, openness and willingness to consult others can be of particular value.

Oxen would also do well to keep their wits about them in social situations this year. An inadvertent comment or lapse could cause problems. Life may not always be straightforward in Tiger years, but despite the variable aspects, there will be social occasions that Oxen can greatly enjoy and the chance to relax will do them good.

Overall, Oxen may not welcome the volatility seen in Tiger years, but by making the best of situations, they can discover new strengths, and sometimes new interests too, as well as derive pleasure from their home life and shared activities.

Tips for the Year

Be flexible. That way you can gain more from what opens up this year. Also, devote time to your own interests and your home life. They can be valuable in this often pressured and fast-moving year.

OX FORTUNES IN THE YEAR OF THE RABBIT

A much-improved year for Oxen. With focus, they can make good headway at work, while on a personal level, there are good times to be had. While the aspects are supportive, Oxen cannot expect instant results – Rabbit years reward patient endeavour – but the steady pace of the year will better suit the Ox temperament.

Any Oxen who start the year dissatisfied should concentrate on the now rather than feel hindered by what has gone before. With a willingness to move forward, they can take important steps and regain more control over their situation.

For those whose lifestyle has got out of balance, this is an excellent year to rectify matters. If personal interests have had to be set aside due to other pressures, Oxen should ensure they allow time for them this year. With the accent on learning and culture, they could benefit from study and research, as well as enjoy the social occasions Rabbit years are so famed for.

Attention to their own well-being can also be of advantage. Some Oxen will give some thought to their appearance and decide to overhaul their wardrobe. Over the year, helpful decisions can be made which have a positive bearing on other aspects of life too.

Personal relationships are particularly well aspected, and for Oxen enjoying romance or who find it this year, these can be exciting times. In addition, personal interests will bring Oxen into contact with many people and this is an excellent year for them to engage in activities and raise their profile.

Being on inspired form, they will also busy themselves in the home, often redecorating, tidying up certain areas and making other improvements. With family members also assisting, much can be undertaken. This can be a satisfying year domestically. However, during it, another person could need help with a problem. Here the Ox's support and considered advice can be of great value.

In their work, Oxen like to specialize and build up their expertise in certain areas. Over the Rabbit year, many will be able to move their career forward and take on greater responsibilities. However, while this progress will be pleasing, it will also place new demands on the Oxen concerned, and there will be adjustments to make, challenges to address and new procedures to learn. In Rabbit years, the abilities of many Oxen will be tested.

For Oxen currently dissatisfied with their present position or seeking work, there can be encouraging developments in store. By making enquiries and considering other ways in which they could use their strengths, they can be offered the chance they were hoping for. To make headway, some flexibility will be needed, but what is achieved now can often be to their longer-term advantage. In addition, all Oxen should make the most of any training that is available. Rabbit years encourage self-development and this will help make this both a more successful and personally fulfilling time.

In money matters, Oxen should manage their situation carefully, ideally budgeting for commitments and being wary if involved in any informal arrangement, including lending to another person. Without care, problems and misunderstandings could arise. Oxen, take note and be vigilant.

In general, the Rabbit year can be a constructive and pleasing one for Oxen. It encourages progress and the development of skills as well as offers the chance to make some beneficial lifestyle changes. In addition, personal relations can be special and give added meaning (and impetus) to this promising year.

Tips for the Year
Be adaptable. With a willingness to consider other possibilities, you can gain a great deal. Also set time aside for your interests and consider making some positive lifestyle changes. Attention to your own self can have an uplifting effect and help in all manner of ways.

Ox Fortunes in the Year of the Dragon

Dragon years are bold and dynamic and Oxen are often uncomfortable with their heady pace. This will not necessarily be an easy time, but, despite its frustrations, Oxen can take quiet satisfaction in their achievements.

At work there will be challenges and some disappointments. New developments are likely to have an impact and may leave Oxen feeling they are not given the credit they are due. Some may find new objectives or ways of working difficult and situations may not be made any easier by office politics. However, the Ox philosophy is one of fortitude and patience and in time situations *will* settle. Oxen will have gained new experience in the process and often fresh insights into their own capabilities. Some of the year can be illuminating and suggest possible options (and career paths) for the future.

While many Oxen will remain with their present employer, for those seeking change or looking for work, the Dragon year can open up some interesting possibilities. Although their quest will not be easy, Oxen may find themselves being offered a position that develops their skills in new ways. Chance may well play a part in this and the speed of developments may take Oxen by surprise.

They will need to keep paperwork in good order, however, as they may find themselves troubled by bureaucracy over the year. A lost policy or document could cause problems and financial forms need to be attended to carefully.

Oxen should also remain disciplined in money matters. They could face some repair costs this year or find some activities more expensive than anticipated. This is very much a time for discipline and control.

However, while the Dragon year has its awkward aspects, Oxen can benefit from the very good and loyal friends they have.

If ever they are uncertain or grappling with an issue, talking matters over with someone they trust could be helpful in many important ways. This year many Oxen will find that a problem shared is a problem considerably eased.

With Dragon years invariably being active ones, Oxen should also follow up the social invitations they receive as well as go to events that appeal to them. Contact with others can be good for Oxen, as can making new friends and participating in some of what the Dragon year offers.

Home life will also see much activity and there will need to be good cooperation and flexibility as schedules change. Oxen are good organizers, however, and their talents will be appreciated, although when under pressure or annoyed, they should exercise patience and watch what is said. But amid the activity there will be individual successes and occasions that Oxen and their loved ones will especially appreciate, particularly in view of the effort involved.

With the demands of the year, Oxen should also give some consideration to their own well-being, as well as allow themselves a respite from all the activity. Time set aside to enjoy personal interests can be of especial benefit. In some cases, new equipment or input from others could encourage them to do more or try something different. It is important that they embrace the spirit of the year and are open to possibilities.

If possible, they should also take a holiday during the year. Many of them will appreciate the new places they visit.

The Chinese proverb, 'Slow and steady wins the race' is often apt for Oxen and is very true in the Dragon year. Progress will not be easy and some situations will be exasperating, but through tenacity and application, Oxen can add to their experience as well as gain important insights into themselves, and what they learn now can be built on in the following Snake year. In the

Dragon year the support of others will be of particular value and Oxen will be helped by being forthcoming, as well as by participating in what is going on around them. This is a time for them to adapt, learn and, in the process, prepare themselves for the opportunities that await. A challenging year but an illuminating one.

Tips for the Year
Tread carefully. Times may not be easy, but they can be instructive. Watch developments closely and value your relations with others. Their support can help and shared activities can be of benefit. In addition, when pressures are great or situations concerning, proceed carefully. An outburst or words said in haste could be regretted later.

Ox Fortunes in the Year of the Snake

Deep thinking, quiet and methodical, Oxen have a lot in common with Snakes and can do well in the Snake year. Rather than feel buffeted by events, they can now proceed in their own way and with much in their favour. Encouragingly, they will be able to build on recent experience and see their patience and fortitude paying off. The successes so many will enjoy this year will be well deserved.

At work, the accent is on progress and Oxen will be well prepared to take advantage of opportunities. Oxen are quietly ambitious and tend to know in themselves when the time is right to advance. Now will be such a time. Accordingly, many Oxen will keep alert for openings and quite a few will take on a greater and often more specialist role with their present employer. Oxen like to concentrate on a chosen area in their working life and this is what many will successfully do this year.

Those who may feel unfulfilled in their present situation or are seeking a position will also find that their resolve can deliver. If they show initiative when making an application, their extra effort can often make a difference. This is a year when Oxen can make their strengths count.

However, while good progress is indicated, new positions will often involve a steep learning curve. With Snake years favouring development, Oxen who feel an additional skill or qualification could help their prospects would do well to consider setting time aside to acquire this. What many learn this year can be an investment in themselves and their future.

Personal interests too can bring considerable pleasure, with Oxen again inspired by new ideas or projects. Creative activities are particularly favourably aspected.

Financial prospects too are good. Many Oxen will enjoy an increase in income and some will also find ways to supplement their earnings through an interest they have. This upturn will persuade many to update equipment and spend money on their home. Also, if they are able to add to a savings or pension policy or set funds aside for something they want, this could be helpful. With good management of resources, they can make this a financially rewarding year.

Although Oxen tend to be private individuals, they can also benefit from the social opportunities of the year. Some of the people they meet through their work or interests will, in time, become part of their trusted social circle. For the unattached, romantic prospects can also make the year special and someone met in often fortuitous circumstances can become significant. Here again Snake years favour Oxen, although to benefit they do need to be active and reach out rather than keep themselves to themselves (a tendency of some). Oxen, take note, and join in with what is happening around you. That way, you can make the rewards and pleasures of the year that much greater.

Domestically, there will be busy times ahead and Oxen again need to be forthcoming. By talking over their ideas and thoughts, they will see a lot more happen. Important changes and improvements (especially equipment-wise) will be seen in many an Ox home this year. In addition, personal successes and family news can give rise to a possible celebration.

Oxen should also aim to take a holiday or enjoy some short breaks with their loved ones over the year. If these are considered early on, some exciting plans – including visits to attractive destinations – can take shape. This is an excellent year for joining with others and enjoying shared activities.

Overall, the Snake year is a good one for Oxen, but they do need to be careful not to immerse themselves so much in their own activities that it has a detrimental effect on other aspects of their life. Over the year they should aim to keep their lifestyle balanced and enjoy spending time with others as well as appreciate the pleasures they work so hard for. They have much in their favour this year, however, and their personal qualities will help make this an often special time.

Tips for the Year
Follow up your ideas and make your strengths and special qualities count. Once action is taken, results can soon follow on. Also, enjoy your relations with others and appreciate the opportunities and good times this year offers.

Ox Fortunes in the Year of the Horse

With its emphasis on commitment and hard work, the Horse year is one in which Oxen can do well. There will be good opportunities and pleasing results, although there will also be times when Oxen will be discomfited by its volatility and the 'winds of change'. During the year they will need to keep their wits about them and respond well (and smartly) to its developments.

Work prospects are good and many Oxen will be able to put their skills to effective use and concentrate on areas they favour. For many, these can be fulfilling times. Some Oxen will take on projects and roles they have been working towards for some time. However, while Oxen like to absorb themselves in what they do, they should not work in isolation. By being visible, networking and involving themselves in what is happening around them, they can contribute all the more, as well as help their standing and prospects. Similarly, when problems and pressures arise, their skills and fortitude will often impress. With effort, Oxen are set to do well this year.

For those who feel their prospects can be improved by a move elsewhere, or who are seeking work, the Horse year can also open up exciting possibilities. To benefit, though, these Oxen will need to keep alert and act quickly when opportunities arise. 'The early bird catches the worm' and speed and initiative will count in this fast-moving year.

Headway made at work will increase the income of many Oxen over the year. However, while this will be welcome, Oxen do need to manage their outgoings carefully as well as check the terms and implications if entering into any new commitment. This is no year to be lax or take unnecessary risks.

Oxen should also give some consideration to their own well-being this year. They are naturally hard-working, but they should allow themselves the occasional respite. Without care, tiredness and tension could take their toll and leave some Oxen lacking their usual energy or finding themselves susceptible to minor ailments. To help counter this, they should ensure their diet is healthy and nutritious and, rather than continually drive themselves on, set time aside for relaxation and pursuits they enjoy. If sedentary for long periods of the day, appropriate exercise may help, too. Good lifestyle balance can make a difference.

Although Oxen tend to be selective in their socializing, they should also take up any invitations they receive as well as go to events that appeal to them, rather than isolate themselves or be too independent. Social occasions can do Oxen good this year and regular contact with friends can be helpful. In addition, if troubled by a particular matter or finding themselves in an uncharacteristic quandary, they would do well to talk to those they trust. This can bring clarity to certain issues. In addition, their social life can help their lifestyle balance, which is important in this busy year.

Where matters of the heart are concerned, extra care is advised, however. With time and attention, many a romance can flourish, but should commitment be lacking, the relationship may falter. Oxen need to proceed carefully and be mindful of others.

In their home life, with busy schedules and many commitments likely, there needs to be good communication between everyone involved. Flexibility is advised, especially where practical undertakings are involved. Ideally, these should be scheduled for less busy times. However, with family members pooling together and encouraging each other, some pleasing times can be had and some noteworthy successes or milestones marked. Time set aside for shared interests and a possible holiday can also do everyone good. This is a year encouraging togetherness and a collective approach.

Overall, the Horse year will be a full and busy one for Oxen, and one that can reward them well. At work, their experience and commitment will result in many making impressive headway. However, all Oxen need to be visible and involved rather than isolated and independent. They also need to balance their commitments and set aside time for themselves and those close to them. With care, though, this can be a fulfilling year and an enjoyable one too.

Tips for the Year
Keep alert and respond quickly and positively to developments. There are good opportunities to be had. Also, watch your independent tendencies. Liaise well with others and give time to them. Extra attention in this area can make the year all the more rewarding.

Ox Fortunes in the Year of the Goat

A mixed year. The disciplined Ox will often be uneasy with the volatility and change that are features of Goat years. This is a time for Oxen to keep expectations modest. However, while progress may not be easy, the year will give them the chance to take stock of their situation, decide on future directions and spend time with those close to them.

Home life can bring especial pleasure, with the practical nature of Oxen often coming to the fore. Over the year several home improvement ideas will present themselves and Oxen will tackle them with relish. When one project is completed, another will often suggest itself, and Oxen will take considerable satisfaction in what they do and the benefits that follow on. With Goat years favouring artistic expression, quite a few Oxen will also enjoy refreshing décor and adding embellishments to their home.

As well as practical improvements, Oxen will do much to support family members, especially as some will be facing pressured situations or contending with change. Those close to Oxen will have good reason to value their stalwart natures and honest opinions over the year. It can also be marked by some memorable domestic occasions, including shared interests, trips out and celebrating personal successes. In addition, many busy Oxen will be encouraged to spend more time with those close to them, and this can be a beneficial feature of the Goat year.

Socially, Oxen should take advantage of the many events and activities that tend to happen in Goat years, including in their locality. In addition, by regularly meeting up with their friends, they will not only appreciate the support and camaraderie, but also the ways in which some of them can help and advise.

For some unattached Oxen, a chance encounter also has the potential to become significant. Goat years favour affairs of the heart, and indeed relations with others.

They also encourage the exploring and furthering of talents. Oxen should devote time to their personal interests this year and if a new activity tempts them, find out more. They will frequently be enthused by what the year opens up for them.

However, while the Goat year will have many pleasurable aspects, it will also bring pressures. In many workplaces, Oxen will find their duties affected by change. New procedures and the burden of additional bureaucracy may make progress difficult. Although frustrating, for many the best policy will be to concentrate on their own role and adjust as required. Situations *will* settle, but patience, and some forbearance, will be required. And when progress does come, it will be well deserved.

For Oxen seeking a position, these can again be challenging times, with openings sometimes limited. However, with tenacity and widening the scope of their search, many could secure a position in a different type of work and have the chance to prove themselves in a new way. Flexibility, together with a willingness to adapt and learn, will be key this year.

In money matters, again this is a year for care and close control of the budget. Risk, haste and speculation should be avoided and, especially when considering new purchases or replacing equipment, time should be allowed to assess options and terms and what best meets requirements.

In general, Goat years can be volatile and Oxen can find the changes frustrating and progress difficult, particularly at work. However, by rising to the year's challenges and adjusting as necessary, they can learn from it, and what they accomplish now can often be important in the longer term. Care is needed in money matters, but more positively, time spent developing personal interests and on practical activities can be satisfying, and relations with others, and romantic prospects, are favourably aspected. Not always an easy year, but with some important personal benefits mixed in.

Tips for the Year

Enjoy being with others and look to make more of your personal interests. Both areas can bring you great pleasure this year as well as help your lifestyle balance. While some developments may concern you, particularly at work, make the most of what happens. Experience gained now can be successfully built upon in the future.

OX FORTUNES IN THE YEAR OF THE MONKEY

Interesting times ahead. Monkey years offer considerable scope and although Oxen may not always welcome the speed of developments, there will be some good opportunities.

One of the strengths of Oxen is their willingness to learn and develop. As they realize, to achieve their ambitions and make the most of themselves, it is necessary to assimilate knowledge and build upon their experience. And they continually aim to do so. In the Monkey year, they will have great chances to develop in this way. This can be a constructive time.

At work, the Monkey year can bring unanticipated developments. Colleagues may suddenly leave, opening up the chance of taking on new duties and/or promotion. Sometimes, too, employers will be keen to harness the skills of Oxen in other ways and will offer training and a different role. By making the most of their opportunities, Oxen can not only further their career, but also add to their capabilities.

For Oxen who are currently unfulfilled in their role or seeking work, again interesting openings can be found. However, when making an application, extra effort and showing initiative at interview can make an important difference. In Monkey years Oxen do need to put themselves forward, not only emphasizing their skills but also their willingness to adapt and learn. Going that extra mile will be well worthwhile.

Personal interests are also favourably aspected and many Oxen will be keen to build on what they do, try out new ideas and add to their knowledge. If intrigued by a new activity, they should investigate. Interests and recreational pursuits can bring considerable satisfaction this year, being a good outlet for skills as well as helping lifestyle balance.

Progress made at work will help financially and many Oxen will decide to proceed with plans they have been considering for some time, including updating equipment. By looking at options and what best meets their requirements, they can make some useful acquisitions. Also, advance budgeting, including setting funds aside for a possible holiday, can lead to much going ahead.

With discipline and good financial management, Oxen can do very well this year.

The Monkey year can also offer good social opportunities. Oxen will find their work and interests will bring them into contact with many people and although Oxen like to take their time in building friendships and other connections, they will enjoy a good rapport with some of those they meet this year. Where matters of the heart are concerned, both existing romances and new ones can often develop well. While some Oxen tend to be private and reserved, all should aim to make the most of the social opportunities the Monkey year offers. There will be many good times to be had.

Domestically, this will be an active year, with some Oxen despairing about all that needs to be done. Some weeks in particular could be frenetic, as important decisions need taking and other matters, including home maintenance issues, require swift attention. Being conscientious, Oxen will be keen to ensure the right decisions are taken and will sometimes feel under pressure. However, Oxen are blessed with good judgement, which will help them successfully deal with the more awkward moments the Monkey year can bring. Throughout the year, though, it is important that family members cooperate and share their thoughts.

While some weeks will be pressured, the Monkey year will also bring its domestic pleasures. It has a spontaneity about it and some surprise occasions, including trips away, will be greatly appreciated and capable of doing everyone good.

Monkey years have considerable energy and a lot will happen quickly. Although this may not always suit the Ox's style, the year can bring excellent opportunities. Openings can arise and ideas occur that should be followed up. There will be ample opportunity for Oxen to add to their knowledge and skills and, by doing so, they will be investing in themselves and their future. Used well, these can be significant times. The Monkey year can also bring good social opportunities, although Oxen do need to engage in them! Their home life will be busy, but will also bring much that will be pleasing. An active year rich in possibility.

Tips for the Year
Make the most of your opportunities and add to your skills. This can be helpful now *and* increase your options for later. Also, join with others and enjoy what the year offers. Monkey years can inject new and beneficial elements into your lifestyle and prospects.

Ox Fortunes in the Year of the Rooster

Rooster years favour structure and organization, and this very much suits Oxen. This is a time for them to make plans and act on them. Encouraging developments will help them along too. Deciding on some objectives for the year will give Oxen something to work towards as well as allow them to make more effective use of their skills and opportunities. For purposeful and determined Oxen, these can be significant *and* rewarding times.

Oxen who start the year discontented with their present situation or dissatisfied with recent progress should focus their attention on the present rather than on what has gone before. This is a year offering positive change.

All Oxen will be helped this year by their steadfast manner. Once they have made plans, they will do their best to see them through. And their plans can be wide-ranging. In particular, for Oxen who have thoughts of relocating, now is the time to make enquiries and explore possibilities. As many will find, once they make a start, important wheels can be set in motion. However, for those who do move or are involved in any property transaction, it is important they take professional advice as well as check the terms and obligations of any agreement they make. Although this is an encouraging year, in property and financial matters Oxen need to be vigilant. This need for care also applies if lending to another person or entering into an informal agreement. Financially, Oxen need to be on their guard, as there is a risk some may be disadvantaged or fall victim to a scam. Oxen, take note.

However, this warning apart, Oxen have a great deal in their favour this year and their actions will deliver results.

At work, many will have been giving some thought to their situation recently, and for those who feel in a rut or unfulfilled in what they do, this is a time to seek change. By taking advice and action, these Oxen could secure an important new role that not only better suits their skills and circumstances, but also has the potential for future growth. This also applies to those seeking work. By widening the range of positions they are considering, they can uncover opportunities and take on new challenges.

For the many Oxen following a particular career, this is also a year encouraging progress. Ambitious and determined Oxen can do well. Recent experience will help their prospects and many can take their career to a new level. However, while Oxen can make headway, they do need to exercise care in their dealings with colleagues. The attitude of another person could concern them, but they should not let this detract from an otherwise promising year. There is important work to be done and much to be gained.

The positive aspects also extend to personal interests and some Oxen will be inspired to try something different or take up a new skill. Some may consider lifestyle changes, including giving some thought to their diet and allowing more time for recreation. Here again, decisions made and acted upon can bring considerable benefit. The Rooster year is a time for reappraisal and action.

Personal interests can also have a good social element, and any Oxen who are feeling lonely and would like to meet others will find joining a local group well worth considering. In general, Oxen should make the most of the social events the year will offer. If they are active and participate, they can enjoy some good times. Romances, too, can develop well this year.

Domestically, there will be much activity, especially as some Oxen will move and spend time setting up their new home. Many will be on inspired form, with ideas to implement and improvements to carry out. However, with ambitious undertakings, timescales need to be kept elastic and some projects will prove costlier and more disruptive than anticipated.

Despite the busyness of home life and the considerable changes that many Oxen will see, the Rooster year will certainly have its highlights as individual successes are marked, quality time is enjoyed and shared activities are undertaken. These can all be a special part of the year.

Overall, Rooster years offer considerable potential for Oxen. They are times to make plans and make them happen. Serendipity can be a useful ally, as once actions are taken, helpful factors can often come into play. This is a year for Oxen to build on their strengths and position. Throughout the year, they need to be thorough, especially in financial matters, and proceed carefully if situations concern them. Generally, though, with commitment and skill, they can enjoy this favourable time.

Tips for the Year
Set plans in motion. Look to develop your career, personal interests and self. With resolve, you can accomplish a great deal. Also, enjoy spending time with those who are special to you and work together on plans as well as celebrate successes. If you are alone, aim to meet others. Positive action can bring rewards this year.

Ox Fortunes in the Year of the Dog

Oxen have great resolve and, through willpower and sheer determination, can make much of the Dog year. It will not be an easy one, with obstacles to overcome and much else happening besides, but Oxen are not ones to let things stand in their way. And they won't.

As Oxen realize, problems are there to be dealt with, and in some instances the problems that arise in the Dog year may not be as difficult as first imagined. The Oxen's pragmatic nature can prove a great asset this year.

This is especially the case in their work. Many Oxen will not only be coping with a heavier workload, but with irritations caused by delays and bureaucracy. Over the year, the demands will be considerable, and Oxen, in their usual inimitable way, will knuckle down and concentrate on the tasks to be done. Their achievements in sometimes difficult conditions can bring them some well-deserved credit. In addition, what they can do behind the scenes, whether networking, taking advantage of training opportunities or learning more about their industry, can stand them in good stead. However, with the pressures of the year, they do need to be wary and thorough and also careful not to undermine their reputation with unguarded words. Dog years require adroit handling.

Oxen seeking work, or a change, will have to strive hard for the opportunity they want, but Oxen are tenacious, and with self-belief and the willingness to adapt, they can secure a platform on which to build in the future.

They need to be careful in money matters over the year, however, and should check the terms of any agreement they enter into. Extra attention is also advised when attending to tax returns or other financial or important correspondence, otherwise there is a risk of getting caught up in the slow workings of bureaucracy and wasting time in the process. Oxen, take note, and remain vigilant and thorough. In addition, any Oxen involved in dealings in land or property need to seek advice and proceed with care.

More positively, travel is well aspected and Oxen should take advantage of any chances to go away. For some, this could include visits to family and friends living some distance away and the opportunity to visit areas which have long appealed to them. A break from routine can do Oxen a lot of good this year.

Their personal life can also be especially rewarding, with those who are enjoying romance or who find love this year likely to get engaged, married or settle down with their partner. Affairs of the heart can bring Oxen much happiness this year.

Also, by pursuing interests and taking advantage of local and other activities, they can take much pleasure in the social opportunities these bring. Challenging though some aspects of the Dog year can be, it can give Oxen the chance to spend time with those who are special to them and on activities they enjoy.

Their home life will also be active, with shared undertakings and, for many, a holiday with loved ones much appreciated. However, matters of concern could arise, perhaps involving the attitude or actions of another person or decisions that need careful deliberation. At such times, Oxen should talk matters through with those around them and pay attention to their views. That way, problems can often be addressed and dialogue and communication of value to all.

In general, Dog years can bring their challenges and irritations. Oxen could face increasing pressures and demands, especially at work, but they are never ones to shrink from challenges and with commitment and focus can obtain satisfying results and learn a lot in the process. Money matters require careful attention, but the Dog year will also bring its pleasures, with travel and personal interests favourably aspected and a myriad of activities to share with others. A mixed year, but Oxen, with all their redoubtable qualities, can still take a lot from it.

Tips for the Year

Be watchful and evaluate situations with care. With focus and good sense, your efforts will prevail and the skills and experience you gain be of considerable benefit. Also, give time to your loved ones and remember that dialogue and communication are important, especially when decisions need to be made or you are under pressure. In addition, seize any chances to meet others – new friendships and connections, and maybe romance, can make this year significant and special.

Ox Fortunes in the Year of the Pig

The Pig year is one of interesting possibility for Oxen. Like Pigs, Oxen are hard workers and they can make much of the opportunities that now open up. However, of often greater value will be the personal benefits that can be gained. Pig years encourage Oxen to pay attention to their own well-being and enjoy a better lifestyle balance as well as appreciate the rewards they work so hard for. Especially for Oxen who start the year in low spirits, this can be an improved time, with subtle yet important changes taking place.

Of particular benefit will be the Oxen's relations with others. Although often private individuals, during the year many Oxen will lose some of their reserve and take advantage of opportunities to go out, including to parties, gatherings and special events. The social diaries of many will be busier than they have been for some time. This is a year to engage and participate, particularly for Oxen who are alone or who have had a recent personal difficulty to contend with. For some, joining a special interest or social group would be well worth considering. New friends and acquaintances could enter their life, and Oxen who are enjoying romance or who meet someone new over the year could find their relationship growing in significance as the year develops.

Their home life can also bring Oxen much contentment. If they set time aside for shared interests and helping those around them, a lot can go well. Successes enjoyed by family members can be especially gratifying.

Although travel may not figure prominently this year, any holiday or short breaks that Oxen can take with their loved ones can do everyone a lot of good, and give rise to some enjoyable occasions.

However, while much will go well, as with any year there will be problems to address. Often these will stem from pressure. Whatever the situation, discussion and compromise will help. Over the year, if difficulties are handled well, they can quickly and effectively be defused.

Oxen should also set time aside for personal interests. If they have let these fall away, they should aim to rectify this in the Pig year. Oxen deserve some 'me time' and should give themselves the chance to relax and unwind.

Also, if lacking regular exercise or not having a balanced diet, again, they should aim to address this over the year. Pig years can be personally beneficial for Oxen and an improvement in the quality and balance of their lifestyle can benefit many.

Work-wise, this can also be a constructive year, with many Oxen building on their position. As staff changes occur, promotion opportunities can arise, and Oxen may be well placed to benefit. Those who feel unfulfilled or in a rut should keep alert for openings and actively pursue any that interest them. This is no time to stand still or let unsatisfactory situations continue. Pig years favour the hard-working and can open important doors for Oxen. Similarly, Oxen who are seeking work can see their tenacity rewarded with a position with potential for the future. In addition, Oxen who are studying for qualifications or involved in training will find their commitment can yield important results. Pig years are encouraging for Oxen and can see them broadening their capabilities.

Financially, Oxen can fare well, although, with plans for their home, tempting purchases and increased chances to go out, their outgoings will be considerable. Over the year, they will need to watch their financial situation and ideally budget for their plans. Much can be done – and enjoyed – this year, but it does require control over the purse-strings.

Overall, the Pig year can be a good one for Oxen and in many ways uplifting. They can get a lot of pleasure from it. Personal interests and recreational pursuits are especially well aspected and there will be some good social occasions to enjoy as well. This is a year for Oxen to engage with others *and* improve their lifestyle. The Pig year also encourages growth and there will be chances to progress. Overall a constructive, satisfying and pleasurable year.

Tips for the Year
Make the most of what opens up for you. With purpose and willingness, you can make good gains and enjoy good times. Also, enjoy your personal interests and special relationships. Both can be important and meaningful in this active and rewarding year.

Thoughts and Words of Oxen

The great thing in this world is not so much where we stand as in what direction we are moving.

OLIVER WENDELL HOLMES

The truest wisdom is a resolute determination.

NAPOLEON BONAPARTE

What you ardently and constantly desire, you always get.

NAPOLEON BONAPARTE

Ideals are like stars; you will not succeed in touching them with your hands. But like the seafaring man on the desert of waters, you choose them as your guides, and following them, you will reach your destiny.

CARL SCHURZ

I will act as if what I do makes a difference.

WILLIAM JAMES

I am in earnest – I will not equivocate – I will not excuse – I will not retreat a single inch; and I will be heard.

WILLIAM LLOYD GARRISON

I do not know anyone who has got to the top without hard work. That is the recipe. It will not always get you to the top, but it should get you pretty near.

MARGARET THATCHER

One only gets to the top rung on the ladder by
steadily climbing up one at a time, and suddenly all
sorts of powers, all sorts of abilities which you
thought never belonged to you, suddenly become a
possibility and you think, 'Well, I'll have a go, too.'

MARGARET THATCHER

Live your beliefs and you can turn the world around.

HENRY DAVID THOREAU

I have learned that if one advances in the direction of
his dreams and endeavours to live the life he has
imagined, he will meet with a success unexpected in
common hours.

HENRY DAVID THOREAU

Men are born to succeed, not to fail.

HENRY DAVID THOREAU

31 January 1938–18 February 1939 — *Earth Tiger*

17 February 1950–5 February 1951 — *Metal Tiger*

5 February 1962–24 January 1963 — *Water Tiger*

23 January 1974–10 February 1975 — *Wood Tiger*

9 February 1986–28 January 1987 — *Fire Tiger*

28 January 1998–15 February 1999 — *Earth Tiger*

14 February 2010–2 February 2011 — *Metal Tiger*

1 February 2022–21 January 2023 — *Water Tiger*

19 February 2034–7 February 2035 — *Wood Tiger*

The Tiger

The Personality of the Tiger

With their stripes and stealth, Tigers are impressive creatures. They are noticed and command respect. And those born under the Tiger sign also have great presence and can make their mark in many ways.

Tigers are born under the sign of courage. They are adventurous and have keen, eager natures. Not only are they capable of coming up with many ideas – Tigers are creative and inventive – but they are innovators. If something new comes along or an appealing opportunity presents itself, they are sure to pursue it. However, their quest for the new can lead to moments of recklessness. Tigers do not always think through the consequences of their actions. They are risk-takers and sometimes their haste does not always lead to the most favourable of outcomes. In life, they will experience knocks and reversals, but they are quick to learn and their unquenchable spirit will lead them forever on.

With their zeal and belief in themselves and their ideas, Tigers are natural leaders. They are enthusiastic, compelling and action-driven, although, curiously, at times indecisive, perhaps bewildered by the choices in front of them. They are honourable in their dealings with others and public-spirited. Many have championed causes, fought injustices or helped others in times of need. Tigers are noble. And they have a rebellious streak and will take a stand against authority should the situation warrant it.

With their enquiring natures, Tigers have a great many interests and involve themselves in a myriad of activities. They are rarely still and usually to be found leading busy and fulfilling lifestyles. However, because they thirst for the new and are keen to experience a great deal, there are times when they lack commitment and move from one thing to another. Tigers can be restless, and if they were to be more persistent, their levels of success would sometimes be greater. Also, as they like to be self-reliant, they do not always seek out or listen to advice from others, and sometimes this can be to their disadvantage. There will be times when Tigers learn the hard way.

Being adventurous, Tigers are often keen to travel and to see new places. They also have a wonderful gift of relating to others. They are lively, stimulating company and usually have a wide social circle. They are also very open and upfront in their dealings with others. They have a dislike of falsehood and hypocrisy and speak as they find. There is no pretence with Tigers – they are genuine, honest and personable.

With their independent spirit, they often leave home at a young age, and many will quickly settle down and establish their own homes. As a partner, they can be caring, protective and generous. If a parent, their enthusiasm and wide interests will do much to encourage their children's development. Tigers make fine teachers.

In many ways, Tigers like to impress. Not only have they a vibrant, friendly personality, but they take care with their appearance. Whether wearing smart fashionable clothes or adopting a more flamboyant and striking style, they know what suits them. This is a talent of both male and female Tigers, although the female is possibly more socially aware than her male counterpart. She is observant and perceptive and has a happy knack of getting on well with most people. She empathizes, is attentive and, when it comes to entertaining, makes a marvellous hostess. She cares, and this is what makes a difference.

In their early working life in particular, Tigers are apt to change jobs quite frequently, as they are always trying to improve their lot. And because of their quick wits, their integrity and their willingness to take on responsibilities, they can do well. If their work encourages creativity and nurtures (rather than stifles) their abilities, many can rise to positions of authority. They enjoy challenge and will keenly pursue targets or objectives. Their communication skills can make them effective advocates, campaigners or politicians, as well as inspirational teachers. Humanitarian work could also appeal, as could careers in the arts, media and commerce, all of which would allow them scope for creative input. With their energy and competitive spirit, they could also find sporting careers tempting. Tigers have many skills and considerable potential.

Their earning abilities are considerable too, but they would be advised to remain disciplined in financial matters. Tigers like to live for the moment and can spend freely. They are also generous, and their money can come and go all too easily. Setting funds aside for specific requirements and saving for the future could be to their advantage. Also, if embarking on anything risky, they need to be careful and aware of the implications involved. Trusting to luck can provide some salutary and sometimes painful lessons.

Nevertheless, Tigers are certainly special, as well as generous, inventive and courageous. Some of their endeavours may end in disaster and some of their dreams will never materialize, but they will succeed in a great many things and lead lives that are fulfilling in so many ways.

The poet John Masefield was born under the Tiger sign and he wrote:

Most roads lead men homewards,
My road leads me forth.

This is so very true of Tigers – they are always keen to venture forth.

Top Tips for Tigers

- You have great enthusiasm, but sometimes get carried away in the excitement of the moment and commit yourself to undertakings without thinking through all that is involved. Sometimes less haste and more planning would lead to better results, and often less pressure too.
- You may have a rebellious streak and consider certain rules and restrictions unnecessary. However, pitting yourself against authority (including employers) will not necessarily do you any favours. You would do well to think through the implications of your words and actions rather than be over-hasty.
- You have many interests, but spread your energies widely. If you were to focus more on specific areas, your level of expertise would be higher and your results often more substantial. Curbing your sometimes restless nature could be to your advantage.
- Your inventiveness is a real strength. You are an original thinker and should have belief in yourself. Make the most of your special talents, for they may take you far.

Relations with Others

With a Rat

Active, lively and sharing many interests, these two get on well.

In work, their inventiveness, energy and skills make them a formidable and potentially very successful team.

In love, the Tiger will delight in the Rat's charm and personable manner as well as value their skills as a home-maker. Their different attitudes to money will need addressing, with the Tiger not always meeting the Rat's thrifty standards, but, with goodwill and adjustment, this can be a reasonably good match.

With an Ox

The cautious and measured ways of the Ox do not sit comfortably with the Tiger. Relations between them do not tend to be good.

In work, the Tiger is a pioneer, taking risks and pushing barriers, while the Ox is a traditionalist. Their different approaches will inevitably cause difficulties.

In love, the Tiger will recognize the Ox's many qualities, particularly their sincere and dependable nature, but these two live their lives at different speeds and, as both are strong-willed, tensions are inevitable. A challenging match.

With another Tiger

With all their Tiger energy, ideas and desire for action, which of these two will prevail? With both being self-willed and driven, relations between two Tigers can be tricky.

In work, they may be enterprising and enthusiastic, but each will want to take the lead – and credit. They are too competitive to work well together.

In love, Tigers are passionate and exciting and have much to offer. But they also have a lot of restless energy and like to have their own way. Two Tigers are too vibrant and strong-willed to live in harmony. A difficult match.

With a Rabbit

Their personalities are very different, but these two signs like and respect each other and relations between them are often mutually beneficial.

In work, the Tiger will value – and benefit from – the Rabbit's orderly and methodical approach and their very different skills can make them an effective team.

In love, the Tiger will be very much attracted by the kindly and companionable ways of the Rabbit and there will be a strong physical attraction too. These two are good for each other and each will benefit from the other's strengths. A fulfilling match.

With a Dragon

These two lively, outgoing signs respect each other, and while sometimes their self-willed natures will clash, relations between them are generally positive.

In work, with both being enterprising, resourceful risk-takers, they generate great dynamism. Anything is possible for them, especially when luck is on their side.

In love, there will be hopes, plans and so much to share. Life will be lived to the full, with the Tiger finding the Dragon a loyal and loving companion. They are both strong-willed and value a certain freedom of action, but provided they can forge a good understanding and agree on a division of responsibilities, they can make an exciting match.

With a Snake

The Tiger is open and upfront and finds it hard to understand or relate to the reserved and sometimes perplexing Snake.

In work, their approaches are very different and the Tiger will feel inhibited by the cautious and guarded tendencies of the Snake. With little trust or understanding, they will prefer to work in their separate ways.

In love, the Tiger may be enchanted by the Snake's quiet and seductive charm, but they live their lives at different speeds and the Tiger's outlook will often be at odds with that of the Snake. A difficult match.

With a Horse

The Tiger admires the lively and spirited Horse and relations between the pair will be good.

In work, both are ambitious, hard-working and enterprising, and the Tiger will draw strength from their redoubtable and purposeful Horse colleague. An effective combination.

In love, their passion and many shared interests (including travel) will bind these two together. The Tiger will especially value the Horse's judgement. They are well suited and can make a successful and lively match.

With a Goat

These two like and understand each other and, with both being easy-going, relations between them are good.

In work, both are creative and each will be an encouraging influence on the other. To be successful, however, they will need to be disciplined, especially with finances, and channel their efforts well.

In love, passionate, fun-loving and sharing many interests, these two can find much happiness. The Tiger will particularly value the Goat's caring and supportive nature and home-making skills. As both signs are spendthrifts, they will need to manage their finances well. Overall, though, a good match.

With a Monkey

Both are lively and they will share many interests, but there can still be a certain wariness between these two.

In work, they are probably the most enterprising and inventive signs there are, but the Tiger could have misgivings about the Monkey's approach and guile. With this lack of trust, their shared potential is not likely to materialize.

In love, the Tiger could delight in the Monkey's lively, optimistic nature, but, as both have a huge amount of restless energy and like to have their own way, they will often clash. A challenging match.

With a Rooster

These two may be outgoing and keen socializers, but they are also frank, forthright and strong-willed. Relations can be tricky.

In work, both have great skills, but are competitive and will want to take the lead. To realize their potential, there will need to be a clear division of responsibility.

In love, they both enjoy an active lifestyle, but their redoubtable and forthright natures will invariably clash. Also, the Tiger could find the structured lifestyle of the Rooster inhibiting. A difficult match.

With a Dog

The Tiger and Dog appreciate each other's qualities and relations between the two will be good.

In work, they can combine their talents effectively and the Tiger will respect the Dog's level-headed and stalwart approach.

In love, their relationship will be mutually beneficial, with the Tiger valuing the Dog's love, loyalty, support and often grounded opinions. These two can be good for each other and can find much happiness together.

With a Pig

With their zest, shared interests and fondness of the good life, Tigers and Pigs enjoy each other's company.

In work, both are enterprising and the Tiger will appreciate the Pig's good business acumen and hard-working ways. By channelling their efforts and remaining disciplined, these two can accomplish a great deal.

In love, these strongly passionate and sensual signs can find much bliss together. They can be very close, with great trust and understanding, and with the Tiger valuing the Pig's thoughtfulness and wise counsel. A splendid match.

Horoscopes for Each of the Chinese Years

TIGER FORTUNES IN THE YEAR OF THE RAT

Tigers like to be involved in a great many activities, but in the Rat year they should adopt a more measured approach. To be impulsive or hasty could lead to problems and disappointment. If they can bear this in mind and exercise greater patience, the year can be smoother and ultimately more rewarding for them.

In work, Tigers should concentrate on the areas in which they have most experience and look to build on their current skills.

Additional training or the chance to extend their present duties can be very much to their advantage. In addition, by immersing themselves in the life of their workplace and seizing any chances to network, they can do a lot to help their future prospects. However, they do need to stay focused and avoid going off on tangents or being diverted into unfamiliar or less helpful matters. This is a year for concentrated effort and using skills to advantage.

Similarly, Tigers who decide to move from their present employer or are seeking work should consider areas in which they have experience and which also offer the chance to build on their capabilities. Success this year will come from steady and dedicated effort in the areas that Tigers know best.

Finance also requires a steady approach. Tigers should watch their sometimes impulsive nature and take their time when making purchases. There will be many temptations to spend, but hurried decisions could be regretted later, and without discipline, spending levels could creep up. Also, if tempted to speculate or enter into any agreement, Tigers should check the facts and implications and take sound advice. Vigilance is advised this year.

A particular strength of Tigers is their ability to enjoy good relations with many people, and their personable nature will again serve them well this year. In view of some of its vexations, Tigers will value being able to turn to others for advice and should avail themselves of the support and knowledge available to them. If they are concerned by any matter, they should not feel alone.

In addition, Rat years bring good social opportunities and Tigers will enjoy going out and extending their social network. Certain interests can bring them into contact with other enthusiasts and some good connections and friendships can be made. Tigers who are feeling lonely would find joining local groups worth considering. Rat years encourage the development of personal interests and involvement with others. In addition, with their future in mind, Tigers would do well to consider courses of study and other ways in which they could develop their skills and knowledge. What some start this year could bring later (often substantial) rewards.

Tigers will also see much activity in their home life this year and there will need to be good liaison between family members. But, amid all the activity, there will be some pleasing occasions too. Whether celebrating an achievement or a personal milestone, enjoying a holiday (Rat years can offer good travel possibilities) or sharing quality time together, there will be much for everyone to appreciate. Also, by encouraging openness, Tigers can be helped and advised and benefit even more from the good rapport they share with those around them.

Tigers have a talent for coming up with ideas and this year will see no shortage of projects they would like to get underway. However, these do need to be planned and costed carefully and Tigers should be careful not to commit themselves to too many undertakings all at the same time. Rat years require care, focus and discipline.

Tigers like to get on with things, but despite their noble intentions, results could be slow in coming through this year. This is a time for proceeding steadily and for building on their position and knowledge. Rush and risks could backfire and, especially in money matters, care is advised. However, by drawing on the support and goodwill of others, Tigers can be helped in both their current and future activities. This may not be the easiest of years, but it can be a constructive one, particularly as it will enable Tigers to acquire greater knowledge and skills.

Tips for the Year
Proceed carefully. Think through your decisions and focus on your priorities. Also, seize any chances to add to your knowledge. Liaise well with others and take note of their viewpoints and advice.

TIGER FORTUNES IN THE YEAR OF THE OX

Ox years favour tradition and the action-oriented Tiger may be frustrated by the length of time things seem to take as well as the paucity of opportunities. However, while this may be a challenging year, there is good reason for Tigers to take heart. Next year is their own year and what they do now can prepare the way for better times ahead.

Also, while the slow workings of the Ox year may not always suit their personality, there are ways that Tigers can counter some of the more awkward aspects. In particular, they should control their rebellious streak, otherwise there is a risk it could undermine their position as well as reduce the level of support they enjoy. In any tense or awkward situation, they should watch their words and be considered in their response.

At work, Tigers will, as always, be keen to get on with things and get results. But, as many will quickly find, wheels turn slowly in Ox years and they may be frustrated by delays, bureaucracy and petty irritations. Progress will not be swift, but by concentrating on their duties and doing their best in often difficult situations, Tigers will not only have the chance to prove their capabilities, but also to gain valuable insight into their industry. In addition, if training courses or extra duties become available, even if just covering for an absent colleague, they should take full advantage of them. By developing their knowledge and skills, they will be better positioned to benefit when further opportunities arise. With their own year following, effort made now can prepare them for future success.

For Tigers who are seeking work, or a change in their situation, this can be a significant time. Although obtaining a position will not be easy, by widening the scope of what they are considering, they may be able to obtain a position that can extend their experience as well as offer future possibilities. Things tend to happen for a reason in Ox years and developments (and lessons) now can prepare the way for more rapid advance in the Tiger's own year.

In money matters Tigers again need to be careful, watching spending and making early provision for larger outlays. This is a year for discipline and good management. Also, Tigers should attend to financial paperwork with care. Lapses and delays could work to their disadvantage as well as sometimes be difficult to rectify.

In view of the pressures they may face during Ox years, Tigers should also give some consideration to their own lifestyle and well-being, including their diet and level of exercise, and, if necessary, seek advice on ways to improve. Preserving time for interests and recreation can also be of benefit. Any interest-related skills or additional knowledge gained now can give Tigers the chance to do more in the future.

With their wide interests and engaging manner, Tigers enjoy company and here the Ox year can bring some special times. Many Tigers will find their circle of acquaintances growing and will enjoy the chance to meet new people and attend interesting social occasions. They can build good connections and friendships this year.

Tigers enjoying romance, or who find it this year, will also find that any additional time and attention they can give to the relationship can help strengthen it. However, with the aspects as they are, they need to be careful of lapses and, should a difference of opinion arise, watch their words. Disagreements or a loss of temper could sour relations. Tigers, take note.

In their home life, shared activities and spending time together can make a difference. While Tigers (and others) may be juggling with many commitments, well-planned projects and mutual interests can often be pleasing. A family holiday, too, could do everyone good. However, rather than concentrating everything around a particular time, projects should be spread out over the year and ample time allowed to complete them. Ox years do not favour hurry. Their home can be a valuable sanctuary for Tigers this year, but their domestic life does require good organization and a willingness to adjust as situations require.

In general, the Ox year will have its awkward moments, but with patience and care, Tigers can do much to minimize its more troublesome aspects. It is a year for tact, patience and for Tigers to curb their sometimes rebellious tendencies. But, frustrating though some of the year may be, by adding to their skills, making the most of situations and spending time with those around them, Tigers can see their efforts being rewarded. While not an easy year, this one can nevertheless lay the foundations for better times ahead.

Tips for the Year
Proceed carefully, thinking through your actions and responses. Also, seize any chances to add to your skills and knowledge and involve others in your activities and plans. This may be a challenging year, but its lessons (and potential gains) can be manifold.

TIGER FORTUNES IN THE YEAR OF THE TIGER

Many Tigers will feel excited about their own year and be keen to set about their plans with gusto. And, especially for those who have felt held back in recent years, this is a time to concentrate on the *now* rather than what has gone before. However, while Tigers will have high hopes for their year, to get the best from it they will need to remain disciplined and concentrate on key aims. With focus, planning and effort, this can be a successful and special time.

At work, in view of their recent undertakings and the skills they have acquired, many Tigers will be excellently placed when opportunities arise. And they will. This is a year for progress. Pleasingly, too, many Tigers will have a greater chance to put their strengths to effective use. Their ideas and ability to think round problems or come up with new approaches can prove a real asset. By contributing and being involved, they can come into their own and greatly enhance their reputation.

For those who start the year discontented in their present position or seeking work, again the year can bring important developments. By keeping alert for openings and being swift in making applications, these Tigers can benefit from some good opportunities. Initiative counts for a lot this year and extra effort can often make a difference. With perseverance, commitment and self-belief, a lot can be achieved. Tigers, take note.

Progress at work can also help financially, and some Tigers will enjoy additional good fortune, perhaps through a profitable idea, a gift or a stroke of luck. Tiger years have their surprises and rewards. In addition, some attractive and timely purchases can be made. However, while Tigers can fare well in money matters, they should use any upturn to help their overall position. Whether reducing borrowings, adding to savings or making provision for the future, good management can benefit them both now and in years to come.

In addition, with this being their own year, they should look ahead. Considering their hopes and future aspirations will not only give them something to strive towards but also make them more aware of what they need to do now. The Tiger year can be an important springboard for what lies ahead and is an excellent time to consider, plan and act. It is said that a journey of a thousand miles begins with a single step. Now is the time to take some steps.

With their enquiring nature, Tigers have wide-ranging interests and again can develop and enjoy them this year. Sometimes new equipment or contacts can open up fresh possibilities. And if a new pursuit tempts them, they should investigate. In their own year, benefits can follow on from many of their activities.

The Tiger year can also bring excellent social opportunities and there will be a lot for Tigers to participate in. Tigers who would welcome new friends or have experienced recent personal difficulty can see their own year ushering in a new chapter, with some finding love and also creating a new social circle. Tiger years can brighten the situation of many.

In their home life, too, Tigers will be keen to forge ahead with plans and, whether making purchases or home improvements or perhaps moving, by carefully considering and costing their options, they can see a lot happen. However, while keen to get things done, they do need to be wary of proceeding too hastily. By allowing additional time and planning, they will often be able to make more suitable decisions.

In addition to the plans and activities Tigers instigate this year, they can also look forward some special moments, especially concerning personal news and family successes. Domestically, Tiger years are busy and gratifying.

In so many ways, this will be an important year for Tigers. It is a time for moving ahead and benefiting from opportunities. Tigers will also benefit from the goodwill and support of others and their own year will give rise to many special occasions as well as allow them to widen their social circle. Tigers have a lot in their favour this year and should focus on their objectives. With purpose, they can enjoy many significant achievements.

Tips for the Year
Take the initiative. Opportunities can open up for you this year. Also, look ahead and give some thought to your future aims. What is started now can take root and in time become significant. Your own year is a special one for you.

TIGER FORTUNES IN THE YEAR OF THE RABBIT

In this constructive year, Tigers can make good gains and build on recent achievements. However, while the aspects are encouraging, they will need to rein in the more restless side of their nature. Rabbit years favour consistency and proceeding along established lines, and Tigers who are inclined to rush or take risks will find obstacles in their way. Rabbit years favour thoughtful and more measured approaches.

At work, Tigers will often have the chance to make more of their expertise. This could be through taking on a more specialist role, being offered new objectives or transferring to another position in their place of work. Many can take their career to new levels this year and see their previous commitment and proven skills recognized and rewarded.

There will, though, be some Tigers who feel they could better themselves elsewhere. These Tigers, as well as those seeking work, should keep alert for openings but also talk to experts and contacts and consider other ways in which they could use their skills. With advice and some thought on how they would like to develop their career, they can find some good openings. Work-wise, these can be important and successful times, but they do require a disciplined approach. Tigers who are inclined to rush or 'cut corners', beware. Mistakes and lapses will often get picked up, especially as Rabbits, who are masters this year, are so keen on detail and doing everything right. Also, Tigers should not act in isolation this year. It is by working closely with colleagues that they will be able to demonstrate their qualities and potential.

Tigers can fare well financially and many will benefit from a rise in income over the year or receive funds from another source. To make the most of any upturn, they need to plan key purchases and avoid succumbing to too many impulse buys. Here again, a disciplined and careful approach can make so much difference.

Personal interests are favourably aspected and Tigers should set time aside for pursuits they enjoy rather than expect to be on the go all the time. Activities that allow them to get out of doors could be particularly appealing, as could developing new ideas and getting involved in creative activities. Tigers could find them-selves on inspired form this year. In some cases, additional instruction or personal study could open up new possibilities.

Their personal life can also bring them considerable pleasure this year. Existing romances, especially those started in the previ-ous Tiger year, can often become more meaningful, while unat-tached Tigers will have excellent opportunities to meet others. This can be a special year for affairs of the heart.

Rabbit years also favour social activity and Tigers will enjoy becoming involved in the myriad of events that are happening. Tigers are popular company and the social diaries of many will be busier than usual this year.

Tigers will also enjoy sharing their thoughts and activities with family members. Domestically, the Rabbit year can be satisfying and constructive. Adjustments (including to routine) may need to be made as opportunities arise, but good communication will help. Sharing thoughts will also benefit everyone when major purchasing decisions need to be made or problems faced (all years have their share). The more that can be addressed collectively this year, the better. In addition, if Tigers are able to start a new activity, perhaps to do with keep fit or another interest, with members of their household, this could be both beneficial and fun. Rabbit years favour a coming together.

They also encourage Tigers to make the most of themselves. There will be opportunities for them to develop and new possibilities to pursue. However, to fully benefit, Tigers need to be disciplined, focused and prepared to put in the effort. Acting in haste or jumping from one activity to another is not the way to proceed in Rabbit years. Tigers will need to temper their sometimes over-zealous nature. But, with good use of their time, they can make this a personally satisfying year. They will also find themselves in demand and can benefit from socializing and sharing activities with those around them. A satisfying and constructive year.

Tips for the Year
Strive for a good lifestyle balance. Enjoy and develop your interests and allow time for yourself as well as for those who are special to you. There is no need to rush or overcommit yourself this year. Instead, savour the rewards and the opportunities of this encouraging time.

Tiger Fortunes in the Year of the Dragon

Dragon years have energy and bring interesting times for Tigers. Never ones to sit on the sidelines, they will be keen to forge ahead with their plans and can make good progress. However, Dragon years can also see much volatility and Tigers will need to be vigilant and guard against impulsive actions.

Work prospects are especially promising. When obstacles present themselves and solutions need finding, ever-inventive Tigers will rise to the challenge. Their resourcefulness and ability to think out of the box will serve many well this year, bringing success and helping future prospects. However, here lies the sting: while successes can be enjoyed, Tigers should not become overconfident. If they rush or are inclined to take risks, situations could be misread and mistakes made. Dragon years can lay traps for the unwary and Tigers need to remain on their mettle.

There will, however, be opportunities for many Tigers to improve on their position over the year, and those who are seeking work or keen to progress their career in other ways could find the opening they are seeking. Their drive and sense of purpose can deliver this year, but they do need to commit themselves and give of their best. In particular, when making applications, extra effort can strengthen their chances.

With Tigers frequently feeling inspired, this is also a good year for them to follow up their ideas and explore fresh possibilities. If they wish to gain or extend certain skills, follow up new interests or try out activities that appeal to them, they should make the most of what is available. Creative pursuits could particularly appeal, and develop in encouraging ways.

In money matters, care is needed. While income may increase, risks or hurried decisions could bring regret. If tempted to lend, Tigers may find problems occurring. They should check the terms when entering into any new agreement and look after their possessions with care, as a loss could be upsetting. This is very much a year for increased vigilance.

A further area of concern may involve the situation of a relation or a close friend. If difficulties arise, by listening and offering advice, Tigers can often give important assistance. However, should they not feel competent in certain matters, they should not hesitate to call on professional advice.

However, while the Dragon year can have its challenging elements, Tigers can nevertheless enjoy some good times. For the unattached, romance can beckon, with some Tigers meeting their future partner in an unexpected but fortuitous way. Existing romances can often strengthen and some Tigers will settle down and start a family.

All Tigers will welcome the social opportunities of the year and there will be a good mix of occasions to enjoy. However, with communication and dialogue so important this year, Tigers do need to remain aware of the views of others as well as heed any advice they are given. Something a friend could say could be both significant and prophetic.

Similarly, in their home life it is important there is good communication and cooperation between all concerned, otherwise life could be conducted in a whirl of activity and there is a risk that tensions could result. To prevent this, Tigers should preserve quality time to spend with their loved ones and suggest activities that all can appreciate. Giving that extra bit of time and attention can make a big difference this year.

As usual, Tigers will busy themselves with many activities this year and should follow the correct procedures if involved in any hazardous undertaking. Lapses could be to their detriment. This is a time to be vigilant and thorough.

By the end of the year, Tigers could be astonished by all that has happened and the great amount they have done. It is a time for furthering ideas, skills and interests. But throughout, Tigers do need to channel their efforts wisely and carefully. A lot can go well for them, but this is also a year to be mindful and vigilant.

Tips for the Year
Set about your activities in a positive manner, but avoid rush, risk or, in the wake of success, complacency. Also, liaise well with those around you and value time spent with those who are special to you. Extra care and good communication are so very important in this active and lively year.

TIGER FORTUNES IN THE YEAR OF THE SNAKE

A reasonable year ahead. While Tigers can do well – some very well – they may find it best to moderate their approach. Snake years favour steadiness. If Tigers adapt to the rhythm of the year, they can make this a constructive and satisfying time.

At work, this can be an excellent year to consolidate recent gains. By concentrating on their duties and immersing themselves in their present place of work, many Tigers will enjoy a good level of fulfilment. Also, as situations change, there will be the opportunity for many to make greater use of their strengths. Whether they are promoting ideas, taking on additional duties or benefiting from training, they can do themselves a lot of good this year. In addition, those pursuing a particular career could find it helpful to network more, as well as follow developments within their industry. By raising their profile, they will be investing in themselves and their future.

Many Tigers will remain with their current employer over the year and build on their position, but for those who desire change or are seeking work, the Snake year can bring important developments. By widening the scope of their search, many could have the chance to use their skills in new ways. Although this could involve readjustment, the Snake year can do much to highlight their potential.

Tigers can also derive much satisfaction from their personal interests, but rather than spread their attention too widely, they should set themselves some projects and aims for the year. With focus, their interests and recreational activities can do them a lot of good and be that much more enjoyable. Tigers who lead especially busy lifestyles should allow themselves the chance to step off the treadmill every so often. Snake years are times to appreciate the rewards of previous efforts and restore balance to busy lifestyles.

Travel could appeal and, if possible, Tigers should aim to take a holiday over the year. With their adventurous nature, they could enjoy visiting some exciting places.

In money matters, however, they will need to be disciplined. Money can come and go all too easily in Snake years. In addition, financial paperwork will require close attention. Bureaucratic matters may sometimes be troublesome and any Tigers involved in legal dealings may find them becoming protracted. Good advice needs to be sought.

With their active and outgoing nature, Tigers will enjoy the social opportunities of the year, but here too there may be problems. A disagreement or personality clash may occur or jealousy surface, and Tigers should be wary of placing themselves in an awkward or embarrassing position. While usually so expert in relations with others, they will find Snake years require care, tact and discretion. Tigers, take note. This can be a pleasing year, but it is not one for lapses or risks.

Domestically, Tigers will have quite a few ideas and projects to pursue, and if they allow time for these to take shape, they will be pleased with the outcomes. Again, the best results will come through planning and proceeding in measured ways. Also, the costs (and disruption) of some activities could be far greater than anticipated. Snake years can be expensive. Tigers, be warned and make ample allowance for this.

In addition, Tigers will give important support to their loved ones during the year and their advice and encouragement will be greatly appreciated. With travel likely to appeal, time away can also be valued and do everyone good.

Tigers enjoy doing a lot at a fast pace, but Snake years encourage them to pause, take stock and build steadily. Rather than rush or be over-ambitious, it is a year to proceed calmly and find greater fulfilment in what takes place. Skills and experience gained now can often have important long-term value. Tigers will need to be aware and attentive in their relations with others, but overall will be pleased with how their ideas and plans develop. And the year's more moderate pace will allow them to appreciate that much more too.

Tips for the Year
Concentrate on the present rather than try to rush ahead. Nurture your strengths, spend time on your interests and value those around you and the rewards your efforts bring.

TIGER FORTUNES IN THE YEAR OF THE HORSE

Tigers are quick to latch onto new developments and will find the Horse year full of possibility. As Virgil noted, 'Fortune favours the bold,' and in Horse years, fortune favours bold and enterprising Tigers. These are favourable times for them and they will be able to make the most of emerging opportunities. For any Tigers who are unhappy with their current situation, this is a time for change. With resolve, effort and willingness, many can see their prospects substantially improve.

However, while the aspects are encouraging, to get results Tigers will need to work hard and be persistent. Horse years require application. Those who let chances slip or lack commitment could miss out.

At work, Tigers will have the chance to make more of the skills and expertise they have recently gained. As a result, when staff movements occur and promotion opportunities arise, many will be excellently placed to benefit. In addition, Horse years often see much activity in the workplace, and by being involved in what is going on, Tigers will not only increase their influence but also have more chance to demonstrate particular strengths. The active nature of the Horse year suits their psyche and, enthused and supported, they can make important progress.

For Tigers who feel their prospects are limited where they are and would welcome greater scope, as well as those seeking work, the Horse year can again open up good possibilities. By keeping alert, making enquiries and being persistent, these Tigers can secure a position which offers a platform on which to build. Horse years require effort, but do give Tigers the chance to do well.

Progress made at work can also help income and some Tigers will also benefit from a bonus or gift. These can be improved times financially, although to benefit fully, Tigers need to manage their outgoings and budget for their needs and plans.

Another positive feature of the year will be the way Tigers can develop their ideas. Whether in a professional capacity or with their personal interests, whenever they have something in mind that they feel has potential, they should take it further. Horse years can be inspiring ones and Tigers can benefit from what they do during them. With this in mind, Tigers skilled in creative pursuits should, if relevant, promote their talents. However, while this is an encouraging year, Tigers do need to persevere and not let setbacks or disappointments weaken their resolve. This is no time to be half-hearted or give up too easily, especially in view of the potential gains to be had.

Horse years can also see considerable social activity and Tigers will enjoy the events they attend and the chance to meet new people. Their interests in particular can have a good social element.

For the unattached, affairs of the heart are splendidly aspected. New acquaintances may quickly become special and existing romances more meaningful. These can be busy, exciting and often passionate times. Tigers who start the Horse year discontented will find that positive action can often brighten their outlook. Horse years have great possibilities.

Tigers can also look forward to some pleasing developments domestically. There will be good reasons for a celebration and a holiday and/or visits to special attractions will also be much appreciated.

With Tigers on enthusiastic form this year, domestic changes may also be on the agenda, but these do need to be considered carefully and ample time allowed for them, especially if practical undertakings are involved. The Horse year will be busy enough without adding further pressure or starting too many projects all at once. Tigers, take note.

Overall, the Horse year can be a good one for Tigers. It is one for commitment and hard work, but the drive, ideas and personal qualities Tigers so often show can help them make it both active and fulfilling. Important progress can be made, as this is a year favouring involvement and moving forward. Relations with others can bring Tigers considerable happiness and they will often be buoyed up by the support and goodwill they enjoy. They have much in their favour this year.

Tips for the Year
Be determined and persistent. Rewards can be substantial this year, but need striving for. However, while this is a year for effort, it is a lively one too and will bring opportunities. Enjoy what it offers you.

TIGER FORTUNES IN THE YEAR OF THE GOAT

An interesting year ahead, although Tigers will need to keep their wits about them. As they will quickly find, in the Goat year even the best-laid plans do not always proceed in the manner intended.

However, while Tigers will need to show some flexibility, in some respects this year will suit them. Tigers enjoy rising to the challenge, particularly when ideas are needed or there are solutions to be found, and they also appreciate the satisfying outcomes their efforts bring.

This will be especially true in work matters. Over the year Tigers will be able to put their skills and creativity to good use and many will play an increasingly important role in their workplace. Their experience and input, including their ability to think out of the box, could prove a real asset and result in a greater role or promotion. However, with a lot happening, they do need to remain focused and concentrate on priorities. This is no year to go off on tangents or be diverted into less helpful matters – always a risk in this active year.

In addition, Tigers should pay close attention to their relations with their colleagues and be aware of office politics. The year requires them to tread mindfully.

For Tigers who are seeking change or a new job, the Goat year has good possibilities. Many Tigers will be able to secure a position that not only offers change but also a welcome challenge. The early days could prove daunting, but many Tigers will quickly prove themselves and relish the chance to use their skills in new ways. Goat years can bring some unexpected developments, and by making the most of them, Tigers can really benefit.

With their inquisitive nature, Tigers have extensive interests, and if something intrigues them this year, they should follow it up and see what develops. Those who lead busy lifestyles in particular should ensure time is set aside for recreational pursuits and, if lacking regular exercise, take advice on activities that may be suitable.

Travel could also appeal. Tigers should take a holiday this year if possible, as they will enjoy the chance to visit some often special attractions. In addition, they could be tempted by a wide range of events and enjoy the opportunities and sometimes unexpected invitations the Goat year offers.

With the year's many activities, spending will be high, however, and Tigers need to manage their resources carefully. A lot can happen quickly and they should be aware of – and make allowance for – the cost of some undertakings. Without discipline, some economizing might be needed later. In addition, they should keep their belongings safe. A loss could be upsetting.

Domestically, this can be a busy year and there needs to be good liaison between everyone concerned and time set aside for sharing. If not, sometimes domestic life could be conducted at a heady pace and pressures and tiredness give rise to moments of tension. Tigers (and others) need to be mindful of this and aim for a good lifestyle balance. Also, plans and situations can be apt to change in the Goat year and flexibility will be required.

Socially, this can be a generally favourable year, although with so much going on, Tigers need to take careful note of the views of friends and of the arrangements being made. Being preoccupied, distracted or overcommitted could cause some awkward moments. This year, rather than conduct so much at a fast pace,

Tigers should aim to slow down a little and simply enjoy spending time with others.

In general, Goat years offer good possibilities, but Tigers do need to be on their mettle, as situations can change quickly. By being flexible and aware and acting smartly, however, they can benefit from the developments of the year. At work, their ideas and resourcefulness can impress others, although they do need to remain focused and channel their efforts wisely. To try to overdo things or spread their energies too widely could reduce their effectiveness. Personal interests can bring much pleasure, but, with the year often being busy, Tigers do need to pay close attention to their relations with others and preserve some quality time for their family and friends. This can be a satisfying year, but it requires mindfulness of others and good time management.

Tips for the Year
Plans should not be set in stone this year. Be open-minded and make the most of the situations that arise. With flexibility, you can see more happen. Also, develop your ideas and personal interests, as you can enjoy some good results.

TIGER FORTUNES IN THE YEAR OF THE MONKEY

The Monkey year has energy and is a time of considerable activity, but during it Tigers will need to exercise care. Rather than proceed regardless, they should look to consolidate their position and make the most of situations *as they are*. Hasty or ill-thought-out action could bring difficulties and Tigers need to watch their sometimes over-zealous nature.

At work, rather than looking too far ahead, Tigers should concentrate on the tasks in hand, and, if relatively new to their position, familiarize themselves with the various aspects of their role. All Tigers should aim to work closely with their colleagues this year rather than operate too independently. Not only can more be accomplished that way, but Tigers will find themselves better placed to benefit from opportunities. There can be good possibilities for them to build on their position this year, whether through training, extending their responsibilities or taking part in new initiatives.

However, while steady progress can be made, they do need to be aware and focused. Sometimes office politics or the attitude of another person could concern them. If so, they should do their best to defuse the situation and not let it distract them from their duties. Some parts of the year will require Tigers to tread carefully, but their diligent and perceptive nature can be of value in tricky situations.

For those seeking change or looking for work, Monkey years can be challenging. Extra effort can yield results, however, and commitment and willingness to learn can lead on to other possibilities. Monkey years are times to build steadily, to learn and, in many instances, to prepare for future progress.

Although in many ways Monkey years ask a lot of Tigers, they also offer scope and, as far as their personal interests are concerned, Tigers can very much enjoy the way their activities develop. In some instances, new projects could be particularly inspiring, while in others, new equipment will offer the chance to do more. Tigers have a keen and inquisitive nature and, despite other commitments, time spent on their own projects can do them a lot of good.

In addition, travel could appeal, and as well as any trips they have planned, some Tigers could benefit from late offers or unexpected (but welcome) opportunities.

Financial prospects are reasonably aspected, and if they control their budget carefully, Tigers will be pleased with the way many of their plans and purchases proceed. By taking the time to consider their options, they can make some good decisions and, where household items are concerned, their eye for style and suitability will serve them well. Tigers have a talent for knowing what looks good!

However, where important correspondence is concerned, especially any related to finance, Tigers do need to attend to this carefully and promptly. Delays or mistakes could cause problems. As with so much this year, extra attention *will* make a difference.

Domestic life will be busy for many Tigers, but also marked by some notable celebrations, including some personal achievements and family milestones. Any ideas that Tigers put forward, whether for travel, visits or improvements to the home, can lead to much going ahead. However, with busy schedules, it is important there is good cooperation between all involved. Any extra support Tigers can give will be of great value.

Although often busy, they will welcome the social opportunities that come their way this year, especially those connected with their personal interests. Surprise invitations could be a feature of the year and Tigers could also enjoy occasions that just seem to happen. But there could be snags as well. In some instances, changing circumstances may lead to some friendships falling away or a disagreement with another person could cause some anguish. Monkey years can have their challenging aspects. Tigers, do tread carefully and be alert to areas of possible difficulty.

Tigers will face pressures this year and will need to be mindful of others and aware of prevailing situations. However, while the Monkey year can have a tempering influence on the enthusiastic Tiger, it also has its value. Personal interests can develop well and travel be appreciated. At work, skills gained can prepare the way for future opportunities. In their relations with others, Tigers need to be mindful and alert to awkward undercurrents, but, with care, they can fare reasonably well and often negate the more awkward aspects of this busy and fast-moving year.

Tips for the Year
Make the most of situations as they are. Liaise, engage and build support. This is no time to go it alone or be too single-minded. Spend time with your loved ones and look to develop your skills and interests. The effort you put in now can bear important fruit in the future.

TIGER FORTUNES IN THE YEAR OF THE ROOSTER

Tigers can make good progress this year, but need to channel their time and energy well. This is a time for concerted effort, as Rooster years favour structure and good planning. For Tigers who feel they have been drifting of late, this is an excellent year for reappraisal, but to fully benefit, they need to decide on their route *and act*.

At work, prospects are encouraging, and the experience and in-house knowledge of many Tigers may lead to an increased role. For those who have been in the same position for some time, promotion and/or a new position could beckon, bringing with it new incentive. Tigers who work in a creative environment could particularly impress this year and see some potentially exciting developments. All Tigers can make their talents count in the Rooster year and during it they should look to network and get themselves and their work better known. Resolute, inspired and keen, they can make these rewarding times.

Prospects are also good for Tigers who feel in need of a change and those seeking work. These Tigers should actively investigate openings and make enquiries. Advice from employment agencies, professional organizations and contacts could be helpful. Action taken now can lead to what can be important and timely developments.

This can also be an improved year financially. Many Tigers will benefit from a welcome increase in income, but to make the most of this they need to remain disciplined, otherwise anything extra could be quickly spent or absorbed into everyday spending. They also need to guard against impulse buying, otherwise hasty purchases could be regretted later. Ideally, major purchases need to be carefully considered. This is a year requiring (and rewarding) good control over budget.

Travel could be on the agenda of many Tigers, and here again planning will be rewarded. Some Tigers may particularly appreciate visits made to family or friends living some distance away.

Tigers can also derive much pleasure from their personal interests, especially from the way ideas and new knowledge can be put to effective use. Those seeking new challenges will find that Rooster years can open up interesting possibilities.

In view of the active nature of the year, Tigers can also expect an upturn in their social life. Whether meeting friends or attending occasions or special events (the Rooster year could see several), they will find themselves in demand. Many could form some important connections, both professionally and socially. Tigers can be on impressive form this year.

Home life promises to be busy, and in view of the varying routines and commitments, there needs to be a certain amount of flexibility. Some weeks could be especially demanding and family members may need to rally round. Good communication and sharing thoughts and concerns can be of great value.

But amid the high-level activity, much can be accomplished. If ideas and hopes are talked through, some exciting plans can take shape. Rooster years favour structure and will reward good organization.

In general, this can be a rewarding year for Tigers. If they channel their efforts and develop their skills, they can make important headway. They can be helped by the support and goodwill they enjoy, although, to fully benefit, they should be forthcoming about their ideas and seek advice. This is not a year for being too independent. Overall, though, prospects are good and the Rooster year will encourage and reward the Tiger's many talents.

Tips for the Year
Plan ahead and work towards your goals. Determined action can bring good results. Also, liaise well with those around you and, professionally, raise your profile. Commitment and effort can deliver this year.

TIGER FORTUNES IN THE YEAR OF THE DOG

A lot is set to happen in the Year of the Dog and Tigers need to pace themselves accordingly. To pay too much attention to one area of their life could cause problems in another. However, while Tigers will be juggling with many activities, these are constructive times with much to gain and enjoy.

At work, many Tigers will face a greater workload and sometimes challenging objectives. However, while there will be pressures, there will also be opportunities and some Tigers will be singled out for more specialist tasks or new initiatives. Employers will often be keen to make greater use of their strengths, and their contribution will be recognized and valued. For the ambitious, these can be significant times, with one step forward often leading to others.

Throughout the year all Tigers should take advantage of any training that may be offered. Keeping their skills up to date can help them both now and in the near future.

Tigers who desire change or are seeking a position can uncover some important possibilities. When opportunities arise, though, they do need to act quickly. Chances may not be available for long and, especially when making an application, indicating early interest can often be to their advantage. And, while any new role will bring its pressures, these Tigers will often revel in the chance to develop their skills in new ways. Dog years require application, but do encourage growth and career development.

Some Tigers could even be tempted to start their own business this year. A lot of hard work will be involved, but with good advice and careful consideration, they can set important plans in motion.

In view of the considerable pressures many Tigers will face this year, they would also do well to preserve some time for recreation and, if lacking regular exercise or a balanced diet, aim to correct this. They should also set time aside for their interests, especially any that allow them to relax and unwind. In Dog years Tigers do need a respite from all the activity. Tigers, take careful note.

Travel is favourably aspected this year and Tigers should aim to take a holiday if possible. A break can not only do them a lot of personal good but they may have the chance to see some impressive sights.

They can fare well financially this year, but should aim to budget ahead rather than proceed on an ad hoc basis. With discipline and careful thought, they can make some useful acquisitions and enjoy some good times, including travel.

Their home life can also bring them considerable pleasure and they will be grateful for the support and encouragement of their loved ones. In addition, their own successes or those of someone close can lead to celebrations. The Dog year will have its memorable moments. However, Tigers will also be grappling with many commitments and do need to make sure these do not make too many incursions into their home life or leave them too preoccupied. They need to maintain a good lifestyle balance and preserve some time to share with others. Also, as with any year, problems will raise their head from time to time. When they do, Tigers should address them and aim to defuse any awkward situations. Talking, listening and sometimes adopting a more accommodating approach will help. Generally, however, home life this year will be busy and gratifying.

The Dog year can also bring good social possibilities. For Tigers who would welcome a more fulfilling social life, this year can see quite a transformation, while for the unattached, romantically this can be a significant and memorable time. However, while social prospects are good, Tigers again need to be aware of others and give time to them. Should they take friendships for granted or be dilatory in maintaining contact, difficulties and disappointments could result. For Tigers, Dog years are often a fine balancing act and inattention could bring possible upset. Tigers, take note, and be aware and attentive.

In fact, that is the key message for Tigers this year. It is a constructive and fulfilling time, but, with so much to do, Tigers do need to remain disciplined and manage their commitments and lifestyle well. In this sense, Dog years can be demanding, but also rewarding, bringing career opportunities and some pleasing personal developments. Tigers should appreciate what is on offer and enjoy the rewards they work so hard for.

Tips for the Year
Value your relationships and spend time with those who are important to you. Shared pursuits (including trips) can bring particular pleasure. Also, act quickly when you spot an opportunity. And aim to keep your lifestyle balanced.

TIGER FORTUNES IN THE YEAR OF THE PIG

Enthusiastic and keen, Tigers have commendable spirit and, thanks to their versatility, can often fare well. However, when their initial enthusiasm wears thin, they are apt to turn their attention to something else. In Pig years they do need to curb their restless spirit and concentrate on priorities.

At work, Tigers will get their best results by focusing on areas that draw on their expertise. Especially if on a particular career path or wanting to become more established where they are, they can do their reputation the greatest good by making the most of their situation and concentrating on their duties. Also, they should actively contribute in their place of work. In particular, if they can see a solution to a problem or have a helpful idea, they should be forthcoming. Their contribution and skills can be greatly valued and, especially for those who work in a creative environment, these can be inspiring times.

However, Pig years do require commitment and Tigers should not relax their efforts after initial success. Should they become complacent, let standards slip or push their luck or the goodwill of others too far, problems could ensue. They need to remain focused and give their best. Tigers, take heed. These can be rewarding times, but do not be lax.

Tigers who feel their prospects could be improved elsewhere or are looking for work should actively seek out opportunities and act quickly when necessary. Prospects will often be better in the types of work they are most familiar with this year. Initiative and effort can open important doors, but again these Tigers need to remain determined *and* persistent.

In money matters, Tigers will need to be careful. The first part of the Pig year could see them in often expansive and generous mood, and spending could easily go over budget. Economies may then be required in the latter part of the year and certain plans have to be curtailed. Tigers, take note. Financially this is a year for discipline. It is also a time to be wary of risk or speculation. If tempted, Tigers should check the facts carefully and be aware of the implications. This is a time to be vigilant and thorough.

More positively, the Pig year can give rise to some good travel opportunities, including some which are arranged quite quickly, perhaps due to a special offer or unexpected invitation. During the year, Tigers will enjoy seeing some often impressive sights.

Pig years can also bring some lively social occasions, and for keen partygoers and socialites, these can be busy and exciting, albeit expensive times. All Tigers could see their social circle grow in numbers, and new acquaintances could prove helpful, both personally and professionally. Tigers who have let their social life lapse due to other commitments or who would welcome new friends could find that joining a local social or interest group could bring the companionship they seek.

Home life too can bring much pleasure, although there is an important caveat. Sometimes when pressures are great or Tigers or other household members are tired, patience can wear thin and tempers become frayed. It is important that Tigers recognize such times and are prepared to talk about pressures or matters on their mind. This way others can better understand and help. Pig years do favour openness and good communication. However while, as with any year, there will be pressures, there will also be much to appreciate. Shared activities and some purchases for the home can be particularly pleasing, as can some of the more spontaneous occasions of the year. Pig years certainly have their fun moments.

Overall, Tigers can do themselves proud this year, but they do need to remain disciplined. It is a time for persistence and resolve and making the most of experience. Good progress is possible, but if Tigers relax their efforts and become distracted, disappointments could loom. They should also watch their spending and be wary of risk. Pig years can, though, bring some lively times for Tigers to enjoy and to benefit from.

Tips for the Year
Focus on what you have to do. Also, be thorough. Distraction or risk can undermine your efforts. You can achieve good results this year, but it is a time for care and concentrated effort.

Thoughts and Words of Tigers

You cannot dream yourself into a character, you must hammer and forge one for yourself.

JAMES A. FROUDE

Nothing great will ever be achieved without great men, and men are great only if they are deemed to be so.

CHARLES DE GAULLE

Every man of action has a strong dose of egotism, pride, hardness and cunning.

CHARLES DE GAULLE

I'm sure you have a theme: the theme of life. You can embellish it or desecrate it, but it's your theme, and as long as you follow it, you will experience harmony and peace of mind.

AGATHA CHRISTIE

The mere sense of living is joy enough.

EMILY DICKINSON

Not knowing when the dawn will come, I open every door.

EMILY DICKINSON

The aim of life is self-development, to realize one's nature perfectly.

OSCAR WILDE

Success is a science. If you have the conditions, you get the result.

OSCAR WILDE

The true perfection of man lies not in what man has, but in what man is.

OSCAR WILDE

There is no upper limit to what individuals are capable of doing with their minds. There is no age limit that bars them from beginning. There is no obstacle that cannot be overcome if they persist and believe.

H. G. WELLS

Life is a helluva lot more fun if you say 'yes' rather than 'no'.

SIR RICHARD BRANSON

19 February 1939–7 February 1940 — *Earth Rabbit*

6 February 1951–26 January 1952 — *Metal Rabbit*

25 January 1963–12 February 1964 — *Water Rabbit*

11 February 1975–30 January 1976 — *Wood Rabbit*

29 January 1987–16 February 1988 — *Fire Rabbit*

16 February 1999–4 February 2000 — *Earth Rabbit*

3 February 2011–22 January 2012 — *Metal Rabbit*

22 January 2023–9 February 2024 — *Water Rabbit*

8 February 2035–27 January 2036 — *Wood Rabbit*

The Rabbit

The Personality of the Rabbit

Whether scurrying on rolling downland or enjoying lush meadows, there is an air of serenity about Rabbits. They are peaceable creatures and they like to be with others and be a part of what is going on. And this is true of those born under the Rabbit sign too.

Rabbits are sociable and strive for a secure and settled lifestyle. Calm-natured and agreeable, they relate well to others. They have style and finesse and put themselves across well. They are often articulate and effective speakers. They are also perceptive and adept at reading people and situations. And if they sense discord or difficulty looming, they will do their best to defuse the situation or get out of the way. Rabbits have a profound dislike of unpleasantness and will always aim to avoid it, even to the point of ignoring what is going on in an effort to keep the peace. Because they can be wary and cautious, they can come across as cold and aloof, but this is, in effect, their defence mechanism. Their eternal aim is to stay out of trouble.

Being keen readers, Rabbits keep themselves well informed. They also tend to know where their skills lie and to build up expertise in their preferred areas. They like to specialize and establish themselves in what they do and where they are. They like to feel secure. And although they may lack the competitive instinct of some signs, as well as be averse to risk or change, their skills, good sense and personable manner will ensure many of them go far in their chosen vocation. With their ability to master detail, positions in finance, law and retail could appeal. They also make effective diplomats and negotiators. Their sense of style and creative abilities could lead some to the fashion industry, design or the arts. With their often strong faith, some could also be drawn to religion or to helping others in a counselling capacity. Whatever they do, their careful and conscientious ways, along with their reliability and likeability, are appreciated by colleagues and employers alike.

Rabbits are also skilled in money matters and aim for a good standard of living. In their financial dealings, they proceed carefully, thinking through major purchases and leaving little to chance. They are not comfortable with risk or disposed to speculation. And because they are so attentive, they tend to do well. They know what they want and choose well, especially where style and beauty are concerned. With their appreciation of value and their aesthetic sensibility, many are fond of antiques and *objets d'art*.

Rabbits also enjoy living well and will not stint on themselves or their loved ones. When they go out and socialize, they often have a generous budget, though they will remain within it. Rabbits like to keep tabs on their situation – but also enjoy the finer things in life.

They will not deny themselves when it comes to their home, either. They will make sure it is well appointed and comfortable and will aim for quality and style. Their home will be tasteful, well ordered and neat.

Rabbits often have large families and are loving and supportive partners and parents. But paramount to them is their desire for a calm and stable existence and they are not always comfortable with the traumas family life can bring. They like to keep everything on an even keel.

They also like company, conversation and meeting others. Being well informed and interested in what is going on around them, they make friends with ease. They also have a happy knack of remembering details and names, and their swift recall delights and impresses many. However, while they will enjoy the good times that socializing and companionship can bring, if they sense problems, they are apt to make themselves scarce. They always do their best to avoid anything that could endanger their settled ways.

Both the male and female Rabbit have style and present themselves well. And both use their strengths to advantage, being alert, perceptive and gifted in their own individual ways. The female, in particular, prides herself on efficiency and likes to be in command of her situation and domain. She has impeccable taste, dresses with style and is an engaging and often witty speaker. She also fits a tremendous amount into her day but always finds time to do the things she wants, including to relax, unwind and enjoy quality time with those who are special to her.

Rabbits are born under the signs of virtue and prudence. Mindful and careful, they have good judgement, are perceptive and relate well to others, so enjoy good support in return. While their dislike of risk, change and the unknown may mean they sometimes hold back, their capabilities and good nature bring them respect and an often agreeable and fulfilling lifestyle.

Rabbits are very much their own masters.

Top Tips for Rabbits
- You value security and are not comfortable with change. However, in order to make the most of your potential, it is sometimes necessary to step forward and embrace fresh challenges. If not, there is a risk you could fall into a rut and underachieve. Take note, believe in yourself and be prepared to venture forth.
- When uncertainties cause you anxiety or you worry about the choices before you, listen to your inner voice and be guided by your instincts. You are highly intuitive, maybe even psychic, and your innermost feelings are useful indicators for you. Trust yourself more, for you are your own best friend.

- You dislike tension and disagreeable situations, but these do sometimes need to be faced. If you were to engage more readily in situations you find distasteful, you would learn more, become stronger and have more chance to turn those situations in your favour. Have courage and be proactive!
- In view of the pressures of modern-day life, it is important you give yourself the chance to unwind and spend time in ways you enjoy. Not only will this help your lifestyle balance, but you need time to collect your thoughts, be at one with yourself and delight in activities that bring you pleasure. Interests and recreational pursuits can be akin to a tonic for you. No matter how busy you are, do preserve some time for yourself.

Relations with Others

With a Rat

These two signs are sociable and have great people skills, but the Rabbit could feel ill at ease with the energy and busyness of the Rat. The Rabbit prefers tranquillity, not bustle, and relations between the two will be cool.

In work, their professional skills can, though, go well together and the Rabbit will recognize the Rat's resourcefulness and ability to sense opportunity. With both canny in business, these two could overlook personal differences and make an effective team.

In love, both are committed to family and home, but the Rabbit longs for a peaceful existence and will find the Rat's vitality and candour troubling. An awkward match.

With an Ox

These two value stability and the quieter things in life and will trust each other.

In work, each will have a high regard for the other and the Rabbit will value the Ox's tenacity, work ethic and principled ways. Neither is a risk-taker and together they could enjoy good levels of success.

In love, each will be good for the other. The Rabbit will take great comfort in having such a dependable and protective partner. An ideal match.

With a Tiger

While there are many personality differences between these two, there is also respect. The Rabbit admires the Tiger's sincerity, zest and ebullient manner, and relations between them are often good.

In work, their relationship can be mutually beneficial, with the Rabbit benefiting from the Tiger's enthusiasm, ideas and enterprise. By combining their strengths, they can do well.

In love, the Rabbit will delight in the Tiger's vivacious and confident manner, and with shared interests, including socializing, these two have a lot going for them. A good match.

With another Rabbit

With similar outlooks and values, two Rabbits will feel secure and comfortable in each other's company.

In work, Rabbits have good judgement and set about their activities with care and skill. They are not disposed to risk and their combined efforts are capable of delivering solid results.

In love, two Rabbits will strive for a stable, close and harmonious home life and can find much contentment together.

With a Dragon

The Rabbit and Dragon have a high regard for each other and respect each other's qualities.

In work, their different strengths combine well and the Rabbit will benefit from the Dragon's enthusiasm and drive. A good, productive team.

In love, passionate, sensual and caring, these two can find much happiness. While there will be lifestyle differences to reconcile, with the Rabbit preferring to take life at a steadier pace than the Dragon, this can be a strong match.

With a Snake

Thoughtful, quiet and sharing a liking for the finer things in life, the Rabbit and Snake can enjoy good rapport.

In work, these two have great business skills, but they do deliberate so! To realize their potential, they need to be more action-driven.

In love, their shared tastes, interests and outlook on life can make this a successful match. Both value stability and peace and the Rabbit will delight in having such a thoughtful and wise partner. (Snakes are born under the sign of wisdom!)

With a Horse

While these two may delight in their mutual love of conversation, the Rabbit will be aware of the Horse's restless energy and relations between them will often be reserved.

In work, the Rabbit will not be comfortable with the Horse's hasty style. Their different outlooks will create difficulties and they will not work well together.

In love, the Rabbit seeks a quiet and settled lifestyle, and this may not often be possible with the busy, active and spirited Horse. A challenging match.

With a Goat

With their peaceable natures and preference for the finer things in life, these two like and trust each other and relations between them will be great.

In work, they will encourage each other and nurture each other's strengths. If their work is in any way creative, there is the chance of great success.

In love, both seek a calm, settled and harmonious existence and together they can enjoy much happiness. The Rabbit will appreciate the Goat's sincere and affectionate nature as well as their many shared interests. A happy match.

With a Monkey

There may be personality differences, but these two like and respect each other, and on a personal level relations can be good.

In work, though, problems can arise. The Rabbit will not be comfortable with the Monkey's methods or risk-taking. Relations may be challenging.

In love, these two fare much better, with the Rabbit appreciating the Monkey's warm, outgoing and generally optimistic nature. With many shared interests, they can have a close and meaningful relationship.

With a Rooster

The Rooster is born under the sign of candour and the Rabbit will be uncomfortable with their outspoken and matter-of-fact ways. Relations will be poor.

In work, both work hard but the Rabbit will be wary of the Rooster's structured and sometimes pernickety ways. Their temperaments and overall approaches are very different.

In love, the Rabbit may admire the Rooster's well-meaning and confident manner, but with one introvert and the other extrovert and one preferring peace and quiet and the other activity and bustle, a match will prove challenging.

With a Dog

The Rabbit relates well to the loyal and trusting Dog and the two signs will get on well.

In work, their combined skills and good business sense can make them a powerful combination, although should problems occur, the Dog's anxiety and the Rabbit's dislike of stress could cause problems.

In love, these two are both home-loving and seek a secure and stable existence. The Rabbit will delight in the loyalty and dependability of the Dog and they can make a happy match.

With a Pig

The Rabbit likes the genial and easy-going Pig and relations between them are good.

In work, these two can combine their skills and enjoy considerable success. There is a good level of trust between them and the Rabbit will be encouraged by having such an honourable and robust colleague.

In love, there will be passion and understanding and each will be good for the other. The Rabbit will value the Pig's supportive and good-natured ways, and theirs can be a strong and harmonious match.

Horoscopes for Each of the Chinese Years

Rabbit Fortunes in the Year of the Rat

Rabbits are very perceptive and aware and during the Rat year there will be times when they feel uneasy with the speed of developments and the uncertainty caused. The fast pace of Rat years does not suit the temperament of Rabbits.

During the year Rabbits should proceed cautiously and ideally pay heed to their instincts. They will often sense what it is best to do. In many cases, they will opt to keep a low profile or hold back until situations are more conducive. But, while the Rat year has its awkward elements, there are still gains to be had.

In work, the demands of the year can be considerable. In addition to their usual workload, Rabbits may face change. Whether this involves the introduction of new working practices, changed objectives and/or changes in personnel, there will be pressures and problems as transitions take place. Being conscientious, Rabbits will often worry about developments and the difficulties they foresee. However, despite their misgivings, this can still be a time of opportunity for them, and if there is the chance to take on additional duties, deputize for another person or undertake further training, they should take advantage of it. The challenges of the year can highlight their strengths, which can, in turn, enhance their prospects.

Those seeking work will find that positions taken on now can also give them the chance to develop their skills. What they do this year can provide a good platform on which to build.

In matters of finance, however, care is required. Rat years are not ones for risk and should Rabbits enter into new agreements or commitments, it is important they check the details and are conversant with the implications. They should also handle paperwork with care and keep documents, policies and guarantees safely. A lost or mislaid document could cause inconvenience and incur cost. Rabbits, take note and be vigilant.

In view of the pressures they are likely to face during the year, they should also take good care of themselves. Regular exercise and a balanced diet will help. Setting time aside for their own interests will also be of benefit. 'Me time' can do Rabbits considerable good this year.

They will also value the social opportunities that arise, including the chance to catch up with friends. Their interests can also have a good social element. However, while many occasions will go well, Rabbits need to be on their guard. Rumours, mischief-making or the attitude of another person could all be cause for concern this year. If, at any time, Rabbits have misgivings about a particular issue, they should check it out for themselves. Rat years have their annoyances, petty though some may be.

Rabbits tend to regard their home as a sanctuary and an escape from everyday pressures, and during the Rat year their domestic life can be especially meaningful. Not only will they welcome the support of those close to them, but by sharing their concerns they will often find that anxieties can be eased. In this sometimes demanding year, the help of others will mean a great deal.

Rabbits will also appreciate the range of activities and interests they can enjoy with their loved ones over the year. Whether tackling projects, furthering joint interests or spending time together, they can see a lot can happen. Rat years may sometimes be pressured ones, but Rabbits will find their home life can be special and rewarding.

Overall, Rat years, with their heady pace, are never the easiest for Rabbits. They will need to exercise care and be wary of risks or distractions. However, while some situations will challenge them, there will be opportunities for them to gain what can be valuable experience and prove themselves in new ways. These can be instructive times. Financial matters require care, and vigilance will be an important factor this year, but more encouragingly, personal interests and home life can be a source of considerable pleasure.

Tips for the Year

Be thorough and alert. Unfolding situations can offer you good ways to gain new skills and further your experience. Also, allow time for recreation and for those who are special to you. Both can do you good as well as be important for lifestyle balance.

RABBIT FORTUNES IN THE YEAR OF THE OX

The Ox year can be a demanding one, with progress sometimes slow and results needing to be worked for. This is a time for effort, resolve and patience. However, by remaining persistent and doing their best, Rabbits can still emerge from it with useful gains to their credit.

In work, they will continue to set about their duties in their usual conscientious way. However, although they will enjoy some success, they could also face quite a few frustrations. Whether

these involve bureaucracy, new regulations or changing procedures, they could find themselves impeded by obstacles, and with
an increasing workload adding to the pressure.

However, while Ox years can be demanding, Rabbits will often
have the chance to prove themselves in new ways and, in the
process, gain new insights into their capabilities and add to their
professional knowledge. Despite their demanding nature, Ox
years can be illuminating and of far-reaching value.

While many Rabbits will remain where they are this year, for
those who decide to move on from their present position or are
seeking work, the Ox year can be challenging. Whether through
a lack of openings or responses taking time to come through,
Rabbits will need to be patient and persistent. However, while
developments will happen slowly, they will happen, and many
Rabbits will (eventually) secure a position. What some take on
now can mark a change in what they do and open up other
options for the future. Much of what is started now can be to
their long-term benefit.

As a result of their efforts, many will enjoy a rise in income over
the year and some may find ways to supplement this through an
interest or skill they can put to profitable use. Enterprising Rabbits
can fare well this year. Their often improving situation will tempt
many to proceed with ideas and purchases for the home as well
as spend on their interests. However, when considering equipment
or large outlays, Rabbits should take the time to find out what
best suits their requirements and their budget. As with so much
this year, it will be a case of proceeding steadily and carefully.

The Ox year will also give rise to travel opportunities. Some
may be work-related, but Rabbits should also aim to take a holiday. With the pressures of the year, a change of scene can do them
good, and a carefully considered holiday can be among the year's
highlights.

They should also set time aside for recreation. Rabbits need time to unwind and enjoy favoured pursuits. In some cases, fresh ideas or new equipment could allow them to develop their interests or take them in a new direction.

In addition, with the demands of the year, they should look after themselves. If lacking their usual energy, concerned about any matter or keen to make lifestyle changes (including exercising more), they could find it worth seeking medical advice.

They will appreciate the social opportunities of the year and will enjoy going to a varied mix of occasions. In addition, personal interests will often bring them into contact with others and some good connections and friendships can be forged. Some new connections could be especially helpful in current activities and quandaries.

Home life too will bring its special times, with loved ones supportive and rallying round at times of pressure. And while Rabbits may not want to trouble others, if they are forthcoming it will not only give them a better chance to help, but often the process of talking will give the Rabbits themselves the chance to clarify in their own mind the best way forward. Good communication can make an important difference this year.

As ever, Rabbits will enjoy carrying out practical projects on their home and the benefits (and additional comforts) some purchases bring. Shared interests and time spent with others can also be particularly appreciated, as will travel and enjoying local amenities and attractions. Once again, Rabbits' ideas, input and thoughtfulness can add much to their home life.

In general, however, the Ox year will ask a lot of them. Results will need to be worked for and progress will not always be easy or straightforward. With effort and patience, though, headway *can* be made, important skills gained and, for some, important new aptitudes discovered. Slowly and steadily, Rabbits will build and move forward. Personal interests and travel are favourably aspected, and Rabbits will also benefit from the support and advice of friends and loved ones. A demanding year, but one of long-term value.

Tips for the Year
'Slow and steady wins the race.' Use this year to build your knowledge and skills. Races will be won later, often as a result of what is done now. Also, draw on the support and affection of those around you. Their input can be important as well as often reassuring.

RABBIT FORTUNES IN THE YEAR OF THE TIGER

Interesting and improving times ahead. Having experienced several demanding years, Rabbits can now begin to reap the rewards of previous efforts. Their fortunes are on the up. And pleasingly, this pattern is set to continue with the Rabbit's own auspicious year following.

For Rabbits who feel dispirited by recent progress or who have suffered from lack of opportunity, the Tiger year can bring a change. Tiger years can give hopes momentum and this is no time to be held back by what has gone before but to concentrate on the now and look to move forward.

At work, Tiger years are fast-moving ones full of action. And although Rabbits may sometimes be concerned by the pace of change, they can often benefit from emerging opportunities. As staff change, promotion opportunities will arise and Rabbits will often be well-qualified to apply. If in a large organization, they may be tempted by openings elsewhere. The Tiger year will encourage many to advance their career in one way or another. However, opportunities do need to be seized quickly. This is no year for delay or prevarication.

While many Rabbits will make progress with their current employer, for those who are keen to move elsewhere, feel unfulfilled in their present type of work or are seeking a position, these can be important times. By making enquiries and considering other possibilities, these Rabbits may be alerted to a different yet ideal opportunity. Again, to benefit, they will need to act before the chance slips away. However, such is the nature of the Tiger year that even if one application does not go in their favour, another could soon take its place. Tiger years offer scope and opportunity.

All Rabbits should take advantage of any training that is offered to them or, if wanting to develop their career in a particular way, take time for study and research. In addition, if a further qualification could help their prospects, this would be a good time to obtain it. Skills and qualifications gained now can be to their present and future advantage.

Rabbits are generally careful when dealing with money matters and over the year they should not relax their usually disciplined approach. Sometimes, with all the activity, there could be the temptation to rush or not be as attentive as usual. In the Tiger year, this could lead to problems. When dealing with finance or anything with important implications, Rabbits need to be thorough, check the details and, if necessary, seek advice.

Although they will be involved in many activities this year, they should also set aside time for personal interests. If wanting to develop an interest in a certain way, start something new or achieve a personal goal, this would be a good year to act. Tiger years are ones for action.

They also bring an increase in social activity. Not only can existing or new interests bring Rabbits into contact with others, but work changes can also lead to a widening of their social circle. However, while this is a generally positive time for social matters, during the year Rabbits could become concerned about a close friend. Here their support and empathy can be an important asset and they may not only demonstrate the true value of friendship but also win the lasting gratitude of another person. Rabbits are indeed special to many people.

They will see considerable activity in their home life, with much to do, arrange and think about. Here their organizational ability will help. However, while they may be willing, they need to be careful not to shoulder too much single-handed and should ask for more assistance at busy times. Also, if anything is troubling them, rather than worry alone, they should be forthcoming and seek advice. And while this is a busy year, there will still be much to appreciate domestically. Tiger years contain a good mix of special and meaningful times.

In general, while Rabbits may sometimes wish the pressures and pace of the Tiger year were less, they can gain a lot from it. By making the most of their opportunities and developing their skills, they can make important headway and find greater fulfilment in much of what they do. This can be a satisfying year and one which can sow important seeds for their own year, which follows.

Tips for the Year
Watch developments closely and act when opportunities arise. Also, look to further your knowledge and skills. They are an investment in yourself and your future. This is a constructive year for you. Use it well.

Rabbit Fortunes in the Year of the Rabbit

Rabbits are highly intuitive and gauge situations well. And not only will they feel buoyed up by the fact that this is their own year, but they will find a lot moving in their favour. Great indeed are the possibilities of this year and Rabbits should seize the initiative and go after what they want.

On a personal level, they will find themselves in demand. In their home life, there could be pleasing developments and special family occasions to celebrate. For Rabbits who have relations living some distance away, there could be the chance to meet up and enjoy a reunion. In addition, many will see their family grow in numbers this year, with births and/or weddings. Being family-oriented, Rabbits will take pride in much that happens over the year and certain occasions will both surprise and delight them.

With what promises to be a very full domestic year, there does, though, need to be good communication between everyone in the Rabbit household and arrangements need to be planned in advance. By giving the year some structure, Rabbits will find that more can happen, and their organizational talents can play a key part. In addition, they will be pleased with some home improvements they carry out, and their deft touches and good judgement can result in some worthwhile enhancements.

On a social level, they will also find themselves in demand and will enjoy the chance to meet up with others. In the process, some valuable new friendships and connections can be made, and Cupid's arrow will be fired in the direction of many unattached Rabbits this year. Affairs of the heart are favourably aspected and can bring much happiness.

Another rewarding area is personal interests. Rabbits will be on inspired form and whether seeing how their ideas develop, engaging in satisfying pursuits or setting themselves new challenges, they can enjoy what they do in this encouraging year. Rabbits who start the year dissatisfied or unfulfilled could find taking up a new interest just the tonic they need.

At work this can also be a successful time. With the experience many Rabbits have behind them, their good colleague relations and fine reputation, they will often be excellently placed when promotion opportunities arise. In addition, some could be keen to take their work in a new direction and seek out fresh challenges, and by keeping alert for openings and exploring possibilities, they can uncover some excellent opportunities. Again, instinct can be a reliable factor this year. Many Rabbits will feel in themselves that now is the right time to venture forward.

For those seeking work, again their own year offers opportunities. These Rabbits should not be too restrictive in what they are prepared to consider. Rabbits can do very well in Rabbit years, but they need to put themselves forward and use and build on their strengths.

Financial prospects too are favourable, and in addition to an increase in income, some Rabbits could benefit from a gift or profit from interest. To make the most of this, they could find it helpful to look at their general situation and, if applicable, reduce borrowings as well as set funds aside for future requirements. Rabbits are often adept in financial matters and, with good management, many can strengthen their overall position this year as well as be pleased with the decisions and purchases they make, including for themselves and their home.

Overall, Rabbit years can be very special for Rabbits themselves, but there is a big 'but'. To make the most of their own year, they do need to act. They can prosper both professionally and personally, but they do need to seize their opportunities. With commitment, skill and the support of others, however, they can make this a very successful time.

Tips for the Year
Enjoy what the year opens up for you, but also act with purpose and be determined to make things happen. This is no year to waste, especially when there is so much to be gained.

RABBIT FORTUNES IN THE YEAR OF THE DRAGON

A fast-paced year with Rabbits contending with a mix of pressures and demands. A lot will be asked of them, but while there will be some uncomfortable times, with care and their usual adroit manner, they can still make useful headway.

At work, many Rabbits will experience times of change. Dragon years favour innovation and fresh approaches and Rabbits will sometimes be concerned about the proposals under consideration. Situations may not always be helped by staff changes and some weeks will be pressured and unsettling. However, despite the challenges, Rabbits should remain focused and concentrate on the tasks in hand. Their experience and steady approach can be especially appreciated. Rabbits can be depended on and many will prove this in this busy year.

They would also do well to keep track of developments in their industry. In some cases there could be openings or developing trends that appeal to them. If they follow these up, they could make useful headway. In addition, all Rabbits should take advantage of any training available to them and any chances to widen their remit. What they do this year can often have far-reaching implications. Dragon years may not always be easy, but they can leave a valuable legacy.

For Rabbits who decide to move on from where they are (and impending changes could be a factor) or are seeking work, the Dragon year can be tricky. Not only will competition be fierce in the job market but vacancies in their preferred areas could be limited. However, Rabbits are resourceful, and by taking advice and considering possibilities, many could succeed in their quest. Although the positions some take on could involve much readjustment, what they can accomplish this year can be to their future benefit.

Dragon years favour a disciplined approach and this extends to money matters. When conducting large transactions, Rabbits need to check the terms and obligations, and, if tempted by anything speculative, be aware of the risks. This is no year to be lax or to accept information at face value. Where finance is concerned, it is a time to be cautious and wary.

However, while Dragon years have their challenging aspects, they do have their pleasurable elements too. During the year, Rabbits will particularly enjoy their opportunities to go out, unwind and spend time with friends. They could be introduced to new people too, often through those they already know, and their social circle is set to widen. Rabbits who are alone or, through changed circumstances, feeling unhappy, will find that by taking advantage of the opportunities that will arise over the year, and perhaps starting a new interest, they can meet likeminded people who can quickly become friends. Romantic prospects too are encouraging, with both new and existing romances capable of bringing much happiness.

Rabbits will also derive much contentment from their home life this year, especially as many regard their home as a sanctuary from outside pressures. At home, they will devote time to their loved ones, set about satisfying projects and enjoy shared interests. They could also make improvements, including adding new comforts and freshening the décor of certain rooms. Their creativity and fine taste will be much in evidence and their domestic life can bring them a lot of pleasure.

Personal interests too can bring considerable benefit, especially as they will offer Rabbits a respite from other pressures. Over the year, all Rabbits should allow themselves regular 'me time'.

The Dragon year can have its challenging aspects and Rabbits will not be comfortable with the speed of developments and the pressures that changes bring, especially work-wise. However, by focusing on their objectives and furthering their knowledge, they can make progress as well as help their long-term prospects. But it will be their home and social life that will be their greatest sources of pleasure this year. And for the unattached, romance, too, could bring much happiness.

Tips for the Year

Be alert. Watch developments closely and seize any chances to add to your skills. Amid all the activity, there is valuable experience to be gained. Also, value your relations with others and allow time for your interests. Both can be very important in this busy year.

RABBIT FORTUNES IN THE YEAR OF THE SNAKE

Rabbits can fare well in the Snake year and can look forward to some good times and successful results. Also, Rabbits enjoy the tenor of Snake years. Rather than being rushed, they will have the time to reflect on what is going on and to savour it. And as well as being a pleasing year, it is also a constructive one.

At work, Rabbits will find this a year full of interesting possibilities. For those who are established where they are, their experience and standing can lead to the offer of greater responsibilities and the chance to become involved in new initiatives. The efforts of recent years can now very much pay off. Also, Rabbits will feel more in charge of their destiny this year and be able to move their career in the direction *they* want.

The majority will make good headway with their present employer, but for those who feel the time is right for a new challenge or are seeking work, again interesting opportunities await. By keeping alert for vacancies, many will secure a position offering both change and the chance to develop their strengths. Work-wise, Rabbits can do well in Snake years and feel more motivated and fulfilled.

Progress made at work can also help financially. However, the Snake year can also see much outlay, with Rabbits often tempted by expensive purchases and travel offers. Ideally, they should budget ahead as well as consider more major purchases with care. That can lead to some fine choices. Rabbits have a sense for quality and a good deal.

Something they should try to make provision for is a holiday, as the Snake year favours travel. Getting away and seeing new places can bring Rabbits great pleasure, as can some short breaks and opportunities to visit others.

Snake years also favour personal development and Rabbits should allow time for their interests as well as seize any chances to extend their knowledge. They have a naturally enquiring mind. Also, rather than rushing, they will appreciate the quieter and more settled moments of the year and the chance to take time for reading and other relaxing pursuits. Snake years suit the Rabbit psyche.

They are also excellent for lifestyle changes and if Rabbits have let certain interests fall away in recent times or feel they are lacking regular exercise, now is the time to address this. Snake years are excellent for taking stock and introducing positive change.

There will also be convivial times to be had socially, although an issue could be of concern. This may involve an unfortunate remark made by another person, some gossip or an awkward situation. Rabbits should keep matters in perspective, tread carefully and, if appropriate, seek advice. The difficulty may quickly pass or be resolved, but Rabbits will, on occasion, need to be wary and circumspect.

This will be a busy year domestically, especially as loved ones will face decisions and other changes will need addressing. Here Rabbits' wise counsel and organizational abilities will once again be much appreciated. Any troubling matters should be talked through, as openness and good communication will be an important part of family life this year.

Although parts of the year will bring domestic pressures, Snake years also have many delights and a family holiday and some personal or family achievements may be among the highlights. Domestic activities and projects could also be inspiring. Snake years encourage Rabbits to spend time with those who are special to them and to enjoy a more balanced lifestyle.

In general, these can be constructive and fulfilling times. During the year, Rabbits will have good opportunities to use and develop their strengths and enjoy some deserved success. Travel can be delightful and many relationships go well, although a particular issue or some gossip may be concerning. However, with care, this can be a favourable time, with Rabbits benefiting from their many actions during it.

Tips for the Year
This is a year of important possibility. Look to move forward. Also, consider ways in which you can improve your lifestyle balance and enjoy travel, your interests and the time you spend with your loved ones.

Rabbit Fortunes in the Year of the Horse

Rabbits can expect a flurry of activity this year. The pressures will be considerable, but there will also be pleasing times in store. Rabbits will be helped by the support and goodwill of those around them and this can be an encouraging factor in what unfolds during the year.

At work this can be an especially active time, with Rabbits facing a heavier workload and having some challenging objectives to meet. While they will sometimes despair of the pressures and would welcome more time to accomplish certain tasks (Rabbits do not like time constraints), by focusing on what needs to be done, they can achieve some impressive results. Their diligence and good communication abilities can prove real assets, and recently acquired skills can also help their situation. In view of the pace of developments this year, opportunities could arise at short notice, and if certain positions or specialist projects appeal to them, Rabbits should waste no time in applying. Speed is of the essence this year.

While many Rabbits will stay with their present employer, for those who feel they can better their prospects elsewhere or are seeking work, the Horse year can again bring important developments. By making enquiries and showing initiative in their application and at interview, many will secure a position with the potential for future development.

Also, throughout the year, Rabbits will find their connections helpful. Some of their contacts who have considerable influence could offer useful advice or assist in another way. It has often been said that the more people you know, the more likely you will be to benefit from opportunities, and this will be the case for many Rabbits in the Horse year. In addition, Rabbits should look to raise their profile. By networking and being involved, they can do their prospects a lot of good.

Progress at work can help financially, but outgoings will need to be watched this year. Although usually careful, Rabbits will have an often busy lifestyle and should be wary of making too many unplanned purchases. These can mount up and spending be greater than anticipated. Rabbits, take note and remain disciplined.

The active nature of the year will also extend to home life. The Horse year favours togetherness and Rabbits will be encouraged by the support and advice of those around them. There will be good times to enjoy as well as domestic plans to advance. However, while much is set to go well, activities should be spread out over the year rather than concentrated on one particular time. In addition, treats or trips out could provide a respite from busy lifestyles and be especially appreciated. As ever, Rabbits will be instrumental in a lot that takes place.

The Horse year is also an excellent time to meet others. Whether through work, mutual friends or personal interests, Rabbits will get to know many new people this year, some of whom can become helpful and potentially important. In addition, there will be a variety of occasions to enjoy. Any Rabbits who are feeling lonely will find their situation brightening if they involve themselves in activities and take advantage of local amenities.

Romance, too, can play a part this year, although for some (but certainly not all), there could be challenging moments to overcome.

In view of the busyness of the year, Rabbits should aim to make sure their own interests and recreational activities do not get sidelined. These can be akin to a tonic for them. Outdoor and activity pursuits will often have considerable appeal this year.

In general, the Horse year will bring its demands, and although Rabbits may not welcome its pressures, there will be good opportunities for them to pursue. By making the most of developments and working hard, they can build on their present situation as well as help their future prospects. Their relations with others are well aspected and whether making new friends, forging connections at work or sharing plans with their loved ones, they can enjoy some good times amid this busy year. It might be pressured, but it can be rewarding too.

Tips for the Year
Seize the moment. Act quickly when opportunities come your way and look to build on your strengths. You can make good progress in this active year. Also, make the most of your chances to meet people. Support can make a lot happen for you.

Rabbit Fortunes in the Year of the Goat

When situations are conducive and Rabbits feel the time is right, they set about their aims with considerable might. And this will be such a year. Rabbits who have felt buffeted by events in the preceding year will enjoy this more settled time and all Rabbits will be better able to implement their plans in their own way. Goat years suit the Rabbit psyche.

One of the strengths of Rabbits is their ability to get on well with many people and over the year they should value their connections and contacts. In particular, by talking over their hopes, they may not only benefit from useful advice, but also find that some of their ideas can be set in motion. Synergy can be an important factor this year.

At work, this can be a successful and satisfying year. For Rabbits who are relatively new to their present position, this is a time to become established and learn about the different aspects of their work. With commitment and involvement, they will not only feel more fulfilled by what they do, but also make a valued contribution. Those who work in creative environments could feel especially inspired and enjoy some notable success. For some, substantial promotion could be in the offering.

For Rabbits who would welcome fresh challenges or are seeking work, the year can again hold some helpful and sometimes surprising possibilities. By talking to others and keeping themselves informed of developments in their area, many could secure the chance to establish themselves in a different capacity. Goat years are encouraging and will see Rabbits on inspired form.

This also applies to their personal interests and over the year they should use their talents to good advantage. Those who enjoy writing, art or some other creative pursuit, should look to extend as well as promote what they do. Also, with culture strongly featured this year, they could enjoy the variety of events, concerts and exhibitions taking place. The Goat year can indeed provide a good mix of social opportunities and Rabbits who are feeling lonely, perhaps after a recent change in circumstances, could see an improvement in their situation. By involving themselves in their community and undertaking shared activities, they can make new friends and, in quite a few cases, meet someone special. This can be an important year for affairs of the heart, with some Rabbits meeting their future partner in a way that seems destined to be.

Rabbits will also derive much pleasure from their home life this year. With their own progress and the successes of family members to mark, there can be joyous times in many a Rabbit home. In addition, the creative natures of many Rabbits will come to the fore and they will enhance their home with deft touches and carefully considered purchases.

Travel, too, can bring pleasure and Rabbits should aim to take a holiday with their loved ones at some time during the year. A rest and change of scene can do everyone good.

Although Rabbits are usually careful in money matters, they do need to remain vigilant this year. To make assumptions or be dilatory when dealing with forms and correspondence could be to their disadvantage. In addition, while income can increase, so can outgoings, and spending levels need to be monitored. This is a year for good management.

This advice also holds good for other areas. When problems occur (as they will in any year), it could be because Rabbits have made assumptions or not given matters sufficient attention. This is no year for complacency. Even though prospects are good, Rabbits do need to remain their conscientious and thorough selves.

However, in so many ways, these can be rewarding times. At work, Rabbits will have the chance to use their skills to advantage, and their personal interests can inspire them. Many Rabbits will enjoy expressing their ideas and creativity this year. Their personal life can also be a source of much happiness and can help underline the specialness of the Goat year. It is a time for Rabbits to enjoy and prosper.

Tips for the Year

Share your ideas with others and act on them. With goodwill and support, you will find a lot opening up for you now. Also, use your talents to advantage – they can be instrumental in the success you enjoy.

RABBIT FORTUNES IN THE YEAR OF THE MONKEY

Rabbits will need to keep their wits about them this year. Situations may not always be straightforward and there may be some pressures and problems to address. However, while this is not an easy year, Rabbits have several factors in their favour. One is the big network they have around them, and a worry shared will be proved to be a worry halved during the year. Their own adroit nature will also help, and when situations are uncertain or volatile, their collected and reasoned approach can again be effective.

Rabbits will see much activity in their domestic life this year, especially as they or a loved one could experience a change in routine which impacts on others. Good communication could be needed, but with openness and cooperation, some keynote changes can be effected. In addition, some early misgivings Rabbits may have about certain developments could be misplaced.

Although the year will see some pressured times when a lot seems to occur at once, there will also be much to appreciate, possibly including a special family event, an academic success or the realization of a particular aspiration. There will be a spontaneity to the year and some hastily arranged trips or spur of the moment suggestions can lead to some fun times. Monkey years have the capacity to surprise.

Rabbits will also enjoy the social opportunities of the year and will have the chance to attend an often wide mix of occasions and events.

Rabbits enjoying romance could find this becoming more meaningful during the year, while those who are unattached or have recently experienced heartache could find someone new and supportive entering their life. This can be an often special year for affairs of the heart.

With the new ideas and opportunities that come to the fore in Monkey years, many Rabbits could also be attracted by new subjects and interests. Again, where possible, they should follow these up. These can be interesting and rewarding times.

With their busy lifestyles Rabbits should also give some consideration to their own well-being. Regular exercise and a good diet will help, but if anything concerns them over the year, they should seek advice.

Similarly, in money matters, they need to be vigilant. This is no time for risk or complacency, and if entering into a new commitment or making a large transaction, they should check the terms and obligations. Official correspondence should also be attended to promptly and thoroughly. Uncharacteristic lapses or mistakes could be to their disadvantage. Bureaucratic matters could prove troublesome this year. Again, if Rabbits are concerned at any time, expert help is available.

At work, Monkey years can be challenging. There will be much innovation and change taking place and conscientious Rabbits could be concerned about their work levels and the expectations being placed upon them. However, demanding though parts of the year will be, they will have excellent chances to develop their skills and knowledge. It is by being challenged that strengths become apparent, and the reputation of many Rabbits will increase over the year.

For Rabbits who are keen to move on, some surprising developments are in store. Opportunities can arise quickly and positions may be offered that, while necessitating readjustment and learning, can take many Rabbits further in their career.

Rabbits who are seeking work will need to persist in their search as well as widen its scope. Monkey years can take curious courses and these Rabbits should not be too restrictive in what they are considering.

Overall, the Monkey year will demand a lot from Rabbits. There will be changes to contend with and issues that will concern them. Also, they will not like some of the volatility and could worry about particular developments or decisions. However, by drawing on the advice of others, proceeding carefully and adjusting as required, they can further their skills as well as appreciate (and potentially gain from) new interests and opportunities. They will need to be careful in money matters and also pay attention to their own well-being, but romantic prospects are promising and they will enjoy spending time with their family and friends. Despite its vexations, the Monkey year offers scope and a great deal to build on.

Tips for the Year

Watch developments closely and be prepared to adjust as required. This is a year to be flexible and rise to the challenges presented. Also, draw on the support that is available to you. Attention to your well-being and lifestyle balance could be to your advantage, as could taking up new interests.

RABBIT FORTUNES IN THE YEAR OF THE ROOSTER

Although the Rabbit's style and creativity may sometimes be cramped by the structured nature of the Rooster year, it can still hold many delights. With care, combined with their usual good judgement, Rabbits can make worthy progress.

One particularly well-aspected area is their own personal development. Rabbits enjoy furthering their knowledge and there will be excellent opportunities for them to do so during the Rooster year. Where personal interests are concerned, they could set themselves new projects or challenges or decide to buy equipment to help extend their capabilities. By doing something purposeful, they can derive a lot of satisfaction from their activities. Any Rabbits who, because of a busy lifestyle, have let their interests fall away will find this an ideal year to rectify this. All Rabbits could benefit from joining local enthusiasts, enrolling on a course or using the amenities available to them. These can be illuminating and constructive times.

Rabbits who lead sedentary lifestyles should also consider fitting more exercise into their schedule. With expert advice, many could soon notice an improvement in their energy levels. Some could even start an exercise regime they especially enjoy.

Throughout the year all Rabbits will appreciate meeting up with their friends and the opportunity this gives to seek advice on certain vexations. Some of the people they know will have expert knowledge or first-hand experience that could prove especially useful.

Also, the Rooster year will see a lot taking place and Rabbits will enjoy going out and being a part of it. For the unattached and those who are perhaps feeling lonely, the year could bring the gift of an important new friend. On a personal level, the Rooster year can surprise and frequently delight.

At home, too, there will be much to occupy Rabbits. Again, the year will see various activities taking place and there will be news and individual achievements to enjoy. When plans need making or occasions arranging, Rabbits will find their organizational talents particularly appreciated. Throughout the year they will do a great deal for their loved ones, including dispensing timely advice. Shared interests and projects can be especially satisfying and make home life all the more gratifying.

At work, however, the pressures will be considerable. As well as grappling with a large workload, some Rabbits could feel hindered by bureaucracy and office politics. There will be times that will be particularly exasperating. However, when the going is tough, Rabbits often choose to keep a low profile, and this is what many will do this year. If they concentrate on what needs to be done, their judgement, focus and experience can serve them well, and the progress they make will be well earned.

For Rabbits seeking work, great effort will be required and there could be disappointments along the way, as well as frustration as delays occur in the processing of applications. However, with self-belief and persistence, they will see doors opening for them and the opportunities that do come will often have long-term potential. Rooster years can be challenging, but tenacity *will* prevail.

Rabbits will need, however, to exercise care in financial matters. Not only could they face additional costs as repairs become necessary or equipment needs replacing, but they also need to be wary of risk or accepting what they are told at face value. Without care, they could find themselves misled. Rabbits, be on your guard and do keep track of spending as well.

The Rooster year will certainly bring its challenges. However, by showing commitment and using their skills to advantage, Rabbits can emerge from it with much to their credit. It is an excellent year to add to knowledge and skills, and personal interests will often develop in encouraging manner as well as bring additional benefits. Money matters require careful attention, but the Rabbit's home and social life both offer an array of possibilities and a good mix of activities to enjoy. Overall, a demanding year, but also an illuminating and potentially rewarding one.

Tips for the Year
Enjoy quality time with those who are special to you and also set time aside for your personal interests. In this busy year, both can help your lifestyle balance. Also, when pressures arise or situations concern you, keep focused. The good you can do in sometimes difficult situations can enhance your reputation and prospects.

Rabbit Fortunes in the Year of the Dog

This is a constructive year for Rabbits. They will be able to build on recent developments and make pleasing headway. Their personal life can also be delightful, with much to do and share.

At work, the aspects are encouraging, and in view of their recent undertakings and often improved reputation, Rabbits will often be excellently placed to benefit when opportunities arise. In many instances, their current employers will encourage them to take on greater duties and/or offer promotion as situations fall vacant. This is very much a year for growth and career progress.

Rabbits who feel their prospects can be improved by a move elsewhere will also find that reputation standing them in good stead. By making enquiries, they may uncover some excellent opportunities. Those seeking work will also find that contact with employment agencies and professional organizations can lead to helpful suggestions and openings to consider. By showing initiative in applications and at interview, many Rabbits will secure a position on which they can build in the future.

Throughout the year all Rabbits should take advantage of any training or refresher courses that become available. Keeping their knowledge and skills up to date will not only help their present situation but also improve their future prospects. Some of the people they meet now can also prove helpful, especially in the area of future decisions and opportunities. With excellent aspects in the following Pig year, what happens this year can often pave the way for even greater successes next.

However, while good progress can be made, Rabbits do need to keep alert to what is going on around them. Office politics or the grievances of another person could be a cause for concern. If so, Rabbits need to be wary and discreet. Dog years can have their distractions and ideally Rabbits should concentrate on what they have to do and leave politics to others. (In Dog years, ideals and various causes invariably get championed.)

Progress made at work will help financially, and in addition to an increase in income, some Rabbits can also look forward to a bonus payment or gift or put an idea to profitable use. Their improving situation will persuade many to go ahead with plans for the home, recreational pursuits and travel. Rabbits work hard and should appreciate the rewards of their labours. However, if possible, they should also consider setting funds aside for the longer term, including perhaps starting a savings scheme or adding to a pension policy. In future years, they could be grateful for this.

They will derive a lot of pleasure from their personal interests this year, especially from following through their ideas and adding to their skills. Furthering knowledge is a key facet of the Dog year. Projects started now could also highlight aptitudes that Rabbits could make more of in the future.

On a social level, Rabbits will find themselves in demand, with many opportunities to go out. Those who would welcome more company will find that by making the most of their chances to meet those with similar interests, perhaps at a local group, they can make some important new friends. For some, serious romance can beckon, transforming their situation and prospects. Many will recognize and value the special qualities of the Rabbit this year.

Domestically, Dog years can see a lot of activity and there may be good cause for both personal and family celebrations. Rabbits will also appreciate the support of their loved ones throughout the year. If they are open about their ideas, and any concerns, they can be well supported. A lot can happen this year, including some notable home improvements, but it is a time favouring collective effort.

In general, the Dog year can be a rewarding one for Rabbits, and by looking to build on their present position and furthering their skills and ideas, they can accomplish a great deal. Importantly, this can often be taken further in the auspicious Pig year that follows. Rabbits will be encouraged by the support they are given and networking can be to their future benefit, while on a personal level there will be some very special times and a possible celebration too. A pleasing and constructive year.

Tips for the Year
Look to develop your skills. What you learn now can be built on in the near future. Use this year well, for its significance can be considerable.

RABBIT FORTUNES IN THE YEAR OF THE PIG

A fine and important year ahead. Rabbits will find themselves benefiting from the expansionist nature of the Pig year and can look forward to making excellent progress and enjoying some special moments.

Personal relations are particularly well aspected, and for Rabbits enjoying romance, or who find it this year, these can be exciting times. Quite a few Rabbits will settle down with a partner or become engaged or married, such are the aspects.

For those with a partner, there can be exciting developments to share. In some cases, much-discussed plans will be set in motion and long-held hopes realized. This is very much a year for action and a certain amount of luck will assist.

Home projects could also be pleasing and the Rabbit's sense of style be both admired and appreciated. Rabbits will be on inspired form this year, although, when one home project is finished, another will surely present itself.

In addition to the practical activity, Rabbits will follow the activities of their loved ones with fond interest. In many a home, there will be successes to mark and personal and family milestones to commemorate. Also, if Rabbits are tempted by events or activities in their locality, they should go along if they can. Pig years favour involvement and there will be fun times to be had.

Rabbits will also appreciate the other social opportunities of the year. Any Rabbits who are feeling lonely, are in a new environment or have had some recent difficulty to overcome can see a marked upturn in their situation this year. To help the process along, they should consider joining local groups or even assisting in their community in some way. Their involvement could add an important element to their lifestyle.

All Rabbits should also allow time for their personal interests. Not only can they help their lifestyle balance but also enable them to make more of certain talents. For creative Rabbits, this can be an inspiring and potentially successful time. If they can promote their work, they should do so. They could be heartened by the response.

The year can also give rise to some good travel possibilities and all Rabbits should aim to take a holiday and/or enjoy a short break if possible. If they plan ahead, not only can some exciting decisions be taken, but their trip can be something to look forward to.

At work, Rabbits will be able to use their strengths to advantage and will often benefit from emerging opportunities. Those who are established in a career may have the chance to move to new levels and take on greater responsibilities. Although possibly involving a considerable learning curve, these can make their working life all the more fulfilling. And Rabbits nurturing certain aspirations should actively seek out openings. Their initiative will enable many to move forward.

Similarly, Rabbits seeking work will find their persistence can often lead to openings being found. Positions taken on now can be a useful stepping stone to other possibilities. Some Rabbits may embark on a different type of work and find it an excellent outlet for their talents. As many will discover this year, things happen for a reason, and much of what happens now will be to both their present and future advantage.

Progress made at work will often lead to rise in income, but with so much happening, the year will be an expensive one. To help, Rabbits should set themselves a budget for certain activities and aim to keep within it. Without watchfulness, outgoings could creep up. Also, if they have misgivings over any transaction or are uncertain about any financial paperwork, they should seek clarification rather than make assumptions. While this is a good year, it is not one to be lax.

Overall, however, this can be a very successful year. Work prospects are good and important progress can be made. Personal interests, especially creative ones, can also be very satisfying. Rabbits will value the backing and help they are given and their relations with those around them can be encouraging. Throughout the year, home life, shared activities and socializing can lead to some very enjoyable times, and for the unattached and those newly in love, romantic prospects are excellent. Pig years suit Rabbits, although to benefit fully from them, they do need to make the most of the opportunities that come their way. It rests with them, but the rewards can be many and considerable.

Tips for the Year
Seize the moment. Take your chances. Promote your talents. Make things happen. This is a year for determined action. It is also one to enjoy.

Thoughts and Words of Rabbits

There is no man, no woman, so small that they
cannot make their life great by high endeavour.

THOMAS CARLYLE

I know the price of success: dedication, hard work,
and an unremitting devotion to the things you want
to see happen.

FRANK LLOYD WRIGHT

The thing always happens that you really believe in,
and the belief in a thing makes it happen.

FRANK LLOYD WRIGHT

We create our fate every day that we live.

HENRY MILLER

The talent of success is nothing more than doing what
you can well and doing well whatever you do,
without a thought of fame.

HENRY WADSWORTH LONGFELLOW

Our deeds determine us, as much as we determine our
deeds.

GEORGE ELIOT

It's never too late to be what you might have been.

GEORGE ELIOT

Let every dawn of the morning be to you as the beginning of life. And let every setting of the sun be to you as its close. Then let every one of these short lives leave its sure record of some kindly thing done for others, some good strength or knowledge gained for yourself.

JOHN RUSKIN

8 February 1940–26 January 1941 — *Metal Dragon*

27 January 1952–13 February 1953 — *Water Dragon*

13 February 1964–1 February 1965 — *Wood Dragon*

31 January 1976–17 February 1977 — *Fire Dragon*

17 February 1988–5 February 1989 — *Earth Dragon*

5 February 2000–23 January 2001 — *Metal Dragon*

23 January 2012–9 February 2013 — *Water Dragon*

10 February 2024–28 January 2025 — *Wood Dragon*

28 January 2036–14 February 2037 — *Fire Dragon*

The Dragon

The Personality of the Dragon

Flamboyant, colourful, mesmerizing, the Dragon takes the lead in many a carnival. And enjoys it. The Dragon is a spectacle – there to be noticed, to excite and to inject energy into the proceedings. Born under the sign of luck, Dragons are vibrant, like to be active and like to get things right. And this applies to many born under the Dragon sign.

Dragons are outgoing, engage with others and involve themselves in many activities. They have great enthusiasm and, when inspired or motivated, will let little stand in their way. They are doers, and their willpower and self-belief will enable them to do a great deal.

Dragons also have high standards and their passion for the things they do brings them good support. They are leaders – inspiring, confident and convincing. But they are also risk-takers, and in their eagerness to secure results can be impulsive, impatient and ignore the finer details. Should setbacks occur, they will feel them deeply, but will not be kept down for long. Dragons are resilient and thrive on challenge. George Bernard Shaw was a Dragon and he wrote, 'The people who get on in this world are the people who get up and look for the circumstances they want, and, if they can't find them, make them.' This is what Dragons do.

With their leadership abilities, Dragons can make their mark in many professions. They are ambitious and work hard to achieve their objectives. They are also honourable and principled in their dealings, which again encourages others to have faith in their abilities. Demanding they may be, and frank and forthright too, but they do deliver. They are usually at their best when facing a challenge or when they have a worthwhile objective in mind. They easily get bored with routine. If what they do places them in the spotlight, so much the better, and they do like to have others around them. For a choice of vocation, marketing, PR, the media, show business or being a manager or entrepreneur could appeal, as could positions involving travel. Dragons need purpose and an outlet for their talents.

Their skills, energy and enthusiasm can reward them financially and quite a few Dragons are materially well off in their middle and later years. For Dragons, the money they have is recompense for their hard work and is there to be enjoyed. As a result, they like to indulge themselves as well as be very generous to their family and friends. There can be times when impulsiveness or a rash decision costs them dear, but if ever they find themselves in deficit, they will work hard to rectify their position and make good.

However, while Dragons are scrupulous in their undertakings, their trust in others can sometimes be misplaced and leave them vulnerable. If they ever have doubts or concerns over any undertaking, it would be worth them clarifying the facts rather than take a risk or accept what they are told at face value. Unfortunately, not everyone is as honourable and ethical as they are.

With their outgoing nature, Dragons enjoy socializing and are rarely short of admirers and friends. However, they value their independence and some will prefer to remain unattached rather than compromise their way of life. Dragons like to be masters of their situation.

Those who do settle down with a partner will often do so in their early adult years and will enjoy setting up their home and styling it in their own way. Dragons do not like to feel restricted, however, and will want to maintain a full and busy lifestyle. With a like-minded partner, there will be fun, laughter and an abundance of hopes to realize, and if a parent, the Dragon's exuberance and enthusiasm are sure to inspire and captivate.

Both male and female Dragons enjoy wide interests and are hard and conscientious workers. They drive themselves to do well. The female has particular allure as well as a mind of her own. Being practical, she uses her time well and she has a happy knack of getting her way. Charming and disarming, she has style and confidence and, as with all her sign, likes a challenge and sets herself (and others) high standards. Tenacious and ambitious, she enjoys success in many of her activities.

Dragons are renowned for their energy and like to channel it into pursuing an objective or contributing in some way. They like to be active and engaged. They also like to take the lead! Their enthusiasm, confidence and ability to relate to others will ensure they lead a rich and busy life, and one that has a goodly element of Dragon luck in it.

Top Tips for Dragons

- You may value your independence and the chance to set about your activities in your own way, but occasionally you would do well to consult others and seek advice. It is important you do not undermine your efforts by being too single-minded or self-reliant. With support, backing and input, so much more can be realized. Take particular note!

- With your full and busy lifestyle, you use up a lot of nervous energy and you drive yourself hard. Allow yourself some time to recharge your batteries now and then. It can do you a lot of good. To be on good form, you do need to have a good lifestyle balance.

- As you involve yourself in so much, you can spread your energies widely and this may lead to mistakes and oversights. To prevent this, be careful not to overcommit yourself and focus more on key priorities. With concentrated effort, you can enjoy even more substantial rewards.

- You are adept at thinking on your feet and making the most of your situation, but longer-term planning could help you channel your efforts more effectively. Acquiring qualifications or skills for the future, saving up for a particular item or plan, or setting yourself a goal could all enable you to make good use of your time and energy.

Relations with Others

With a Rat

With both signs being lively and resourceful, relations are often excellent and great times can be had.

In work, these two are enterprising and have ideas aplenty. The Dragon will especially appreciate the Rat's skills in identifying opportunities and finding ways forward. An effective combination.

In love, their passion, energy and many interests make for a lively and fulfilling lifestyle. These two understand each other well and the Dragon will respect the Rat's judgement as well as value their support. An excellent match.

With an Ox

These two may recognize and respect each other's qualities, but they conduct themselves in very different ways. Relations may not be easy.

In work, both are hard-working and have high standards, and if they can unite in a common objective and cope with their forthright tendencies, they can combine their different strengths to good effect.

In love, the Dragon values the Ox's dependable and straightforward manner, but enjoys a more active lifestyle. As both are redoubtable and self-willed, there could be challenging times ahead.

With a Tiger

With both enjoying active, lively lifestyles, relations between them will be good, even if sometimes volatile.

In work, with their zeal, enterprise and ideas, they can make a dynamic duo, but they need to remain focused and channel their efforts if they are to succeed.

In love, there will be passion, thrills, plans and hopes, and life can be wonderful, *and* exciting, but both are forthright and like to retain a certain independence. They will need to come to an understanding if this exciting match is to last.

With a Rabbit

They may have different temperaments, but these two like and respect each other and relations between them will be good.

In work, both set themselves high standards and the Dragon will appreciate the Rabbit's work ethic and ability to plan and organize. They will work well together.

In love, these two passionate signs will greatly admire each other's qualities. The Dragon will value the calm, caring and collected ways of the Rabbit. They will have differences to reconcile, but can enjoy a strong and meaningful match.

With another Dragon

Lively and sociable, two Dragons can enjoy each other's company but, with both being domineering and forthright, there will be some clashes too.

In work, these two have huge potential, and ideas, enterprise and enthusiasm in abundance. But each will vie for dominance and their competitiveness could undermine their joint effectiveness.

In love, there will be passion, fun and high hopes, but also two strong-willed natures. They will need to come to a workable arrangement.

With a Snake

The Dragon very much admires the quiet and thoughtful Snake and relations between the two will be excellent.

In work, these two can combine their different strengths to good effect, with the Dragon respecting the Snake's judgement and business skills. Together, they could enjoy considerable success.

In love, these two complement each other and the Dragon will be attracted by the Snake's calm, alluring and thoughtful ways. The Snake can also bring order and a certain serenity to the Dragon's often busy schedule. They are ideally suited. A great match.

With a Horse

The Dragon enjoys the company of the active and spirited Horse and relations between the two will be good.

In work, their combined energy and enthusiasm can lead to considerable success, with each being a useful spur to the other.

In love, their passion and shared outlook will make for a busy and fulfilling life together. The Dragon will appreciate the Horse's lively, eloquent and practical nature. A rewarding match.

With a Goat

These two may enjoy each other's company for a time, but differences in outlook and character could lead to problems.

In work, by harnessing their different strengths these two can do well, with the Dragon recognizing and encouraging the Goat's creative input.

In love, both are passionate, fun-loving and enjoy active lifestyles, but the Dragon could, in time, become exasperated by the Goat's fickleness, mood swings and sometimes lackadaisical manner. Portents are not good.

With a Monkey

Highly sociable and enjoying wide interests, these two like each other and there will be good camaraderie between them.

In work, their enthusiasm, energy and many ideas make them a powerful combination. The Dragon will appreciate the Monkey's inventive flair and also keep everything above board.

In love, these two can enjoy a close, loving and often special relationship. They will understand and support each other and the Dragon will admire the Monkey's many talents and *joie de vivre*. An excellent match.

With a Rooster

These are two redoubtable signs with a great liking and respect for each other.

In work, the Dragon will admire the Rooster's orderly and efficient ways. With both being hard-working and keen to get results, they can combine their talents to good effect.

In love, these two can be good for each other. Both enjoy wide interests, are keen socializers and like an active lifestyle. The Dragon will respect (and benefit from) such an ordered and caring partner. A good match.

With a Dog

With their different outlooks and attitudes, there is little accord between these two.

In work, with different approaches and styles, but both being forthright and keen to take the lead, there will inevitably be problems.

In love, the Dragon will value the loyalty and sincerity of the Dog, but as both are strong-willed and the Dragon may not always understand the Dog's tendency to worry, relations could be challenging.

With a Pig

With both signs active, sociable and having an abundance of interests, relations can be good.

In work, their hard work, skills and mutual respect can make them successful team. The Dragon will particularly value the Pig's persistent approach and commercial acumen.

In love, the Dragon will enjoy the joyful, easy-going and affectionate ways of the Pig. They will have much to share and are well suited.

Horoscopes for Each of the Chinese Years

DRAGON FORTUNES IN THE YEAR OF THE RAT

A lively year ahead. Like the Rat, Dragons enjoy life to the full, busy themselves in a myriad of activities and embrace the thrill of opportunity. Rat years promise active and special times, and Dragons will find that once they set plans in motion, fortunate developments will often follow on. There will be a strong element of serendipity to the year. For Dragons who are nurturing particular hopes or aspirations, *now* is the time to act. As Virgil noted, 'Fortune favours the bold,' and the Rat year very much favours bold and enterprising Dragons.

At work, the aspects are especially encouraging and many Dragons will take on greater responsibilities where they are or successfully transfer to another, often more remunerative position elsewhere. This is no year to stand still. For some Dragons, what opens up for them will involve considerable change and they will relish the chance to prove themselves in a new way. For those who feel they have become staid recently, the developments of the year can re-energize their prospects. Chances do need to be taken, but once Dragons start to explore options and make enquiries, important (and unstoppable) wheels can be set in motion.

Dragons seeking work should actively follow up vacancies, but also take advantage of the advice and other resources available to them. In some cases, employment officials could suggest different ways forward or advise on relevant refresher courses and schemes. With commitment, many Dragons can successfully secure a position which they can build on in the future. For some, this Rat year can mark the start of a new chapter in their working life.

Progress made at work can often bring a welcome increase in income, and some Dragons will also find ways to supplement their means through an enterprising idea. However, with their commitments and plans, their outgoings will be high and throughout the year they should keep watch on their spending levels. It could be easy to overindulge this year. Also, when entering into important agreements, they should check the terms carefully, otherwise mistakes could be made and unnecessary outlay be incurred. Dragons, take note.

Dragons will derive a lot of pleasure from their personal interests over the year and often be on inspired form. For those keen to make more of a particular talent, now is a good time to seek expert guidance. With an earnest approach, this is a time of great possibility.

The active nature of the year will also be evident domestically. Dragons will often be keen to make some home improvements, including updating equipment and altering certain rooms. However, while enthusiastic, they do need to allow ample time to complete their projects. Some undertakings could be more protracted than anticipated. In addition to the often considerable practical activity of the year, there will also be domestic occasions that Dragons will particularly appreciate, including the marking of their own achievements and the successes of family members.

They will also make the most of what is happening during the Rat year, including events held in their area. If they go along with family and friends, they can enjoy some lively times. In addition, they will find their social circle widening, as their work, interests and friends can all lead to them meeting others.

For unattached Dragons or those who would welcome a more active social life, the Rat year can see quite a transformation in their situation. A chance meeting could lead to many an unattached Dragon finding love, and interests and activities started now can help to open up new social opportunities.

Dragons are quick to latch onto all forms of opportunity and many will appreciate the possibilities the Rat year offers. It is a time to seize the initiative and look to advance. On a personal level, there will be much to share, and for some Dragons, love can make the year all the more special. However, while so much can go well, Dragons do need to be wary of taking unnecessary risks, spending too freely and pushing their good fortune too far. When times are good, it is easy to go overboard, but, this warning apart, this can be a lively and fulfilling year and Dragons can benefit from it in many ways.

Tips for the Year
A year for action. By making the most of your situation and seizing your opportunities, you can make good headway. Value your relations with others and share the good times the year will bring.

DRAGON FORTUNES IN THE YEAR OF THE OX

The Ox year is a generally encouraging one for Dragons, although they will need to remain mindful of others and toe the line. Ox years favour tradition and proceeding along established lines. 'Follow proper procedures and enjoy success in whatever you do', as the Chinese proverb says. That success could be slow in coming, though, and patience will be needed – not always a Dragon strong point!

At work, Dragons will fare best by concentrating on areas where they have the greatest expertise. If new to their position, this is an excellent year for them to become established, learn more about the different aspects of their work and immerse themselves in what is going on around them. With commitment, these Dragons can not only help their present standing, but also find greater fulfilment in what they do. Rather than look or rush ahead, it is a case of making the most of the present. Also, as the year develops, many Dragons can benefit from the developments that take place. In some cases, staff movements will create roles to fill or give them experience in another capacity. By making the most of such chances, Dragons can do much to enhance their reputation. This is a year favouring steady progress.

Throughout the year, Dragons should work closely with their colleagues and be aware of the viewpoints of those around them. While they may have their own ways of doing things, this is not a time to go out on a limb. More independent Dragons, take careful note.

For Dragons seeking work or who decide to move on from where they are, the Ox year can present some good opportunities. However, Dragons will again find it best to concentrate on areas which draw on their skills and expertise rather than trying for anything very different. The job-seeking process can be slow and, at times, frustrating, but by remaining patient and persistent, these Dragons may be rewarded. Results this year will come through hard, steady effort.

Many Dragons will enjoy a rise in income over the year and some could also benefit from a gift or the receipt of something extra. To make most of this, they should manage their situation well, ideally setting funds aside for specific requirements and, if possible, making provision for the future. With control and careful consideration, they can fare well.

Travel could appeal this year and Dragons should try to go away at some point if they can. A change of scene and the chance to see some new areas could do them a lot of good. Some could successfully combine their travels with an interest-related activity or a visit to a special attraction. Planning ahead can lead to some very agreeable times.

As always, Dragons will appreciate the social opportunities of the year and, while they may not go out as regularly as in other years, the Ox year will bring a pleasing mix of social occasions. Those related to personal interests could be especially appealing and many Dragons will enjoy meeting up with other enthusiasts. As a result, some important connections can be forged.

Dragons enjoying romance could find their relationship strengthening over the year and some Dragons will settle down or marry. However, while Dragons will enjoy good relations with many of those around them, a word of warning does need to be sounded. In the Ox year Dragons need to be wary of rumour or getting caught up in what could be complicated situations. In their dealings with others, they should remain open and upfront. Indiscretions or lapses are liable to cause problems. Dragons, take note.

Their home life can be a source of much pleasure, however, and preserving time to share with others will not only be good for relationships but also lead to many enjoyable times, including trips away. Ox years encourage Dragons to have a good lifestyle balance and their domestic life is an important part of this. Also, many Dragons will give sterling advice to family members and their judgement will be of considerable value. During the Ox year, the Dragon's perceptiveness and special empathy with others can be great assets.

Although the Ox year may lack the pace and vigour Dragons like, it will nevertheless allow them to proceed steadily and enjoy a greater level of fulfilment in their activities. It can be a satisfying year and bring many pleasures, including travel possibilities and some rewarding personal and family times.

Tips for the Year

Rather than rush through the year, savour it. Enjoy your interests, spend time with your loved ones and add to your skills. These can be fine and constructive times for you.

DRAGON FORTUNES IN THE YEAR OF THE TIGER

Tiger years have great energy and vitality, and with hopes to fill and plans to realize, Dragons are set to do well.

At work this can be a time for progress. With many Dragons having now proved themselves in their present capacity, they will feel ready to move ahead and take on new challenges. And by keeping alert for openings in their present place of work as well as elsewhere, they could discover attractive possibilities. Sometimes these could be a considerable change from previous roles, but give them new incentive and the chance to prove themselves in another area. Tiger years offer scope and many Dragons will welcome new opportunities.

This also applies to Dragons who are discontented in their present role or seeking work. By not being too restrictive in what they are considering, they could uncover interesting new opportunities and be offered a role which suits their capabilities. The Dragon's drive and initiative can bear considerable fruit this year.

However, while the aspects are encouraging, Dragons still need to be focused and aware of what is going on around them. In setting about their duties, they should be thorough and wary of jumping to conclusions or taking risks. Haste or lapses could undermine some of the good they have done. Also, throughout the year, they should work as part of a team rather than too independently. This way not only will support be more forthcoming, but they will benefit from the pooling of talent and ideas. In Tiger years, Dragons need to watch their independent streak.

Progress made at work can increase the income levels of many Dragons this year and some could also benefit from an additional sum. However, Tiger years do call for fiscal discipline. With some expensive purchases tempting and their current commitments needing to be met, Dragons could find their outgoings high. While they will be keen to go ahead with their plans, particularly for their home, if they take the time to consider options, ranges and costs, they can make better decisions. In money matters, care and time need to be allowed this year.

This need for care also extends to relations with others. Although much is set to go well, problems can still their raise their head. In their home life, Dragons could find busy schedules and work pressures could lead to tiredness and tension, and quality time could suffer in the face of competing demands. They do need to be aware of this and preserve time for family life as well as communicate well with their loved ones. Dragons are usually mindful in this respect, but pressures can be intense this year and they need to ensure that they do not give rise to domestic difficulties. In this busy year, it is important to strike a good lifestyle balance.

However, despite these cautionary words, there will be a lot to enjoy, including what can be extensive home (and for some, garden) projects. There will also be individual successes to mark and the chance of a special occasion and family gathering.

When possible, Dragons should also aim to fit some travel into the year. A holiday with their loved ones can do everyone good.

The Tiger year can also bring a good mix of social opportunities, with Dragons enjoying the broad range of activities they engage in and the chance to meet new people. Some of their contacts could be particularly helpful with a certain matter or aspiration, although, to fully benefit, Dragons need to be forthcoming and listen carefully to what is advised.

Where matters of the heart are concerned, Dragons also need to be attentive. With care, romances can flourish and bring considerable happiness, but if Dragons start to take the love or affection of another person for granted, problems could ensue. Dragons, take note.

With the year's demands, it is also important that Dragons take good care of themselves. This includes taking regular exercise, paying attention to diet and allowing time for interests and recreation. With the Tiger year often abundant with ideas and possibilities, many Dragons could become attracted by a new activity or set themselves a personal goal. Tiger years offer scope, but to benefit Dragons need to use their time well and make the most of their opportunities.

In general, the Tiger year promises to be a busy and full one and Dragons will welcome the opportunities it brings. A lot can be accomplished, although Dragons do need to remain watchful and alert, otherwise difficulties and misunderstandings could arise which, with greater consideration, could often have been averted. Dragons, take note. Enjoy the year and its well-deserved successes, but do be mindful of others too.

Tips for the Year
This is a time of considerable potential – make the most of it and seize your opportunities. But do balance out your activities and preserve some time for those who are special to you. Inattention could bring problems. Take note and make the most of this encouraging year.

DRAGON FORTUNES IN THE YEAR OF THE RABBIT

Dragons like to lead busy lifestyles and put a lot of energy into their various activities. But even they need time to reappraise their lives and build up their reserves. And the Rabbit year will be such a time. This will be a steady and settled year, and ideal preparation for the Dragon's own auspicious year, which follows.

One area which is particularly well aspected is personal development. This is an excellent year for Dragons to develop skills and, if they feel a further qualification or additional knowledge could help their prospects, set aside time to acquire this. Study and self-development can be a satisfying and potentially important element to the year.

Personal interests can also allow Dragons to develop their talents, as well as be a source of much pleasure. This year all Dragons deserve some 'me time', and any Dragons who have let their interests fall away would do well to rectify this and perhaps consider taking up something new. This can provide balance to their current lifestyle and additional benefits can follow on.

Rabbit years also favour culture, and if attracted by specific events, Dragons should see what can be arranged. There will be a lot they can appreciate this year.

Many of their activities can have a good social element too. However, while they can have a lot of fun and make new friends, they do need to be aware that an inadvertent or flippant remark could cause problems. Dragons, take note and be careful.

More positively, Dragons will enjoy sharing much in their domestic life, including advising and supporting loved ones when they are facing decisions. This is an excellent year to share interests and activities and make the most of local amenities. Rabbit years can give rise to many enjoyable occasions. However, throughout the year, Dragons do need to consult others *and listen to what they have to say.* With their forceful personality, they do like to hold sway, but in some instances greater consultation and flexibility would be to the benefit of all.

At work this can be a constructive year. Any Dragons who have recently taken on new responsibilities, or who do so over the year, should aim to establish themselves and learn about the different aspects of their role. With commitment, they can gain an excellent reputation and become an integral member of any team. They should also use any chances to network and build connections, as this can be to their later advantage.

For Dragons seeking work or a change from their current role, the Rabbit year can be an excellent one in which to reappraise their situation. By considering how they would like their career to develop and seeking advice, they can see some interesting possibilities emerging. When they have found an opening that interests them, they should be quick to follow it up. What is achieved this year can have an important bearing on developments next year.

Dragons can also fare well financially. Their fine taste and eye for a good buy will be on fine form, and they could enjoy some luck too, possibly buying a desired item at a favourable price or finding just what they wanted in an unusual outlet. However, in view of their commitments, they do need to stay disciplined and manage their budget well.

When possible, they should also make provision for travel. Many Dragons will enjoy a holiday this year and if there are specific sights they would like to see or destinations they would like to visit, they should make enquiries. Interesting possibilities can open up this year.

Although the Rabbit year may lack the activity of some, it can still be a satisfying one. Rather than overcommit themselves or conduct life at a fast pace, it is a year for Dragons to take stock, to appreciate where they are and to build steadily on their position. Their home life, social life and personal interests can bring them a great deal of pleasure and many will also be able to enjoy a better lifestyle balance in this settled and steady year.

Tips for the Year

Enjoy the present, but also consider the future. This is an excellent time for personal development, and skills and knowledge gained now will help your future prospects. This is a year of preparation for the opportunities that lie ahead.

DRAGON FORTUNES IN THE YEAR OF THE DRAGON

As the Dragon year starts, many Dragons will celebrate in style and be determined to make the most of the next 12 months. And with their energy and drive, along with an element of Dragon luck, they can make this a special time.

For Dragons who are nurturing particular ambitions or have felt held back in recent times, this is a year for action. Dragons are in the driving seat and fortune will favour the bold and enterprising. For some, their year can mark a new chapter in their life and, in some cases, a fresh start.

At work the aspects are especially encouraging. For Dragons who are already established a career, there will be the chance to move to new levels. Here recent activities can stand them in excellent stead, and when openings arise, they should actively pursue them. This is no year to stand still and many Dragons will make progress in their existing place of work or further their career elsewhere. In addition, many will have more chance to draw on their field of expertise and enjoy some notable achievements.

For those who feel unfulfilled in their present type of work or are seeking work, the aspects are also promising. By keeping alert for opportunities and exploring different possibilities, many of these Dragons can secure what will prove to be an ideal position. Events can happen quickly in their own year and they will need to move fast, but what many succeed in doing now can help re-energize their career.

All Dragons should also take advantage of any training that is available as well as build connections in their area of work. By being active and involved, they can impress others and strengthen their reputation.

Progress made at work can help financially and many Dragons will enjoy an increase in earnings over the year. However, with their many ideas and plans, they do need to watch their spending levels. Also, if they have any funds they do not immediately need, it could be to their advantage to make some provision for the future. The Dragon year is a good one in which to give thought to the longer term.

With their genial and outgoing nature, Dragons will often be on impressive form this year and will have the opportunity to meet many people, some of whom will become important friends and connections.

For the unattached, their own year can bring wonderful romance. Affairs of the heart are splendidly aspected and some Dragons could meet their future partner. Any who have suffered recent hurt will find their own year offering much brighter prospects. This is a time to move ahead and, for some, make a new start.

Dragons can also look forward to an active home life, although, with their own commitments and those around them leading busy lifestyles as well, there needs to be good cooperation. This includes assisting one another at busy times, sharing tasks and, importantly, preserving quality time to spend together. Without care, there is a risk that home life could be conducted in a whirl, with Dragons not fully enjoying the rewards of their efforts. In this exciting year, they do need to take the time to pause, unwind and value the pleasures of home life.

Throughout the year, they should also be forthcoming and willing to talk about their hopes and activities. This way, not only can they gain from the advice of those around them but also be assisted in unforeseen ways. In addition, the year may be marked by special celebration. In so many ways, the Dragon's own year can be meaningful and memorable.

During it, Dragons should aim to make the most of their ideas, and some of these will be connected with their personal interests. Travel, too, could be tempting, and if possible, Dragons should aim to take a holiday this year. By planning their itinerary in advance, they can look forward to visiting some major attractions. Their own year offers great possibility.

Overall, the Dragon year is a highly auspicious one for Dragons. It is a time for them to forge ahead with plans and look to build on their position. However, to make the most of their year, they do need to be the drivers of change. As they will find, once they start to take action, much can follow on. This year they have much in their favour and can see some impressive results.

Tips for the Year
Act. Make the most of your strengths now and give some thought to your future. What you accomplish can not only help your present situation but also lead on to later successes. Your own year is indeed significant and special for you. Use it well.

Dragon Fortunes in the Year of the Snake

A constructive year ahead. Dragons will have a good chance to build on their recent success and move ahead. Also, the steadier nature of the Snake year will give them more chance to concentrate on their priorities.

At work, the recent efforts of many Dragons can now bear fruit. As opportunities arise, they will often be well placed to benefit. Some could be asked to take on a more specialist role or secure promotion. Certainly this is a year when their special talents can be nurtured and many Dragons are set to make impressive headway. In addition, if they have particular goals or aspirations, this is a good time to pursue them. Their skills and resolve can be a compelling combination this year. In addition, all Dragons should seize any opportunities to further their knowledge, including taking advantage of any training that is available.

The majority of Dragons will remain in their current area of work, but for those who decide to make a change or are seeking work, important opportunities can open up. By considering different ways in which they could use their strengths and looking at options, many of these Dragons will secure an opening on which they can build, often very quickly. And if certain applications do not go their way, they should not lose heart. This year success can come in curious ways. The Snake, who rules the year, is a master of mystery and surprise. A lot happens for a reason in the Snake year, and often it is in the Dragon's favour.

The encouraging aspects also extend to personal interests. If Dragons have been nurturing ideas or become intrigued by a new activity, they should follow it up this year. By applying themselves and taking advantage of their opportunities, they can make this a rewarding and inspiring time. Snake years encourage Dragons to make more of themselves.

Dragons can also fare well financially this year. Many will enjoy an increase in earnings and some may also benefit from an enterprising idea. However, all Dragons do need to control their outgoings, otherwise anything extra could become absorbed by everyday spending and not always used to best advantage. Good budgeting will help, including saving for more substantial purchases.

With their broad interests and outgoing personality, Dragons know a great many people and will enjoy regular contact with their friends during the year as well as the chance to meet new people. Work developments and personal interests can both have a good social element.

For Dragons hoping for or enjoying romance, the Snake year calls for care. If a relationship is to develop, Dragons need to give it time and attention. Should they come across as preoccupied or start to take the affection of another person for granted, problems could ensue. Dragons, take note and take the time to nurture romance.

This need for awareness and care also applies to home life. With their various commitments, Dragons need to make sure that quality time with their loved ones does not suffer. Also, when projects need tackling or decisions taking, they should consult those around them rather than take on too much single-handed. Dragons should watch their independent tendencies in Snake years. However, the year will also see some key domestic plans advanced, some of which will add new comforts and be much appreciated. Dragons will also enjoy some of the more spontaneous occasions of the year.

The Snake year has the capacity to surprise and delight. It also harnesses Dragons' abilities and encourages them to progress. With concerted effort, they can look forward to making important advances and enjoying favourable outcomes. This is a year for them to profit from their strengths. However, while much can go well, they do need to exercise care in their relations with others. This year may be rewarding, but Dragons do need to keep their lifestyle in balance and take others into consideration.

Tips for the Year
Make the most of your skills and experience. Much can be achieved this year. In your personal life, do give time to those who are special to you and be mindful of their views. Extra attention can make an appreciable difference.

DRAGON FORTUNES IN THE YEAR OF THE HORSE

With their resolve, personality and drive, Dragons make the most of situations. Even when those situations are not so favourable, their resourcefulness and skills invariably see them through. These qualities will again serve them well in the Horse year. While it is a generally good one, throughout Dragons need to keep alert and be wary of complacency or taking one risk too many. Horse years can have salutary warnings for the careless.

A particular feature of the Horse year is that situations move quickly. In the workplace, changes can occur suddenly. Colleagues may move on or new initiatives be launched, and experienced Dragons will be excellently placed to benefit. They do, though, need to act quickly – 'the early bird catches the worm', as the saying goes. In the Horse year, enthusiasm and commitment will count for a lot. Also, Dragons do need to remain thorough and give of their best. Should they take risks or short cuts, problems could arise. Horse years call for care *and* thoroughness.

While many Dragons will make progress in their present place of work, some may feel they can better their prospects elsewhere. For these Dragons, and those seeking work, the Horse year can bring surprising developments. By considering different possibilities and following up openings, many of these Dragons could secure a position which offers the chance to prove themselves in a new way. Although this could entail much learning and adjustment, these Dragons will welcome the challenge. Horse years reward effort and industry, and committed Dragons are set to do well.

Progress made at work can help financially, although, with their busy lifestyle, Dragons need to keep a close watch on spending. When considering any major outlay, they need to be conversant with the costs. With care, however, they can see the realization of some key hopes this year and make substantial purchases for themselves and their home.

Travel will tempt many, and by planning ahead, they can enjoy some exciting times away. Horse years are rich in possibility, but require a disciplined approach. Also, while Dragons could enjoy some good fortune, they should not tempt fate by taking unnecessary risks or ignoring finer details. At all times, Horse years require vigilance.

With their outgoing natures, Dragons will also enjoy the social opportunities of the year and will have many chances to go out, meet others and attend events. For the unattached, there could be excellent romantic possibilities, although circumstances (such as distance or conflicting routines) may not always make things easy. With care and time, though, many new relationships can often become more meaningful.

However, while the Horse year will be busy and active, Dragons need to be on their guard. At times a rumour or some disturbing news may be of concern. To help clarify matters, Dragons should check situations themselves rather than accept what they may hear. Also, if agonizing over a decision, they could find it helpful to talk to someone they trust. Situations can often be defused and worries prove groundless, but Horse years can have their concerning moments.

The busy nature of the year will also be seen domestically, and whether assisting their loved ones, giving advice or setting about practical projects, Dragons will once again undertake a great deal. In addition, a personal success and possible holiday can bring some special times. However, throughout the year, there needs to be openness and good communication, and activities need to be planned and spread out to avoid undue pressure.

With their active lifestyles, Dragons should also preserve some time for their own interests as well as give some thought to their well-being. Taking regular exercise and improving the quality of their diet could make a real difference.

The Year of the Horse will see a great deal happen and, Dragons can make gratifying progress. It will require effort, and sometimes adjustment, but the rewards can be substantial and many Dragons will successfully advance their career as well as be pleased with how many of their personal plans go forward. However, throughout the year they do need to be thorough and avoid unnecessary risk. This can be a fulfilling year, but Dragons need to stay disciplined and make the most of situations.

Tips for the Year

Be aware of how situations are developing and if an opportunity arises that appeals to you, act quickly. Also, be prepared to adapt and learn. By embracing what the year brings and remaining thorough, you can enjoy some good results.

DRAGON FORTUNES IN THE YEAR OF THE GOAT

Although not a bad year, Dragons could find this one frustrating. Progress will not be as easy or substantial as they may like and they may have to rein in certain ambitions. However, while the Goat year will have its vexations, it will also have its benefits, including improving lifestyle balance as well as developing knowledge and skills.

At work, rather than looking to make major advances, many Dragons will decide to concentrate on their present position. As a result, they will not only have the chance to make more of their expertise but also enjoy some professionally pleasing results. In addition, many will benefit from training opportunities as well as the chance to widen their remit. This is a year to build steadily on what they do and use their strengths well.

Dragons who work in creative environments could find this an inspiring time and will relish the chance to be part of the idea-generating process. Goat years are encouraging for Dragons in this respect, although Dragons do need to work within the parameters laid down and closely with their colleagues rather than too independently.

For Dragons who desire change this year or are seeking work, times will be challenging. Obtaining a new position will require effort and Dragons will not only need to persist but also to broaden the scope of their quest. However, with tenacity and self-belief, they *can* succeed, and often what is obtained now will be a springboard for greater progress next year.

A feature of the Goat year is that it will give Dragons the chance to take stock and appreciate their personal interests and talents more. Some may give time to projects they have long been considering or take up subjects and pursuits that have intrigued them. Some could decide to enrol on study courses or self-improvement programmes and further their abilities (and sometimes prospects) in some way. By using their time well, they can find the year both satisfying and beneficial.

Travel will appeal to many and they should aim to take a holiday during the year as well as visit local attractions that interest them. Goat years can bring pleasurable times, but ideas do need acting upon. To delay could lead to disappointment or missed opportunities. Dragons, take note and do not let chances slip.

With travel possibilities and other commitments, this will be an expensive year and Dragons need to manage their finances well. Important purchases and other transactions should be carefully considered and costed, and, if tempted by anything speculative, Dragons should check the terms and be aware of the implications. Without sufficient attention, there is a risk of misjudgement and loss this year. It is a time for careful control.

More positively, Dragons can look forward to a lively social life. As always, they will appreciate spending time with their friends and coming into contact with others through a range of activities. As a result, some good connections can be made. Romantic prospects are promising and potentially significant this year.

Domestically, Goat years also favour a coming together and Dragons should ensure that time is set aside for activities everyone can appreciate – perhaps watching a film, enjoying a good meal or having a trip out. Goat years are ideal for putting lifestyles into balance and valuing times with those who are special. Shared interests could be particularly gratifying and lead to some fun times.

Overall, this is a year favouring personal development, adding to skills, giving time to interests and striving for a good lifestyle balance. It is also a time to join forces with others and to share – and enjoy – what is going on. In many ways Goat years, with their encouraging yet slower pace, can be a tonic for Dragons and be of present *and* future value.

Tips for the Year
Focus on the present and follow through your ideas. Also, cultivate your interests and value your relationships with others. There is much to appreciate and gain personally from what is done over the year.

DRAGON FORTUNES IN THE YEAR OF THE MONKEY

As the Monkey year starts, many Dragons will have high hopes and be feeling in inspired mood. And this *is* a year of scope and possibility. However, while the aspects are generally favourable, Dragons do need to be careful not to overreach themselves. The Monkey year can trip the unwary and haste can lead to possible mistakes and oversights. Care will be needed to make the most of the year.

A key feature of the Monkey year is that it favours personal development. Over the year Dragons should make the most of this trend and enjoy what opens up for them. Particularly as far as recreational pursuits are concerned, if a new activity appeals to them, they should find out more or, if equipment or a new product becomes available that would enable them to do more, they should check it out. The Monkey year is an encouraging one and can provide an interesting mix of things to do as well as, sometimes, new outlets for Dragons' many talents.

Dragons will find themselves in demand on both a domestic and social level this year. However, it is important they remain mindful of those around them and consult them over their ideas and plans. That way they can benefit from advice and support as well as sometimes be alerted to considerations they may have overlooked. The more feedback Dragons can get this year, the better.

Monkey years also have a strong social element, and more independent-minded Dragons would certainly find it worth embracing the spirit of the year and involving themselves more readily in things that are going on around them. Participation can be rewarding this year, bringing good times as well as helping forge useful connections.

In their home life, Dragons will be busy and good communication and cooperation will be needed. In view of the general level of activity, it will be helpful if the timescales of certain projects are kept elastic. There is only so much that can be done at any one time. Also, Monkey years can sometimes throw up their quandaries and these need to be addressed before proceeding. Here again, all need to pool together to come up with the best solution.

However, despite some demanding times, Monkey years also bring their pleasures, and home improvements, spur of the moment trips and unexpected travel opportunities can all be appreciated. There is certainly a spontaneous element to the year.

At work, Monkey years are also times of opportunity. In many a workplace, considerable change will be seen as new ideas and systems are introduced. And Dragons, with their usual zeal, will often latch on to developments and be excellently placed to benefit. Over the year many will enjoy promotion or successfully transfer to a greater position elsewhere. Monkey years offer scope and Dragons will welcome the chance to prove themselves in a greater capacity. A few Dragons will embark on a complete career change this year and will relish the opportunity.

Many Dragons who are seeking work will also find interesting possibilities arising. While some may come with a steep learning curve, what is started now can often have excellent potential for future growth.

With such a busy lifestyle, outgoings will be high and Dragons will need to keep a close watch on spending. Also, if entering into any new agreement, they should thoroughly check the terms and obligations. This is no year for rush or risk. In addition, if they can make early provision for key requirements, this will lead to more happening. Monkey years favour preparation and working (and saving) towards desired outcomes.

This can be a rewarding year for Dragons, but it does require determined effort and close liaison with others. With support, much can be accomplished. Dragons will need to proceed carefully, avoiding rush or risk, and in many matters, including finance, be thorough. But, with their usual consummate skill, they can enjoy this year and do well.

Tips for the Year
A year of considerable possibility. Improve your skills and look at ways in which you can gain support and move your plans forward. Whether professionally or personally, if you make the most of what opens up, these can be fulfilling times.

DRAGON FORTUNES IN THE YEAR OF THE ROOSTER

Dragons are very adept at making the most of their situation. And in the Rooster year, many will find themselves in the right place at the right time and benefiting from fortuitous developments. In addition, a certain serendipity will be seen this year and once Dragons set their plans in motion, circumstances will assist. The Dragon is, after all, born under the sign of luck. Also, while many Dragons will have made important headway in recent times, for those who start the year nursing disappointment or experiencing problems, this is very much a time to focus on current objectives. With purpose, they can move forward.

At work, the aspects are especially encouraging. Often as a result of their recent activities, many Dragons will find employers keen for them to take on greater responsibilities. When promotion opportunities or other openings occur, they can be well placed to benefit.

Those who feel their prospects could be bettered by a move elsewhere, as well as those seeking work, should make enquiries and actively explore possibilities. In some instances, contacts may alert them to openings or give them ideas to consider. Others could benefit from companies expanding in their area. The Rooster year offers scope and many Dragons will make deserved progress.

This will also help financially, and some Dragons will benefit from an additional payment as well. However, while this is an improved year, they do need to watch outgoings and budget for key requirements. With good management, they will, though, be able to proceed with many of their plans and make useful acquisitions for themselves and their home.

Another positive feature of the year will be the way Dragons can develop their knowledge and skills. Often this will come through training at work, but those who feel another skill or qualification would help their progress should set aside time to study. This can not only be personally satisfying but also reinforce the favourable aspects of the year.

Similarly, personal interests can develop well. Whether enthused by ideas or encouraged by others, Dragons will often enjoy the way their activities can broaden out and sometimes lead in new directions. Those whose busy lifestyles have led to interests falling away should look to rectify this. Purposeful action can be well rewarded this year.

The Rooster year can also bring some good travel opportunities, which will satisfy the adventurous natures of many Dragons.

However, while the aspects are generally encouraging, the Rooster year does have its more cautionary elements. In particular, Dragons need to take careful note of the views of those around them. If they are too preoccupied with their own activities or appear distracted, strains and tensions may arise. Similarly, pressures and tiredness could lead to disagreements and this is not a time to take feelings for granted or make assumptions. Dragons, take note. Without proper care and attention, certain relationships could be put to the test.

There will, however, be social events to enjoy. Dragons can look forward to many convivial occasions and the chance to make new connections. Where romance is concerned, however, care is advised. New relationships should be built up steadily rather than hurried.

Dragons should also make sure their various commitments do not impinge on their home life. At times they could find it difficult to balance their busy lifestyle, but preserving quality time to share with their loved ones can be to the advantage of all. In addition, the Rooster year can give rise to many enjoyable occasions. And, when certain activities are started, serendipity (which can include some advantageous offers) can assist.

Overall, the Rooster year will contain some excellent opportunities for Dragons. Their enthusiasm and determination can enable them to benefit from these, and timely developments will often help the process along. However, Dragons do need to take care in their relations with others and, importantly, give time to those who are special to them. Inattention and preoccupation could cause problems. Provided Dragons remain mindful of these cautionary aspects, they are set to do well in the Rooster year.

Tips for the Year
Act with determination and move your plans forward. Much can now be accomplished. Also, seize any chances to further your skills. They are an investment in yourself and your future. And importantly, pay attention to those around you, listen to them and give them your time.

DRAGON FORTUNES IN THE YEAR OF THE DOG

Although Dog years have their opportunities, they also have their more difficult aspects, and Dragons need to be cautious in their undertakings. The Dog year is not a time to proceed regardless or take unnecessary risks. However, while Dragons may sometimes feel restricted by developments, the progress they do make can often pave the way for the successes that await in the following year.

At work, Dragons should make the most of current developments and add to their skills and experience. By networking, taking advantage of training and following developments in their industry, they will not only be helping their present situation but also learning of possible ways forward. Dog years are very rewarding of commitment, and effort made now will enhance Dragons' reputation *and* prospects.

Many Dragons will decide to remain with their present employer this year and develop their role, but for those eager to move elsewhere or to find work, the Dog year can bring interesting developments. Obtaining a new position will require time and persistence, but what many Dragons take on now will not only broaden their experience but also open up possibilities for the future. The Dog year can leave an important legacy.

In addition, all Dragons should use any chances to network and build connections. These can, in time, prove significant.

In money matters, however, great care is needed. This is not a year to take risks, and if entering into any new agreement, Dragons should check the terms and obligations. Similarly, paperwork should be attended to with care and documents kept safely. Lapses and losses could be inconvenient. Dragons should also proceed carefully when making major purchases. Haste or impulsive decisions could lead to regret.

One expense many Dragons will have this year will be travel. Again, they should plan this carefully, including reading up about their destination beforehand. The more thorough and prepared they are, the more they can get out of their trip. Some may also find their work or interests giving rise to additional travel possibilities.

A particular feature of Dog years is that they are a time when many find themselves championing causes, and some Dragons will be speaking out on matters close to their heart, helping other people or becoming caught up in a new interest. Dog years can open potentially worthwhile doors.

With their busy lifestyles, Dragons should also give some thought to their own well-being. To drive themselves too hard or pay scant attention to their diet or exercise levels could leave them prone to minor ailments. If lacking their usual sparkle or considering new exercise or diet regimes, they would do well to seek advice.

As ever, their social life will see considerable activity. Travel, work and other interests could all lead to them meeting other people this year. Dragons who would welcome more companionship will find local activities and interests excellent ways of meeting others, and their many qualities will win them new friends. Again, this is an excellent year to network and to participate in what is going on.

Dog years do, though, have their trickier aspects. In their home life, Dragons need to be attentive to those around them, as pressure and tiredness could give rise to irritability or patience wear thin. Failure to communicate properly or give adequate attention to domestic matters could also bring problems. Dragons do need to be aware of this and set aside time to spend with family members. Shared interests and activities can be of particular value and a possible family holiday also much appreciated. Extra attention would definitely not come amiss this year.

Dragons have a canny knack of making the most of many situations, however, and while the aspects may be variable, by building on their skills and knowledge and seizing their opportunities, they can prepare the way for future success. Financial matters need care and Dragons should make sure their commitments and busy lifestyle do not lead to problems in their domestic life. But forewarned is forearmed, and many Dragons will successfully side-step the year's trickier aspects and use their time in constructive ways.

Tips for the Year

Avoid rush. Be willing to extend your knowledge and skills and draw on the support of those around you. Also, preserve time for your loved ones and be attentive towards them. Time and care can make an important difference this year.

Dragon Fortunes in the Year of the Pig

Pig years favour the bold and enterprising, and for Dragons who are nurturing ambitions and keen to make headway, this is a time of considerable promise. For any Dragons who are in low spirits, it is a time to draw a line under what has gone before and focus on the present. Much is possible this year and with a positive 'can do' attitude, Dragons can achieve a great deal.

At work, prospects are particularly encouraging and Dragons will be able to profit from their experience. In many a workplace, there will be the chance for them take on greater duties and make important progress. Also, as a result of developments, some may be persuaded to take on a different role and they will relish the opportunity. Pig years are times to make headway and many Dragons will enter a new stage in their working life.

Those who start the year feeling unfulfilled or staid should make enquiries and explore possibilities. This is no time to drift or stand still and they could identify some appealing new opportunities.

Similarly, those seeking work should give serious thought to what they really want to do. Talking to professional organizations and employment experts could alert them to possibilities worth considering. In addition, some may find refresher or training courses helpful in their quest. In this favourable year, effort and initiative can certainly pay off.

Progress made at work can also help financially and many Dragons will not only enjoy an increase in income but also benefit from the receipt of extra funds or a gift. However, to make the most of any upturn, they should manage their money well, including perhaps looking to reduce borrowings or make savings. With care and thought, they can make a difference to their overall situation as well as appreciate their more substantial purchases. This is a year rewarding planning and discipline.

Travel will appeal to many Dragons and they may have the chance to visit some impressive attractions. Even those who do not venture too far could enjoy visiting places of interest in their own locality. Pig years encourage Dragons to engage in what is going on around them.

In their home life this can be an especially active year, with Dragons helping and advising their loved ones as well as overseeing many activities. Here their judgement and foresight can be much appreciated, although where practical undertakings are concerned, ample time needs to be allowed. Some plans can be problematic and more extensive than anticipated and will be ideally best tackled in stages. Throughout the year it is also important that there is openness and good communication between everyone in the Dragon household. Pig years favour collective effort, and certain family occasions, successes and shared activities will give a lift to the year.

Social prospects are good too. In addition to meeting up with their friends, Dragons could find their work and interests having a pleasing social element. There will be much to enjoy this year and any Dragons who start the year feeling lonely or dispirited will find that new activities can bring new friendships and brighten their situation considerably.

There can be interesting romantic prospects too, although new relationships should be built up steadily. Rush or pressure in the early stages may bring heartache. This is a year to enjoy the present and see what results. *Que sera, sera.*

Although Dragons already pack a lot into their days, it is also important that they do not let their own interests and recreational activities fall away. Not only can these be a good outlet for their talents and energy, but they can give them the opportunity to unwind in ways they enjoy. Some could offer the benefit of exercise too. In this already full year, it is important that Dragons preserve some 'me time'.

In general, the Pig year has considerable potential for Dragons, but it will be a case of seizing the moment and acting with determination. 'Diligence leads to riches', as the Chinese proverb reminds us, and diligence (and effort) can deliver this year. At work, it is a time to look to advance, while financially, good management can pay off. Dragons can also look forward to some special times with others. Both their home and social life can be active and rewarding. They do need to watch their independent tendencies and communicate well with those around them, but if they do this, they can really enjoy this pleasing and rewarding year.

Tips for the Year
Act with purpose and determination. A lot can open up for you, but you need to seize your chances and set about what you want to do. Value the input of those around you and watch your independent tendencies. Support can help you achieve a lot this year.

Thoughts and Words of Dragons

To accomplish great things, we must not only act, but also dream, not only plan, but also believe.

ANATOLE FRANCE

We can do anything we want to do if we stick to it long enough.

HELEN KELLER

Life is either a daring adventure or nothing.

HELEN KELLER

Never bend your head. Hold it high. Look the world straight in the eye.

HELEN KELLER

Determine that the thing can and shall be done, and
then we shall find the way.

ABRAHAM LINCOLN

Always bear in mind that your own resolution to
success is more than any other one thing.

ABRAHAM LINCOLN

Either you reach a higher point today, or you exercise
your strength in order to be able to climb higher
tomorrow.

FRIEDRICH NIETZSCHE

Everything happens to everybody sooner or later if
there is time enough.

GEORGE BERNARD SHAW

Life is not a 'brief candle'. It is a splendid torch that I
want to make burn as brightly as possible before
handing on to future generations.

GEORGE BERNARD SHAW

Far away there in the sunshine are my highest
aspirations. I may not reach them, but I can look up
and see their beauty, believe in them and try to follow
where they lead.

LOUISA MAY ALCOTT

27 January 1941–14 February 1942 — *Metal Snake*

14 February 1953–2 February 1954 — *Water Snake*

2 February 1965–20 January 1966 — *Wood Snake*

18 February 1977–6 February 1978 — *Fire Snake*

6 February 1989–26 January 1990 — *Earth Snake*

24 January 2001–11 February 2002 — *Metal Snake*

10 February 2013–30 January 2014 — *Water Snake*

29 January 2025–16 February 2026 — *Wood Snake*

15 February 2037–3 February 2038 — *Fire Snake*

The Snake

The Personality of the Snake

The Snake may remain still for a very long time. Silent, patient, but ever alert. And when the moment comes to act, it moves swiftly and with might. It would be folly to underestimate the Snake, and those born in the Snake year have great depth and strength of character.

Born under the sign of wisdom, Snakes are thinkers. They like to plan, to work through possibilities and to choose the way that is best for them. They keep a lot to themselves and are masters of their own destiny. Some may find their secretive tendencies an enigma, but this is part of their charm. They are thoughtful, perceptive and, while not as outgoing or garrulous as some, have a rich, caring and gentle character. Many also have a fine sense of humour and lace their conversation with timely anecdotes or an amusing choice of words. In their own way and style, Snakes can be effective and engaging. Many qualities lurk behind their quiet persona.

Snakes are also patient. They not do not like hurry or haste, or to be in frenzied or pressured environments. Instead they prefer to take their time and pick their moments. Many know in their own mind what they want to do and work steadily towards their aim. They do not leave much to chance and will study, work and prepare well.

Snakes also rely a lot on intuition and their reading of situations. Here their instinct rarely lets them down unless they are gambling. Out of all the Chinese signs, the Snake is one of the worst gamblers, as the risk and pressure involved are not suited to their psyche.

Being such deep thinkers, Snakes are capable of coming up with very original ideas. They are innovators and are prepared to be different. Accordingly, Snakes have made an important contribution to many walks of life.

As a vocation, Snakes tend to prefer cerebral activities to more physical ones. Unlike some signs, they tend not to have great stores of energy and need time to rest and regain strength after great physical exertion. With their analytical and questioning mind, they can often enjoy success in the sciences, law, education and the financial sector. Religion, psychology and counselling could also appeal, and some could find an outlet for their creativity in the arts and media. Snakes do have diverse talents, although it can be a little while before they establish themselves in their chosen area.

Snakes are adept in money matters and carefully plan their purchases and investments. They are shrewd and astute, and many enjoy a comfortable lifestyle. They do, though, possess an indulgent streak and enjoy spending on themselves and their loved ones. However, those outside their immediate circle may not fare so well, as Snakes like to keep careful control over their assets and outgoings.

Snakes like to appraise and judge situations, and this also applies to the people they meet. Until they know someone well, they can be reserved and guarded. Rather than having a wide social circle, they prefer to have a few close friends whom they trust and with whom they enjoy a good rapport. And while they very much enjoy the passion and excitement of love, they like to take their time before settling down with another person. Snakes are never ones to rush, preferring to wait until they feel everything is right.

Snakes enjoy setting up their home and stamping their personality on it. In addition to their many books and other resources (for Snakes enjoy reading and have wide interests), they will add their own distinctive touches. Snakes have a penchant for the unusual and eye-catching. They also like the finer things in life and will ensure their home is well equipped.

The female Snake in particular has a great sense of style. In appearance, she is often elegant and could have a fondness for jewellery and an expensive taste in clothes – or at least a taste for good-quality ones. She carries herself in a calm, confident and serene way. She has a quiet manner, but relates well to those around her and many place great trust in her. She is also a good organizer and uses her time well.

The family unit is very important to Snakes and they take a caring and protective interest in their loved ones. If a parent, their imagination, wide interests, gentle humour and placid nature will often create a strong bond between them and their child. All Snakes can find much contentment in the love and security their family can offer.

The German writer Johann Wolfgang von Goethe was a Snake and he wrote, 'Just trust yourself, then you will know how to live.' And Snakes do place great trust in themselves. They forge their path in life in their own way and style. And often successfully too.

Top Tips for Snakes
- You may be a private individual, but if you have worries, are concerned over a decision or feel wronged or jealous, you can let the situation gnaw away at you. At such times, it would be to your advantage to be more open and talk to those you trust. With helpful input, many worries can be considerably eased and lift what could be a heavy burden preying on your mind.
- In your early years in particular you can sometimes be lacking in confidence and shy and retiring. Have faith in yourself, draw on your inner reserves and let others see the richness of your character, ideas and potential. If you interact

more readily with others, it will give them a better chance of appreciating you.

- You are capable of coming up with ideas, new approaches and solutions to problems – make the most of your creative abilities and nurture your talents. Whenever appropriate, put your ideas forward. You have much to offer.
- You may like to reflect and plan, but there will be times when the theorizing has to stop and action is needed. As Goethe famously wrote, 'Whatever you can do or dream, you can begin it. Boldness has genius, magic and power in it. Begin it now.' By beginning, you will have more chance of unleashing the magic and power within you.

Relations with Others

With a Rat

The Snake enjoys the charm and vivacity of the Rat and relations between them are good.

In work, these two recognize each other's strengths and can combine them to good effect. With a resourceful Rat colleague, the Snake can feel inspired and energized.

In love, there is a powerful chemistry between them. Both are home-loving and they share many interests. The Snake will enjoy the Rat's enthusiasm and buoyant manner. An often happy match.

With an Ox

With both being quiet and thoughtful and preferring to take things at a more measured pace, there is good respect and understanding between these two.

In work, both are ambitious and persevering. They respect each other and the Snake admires the Ox's tenacity and strong sense of purpose. A formidable team.

In love, with similar tastes and temperaments, these two understand each other well and the Snake will especially appreciate the Ox's practical and dependable nature. An often excellent and fulfilling match.

With a Tiger

The restless energy and busy lifestyle of the Tiger does not sit comfortably with the Snake and relations between the two are generally poor.

In work, the Snake likes to plan and prepare, while the action-orientated Tiger is more gung-ho. With little understanding of each other, theirs is not an effective combination.

In love, the Snake may initially be attracted by the Tiger's warm and lively nature, but the Snake prefers a calm and settled lifestyle and will find the Tiger's high level of activity and desire for independence disquieting. A difficult match.

With a Rabbit

Their mutual liking of the finer things in life and similar tastes and attitudes mean these two signs get on well.

In work, both have good business sense but like to plan and deliberate, and together they could lack the drive and oomph needed to maximize their potential.

In love, these two value an orderly, stable and settled lifestyle, love their home and enjoy their comforts. An excellent and often successful match.

With a Dragon

Somehow the different personalities of these two just gel! Each will be intrigued by the other and relations between them are often excellent.

In work, the Snake will be encouraged and enthused by having such an enterprising colleague. Together, they can combine their strengths to excellent effect.

In love, these two signs complement each other perfectly. The Snake will be particularly attracted by the warmth, vitality and sincerity of the Dragon. Their love, passion and understanding can be very special. An excellent match.

With another Snake

With the Snake being such a profound thinker, time spent with another Snake could be fascinating and intense, but there could still be a certain reserve between the two.

In work, two Snakes will have ideas, plans and high hopes, but with both being deliberators, they could lack the spark needed to fulfil their potential.

In love, two Snakes could bewitch and mesmerize each other. Allure and passion could be strong, but Snakes are possessive, jealous and private, and once differences of opinion arise, there could be difficulties. It is said that two Snakes cannot live under the same roof. In the longer term, a challenging match.

With a Horse

Snakes and Horses like each other and admire each other's qualities, but their lifestyles and natures are very different.

In work, their different skills and strengths can make these two an effective force, with the Snake benefiting from the Horse's more assertive and action-orientated approach.

In love, their personality differences may initially be attractive, with the Snake enjoying the vivacity and spirited nature of the Horse, but the Horse's busy lifestyle will not sit comfortably with that of the more placid Snake. A tricky match.

With a Goat

With both being calm, easy-going signs and having interests in common, understanding between these two can be good.

In work, if their work is in any way creative, these two could enjoy much success, with the Snake valuing the Goat's imaginative input. Great possibilities here.

In love, these two enjoy a wonderful rapport. The Snake will especially appreciate the Goat's kindly and engaging nature. With both seeking a loving, stable and peaceable existence, they are well suited to each other.

With a Monkey

Each finds the other fascinating company and relations between the two are generally good.

In work, however, their styles could clash, with the cautious Snake being wary of the Monkey's haste and more freewheeling approach. With both being evasive and secretive, working relations could prove tricky.

In love, these two signs can be intrigued by each other and stay that way. The Snake will especially like the Monkey's *joie de vivre* and positive nature. With shared interests too, these two complement each other very well.

With a Rooster

Each of these signs admires qualities in the other and they get on well together.

In work, their different strengths can spur each other on, with the Snake drawing confidence from the meticulous planning and skill of the hard-working Rooster. With both being ambitious, they could enjoy considerable success.

In love, these two complement each other well, with the Snake particularly appreciating the loyalty and thoughtfulness of the Rooster as well as their orderly nature. Each has great faith in the other. A happy match.

With a Dog

Both signs take time to lower their guard and feel at ease with another person, but Dogs and Snakes can become good and loyal friends.

In work, the approach and motivation of these two can be very different and, with both being cautious, they do not bring out the best in each other.

In love, the Snake will value the Dog's attentive, loyal and dependable nature and they will both strive for a secure and settled lifestyle. But there will be differences to reconcile and the Snake will need to be tolerant of the Dog's tendency to worry. With care and understanding, a reasonably good match.

With a Pig

The Snake is quiet and reserved and the Pig outgoing and upfront. This does not make for easy or close relations.

In work, the Snake likes to plan, while the Pig is more spontaneous and, to the Snake's mind, impulsive. They do not work well together.

In love, both may appreciate the good things in life, but their personalities and approaches are so very different that for a relationship to work, major adjustments will be needed. A difficult match.

Horoscopes for Each of the Chinese Years

SNAKE FORTUNES IN THE YEAR OF THE RAT

Snakes like to think ahead, and as the Rat year begins, many will have ideas and aims for the next 12 months. And during the year, their tenacity and skills can lead to some pleasing results. However, the Rat year does require effort, and for those who sit back or take risks, disappointments could loom. This can be a good year, but it will also be a demanding one.

A feature of Rat years is that they favour innovation. And Snakes are capable of coming up with some very original notions. Accordingly, those whose work or personal interests have an element of creativity about them should make the most of their talents this year. Whether they are promoting ideas or putting forward proposals, their efforts could meet with a pleasing response. These can be inspiring times, with Snakes often enjoying the chance to express themselves more fully.

For Snakes who have let their interests lapse and would

welcome new challenges, this is also an excellent year to consider taking up new activities. By giving themselves something purposeful to do and an outlet for their talents, they can add much value to their year – and life! The Rat year is an encouraging one, but to benefit fully, Snakes need to make the most of it.

At work, this can be a year of important developments. Snakes will find that their strengths and determination will help their progress. Those established in a particular line of work could find situations changing and new initiatives giving them a chance of greater involvement. Some may transfer elsewhere, but whatever they choose to do, by looking to further their position and seizing the (sometimes unexpected) opportunities of the year, they can make good progress. Those who work in a creative environment could fare especially well.

For Snakes who are seeking work or feeling ready for a change, this is also a year of interesting possibilities. By keeping alert for openings and talking to contacts and employment experts, many could secure a position which not only offers a fresh challenge but also has the potential for future development. Determined Snakes can gain a lot from the year. Even though some may experience disappointments in their quest, with persistence and self-belief, they will have the chance to move forward.

Although the income of many Snakes is set to increase over the year, they will, however, need to remain disciplined in financial matters. Without care, spending levels could creep up. Rushing purchases or acting on impulse could also be disadvantageous. Time should be taken to compare options and be certain about terms and obligations. Rat years require careful management of outgoings and resources.

Domestically, the year can see a lot of activity, although Snakes do need to be mindful of those close to them. To keep their thoughts too close to their chest (as some do) could deny them support and useful input. In Rat years, Snakes need to open up more. The year can, however, see some pleasing activities and there will be a lot to appreciate, including individual and family successes. Many Snakes will also delight in some unexpected travel opportunities.

Although Snakes tend to be selective in their socializing, the Rat year can provide some good opportunities to go out, and by making the most of them, Snakes do stand to gain. This is no year for them to be too reserved or independent in outlook. Rat years encourage Snakes to make more of themselves and to show their talents *and engage*. More reserved Snakes, take note and do aim to participate more in the year's happenings. Much can follow on as a result.

The Rat year marks the start of a new cycle of animal years, and for many signs, what is started now can have an influence on following years. For Snakes, efforts made during the Rat year can leave an important legacy. Commitment will be required and Snakes do need to put themselves forward, but by making the effort, they can not only accomplish more but also enjoy developing their capabilities and strengths. This is a year to have self-belief and act with determination. The rewards can be far-reaching.

Tips for the Year
This is a year of good possibilities. Be active and respond to what it opens up for you, even if it means stepping out of your comfort zone. Watch your independent tendencies, liaise well with those around you and build support. With action and belief, you can go far.

SNAKE FORTUNES IN THE YEAR OF THE OX

The Ox year suits the Snake's psyche. This is a year favouring a steady approach rather than a heady pace. However, the Ox is a hard taskmaster. As a result, Snakes could find parts of the year demanding, but, as the Chinese proverb reminds us, 'Diligence leads to riches.' Diligence in the Ox year will reward Snakes well.

At work, they will need to remain disciplined and focused. A lot will be expected of them and many will be facing new challenges and greater responsibilities. However, what arises over the year will give them the opportunity to develop their skills and often prove themselves in a new capacity. Whether covering for absent colleagues, being trained for a greater role or being assigned to particular initiatives, many will be able to do themselves and their prospects a lot of good.

For Snakes who are eager to move elsewhere or are seeking work, the Ox year may not be the easiest. Sometimes openings will be limited and competition fierce. However, here again a disciplined approach can prevail. By finding out more about positions they are applying for and stressing their suitability, Snakes may find their efforts rewarded. Results will need to be worked for this year, but this will help underline the skills of many Snakes.

The Ox year is an excellent one for self-development and if there are skills or activities Snakes feel could be helpful to them, they should find out more. Snakes are naturally curious and some may enrol on study courses and/or carry out some research on their own this year. For those in education or studying for qualifications, this can often be a successful time and focus and hard work will deliver some pleasing results.

Snakes should also give some thought to their well-being and lifestyle this year and, if lacking in regular exercise or feeling dietary changes could help, seek advice on the best ways to proceed. Some may set themselves personal objectives such as correcting certain habits or striving for a particular goal, and by remaining disciplined and keeping in mind the potential benefits, they can accomplish a great deal. Ox years reward effort and application.

In money matters, Snakes will need to be vigilant. Over the year many will not only have some expensive plans and purchases in mind but also find their general level of outgoings increasing. Ideally, all Snakes should keep watch on their budget and save for forthcoming purchases. In addition, where paperwork is involved, Snakes need to check the small print and clarify anything they are uncertain about.

Domestically, this can be a full and pleasing year. In addition to celebrating individual successes, Snakes will appreciate sharing various activities and plans, many of which they will instigate. It is important that there is good communication and cooperation, but again the Snake's thoughtfulness and input can be a valuable ingredient in family life.

The Ox year will also bring some good social opportunities. Parties, celebrations and other events (and there could be several) will give Snakes the chance to relax, unwind and meet others. With their quiet yet genial manner, they can make some good friends and contacts this year, and for the unattached, serious romance could beckon. The Ox year is full of possibility, but Snakes do need to be active and engage. Private and reserved Snakes, take note, and do make the most of your opportunities. It will be worth the effort.

Overall, Snakes can do well in the Ox year. It is an excellent time to refine skills and go after personal objectives. With purpose and resolve, much can be accomplished. Snakes will be encouraged by the support of those around them and their domestic and social life can be gratifying. New contacts (and, for the unattached, romance) can also be helpful and inspiring. Snakes have a lot in their favour this year. It may sometimes be demanding, but its rewards can be many.

Tips for the Year
Go after your aims and objectives and seize any chances to develop your skills. By making the most of your opportunities, you can gain a considerable amount.

SNAKE FORTUNES IN THE YEAR OF THE TIGER

Snakes prefer to proceed in measured ways and will not always welcome the volatility and haste that tend to characterize the Tiger year. As a result, many will opt to keep a low profile. However, although the year may not be an easy one, it can be of considerable personal benefit.

At work, Snakes will often feel the effects of change. New ways of working may be introduced and there may be systems to learn, routines to adjust to and initiatives to launch. Snakes will often have reservations as well as face increased pressures as they learn and adapt. Although what happens will give many the chance to extend their role, changes are likely to happen quickly, and some months could be especially demanding. Tiger years certainly challenge the placid Snake!

For Snakes who decide to move away from their present position (possibly due to recent changes) or are seeking work, the Tiger year can again be difficult. Some could find few openings in the type of work they favour, as well as much competition. However, while this may be frustrating, situations can change quickly this year and while one moment Snakes may be in despair, the next they may be celebrating a new job. 'You never know what's around the corner', and the Tiger year can present quite a few Snakes with an unexpected but (very) welcome work opportunity.

In view of the pressures of the year, all Snakes should, however, watch their independent tendencies and be an active part of any team. To appear removed or isolated could undermine their position or place them on the periphery of developments. Also, as many have found, it is in more challenging times that the seeds of success are often sown and, for many, what they do this year can prepare them for the rewards to come.

In money matters, care will also be needed. During the year, many Snakes could have unanticipated expenses, perhaps repair costs, the need to replace equipment or increased expenditure on the family or home. The Tiger year can be an expensive one. Accordingly, Snakes should keep tabs on spending and make early provision for requirements. With good management, they will be able to proceed with many of their plans, but it will require discipline and planning. Also, if they have reservations over any financial matter, they should be thorough in checking the terms and obligations.

Despite this need for fiscal care, in this active and sometimes pressured year it would do Snakes good to take a holiday, and if possible, they should aim to go away and enjoy a change of scene.

With their enquiring mind, Snakes often busy themselves with various interests and may become intrigued by something new this year. Despite the year's vexations, significant seeds can now be sown and take root.

Although relations with others will generally go well, here again the Tiger year requires care. Some Snakes could find themselves being drawn into awkward matters or giving advice on a complex situation. At such times, they should choose their words carefully and think their responses through. Fortunately Snakes are by nature astute, but in Tiger years they need to tread warily.

However, despite the cautionary aspects, there will be a good mix of social occasions to enjoy, including special events and the chance to visit places of interest. By taking advantage of these, Snakes can add valuable balance to their lifestyle.

Their home life can also bring them pleasure. Tiger years have an element of spontaneity and there may be sudden invitations and other possibilities which, due to their unexpectedness, can add fun to many a household. Shared activities can be pleasing and throughout the year Snakes would do well to listen to the words of their loved ones, including when reservations are voiced. Others do speak with their interests at heart and this is a year when Snakes should avoid being too independent in attitude.

Overall, the Tiger year will be demanding and Snakes will often be concerned by the situations that unfold and the expectations that are placed upon them. But by rising to the challenge, they can build on their experience and extend their capabilities. Personal interests can open up in encouraging ways and the activities and lessons of the year can have far-reaching value. Snakes should watch their independent tendencies, value the times they spend with family and friends and make the most of the opportunities the year will bring.

Tips for the Year
Be alert. Amid the activity, there will be lessons to learn and possibilities to explore. Also, liaise with others and value their support. And enjoy spending time with those who are special to you.

SNAKE FORTUNES IN THE YEAR OF THE RABBIT

Snakes can do well in Rabbit years. Rather than be buffeted by events or situations outside their control, they can be more in charge of their situation and destiny. This can be a constructive time for them and they will have the chance to make more of specific talents. However, while the aspects are good, Snakes do need to channel their efforts wisely and keep their lifestyle in balance.

Work prospects are especially encouraging, with many Snakes having the opportunity to make greater use of their strengths and ideas. Especially for those who work in a creative environment, these can be inspiring times, and if Snakes have ideas, or solutions to matters that need addressing, they should put them forward. By being active, doing what they are good at and giving that little bit extra, many can enjoy some notable success.

For Snakes who are keen to build on their present position, some ideal possibilities can arise this year, while for those who are unfulfilled or seeking work, the Rabbit year could provide the chance to re-establish themselves and take on a new and more suitable role. This is very much a time for moving ahead and seeking out opportunity. Snakes who do take on a position or new duties in the year could find other opportunities opening up in the later months. The skills and potential of many Snakes will be recognized and rewarded this year.

Progress at work can bring a welcome rise in income and this can be an improved year financially. However, to fully benefit, Snakes could find it helpful to look closely at their present position, including at various outgoings and commitments. Some changes could make a noticeable difference, with money being saved or outgoings being redirected to a better use. This is a year for good financial management.

Snakes would also do well to make provision for travel this year. If they can combine a holiday with visiting a location or event related to an interest they have, this can add considerable meaning to what they do. By thinking ahead, they can see some exciting plans taking shape. Rabbit years also favour culture and Snakes will enjoy visiting particular attractions or attending some of the special occasions and exhibitions being held.

The Rabbit year can also see many positive developments domestically. With it having an aesthetic quality, many Snakes will be on inspired form and keen to go ahead with home improvements. They will enjoy making choices and seeing their ideas realized. This is very much a year for action, although some undertakings could prove more costly and time-consuming than initially envisaged.

Also, with Snakes and others being busy with various commitments, it is important there is good communication and that other activities do not make too many incursions into home life. Enjoying joint activities (including travel) can be of particular value this year.

Snakes can also benefit from the social opportunities of the year. Their work, travel and interests will all give them the chance to meet others. For the most part, good times can be had and valuable connections formed, but a cautionary note does need to be sounded: any discretion or lapse this year could lead to complications and embarrassment. Some Snakes may also find themselves troubled by rumour. Over the year, all Snakes need to be on their guard, for there can be problems for the unwary and careless.

They can, though, derive much satisfaction from their personal interests. Creative pursuits in particular are favourably aspected. This is a year to develop and promote special talents. Also, with the energy Snakes put into so many of their activities, giving some thought to their well-being would not come amiss. As well as considering their diet and level of exercise, they should also ensure they have adequate rest, especially at busy times.

In general, Snakes can do well in Rabbit years. However, with so much happening, pressures will at times be considerable and it is important that Snakes keep their lifestyle in balance, value the time they spend with family and friends, enjoy their interests and appreciate the rewards they work so hard for. This can be a successful year, but maintaining a good lifestyle balance is key.

Tips for the Year
Make the most of your strengths, ideas and opportunities. A lot can now be achieved. Also, enjoy pursuing your interests and spending time with those who are close to you. This can be a satisfying and rewarding year. Use it well.

SNAKE FORTUNES IN THE YEAR OF THE DRAGON

While Snakes may not always welcome the bustle and razzmatazz of Dragon years, they can enjoy some pleasing developments during them. And what is set in motion now can have long-term value.

At work, Snakes often like to specialize in certain areas and build up their career steadily. They do not favour rush. In Dragon years many Snakes will decide to concentrate their efforts on their current role and to continue to develop their skills and expertise. And although there may be change and some volatility in their workplace, their calm, dependable ways can be particularly appreciated, and what they do, often without fuss and in the background, can do their reputation and prospects much good.

During the year Snakes can help their situation by taking advantage of training. If they feel an additional qualification or skill could help their prospects, they should look at ways in which they could obtain this. Much of what they do now will be an investment in their future, and their approach will impress many, including some who have considerable influence.

For Snakes who decide to move from where they are or are seeking work, the Dragon year can open up interesting possibilities. By considering different ways in which they can draw on their experience, these Snakes may be able to find a new position, and once they have a foothold, they may soon be able to go further. Again, what is accomplished now can be an important factor in subsequent progress.

Personal interests can be satisfying and this is an excellent year to both enjoy and add to skills. By setting about what they do with purpose and commitment, Snakes will find that benefits can often follow on. In addition, some could find instruction or expert input concerning a particular interest or idea of especial value.

In money matters, Snakes will, however, need to remain disciplined, otherwise outgoings could creep up and impulse buys be regretted. Also, when entering into agreements, they should check the terms and implications and seek clarification if anything is unclear. They cannot afford to be lax this year. They should also take steps to safeguard their possessions. A loss or theft could be upsetting. Snakes, take note and take extra care with security.

Domestically, Snakes will find themselves in demand, especially as loved ones may need help over certain decisions or extra assistance with activities. The advice and time Snakes give may often be of more value than they realize, and their words and foresight may be highly pertinent. Many hold the Snake's judgement in high regard. However, just as Snakes will assist those around them, they too should be forthcoming about any concerns as well as any hopes and ideas they may be nurturing. As with so much this year, input and action can have important consequences.

Also, with the active nature of Dragon years, any suggestions Snakes may make for family activities, including treats and trips out, can lead to highly enjoyable times as well as do everyone good.

With the busy nature of the year, Snakes will be more selective in their socializing, but will nevertheless enjoy their chances to meet friends and attend events. Personal interests can often have a pleasing social element. However, while a lot will go well, Snakes still need to remain alert, as rumours and gossip could sometimes be troubling. If affected or concerned, they should check the facts as well as correct any untruths. Dragon years do tend to have their niggles, but, with care and time, many concerns will quickly pass. And patience and cool thinking are Snake virtues.

The Year of the Dragon will be a full and interesting one for Snakes, and by setting about their activities with care and seizing any chances to add to their skills and experience, they can profit from much that they do. With next year being their own, this one can pave the way for successes to come. It will also contain some gratifying times. Shared domestic activities will be pleasurable, as will furthering interests. However, this is also a year to guard against carelessness and Snakes need to remain alert and seize their opportunities. Overall, a valuable and potentially significant year.

Tips for the Year
Develop your skills and strengths and be prepared to adapt as required. Effort made now will be an investment in yourself and your future. Also, be mindful of others and do liaise well with those around you. With support, commitment and your consummate skills, you are set to impress this year.

SNAKE FORTUNES IN THE YEAR OF THE SNAKE

There is a Chinese proverb which states, 'With aspirations, you can go anywhere; without aspirations, you can go nowhere.' Their own year is one in which Snakes should act on their aspirations. With determination, they can enjoy excellent results. Any Snakes who start the year disenchanted and in low spirits should try and draw a line under what has gone before and focus on the present. With resolve, they will find that their situation can be transformed.

One important feature of the year will be the support that Snakes enjoy. Domestically, their own year can be marked by some special occasions. Also, Snakes will instigate many activities this year, including some ambitious home projects as well as a possible holiday. Their input can make this a full and satisfying year. However, while a lot will go well, as with any year, difficulties may arise, and sometimes be exacerbated by tiredness or lack of communication. At such times, Snakes should tackle issues rather than risk them souring an otherwise promising year. Fortunately problems will be few, but they should not be ignored.

The Snake year can, however, give rise to some good social opportunities, and Snakes should make the most of them. As has been shown, the more people you know, the more opportunities come your way, and by raising their profile, Snakes can benefit from support and advice as well as enjoy the chance to make some important new friends. This is no year for them to keep themselves to themselves. Particularly in their work, it is an excellent time to network and build connections.

During the year Snakes will also enjoy going to some lively occasions, and if particular events appeal to them, they should aim to attend. For the unattached, there can also be the chance to meet someone who is destined to become significant. Snake years look after their own sign well.

At work, the prospects are encouraging. For Snakes who are established in a career, there will be excellent opportunities to make progress. As more senior staff move on and promotion opportunities occur, many Snakes will be well positioned to take on a greater role, while others may be tempted by vacancies in other sectors and have the chance to broaden their experience. This is a year to move forward and many Snakes will be able to take their career to a new level. Especially for those who have languished in the same position for some time, this is a year to look to move on.

For Snakes seeking work, again there can be important developments in store. By actively following up vacancies that interest them, many will secure a position with potential for the future. This could come with a steep learning curve, but Snake years will provide many Snakes with the chance they have been seeking.

Progress at work can also help financially, although Snakes cannot afford to be lax in money matters. With some expensive plans and good travel possibilities, together with their existing commitments, they could see outgoings creeping up. Also, while usually astute, they should be wary of risk or acting in haste. Their judgement may not always be as good as usual, and when conducting important transactions, they need to be aware of all the terms, implications and requirements.

This is, however, an excellent time for enjoying interests, and Snakes who would like a new challenge or are keen to use certain talents more fully will find it an ideal year to take things further. Creative activities are especially well aspected. Also, personal interests can be a good way for Snakes to reconnect with themselves, which is important for the Snake psyche. Any Snakes who are nurturing certain aspirations, whether connected with their work, personal interests or a particular goal they would like to reach, should look to take these forward. Snakes can be masters of their own destiny this year.

Overall, this can be a special and fulfilling year. By moving their plans forward, Snakes can accomplish a great deal and enjoy many positive results. This is a time for them to have belief in themselves and seize the initiative. They will be encouraged by the support they receive, and their colleagues and loved ones will be keen for them to make the most of their potential. As well as success at work, their own year can bring some personally happy times. A great year and one rich in possibility.

Tips for the Year
Act with determination. Set your plans in motion and make the most of your opportunities. Also, look to raise your profile and value the positive relations you enjoy with those around you.

SNAKE FORTUNES IN THE YEAR OF THE HORSE

A mixed year when Snakes will need to keep their wits firmly about them. Events can move swiftly and Snakes may find a lot being expected of them. However, while it is not an easy year, useful progress can still be made.

At work, many Snakes will find their situation affected by change. Systems and initiatives may be introduced and objectives altered. With so much going on, Snakes need to be alert and keep themselves informed. This is no time to immerse themselves in their own role and lose sight of the broader picture. Also, they should take careful note of developments within their industry. Changes could be afoot, with new trends emerging, and by being aware, Snakes can better prepare and adapt. Indeed, looking ahead and considering new possibilities is one of their strengths.

However, Horse years are very hands-on and require active involvement rather than the planning and theorizing that some Snakes prefer.

Many Snakes will continue to build on their present position and will have the opportunity to demonstrate their skills as well as gain greater insights into their industry. What is undertaken now can have an important bearing on future prospects, particularly in the following, more favourable Goat year.

For Snakes seeking change or looking for work, speed is of the essence. Emphasizing their (relevant) experience and desire to learn will also help their prospects. Horse years require effort, but are also times of opportunity and professional development.

Financial prospects are reasonable and many Snakes will enjoy an increase in income over the year. Some will also be able to supplement their means through additional work or an enterprising idea. The resourcefulness of many can bring a good return, but while income levels may increase, Snakes still need to budget carefully and manage their outgoings well. Key purchases and plans need to be costed in advance and Snakes should not enter into any commitment until they feel ready and satisfied. Snakes, take note.

If able, they should make provision for a holiday, however, as in this active year, a break and change of scene can do them considerable good.

In view of the pressures of the year, it is also important that they give some consideration to their own well-being. Having time to rest, chill out and unwind is very necessary to their psyche, and without this there is a chance that some could become prone to stress or, if overly tired, susceptible to niggling ailments. If they have any concerns over the year, they should get these checked out.

Personal interests can bring them pleasure, and by absorbing themselves in activities they favour, they can help their lifestyle balance.

In addition, they should make the most of their social opportunities. While some Snakes prefer to keep their social life low key, this year they should look to engage with others, enjoy the activities that are going on around them and spend time with their friends.

However, as with so much this year, they do need to be aware of the views of others. For Snakes who are enjoying romance, or who find it this year, care is advised. Preoccupation or a minor disagreement could bring problems. Snakes need to tread particularly carefully in volatile or delicate situations. Where matters of the heart are concerned, Horse years may bring tricky moments. Snakes, take note and be attentive.

This need for awareness also applies to domestic life. A lot will be happening, and preoccupation, pressure and tiredness could give rise to some awkward moments. Here greater openness can be of particular value. With good communication, some problems or disagreements can be skilfully avoided. Shared activities should be encouraged, as these will help rapport as well as lead to some enjoyable occasions. If possible, a holiday and, at busy times, an occasional treat can do everyone a lot of good.

Overall, the Horse year will be a demanding one for Snakes. A lot will be expected of them. And although Snakes like their independence, this is a year to adapt, work with others and make the best of situations. In the process, new skills and knowledge can be gained. There will also be possibilities to build on. For many Snakes, Horse years can be times of preparation for the opportunities that lie ahead. In the meantime, they need to be mindful of others and give time and attention to all their relationships. Shared activities can be of particular value. They should also give some thought to their own needs, including preserving time for rest, relaxation and personal interests. This may not be the smoothest of years, but its demands and expectations can be instructive, and often important in the longer term.

Tips for the Year
Watch your independent tendencies and be involved in what is going on around you. That way your talents and qualities can be seen and your skills furthered. Also, put in the effort where required, but give time to those who are important to you and set aside some for yourself as well.

SNAKE FORTUNES IN THE YEAR OF THE GOAT

A constructive year ahead, with Snakes making good progress. With this being a year favouring creative endeavour, they can find it an inspiring time. However, while the aspects may be promising, Goat years can be fickle and there will be times when plans have to be altered to fit in with changing circumstances. Here Snakes will find their skills and adroit nature serving them well.

At work, there may be changes afoot. Internal reorganization and staff movements may create opportunities requiring particular expertise, and by acting quickly, Snakes may succeed in taking on a greater role. Also, when certain problems in the workplace need addressing, their input can be used to telling effect. Their strengths can be of great benefit this year.

The majority of Snakes will make important progress in their current place of work, but there will be some who feel their prospects can be bettered by a move elsewhere. For these Snakes, and those seeking work, the year can hold significant developments. By keeping alert for vacancies and considering ways in which they can use their experience, they may find some good opportunities. This is a year to be open to possibility. What some Snakes take on now could also give them the chance to develop their skills in new ways and lead to them discovering a type of work for which they are ideally suited. Also, for those who work in a creative environment, this is very much a time to promote their talents.

The progress many Snakes make over the year will lead to an increase in income, and this will persuade them to go ahead with certain plans, including purchases for themselves and their home. By carefully considering their requirements and the options available, they could be particularly satisfied with what they acquire and the improvements that follow on. Their eye for quality, suitability and value can be on excellent form this year. Also, if some funds are not immediately needed, they should consider setting them aside for the longer term. With care and diligence, Snakes can fare well this year and improve their overall financial position.

Personal interests are also well aspected, particularly those that encourage Snakes to develop their ideas and enjoy their creativity. Snakes could have some novel ideas this year, for the Goat year is an inspiring time.

With the positive aspects in mind, Snakes should also give some thought to their current lifestyle and, if lacking regular exercise or not having a sufficiently balanced diet, seek advice on ways in which they could improve this. A few modifications could make a noticeable difference.

Although some Snakes can be private and reserved, in the Goat year much benefit (and pleasure) can also be had by being more forthcoming and involved. Being alone or on the periphery of events could deny Snakes some good opportunities and pleasing occasions. This is a year to engage, keep in regular contact with friends and enjoy the mix of things happening. In the process,

Snakes will often have the chance to meet like-minded people and make some important (and sometimes influential) friends.

For the unattached, romance can add considerable sparkle to the year too, but new relationships should be allowed to evolve and strengthen over time.

Home life will also see many pleasing developments. Not only will loved ones give valuable support and advice when decisions have to be made, but may enjoy some notable achievements of their own. Over the year there could be several successes to mark. However, while much will go well, Goat years have their awkward elements, and delays and setbacks to certain plans may lead to some being altered and rescheduled. At such times, flexibility will be needed. Here the Snake's resourcefulness can be of particular value. However, despite the problematic nature of some undertakings this year, family successes can make this a gratifying time.

In general, Snakes can do well in Goat years. At work, their strengths can come to the fore and many will be encouraged to take their career to new levels. Their interests, too, will give them the chance to enjoy their creativity and try out new ideas. They will be helped by the support they receive and will enjoy sharing their thoughts and activities with those around them. Most of all, this is a year for action and if Snakes are to make the most of themselves, *act they must*. Shy and more reserved Snakes, take note, for luck and opportunity await those who are ready to put themselves forward and make the most of what this most interesting year offers.

Tips for the Year
Be proactive and seize opportunities. Adapt as required. There is much to be gained in this favourable year. Use it well and enjoy reaping the benefits.

Snake Fortunes in the Year of the Monkey

Monkey years are invariably busy, with a lot happening at a fast pace. Accordingly, Snakes will need to keep their wits about them. Situations may not always be as clear-cut as they may think and some matters may be problematic. This is a year to exercise caution, be alert and focus on specific areas. Snakes would do well to remember the saying, 'It is better to be safe than sorry.'

At work, the skills and patience of many Snakes will be tested, as obstacles and delays will occur and there may be a possible difficulty with a colleague. At such times Snake should concentrate on their responsibilities and adopt a low profile. This is not a year to be drawn into office politics or diverted into less helpful matters. However, while they will need to be wary, the Monkey year is not without opportunity, and if they see an opening which appeals to them, they should put themselves forward. Over the year many Snakes will have the chance to extend their role and, in the process, develop their skills.

For any Snakes who feel their prospects could be improved by a move elsewhere, as well as those seeking work, the Monkey year can also have important developments in store. Although the job-seeking process will not be easy and many Snakes will face disappointments in their quest, openings *can* be found. Monkey years require effort, but it is through rising to challenges (and overcoming some difficulties) that Snakes can gain experience as well as insights into their capabilities. Much can follow on from what they learn about themselves now.

In money matters they will need to exercise care and be wary about accepting all they are told at face value. If they have reservations over any transaction, they should check the facts and, if appropriate, obtain professional guidance. Without this, some Snakes could be misled this year. They also need to safeguard their possessions. A loss could be upsetting and inconvenient. However, while caution is required, by managing their resources carefully and taking their time over key purchases, Snakes can nevertheless be pleased with their acquisitions both for themselves and their home. But Monkey years do require a careful and disciplined approach.

With the pressures of the year, Snakes should aim to set aside some time for their own interests. These can bring them considerable pleasure and many Snakes will be inspired by new ideas and possibilities that arise over the year. However, when setting about more demanding activities, Snakes should follow the guidelines and not compromise their personal safety.

Similarly, some travel plans may prove problematic, and if planning long journeys, Snakes do need to check the times and connections and go well prepared. Extra care is advised this year.

In their relations with others, Snakes will again need to be alert. While they can look forward to some very agreeable occasions – the Monkey year certainly has a lively element to it – a disagreement or awkward situation could be troubling. And if Snakes find themselves in a volatile situation or sense impending difficulty, they should remain their diplomatic selves. By being alert and guarded, they could avert or considerably lessen some of the year's trickier moments.

However, Monkey years also have their brighter times. Romantic prospects are good and some relationships will grow in significance over the year. Snakes tend to choose their friends well, and some close and true friends can prove important at this time.

Home life will be busy this year, and with a myriad of activities and plans going forward, there needs to be openness and good communication between everyone in the household. By sharing matters, talking over developments and deciding on plans together, Snakes and their loved ones can see a lot happen, including some appreciated home improvements. In addition, some personal or family successes can be much enjoyed, along with some of the year's more spontaneous occasions. A surprising amount can happen in Monkey years and close family ties are always special to Snakes.

Overall, the Monkey year will bring its pressures and Snakes need to be vigilant. In work matters, situations will be testing, but Snakes can develop their skills and often improve their prospects. Their personal interests can be satisfying and new activities will often appeal. Some relationships (often with colleagues) and situations may give rise to concern, but with care and their usual consummate skill, Snakes will often steer their way around the year's more awkward aspects and emerge with much to their credit. And affairs of the heart can be meaningful and special in this busy and sometimes – to their mind – crazy year.

Tips for the Year
Be vigilant and thorough and think through your responses to situations and developments. Seize any chances to broaden your skills and value your relations with those who are special to you. This may be a demanding year, but it is not one without possibilities.

SNAKE FORTUNES IN THE YEAR OF THE ROOSTER

An excellent year ahead. When Snakes feel inspired and consider conditions are right, they act with considerable might, and this will be such a year. In almost all aspects of their life, prospects are good. Also, Snakes appreciate the structure and order that exist in Rooster years, and this too will encourage them. For Snakes who start the year dispirited, perhaps bruised by recent developments, this can be the year for a new start. For all Snakes, it is a time for setting about their aims and aspirations with renewed vigour.

The aspects are especially promising in work matters. With the skills Snakes have built up and the strengths they have shown in recent times, many will be excellently placed to take advantage of opportunities to play a greater role. And if possibilities are limited where they are, they should look elsewhere. Snakes in large organizations could successfully transfer to a different position and/or department, and a few may even relocate. Rooster years are encouraging and Snakes will often be ready in themselves to move their career forward.

For Snakes who are currently unfulfilled and would welcome change, as well as those seeking work, again the Rooster year can open up excellent possibilities. By making enquiries and considering different ways in which they could use their skills, many could secure a position in a new capacity and with the potential for development. In some cases, a friend or contact could be especially helpful in alerting them to an opportunity or in giving a recommendation. Snakes will have many factors working in their favour this year and their own initiative will reward them well.

Snakes also like to keep themselves informed of developments and keep their skills up to date. To help with this, if training is available in their place of work, they should see what can be arranged, or, if they feel an additional skill or qualification could be of advantage, they should investigate. By seizing any chances to further their knowledge, they will be investing in themselves and their future.

This also extends to their personal interests. Inspired and keen, some Snakes could become absorbed in a project they set themselves over the year or take a particular interest in a new direction. This can be a source of much personal pleasure over the year, as well as good for their psyche.

Financial prospects are also encouraging, with progress at work likely to bring a welcome increase in income. However, Snakes will often be tempted by some expensive undertakings, and while money may flow into their accounts, it could quickly flow out. This year they do need to watch spending and budget ahead. The better their control, the more satisfying their purchases and decisions.

If able, they should make provision for travel, however, as a change of scene and the chance to visit some interesting attractions or attend interest-related events can bring them a great deal of pleasure.

In their home life, the year can often be special, and made all the more so by personal successes and family news. Over the year there could be celebrations in many a Snake household. Snakes will also find that their enthusiasm and imaginative input can lead to many plans going ahead. The Rooster year is a time for sharing and rich in possibility. The one proviso is that at busy times Snakes should prioritize their commitments and concentrate on what is practical rather than overcommit themselves. Rooster years favour planning and working together for desired outcomes.

Snakes will also value their social life and could find their circle of contacts increasing. By being involved in what is going on around them and raising their profile, they can often add an interesting element to their lifestyle.

For the unattached, the year also has good romantic possibilities and a chance meeting may be significant.

So much good can happen for Snakes this year, but to benefit fully they do need to put themselves forward and seize the moment. With purpose, resolve and self-belief, they can make the most of these exciting times. In work, some good opportunities can open up, while personal interests can also be inspiring and offer new possibilities. Snakes will benefit from the support of those around them, although to maximize this they do need to be open, receptive and prepared to consult others. Both their home and social life offer rewarding times with much to share and enjoy. This is a highly favourable year for Snakes and their skills, qualities and initiative can bring them many pleasurable and successful results.

Tips for the Year

Build on your position and capabilities. With action and resolve, you can achieve a lot. Also, share your thoughts and activities with others and be a part of what is going on around you. That way far more can open up for you.

SNAKE FORTUNES IN THE YEAR OF THE DOG

A constructive year with some good opportunities to pursue. Encouragingly, Snakes will be able to build on recent successes and see the successful culmination of various projects and plans. Also, Dog years proceed in steady and measured ways and this suits the Snake temperament. Never ones for rush, Snakes will prosper steadily this year.

At work, many Snakes, especially those who have been involved in recent change, will be content to focus on their role and use their skills to good effect. By immersing themselves in their workplace and seizing any chances to raise their profile, they will not only enjoy a greater level of fulfilment in what they do but also have the chance to contribute more. Snakes like to build their career steadily, one stage at a time, and Dog years enable many of them to do just that. In addition, there may be the chance to become involved in a new project, assist with the implementation of changes or train others. By expanding their role in these ways, many Snakes could discover new talents as well as help their future prospects. Dog years are encouraging ones for Snakes.

There will, though, be some Snakes who feel in a rut and would welcome the chance to progress in other ways. For these Snakes, and those seeking work, the Dog year will also bring new possibilities. By actively following up vacancies and taking advice from employment officials, many could succeed in securing the change they need. For some, a steep learning curve could be involved, and much readjustment, but what they take on will reinvigorate their career prospects. Many Snakes will have the chance to set their career on a brighter path this year.

Progress made at work will increase the income of many Snakes over the year and some will also benefit from the receipt of extra funds. However, Snakes still need to manage their situation well. In particular, they could find it helpful to think ahead, including making early provision for forthcoming plans as well as possibly saving for the longer term. With discipline and good control, the financial position of many Snakes can improve over the year.

Travel is also well aspected and Snakes should take advantage of any chances to go away. By considering possibilities and planning an itinerary, they can see some exciting plans taking shape and a change of scene will do them good.

Personal interests can also bring much pleasure, and with the expertise some Snakes have built up, certain activities and projects could prove especially satisfying. Snakes can make their talents count in many ways this year.

In addition, they should pay some attention to their own well-being, including giving themselves the opportunity to relax as well as take appropriate exercise. Some Snakes could be attracted to a new fitness discipline or set themselves a personal goal, but whatever they choose to do, some extra attention to their own lifestyle can be to their advantage. Also, if at any time they feel below par, it would be worth them seeking medical advice.

Snakes will have good reason to value their domestic life over the year. Those close to them could offer sterling support with certain decisions as well as offer additional help when pressures are great. Snakes do a lot for others and in Dog years there will be good chances for others to reciprocate. The year can also see the marking of several achievements and there could be some delightful family news. If embarking on practical projects, ample time needs to be allowed, however, as some could be protracted. Dog years may be rewarding, but they can be slow-moving ones too.

In view of all their commitments, Snakes may be tempted to cut back on their social life this year. However, it is important that they keep in regular contact with their friends as well as go to social events that appeal to them. This will not only help their lifestyle balance but also lead to some very agreeable occasions. Some people they know, or meet over the course of the year, could also be helpful with certain activities. More independent-minded Snakes, take note and do engage more readily with others.

In general, the Year of the Dog rewards effort and commitment, and Snakes are set to do well. At work, they can use their skills and experience to good effect and make satisfying progress. Personal interests and projects can also develop well and any extra attention Snakes can give to their lifestyle (including lifestyle balance) can be to their advantage. Finance and home life are both well aspected and Snakes will also benefit from the support and goodwill of many in this fulfilling and encouraging year.

Tips for the Year

Develop your skills and knowledge. Commitment and steady effort will reward you well. Also, look after yourself and ensure you have a good lifestyle balance. Time shared with others can be of great personal value too.

SNAKE FORTUNES IN THE YEAR OF THE PIG

For Snakes, Pig years can be challenging, with progress difficult and situations not always straightforward. But Snakes are patient and aware that in time things *will* move back in their favour. The Chinese proverb, 'You won't get lost if you frequently ask for directions' will be helpful this year, and whenever Snakes find themselves in a quandary or facing a complex situation, they should seek the opinion of those they trust. There is no need for them to feel (or act) alone.

At work, Snakes should remain focused on their duties and concentrate on the areas they know best. To spread their energies too widely, become distracted by lesser matters or venture into areas in which they lack experience could all undermine their effectiveness. Also, throughout the year, they should work closely with others rather than independently. That way, not only will more get done but they will benefit from the support and advice available to them.

Many Snakes will remain with their current employer this year and add to their professional knowledge, but for Snakes who are seeking work or who decide to make a change, the Pig year will require a careful approach. With openings sometimes limited and competition fierce, Snakes will need to put extra effort into their applications, including stressing their experience and suitability. Progress in the Pig year does need to be worked for, but while there may be disappointments in their quest, with self-belief and persistence, many Snakes will succeed. Most will find their best chances are in the type of work they are most familiar with.

Another area requiring care is finance. In Pig years, Snakes cannot afford to be lax or take risks. If they have reservations over any money matter, they should ask questions and, if necessary, seek professional advice. They should also be wary about acting in too much haste, including succumbing to expensive impulse buys. This is a year for caution and good control over the purse-strings. In addition, financial correspondence and other important paperwork requires careful attention, otherwise there is the possibility of some Snakes finding themselves disadvantaged or caught up in a bureaucratic tangle. Snakes, be thorough and vigilant.

With the pressures of the year, it is also important that Snakes give themselves a respite from the activity and allow themselves some 'me time'. Here personal interests can be akin to a tonic. Creative activities could be especially pleasing. Also, with so much happening in Pig years, if Snakes learn of interest-related events, including concerts and sporting fixtures, that appeal to them, they should follow these up. Recreational pursuits can be a source of much benefit this year and should not be ignored.

Snakes should also make the most of the year's social opportunities. Contact with others can add an important element to their lifestyle. Personal interests can lead to meeting like-minded people and making some useful connections and friendships.

Domestically, this can be a busy year, and whether assisting loved ones, making arrangements or dealing with their own commitments, Snakes will find their ability to keep tabs on a great many things will be valued by those around them. However, with such a lot happening, it is important that there is good communication and that any worries and concerns are talked through. That way, some of the pressures and more awkward matters of the Pig year can often be resolved or eased. Also, Snakes should encourage joint activities, including attending any local events that appeal. Their thoughtfulness and input can lead to some special times.

Overall, the Pig year will ask a lot of Snakes. Progress will be difficult and objectives sometimes challenging, but by doing their best, concentrating on their areas of expertise and furthering their knowledge, they can often prepare the way for success in following years. This year they should also value their connections with others, as their home and social life as well as their personal interests can be of particular importance in this often testing year.

Tips for the Year
Proceed carefully, draw on the support of others and do not go against your instincts. Be wary, check facts and consider the implications of your actions. Whenever you are concerned, remember 'You won't get lost if you frequently ask for directions.'

Thoughts and Words of Snakes

Happiness lies in the joy of achievement and the thrill of creative effort.

FRANKLIN D. ROOSEVELT

The only limit to our realization of tomorrow will be our doubts of today. Let us move forward with strong and active faith.

FRANKLIN D. ROOSEVELT

To reach a port, we must sail – sail, not tie at anchor, sail, not drift.

FRANKLIN D. ROOSEVELT

If you want to be respected, the great thing is to respect yourself.

FYODOR DOSTOEVSKY

We are all of us richer than we think we are.

MICHEL DE MONTAIGNE

A man is a success if he gets up in the morning and gets to bed at night, and in between he does what he wants to do.

BOB DYLAN

Within yourself are the riches of your tomorrow.

NEIL SOMERVILLE

Took the nowhere road.
Glad I did. Met no one.
But I found myself.

NEIL SOMERVILLE

Just trust yourself, then you will know how to live.

JOHANN WOLFGANG VON GOETHE

I am what I am, so take me as I am!

JOHANN WOLFGANG VON GOETHE

Knowing is not enough, we must apply; willing is not enough, we must do.

JOHANN WOLFGANG VON GOETHE

15 February 1942–4 February 1943 — *Water Horse*

3 February 1954–23 January 1955 — *Wood Horse*

21 January 1966–8 February 1967 — *Fire Horse*

7 February 1978–27 January 1979 — *Earth Horse*

27 January 1990–14 February 1991 — *Metal Horse*

12 February 2002–31 January 2003 — *Water Horse*

31 January 2014–18 February 2015 — *Wood Horse*

17 February 2026–5 February 2027 — *Fire Horse*

4 February 2038–23 January 2039 — *Earth Horse*

The Horse

The Personality of the Horse

Whether competing in a race, working on a farm or frolicking in a field, Horses have an exuberance about them. And they also have style. Horses are engaging, versatile and, in Chinese astrology, born under the sign of elegance and ardour.

Those born under the Horse sign are also blessed with many qualities. Skilful and articulate, they delight in conversation and relate well to others. They can also be most persuasive and this, backed by their charm and determination, ensures that many get their way. Horses are strong-willed and use their talents to good effect.

They are also strong-minded, and when they have formed an idea or set themselves an objective, they are not ones to change it. They can be stubborn and intractable and do not always take on board what others say. They have a mind of their own and like to do things in their own way. They can have a quick temper too, and while their outbursts are often short-lived, in the heat of the moment Horses can sometimes say things they later regret.

However, while they value their independence and freedom of thought, Horses are very sociable. Many will enjoy being a member of a group or club, or, if appropriate, a team or workforce. Horses love to participate and their lively nature and quick wits make them popular company. Never liking to turn an opportunity down, they can, however, sometimes overcommit themselves and find their social diary incredibly full. Horses certainly pack a lot into their days.

Many enjoy sport and the outdoor life and, if participating in an event, can be competitive. They like to do well – and often come out winners.

Horses are also adventurous and like to travel. They enjoy seeing new places and having the experiences that travel makes possible.

They usually keep themselves well informed and have wide interests. However, they sometimes lack persistence and can be easily tempted into dropping what they are doing when something new comes along. When motivated, though, and with an objective to reach, they are prepared to work long and hard to achieve their aims.

Strong-willed, determined, versatile and with the ability to enjoy good working relations with many, Horses are destined to do well in many a profession. They are adept at mastering detail and assimilating facts, and quite a few are skilled linguists. They are good multi-taskers, and the media, marketing, travel, tourism or positions which bring them into contact with others can suit them well. Being skilled in presentation, some could also be attracted to the entertainment industry, and, with their agility and liking of the outdoors, sport and the fitness industry could also appeal. But whatever vocation they choose, they do need to *persist* rather than change course too regularly. Some Horses do lack staying power. Also, Horses like to do things right and sometimes a fear of failure can inhibit them. Yet they have much to offer and their skills will ensure they prevail on many an occasion.

Horses enjoy their earnings and usually put their money to good use. Rather than being materialistic, they regard money as a tool, and once their commitments are covered (as they do take their responsibilities seriously), they will enjoy spending it in the way they want, whether on their loved ones, socializing or indulging in their love of travel.

Horses are passionate and caring and welcome having someone to love and to love them in return. As a partner, they can be loyal, protective and generous, but they also need space for their own interests and dislike a restrictive or routine lifestyle. While their home will be orderly and well equipped, they are not ones for spending hours in it. There is too much else to do.

Like her male counterpart, the female Horse has diverse interests and is alert to everything going on around her. Well informed, intelligent and versatile, she is practical and has clear-cut views and desires. She is also conscientious, and when she sets herself a task, she likes to do it well. A keen socializer, she possesses a ready wit and has a good understanding of human nature. With her often excellent dress sense, she may be renowned for her elegance and style. Determined and articulate, she does well in much that she sets out to do.

As parents, Horses can be encouraging and effective in identifying and nurturing individual talents. And with their wide interests and active lifestyle, they will encourage and stimulate many an eager young mind. They do, though, have high standards and are firm on discipline.

Horses like to be active and have purpose. Although sometimes they can be restless and stubborn, their quick wits, energy and enthusiasm invariably lead to them enjoying a busy and often fulfilling lifestyle. The American showman P. T. Barnum was a Horse and he wrote, 'Your success depends on what you do yourself, with your own means.' And these words are so true for Horses. They like to forge their own path and their drive and exuberance make their life rewarding in so many different ways.

Top Tips for Horses
- With such wide interests and a desire for action, you can be restless. Sometimes you abandon activities for the sake of something new or spread your energies just too widely. Greater discipline would not come amiss. By being more focused *and persistent*, you could enjoy more substantial

rewards. Curb your restless tendencies and have greater sticking power.

- Although you very much enjoy conversation, you are not always that good a listener! Taking note of what others are saying can often be to your benefit, so do not cut yourself off from this potential assistance. Also, although you may know your own mind, listening to the viewpoints of others can help you in your dealings with them.

- You do not like to fail and sometimes a fear of losing face stops you from taking action. But, as the Chinese proverb reminds us, 'The gem cannot be polished without friction, nor man perfected without trials.' You will learn a lot from the challenges you take on.

- Although you like results to come through quickly, time is needed in order to build experience and gain competence. Be patient. When you are feeling frustrated, looking ahead and setting longer-term goals could be especially useful. Give some thought to future glories and work towards them.

Relations with Others

With a Rat

Lively and sociable they may be, but with both also strong-willed and forthright, who will have the last word? Relations could be tricky.

In work, both will be keen to take centre stage and prevail. Furthermore, the Horse will look askance at the Rat's methods and opportunistic nature. Not a good combination.

In love, these two may be fun-loving and enjoy active lifestyles, but their redoubtable personalities will clash sooner or later. And the Horse, who likes a certain freedom of action, could find the Rat's meddling ways troubling. A difficult match.

With an Ox

These two like to live life at different speeds and in different ways. Relations could be poor.

In work, the action-orientated Horse will be keen to get results and could find the more measured ways of the Ox inhibiting. And, with both being strong-willed, working relations could be difficult.

In love, while the Horse may admire the steadfast and dependable ways of the Ox, their adventurous nature will not sit comfortably with the Ox's more traditional style. These two are not suited to each other.

With a Tiger

With their energy, enthusiasm and lively spirit, these two enjoy each other's company and get on well.

In work, their combined enterprise, zeal and hard work can pay off. They can make quite an impact and enjoy a good level of success.

In love, these two will live life to the full. The Horse will draw strength from the Tiger's lively and supportive nature and each will be an encouraging influence on the other. An excellent match.

With a Rabbit

These two may recognize each other's strengths, but their different temperaments and lifestyles do not make for easy relations.

In work, the Horse is geared up for action and could feel restricted by the Rabbit's more cautious approach. Not an effective combination.

In love, both are passionate signs and they could learn a lot from each other. In particular, the Horse could become less restless under the Rabbit's calm and orderly influence. But in time, their personalities and lifestyle differences could be difficult to reconcile. A challenging match.

With a Dragon

Two bold, dynamic characters – relations between them will be good.

In work, their drive, enthusiasm and respect for each other make these two a powerful and effective force. When united in a particular cause, they could enjoy considerable success.

In love, these two passionate signs can find much happiness together. With many shared interests and an active lifestyle, they will keep themselves busy and the Horse will value the enthusiasm, vigour and decency of the Dragon. Admittedly, their forthright natures could sometimes clash, but overall a good and often successful match.

With a Snake

True, there are personality differences between these two, but each finds the other interesting company. Relations between them can be reasonable.

In work, their different strengths and attitudes could combine well. The Horse has a high regard for the Snake's considered approach and business acumen, and these two can make an effective and often successful team.

In love, their personality differences could prove attractive, with the Horse particularly enchanted by the Snake's quiet, alluring and kindly manner. There will need to be considerable adjustments on both sides, so a tricky match, but certainly not an impossible one.

With a Horse

With good rapport, a shared love of conversation and a multitude of interests, Horses get on well together.

In work, their drive, enthusiasm and hard work are certainly capable of delivering good results, but they will need to stay focused and agree on a clear division of responsibility. If not, their competitive instincts could get the better of them, with each jockeying for control.

In love, theirs can be a close, passionate and exciting relationship. With a myriad of activities to enjoy as well as a mutual love of socializing, travel and conversation, life for two Horses can be good. Admittedly both can be forthright and there will be some stormy moments, but, with care, this can often be a special match.

With a Goat

The Horse likes the easy-going nature of the Goat, and with interests in common, these two get on well.

In work, their different strengths can combine well. The Horse will often have a high regard for the Goat's creative input. With trust and good rapport, it will be a good working relationship.

In love, these two are well suited. The Horse will value the Goat's caring and supportive nature and skills as a homemaker. A close and loving match.

With a Monkey

These are two spirited individuals, but each tends to be wary of the other and there will be a lack of accord.

In work, their combined strengths have the potential for great success, but with the Horse often distrustful of the Monkey's motives and methods, these two do not work well together.

In love, they may enjoy lively lifestyles, but both are strong-willed and each will want to prevail. The Horse, who is so open and upfront, could be wary of the Monkey's secretive tendencies. A difficult match.

With a Rooster

These two may share a love of conversation and a multitude of interests, but as both are candid and self-willed, relations could sometimes be tricky.

In work, these two have energy and great commitment and the Horse will value the Rooster's organizational talents and ability to think ahead. Together, they could enjoy considerable success, although both will be keen to take the credit!

In love, these two redoubtable signs can make a splendid and attractive couple. They are also good for each other. The Horse will benefit from the Rooster's orderly and attentive ways. There will be a lot for them to enjoy together, but, with both being stubborn and wanting to prevail, there will be differences to reconcile. A good, although challenging match.

With a Dog

There is great respect and rapport between Horse and Dog and relations between them are very good.

In work, these two combine well, with the Horse often placing much faith in the Dog's thoughtful and considered approach. A successful and competent team.

In love, their rapport and understanding are often very special. The Horse will value the Dog's loyal, supportive and dependable nature and they can make an excellent match.

With a Pig

Outgoing and sociable, the Horse and Pig enjoy each other's company.

In work, these two are hard-working and enterprising and the Horse will value the Pig's commercial flair and persistent, redoubtable manner. Each can be a spur to the other, and together, if they direct their energies well, they can enjoy considerable success.

In love, these two lively, passionate signs can make an excellent match. With good rapport and the Horse valuing the Pig's joyful, optimistic nature and encouraging ways, these two can be good for each other and find much happiness.

Horoscopes for Each of the Chinese Years

Horse Fortunes in the Year of the Rat

The Rat year can be a busy and lively one and Horses may be troubled by its volatility. Progress will be difficult, and while it may not always suit Horses to do so, there will be times when it could be best for them to keep a low profile and wait for situations to clarify and improve. In Rat years, they need to be watchful and patient.

At work, the Rat year can be challenging. Many Horses will be contending with a heavy workload as well as dealing with complex issues. Sometimes delays, bureaucratic problems or the attitude of another person could also make situations difficult. Being conscientious, Horses will often feel frustrated. However, while the year will bring its difficulties, it is at such times that Horses can demonstrate and develop their strengths. By concentrating on the tasks that need to be done and avoiding distractions, as well as adapting as required, they can still achieve some creditable results. As has often been found, problems can be opportunities in disguise, and the Rat year will give Horses the chance to gain invaluable experience as well as highlight their potential. For some, the seeds of later success can now be sown.

Rather than embark on change, many Horses will remain with their present employer and in areas which draw on their expertise. However, for those intent on change or seeking work, the year can again be challenging. Opportunities may be limited and some Horses will be frustrated by the way certain of their applications are processed and their skills ignored. However, Horses are tenacious and by persisting and putting in that extra effort, many will eventually secure an opening this year, and often one they can build on. Effort will be required, but achievements this year can have an important bearing on future prospects.

In money matters, Horses again need to be careful and be wary of haste or rush. More expensive plans and purchases need to be thought through and the terms carefully considered. Should Horses have any concerns, it is important they get these addressed before proceeding. Similarly, they need to be thorough when dealing with important paperwork and ensure that insurance policies are kept up to date and are sufficient for their purposes. Lapses could be to their disadvantage this year and the slow workings of bureaucracy could be troubling. At times, the Rat year can be exasperating!

In view of the pressures of the year, it is important that Horses give themselves an occasional respite. Some 'me time' can do them a lot of good. Not only could some of their pursuits give them the chance of additional exercise, but some could have a social element as well. Any Horses who have let their interests lapse should look to address this, perhaps by giving themselves a project or personal goal for the year.

In addition, all Horses should give some thought to their well-being, and if sedentary for large parts of the day or feeling their diet is in any way lacking, take advice on activities and foods that may help. Some self-care can be of particular value.

With their active nature, Horses set great store by their social life, and the support and camaraderie shown by others can be of particular help this year. By talking over concerns or dilemmas with those they trust, they can not only benefit from advice given but also be assisted in ways they had not envisaged. Horses should not feel alone and will often find that a worry shared is one considerably eased.

They should also make the most of the social opportunities that come their way, as the Rat year can give rise to some enjoyable occasions. Local and interest-related events could be particularly appealing.

Domestically, busy times are indicated. Not only will Horses be contending with their own commitments, but their loved ones could have a lot happening too, and there could be changes to domestic routine and working patterns. With such a lot to be considered, it is important there is good communication and flexibility over arrangements and plans. This is a year for consensus and pulling together. However, while some weeks will seem like a whirl, the Rat year will certainly have its pleasures too, including joint activities and possible trips out. Awareness, sharing and good communication are, though, so important.

Overall, the Rat year will bring its challenges and Horses will need to keep their wits about them. However, by doing their best and adapting as required, they will not only have the chance to demonstrate their skills but also be preparing themselves for the successes soon to come.

Tips for the Year
Be mindful of others and do consult them when taking decisions or in a dilemma. Also, preserve time for your loved ones and personal interests. Both can bring meaning and benefit to this often pressured year.

HORSE FORTUNES IN THE YEAR OF THE OX

Like Oxen, Horses are prepared to work long and hard to achieve results, and this year their efforts will be well rewarded. For those who have been disappointed with recent progress (and the previous Rat year will not have been an easy one) or are nurturing particular hopes, this year offers far brighter prospects. It is a time to move forward and even though results may be slow in coming (Ox years do not favour haste!), there will be good (and well-deserved) gains to be had.

At work, the aspects are particularly encouraging. With the experience they now have, together with the qualities many have shown recently, many Horses will be particularly well placed when opportunities arise. In some cases, senior colleagues will move on, creating promotion possibilities, or Horses will have the chance to use their skills in other ways. Whenever an opening appeals to them, they should put themselves forward. Many will be able to take their career to a new level this year.

To help their prospects, all Horses should take advantage of any training courses that are available to them, as well as keep informed about developments in their industry. This can not only help them in the present but also alert them to possibilities to consider in the near future. In addition, as this is a year of opportunity, they should make the most of any chances to network and raise their profile.

For Horses seeking work and those who feel their prospects could be improved by a move elsewhere, the Ox year can also bring some good opportunities. By making enquiries, talking to employment experts and looking at ways in which they could use and adapt their skills, many Horses could secure a new position that is capable of re-energizing their career.

Work-wise, this is an encouraging year, with effort, skill and persistence rewarding Horses well.

Progress made at work can increase the income of many Horses and some will also benefit from the receipt of extra funds. However, Horses do need to manage their situation well and ideally make advance provision for plans and requirements. With good budgeting, they will be able to proceed with many of their plans and will be especially pleased with the usefulness of certain acquisitions. However, if tempted by anything speculative, they should check both the facts and the implications.

Travel will be tempting (as it usually is to Horses) and if there is a particular destination or event that appeals to them, they should find out more. Similarly, if there are events happening locally, they should investigate. Horses like to keep themselves active and the Ox year will offer a good mix of possibilities, including the chance to visit new locations.

Horses will also appreciate the year's social opportunities and the chance to spend time with their friends. However, while usually they are good conversationalists, this year they need to be on their guard. A *faux pas* or lapse could cause problems. Horses, take note and do be attentive to those around you.

For Horses enjoying romance, or who find it in the Ox year, care is again advised. 'The path of true love does not always run smooth' and Horses need to give time to a relationship and be mindful of the feelings of the other person.

In their home life, too, they should ensure there is good communication and openness. A lot will be happening, and if arrangements are decided on in advance, more will go ahead. Lack of planning, on the other hand, could lead to possible disappointment. Also, if considering practical undertakings, ample time needs to be allowed, as home or garden projects could be more protracted than envisaged, especially as one project gives rise to another. Domestically, Ox years can be busy, with a lot to consider and do, but they can also bring their pleasures, with shared interests, family occasions and travel to enjoy.

Horses generally do well in the Ox year. However, they need to work hard as well as be persistent. It can take time for results to filter through, but filter through they will. In their relations with others, Horses do need to be mindful of the views of those around them. Lapses or inattention could cause problems. But overall Ox years encourage Horses to demonstrate their abilities and strengths and will bring them some well-deserved (and in some cases overdue) rewards.

Tips for the Year
Make the most of the year's opportunities and look to move forward. With effort and determination, you can make good progress. But do be attentive when in company and communicate well with those around you.

Horse Fortunes in the Year of the Tiger

An important year. With Horses in often inspired mood, a lot can happen. There can be a strong element of serendipity to the year too, with helpful influences coming into play.

At work this can be a year of change. For Horses who are established in a career, there may well be the possibility of moving to a new level, often in a more specialist capacity. Some Horses may have been working towards (and hoping for) such an opportunity for some time. With those around them supportive and their skills now proven, many will be well placed to advance.

There will, though, be some Horses who feel they have accomplished all they can where they are and need a new challenge. For these Horses, as well as those seeking work, this is a time to seize the initiative. The Tiger year is no time to stand still and it will bring the Horse's strengths and potential to the fore. By being active in their search, these Horses will find their energy and persistence will be noticed and in many cases lead to them securing an important new platform on which to build. They will relish the opportunity.

Horses should also make the most of their personal interests this year. Those who are keen to develop a specific interest should build on what they do. In some cases, expert tuition or extra practice could make a noticeable difference. Some Horses could also be attracted by a new subject or activity. If keen to try something different in this active year, they should keep alert for possibilities to pursue. Tiger years encourage self-development.

With the busy lifestyle many Horses lead, it is important they give some consideration to their well-being this year too. Regular exercise and a healthy diet could help. Also, during especially busy times, they should allow themselves the chance to rest. To continually drive themselves could sap their energy.

Attention to their lifestyle can be an important consideration this year.

On a personal level, Horses will find themselves in demand, with their home and social life both favourably aspected.

In their home, the year can again bring change. Some Horse households will see a relation moving away, perhaps for the purpose of education or work, and other changes to routine as well. Cooperation will be required, and the better this is, the better home life can be. In view of the pressure some changes and decisions can cause, it is important these are talked through and a spirit of openness encouraged. If not, there is a risk that tiredness or tension could lead to irritability. Horses, be aware of this and do share any matters on your mind.

Busy though home life will be, it will, though, contain many gratifying occasions. There will be individual successes to mark as well as the successful completion of plans and projects that enhance the home.

Many Horses will see an increase in social activity this year and their social circle growing as a consequence. The active nature of the year will bring them into contact with many people and some good friendships and connections can be forged.

For the unattached, the prospects of finding love are good, and for any Horses who are nursing hurt or disappointment, this is a year to go out, explore new interests and meet new people. Positive action will be well rewarded.

Although the aspects are generally favourable this year, one area which requires care is finance. With family commitments, home purchases and a busier social life, Horses will have high outgoings and spending needs to be watched. Also, if they have concerns over the terms or implications of a particular transaction, they should seek advice. With so much going on, control, prudence and discipline are required.

Overall, though, the Tiger year is a favourable one for Horses. It is a time to build, move forward and be open to opportunity. At work, many Horses will be able to make greater use of their strengths, and their personal interests can also develop well and encourage them to make more of their skills and talents. Their home and social life will be busy, with much to do, share and enjoy. But all the activity will make this an expensive time and Horses do need to watch their spending and manage their finances carefully. If they do so, they can make the most of this encouraging year.

Tips for the Year
Remember the words of Virgil, 'Fortune favours the bold.' This is a year to be bold. Go after what you want. Believe in yourself and make the most of your talents. Also, enjoy your relations with others. Their love and support can benefit you in many ways.

HORSE FORTUNES IN THE YEAR OF THE RABBIT

A fine year ahead. While it may lack the activity that Horses favour, a lot can still be accomplished. However, Horses will need to focus on their objectives and watch their independent tendencies. To act alone, in haste or without thinking things through could bring difficulties. While this is an encouraging year, Horses need to keep their wits about them.

At work, Horses should remain focused on what they have to do and show some patience. Sometimes the results of their actions could take time to filter through or they could find themselves affected by delay or the slow workings of bureaucracy. For keen Horses, parts of the year will be frustrating, but in Rabbit years it is a case of persevering and concentrating on the tasks in hand. However, there will also be developments which many Horses can profit from. In some instances, workplaces will see restructuring and/or the launch of new initiatives and their in-house knowledge will enable many Horses to benefit. What happens this year may not necessarily be what they were envisaging, but it will allow many to extend their skills. The latter part of the year could see key developments.

For Horses who are keen to move elsewhere, as well as those seeking work, the Rabbit year can also hold some interesting developments. By widening the scope of their search, many of these Horses could secure a new role that offers the change they want. There could be considerable adjustment involved, but many Horses will have the chance to establish themselves in a new working environment this year. It may take time for opportunities to come through, but when they do, they can be significant.

Progress made at work can help financially, but Horses do need to be careful in financial undertakings. When considering expensive purchases, they should check the ranges and options available as well as the costs involved. If borrowing, the terms need to be clarified, as this is no time for taking risks or making assumptions. Horses should also be disciplined when going out. Too many impulse purchases or social extravagances can lead to them spending more than intended. Financially, this can be a reasonable year, but it does require discipline and control over the purse-strings.

With their keen and active nature, Horses can derive particular pleasure from their personal interests this year, especially those that take them out of doors and/or allow them to make greater use of certain skills. If there is a local activity group or course that could help or provide facilities, they should find out more. Rabbit years encourage participation and Horses will enjoy a lot of the activities they carry out (or start) now. With their public-spirited nature, some could become involved in community activities or help others in some noble way.

Their interests can often have a good social element to them and Horses will appreciate their opportunities to go out and spend time with others over the year. With Rabbit years favouring culture, the arts and entertainment, Horses could be attracted by the many events going on.

However, while Horses will often add to their social circle, for the unattached, matters of the heart require careful handling. Horses need to be attentive and mindful of the feelings of others. Particularly for those who meet someone new, rather than build up high expectations in the early stages, it would be better to show patience and let the relationship develop in its own way and time. Some Horses can find happiness in Rabbit years, but for others, new love could be problematic.

Their domestic life can, though, be a source of great happiness, especially as some Horses will see an addition to their family or have cause to celebrate an achievement or milestone. Some may relocate. A lot can happen this year, although plans could take some time to come to fruition. With determined effort, however, Horses can see some far-reaching results.

In general, Horses can fare well in the Rabbit year, but it is one requiring commitment and effort. Progress may not necessarily be swift and results will need to be worked for, but the year will not be without its opportunities. By focusing their efforts and seizing any chances to further their skills, many Horses can further their career and enhance their prospects. Their home life can also be rewarding, with personal news and family developments that will delight them. Socially, too, the Rabbit year offers good possibilities, although, in matters of the heart, extra care is advised. Overall, a pleasant even if sometimes slow-moving year.

Tips for the Year
Allow time. Rather than rush, appreciate the present and what can be done now. Also, build on your capabilities. What you do this year can be to both your present and future advantage.

HORSE FORTUNES IN THE YEAR OF THE DRAGON

As the Dragon year starts, Horses will often detect change in the air. Rather than feel restricted, many will feel more motivated and enthused and will set about their aims with renewed vigour. Accordingly, both their personal and professional life can see favourable developments.

For Horses who feel frustrated or are nursing some regret, this is a year for action. Rather than feel fettered by what has gone before, these Horses should channel their efforts into what they want to see happen now. With resolve, self-belief and the desire to move forward, they can help open up new possibilities and sometimes make new starts. Horses have much within their reach this year.

At work, developments can happen quickly. Some Horses could have the chance to cover for an absent colleague, take on extra responsibilities and/or benefit from a promotion opportunity. Dragon years will enable many Horses to make good headway. For those who are in a large organization or keen to develop their career in new ways, there may even be the chance to relocate. This is no year to stand still. However, when taking on anything new, Horses do need to give themselves time to learn and settle down. While keen, they need to be realistic and apply themselves to what arises.

Horses looking for work also need to keep alert for openings as well as consider different ways in which they can draw on their experience. With initiative and possibly a widening of their search, they can see important doors opening for them. Quite a few could find themselves working in a different capacity but welcoming the opportunity to develop their career in a new way.

Progress made at work can bring an increase in income too, although to benefit fully, Horses need to remain disciplined. With expensive plans and purchases likely, they should budget ahead. They should also be wary of risk and, if tempted to speculate, be aware of the implications. Without care, misjudgements could be made. In addition, when dealing with important paperwork, Horses need to be thorough as well as meticulous in keeping documents, receipts and guarantees. Losses and lapses could be inconvenient and possibly costly. Horses, take note.

With the busy nature of the year, Horses should also give some thought to their own well-being, including their level of exercise. Horse are usually active, but if they feel they need more exercise or are tempted by a new fitness activity, if they seek medical advice on the best ways to proceed, they could find their actions making a difference to how they feel as well as sometimes introducing them to a fun pursuit.

The Dragon year also offers considerable social opportunities and Horses can see their circle of acquaintances and contacts growing ever wider. They will gel very quickly with some of the people they meet this year and some good friendships can be formed.

This can also be an exciting year for affairs of the heart, with some currently unattached Horses meeting someone who is destined to become significant. Even if some relationships flounder, new ones can often quickly follow, with Cupid's arrow striking many a Horse this year. In some cases, wedding bells will beckon in these exciting and often special times.

Domestically, this can be a full and interesting year. However, with Horses and others grappling with various commitments, some parts of the year will be frenetic with activity. At such times, it will be a case of everyone working together, concentrating on priorities and being flexible over arrangements. Amid all the activity, there will, however, be special times to enjoy, with personal and family successes to enjoy and key plans to carry out.

Travel too can bring pleasure and Horses should aim to go away with their loved ones at some point during the year. A change of scene and the chance to visit new attractions can do everyone a lot of good.

Dragon years can be busy, and even for Horses, who like activity, sometimes a bit too busy. However, a lot can be achieved, and by channelling their efforts and seizing their opportunities, Horses can enjoy many good results.

Tips for the Year

Take action and look to move ahead. With some aims in mind, you can make progress and make more of yourself too. Also, enjoy your relations with others. Their support, friendship and love can add to the pleasures of the year.

Horse Fortunes in the Year of the Snake

Horses are not always comfortable with the mysterious workings of the Snake year. Situations are not always straightforward and some areas of life can be problematic. However, while not the best of years, it will nevertheless give Horses the chance to take stock, immerse themselves in their activities and add to their skills.

In work, rather than looking too far ahead, Horses would do best to focus on their present position and objectives. By concentrating on the tasks in hand and using their skills to good effect, many will not only find this a more fulfilling time but will benefit professionally. Sometimes training will be offered or Horses will have the chance to familiarize themselves with other aspects of their industry and so help their future prospects.

During the year, they should work closely with their colleagues and be an active member of any team. In addition, by using any chances to network and raise their profile, they can impress others and form some influential connections and friendships.

Many Horses will remain with their present employer over the year, but for those seeking change or looking for work, the Snake year will be challenging. With openings often limited and competition fierce, Horses will need to show initiative in their applications. Finding out more about the duties involved and emphasizing their experience could make a difference. Progress in Snake years may not be easy, but will show the stuff Horses are made of. Their fortitude will impress and, in time, deliver.

This will be an expensive year, especially as Horses will be keen to proceed with some major purchases as well as carry out improvements on their home. To do all they want, they will need to control their budget and, if possible, make early provision for outgoings. Also, when entering into agreements, they should check the terms and conditions. This is no year to be lax or rely on assumptions.

One area which can particularly benefit Horses in Snake years is the development of their own interests. By setting time aside for activities they favour and adding to their knowledge and skills, they can take great pride in what they do. Some may enrol on local or online courses or set themselves a certain objective. Any Horses who have let their interests lapse and would welcome fresh challenges should aim to take up something new. Purposeful and inspired action can be highly rewarding this year. And personal interests can help lifestyle balance as well.

With their outgoing nature, Horses will enjoy the social opportunities of the year and on many an occasion will be on sparkling form, with their eloquence and exuberance winning them new friends. However, while a lot can go well, Snake years can also give rise to some difficult moments, and Horses need to be on their guard. In particular, lapses or indiscretions could undermine rapport, and for any Horses who are tempted to stray or take risks, there could be consequences to face. These words of warning only apply to a few, but Horses, do take note.

Also, Horses enjoying romance or who find love this year need to remain attentive and allow time for relationships to develop. In matters of the heart, this is a year to tread carefully and mindfully.

Domestically, this will be a busy year, particularly as many Horses will be keen to go ahead with some ambitious projects. Ample time will need to be allowed for these, and the more that can be tackled jointly, the better. Throughout the year, it is also important that there is good communication and cooperation and that any pressures or concerns are addressed and talked through. A spirit of openness can be to the advantage of all. Shared interests and quality time together can also be of benefit, as will any short breaks or holidays taken. Despite all the activity, their home life can bring many Horses much contentment this year.

Horses like to be active and drive themselves hard, and while they will involve themselves in many activities this year, it will allow many of them to enjoy a better lifestyle balance. Personal interests and times spent with others can be especially satisfying, although Horses are advised to be attentive in matters of the heart. While progress at work may not be as extensive as in some years, by channelling their efforts, Horses can make this a fulfilling time and gain insights, skills and experience which can be to their later advantage, especially with their own year following.

Tips for the Year

Pay careful attention to your relations with others. Many good times can be shared and good connections forged, but lapses and indiscretions risk undermining much. Be especially careful in matters of the heart. Also focus on the present and seize any chances to develop your skills. What you do now can have an important bearing on subsequent developments.

HORSE FORTUNES IN THE YEAR OF THE HORSE

Exciting times ahead, with excellent opportunities, although a word of warning does need to be sounded: in their own year Horses should be careful not to overreach themselves or push their luck or the goodwill of others too far. With care, this can be a highly successful year, but the aspects warn against complacency or unnecessary risk.

In work, what many Horses have recently undertaken can now be rewarded, and when promotion and other opportunities arise, they will be well-placed to benefit. Their in-house reputation can also stand them in good stead and give them the chance to take their career to new levels. Horses who have felt held back or dispirited by recent progress can now see new doors opening and many will make deserved and overdue headway over the year.

For Horses who are keen to take their work in new directions or are nurturing specific aspirations, this is a year to keep alert for openings and pursue ideas. Again, initiative and resolve may be well rewarded, with some of these Horses setting their career on a new and potentially successful track. Many of those seeking work will also be fortunate in securing a position in which they can develop their skills.

Throughout the year, all Horses can be helped by the support of their colleagues and contacts. These may not only alert them to possible openings but also give advice on the best way forward. Horses have much in their favour in their own year, although to fully benefit they do need to watch their independent tendencies and be receptive to developments and possibilities. In addition, they need to be realistic about what is doable. To be overambitious or overcommit themselves could weaken their effectiveness. Horse years provide salutary warnings for those who rush, take risks or are less than thorough.

In money matters, this can be a successful year, with many Horses enjoying a noticeable rise in income. However, they need to remain disciplined. Too many unplanned or hasty purchases could soon mount up and impulse buys could come to be regretted. Good planning would be useful this year.

Travel will appeal to many Horses, and if possible they should make provision for a holiday as well as take up any chances to visit attractions that appeal to them, including some that are local. Over the year, the adventurous and enquiring nature of many Horses will be well satisfied.

Horses like to fill their time with a good mix of activities and their own year will open up an array of possibilities. New interests, ideas and activities could all appeal and outdoor and creative pursuits be particularly satisfying. Also, with the busy lifestyles many Horses lead, it is important that they give some consideration to their own well-being, including their diet and level of exercise. If they feel any modifications would help, they should seek advice. And if they have any concerns, they should get these checked out.

They can see a lot of activity in their home life and the year may be marked with some special and proud moments. In many cases, some long-considered plans can be advanced, including perhaps relocation. This is a year for concerted action, and once decisions are taken, helpful developments will many times assist.

However, with all their undertakings, Horses need to be aware of the cost implications and take careful note of the views of others. Rushing or being too dogmatic could cause problems. This is very much a year favouring joint effort and working towards desired outcomes.

There will also be an increase in social activity and some parts of the year could be especially busy. Horses who see changes over the year will have excellent chances to meet new people, some of whom they will get on with very well.

Romantic prospects are also good, although rather than rush into a commitment, it would be better to let any new relationship develop gradually. As with so much this year, the aspects are promising, but rush and haste can undermine efforts.

Overall, though, the Year of the Horse can be a special one for Horses themselves. Their work prospects are especially promising and their home and social life likely to be gratifying. For the unattached, there will be romantic opportunities too. However, while Horses will have much in their favour, they need to remain disciplined and focused. Haste, rush or acting too independently could all reduce effectiveness. In their own year Horses will be very much the arbiter of their own fortune. Horses, take note and do make the most of this year which is so rich in possibility.

Tips for the Year
Seize the moment and make the most of your opportunities. A lot can be accomplished in this busy year. Also, value the support of others and enjoy your relations with those who are special to you. These can be rewarding times, but with so much happening, remain vigilant and mindful of others.

Horse Fortunes in the Year of the Goat

This can be a pleasing year for Horses. During it they will be able build on recent gains and enjoy good progress. Also, rather than having their attention drawn in many different directions, they will be able to concentrate more on the things *they* want and will feel more in charge of their destiny.

To help, as the Goat year gets underway, Horses should decide on some objectives for the next 12 months. By having thoughts in mind, they will not only have something to work towards but can use their time and energies more effectively. Any who may be discontented or nursing disappointment should focus their attention on the present rather than what has gone before. With resolve and the willingness to move on, they can make a lot happen.

Work prospects are encouraging, and for Horses who are keen to move forward and build on their present position, good possibilities can open up. Some Horses will make progress in their existing place of work and their in-house knowledge will be a real asset, while others will keep alert for openings elsewhere. Whatever they do, important doors can open for them this year.

For Horses who are feeling staid and unfulfilled in what they currently do and would welcome a fresh challenge, as well as those Horses seeking work, the Goat year can bring interesting possibilities. By keeping alert for openings, thinking of different ways in which they could use and adapt their skills and making enquiries, many will find a position which can re-energize their career. The determination and enthusiasm Horses display can be important factors in the headway they now make.

Progress at work can also lead to rise in income for many Horses. However this can be an expensive year. For those who may have recently moved or who now do so, there may be many accommodation costs. In addition, with commitments, plans and good travel opportunities, outgoings will be considerable, and Horses need to watch their spending and budget accordingly. This is a year for good management.

Horses can derive much pleasure from their personal interests this year, with creative pursuits being particularly satisfying. By giving themselves the time to follow through their ideas, Horses can enjoy the way certain activities develop. For some, new equipment can open up new possibilities.

Domestically, Goat years can be busy and see Horses eager to go ahead with plans they have long been considering. For some this could include relocation, while others may content themselves with ambitious practical projects. Over the year the homes of many Horses will be considerably enhanced, although projects will often become more wide-ranging than initially envisaged. However, by focusing on what needs to be done and drawing on the expertise available to them, Horses can be pleased with what is accomplished.

In addition to practical undertakings, the Goat year will also contain a good mix of things to do. Whether enjoying special activities, a holiday and/or helping each other with interests, by spending time together, the whole Horse household can benefit.

Social prospects are good too, and Horses will enjoy the variety of events and occasions the Goat year offers. Entertainment, the arts and culture are particularly favoured in Goat years and Horses will make the most of their chances to go out and be with their friends. They could be particularly grateful for a close friend's advice on a matter of concern. However, to fully benefit, they do need to be receptive to what is said.

For the unattached, romantic prospects are promising. For some, a chance meeting could become significant. Time and care will cement many a relationship this year. And for Horses nursing personal hurt, new friendships and love are capable of changing their situation. Goat years can be good for Horses in many different ways.

By the end of the year, Horses could be astonished by all they have done and how their achievements have built up. At work, their experience and diligence can lead to important advances being made, while with their personal interests, their special talents and creativity can make this a rewarding time. They will value the support and friendship of others, and romance can help make the year special. All the activity of the year will make it an expensive one and they will need to manage their outgoings with care. But by using their time well and seizing their opportunities, they can make this a satisfying time.

Tips for the Year
Act with purpose. Make the most of your strengths and experience. They are assets of great value and can open up possibilities for you. Also, enjoy your relations with others and the good times this lively year offers. It is one to appreciate.

HORSE FORTUNES IN THE YEAR OF THE MONKEY

Horses will enjoy the energy and opportunities of the Monkey year and are set to do well. However, they do need to remain disciplined and focus their efforts. To spread their energies too widely could reduce their overall effectiveness. In addition, they should pay heed to their instincts. Sometimes seemingly good chances can arise which they have misgivings about. And if they have reservations, they should be wary. Monkey years, while exciting, have their distractions, and Horses need to stay focused on priorities.

At work, this can be a year of swift-moving developments. Whether as a result of staff movement, new management or changing workloads, the roles of many Horses will alter. At times, pressures may be great and adjustments necessary, but by making the most of what opens up, many Horses will have the chance to prove themselves in a different capacity.

For those who feel their prospects can be improved by a move elsewhere, as well as those seeking work, the Monkey year has scope and possibility. By keeping alert for openings and not being too restrictive in what they are considering, many of these Horses could succeed in taking on a different role with the potential for future development. Monkey years have a capacity to surprise and can offer what can sometimes be substantial change.

With their outgoing nature, Horses can also be helped by the good working relations they have with many people. If in a new working environment, their early efforts to get to know others and immerse themselves in what is happening will impress. However, in setting about their duties, they need to remain disciplined. To be distracted, take short cuts or be less than thorough could lead to mistakes and regrets. In Monkey years, Horses need to be on their mettle.

Discipline is also needed in money matters. This is no year to be lax. If Horses have reservations over any financial matter, they should exercise caution and, if appropriate, seek professional advice. Without sufficient care, some could find themselves disadvantaged or let down in some way. Monkey years have their temptations too, and to succumb to too many impulse buys or seemingly good offers could prove costly. It is a year for financial care.

Monkey years can, though, open up some interesting possibilities and many Horses will be enthused by their recreational activities. Some could be tempted by a new pursuit and enjoy using their abilities in new ways. For the creative, ideas and projects could be particularly inspiring.

However, while a lot is set to go well, Horses would be advised to pay attention to their well-being this year, and if involved in any hazardous activities, follow the correct procedures. This is no time for risk or neglect.

Socially, with their eloquence and wide interests, Horses are set to impress many and will enjoy the variety of occasions the Monkey year offers. Lonely and unattached Horses should aim to go out more and perhaps join a local society or interest group. Positive action can be of great benefit and new friends (and love) may transform their situation.

Domestically, too, Horses will be on inspired form and often keen to go ahead with improvements, including updating equipment and adding to home comforts. However, while eager, they need to be realistic about what is possible and ideally focus on one task at a time. The year will be busy enough without over-committing themselves.

During the year, they could also feel that a close relation is in need of support. Here their thoughtfulness and empathy can be of especial value. Similarly, if they themselves become anxious over a certain matter, they should speak of it and, if necessary, seek advice. Horses may be strong and redoubtable, but they cannot expect to handle everything on their own. Horses, take note and be forthcoming.

Overall, Horses can do well this year. Many can make pleasing advances in their work as well as enjoy the way both new and existing interests develop. In money matters, they need to be vigilant and wary of risk, but domestically and socially this can be an active, full and encouraging year.

Tips for the Year
Remain focused and use your time, skills and chances effectively. Also, enjoy the possibilities that open up for you, including new

ways of developing your strengths and interests. This is a reward-ing and satisfying year, although it does require concentrated effort.

Horse Fortunes in the Year of the Rooster

Horses are strong-willed and enjoy a certain freedom of action and could find the structured nature of the Rooster year inhibit-ing. This is a year for sticking to the tried and tested.

At work, Horses will find their best results will come from concentrating on their areas of expertise. This is not a year favouring radical change. Horses who are relatively new to their present position should aim to become better established and learn about the different aspects of their role. All Horses should take advantage of any training that is available as well as keep themselves informed of developments in their industry. By immersing themselves in their situation and developing their skills and knowledge, they will not only be helping their present position but also preparing the way for future progress.

Over the course of the year they could, however, find some situations irksome, especially as delays occur, bureaucracy impedes their progress or the attitude of another person concerns them. At such times they should show patience and wait for situations to resolve themselves. This may not suit their mentality (Horses just like to get on and do), but the problems and lessons of the year can leave them wiser *and* considerably more experienced.

The majority of Horses will remain with their present employer, but for those keen to move on or seeking work, the Rooster year can be significant. Obtaining a position will not be easy, but by keeping alert for opportunities in their area of expertise, these Horses can take on new positions and enjoy the chance to re-establish themselves.

While many will enjoy a modest rise in income, financially this is also a year for care, especially as they could face additional expenses, including repairs and the cost of updating equipment. In view of this, they should keep a close watch on their spending and, when possible, budget ahead for forthcoming expenses. Also, when making large purchases, they should ensure that their requirements are being met and that they are conversant with the costs and implications of the transaction. Without vigilance, problems could arise and bureaucratic correspondence and procedures be troublesome.

The Rooster year can, though, bring some good travel opportunities, and by planning a holiday in advance, many Horses could fit some exciting sights and attractions into their time away.

Personal interests can also bring them much pleasure. Although they may be grappling with many commitments, preserving time for activities they favour can help them relax (important in this sometimes stressful year) as well as be a satisfying outlet for their talents and ideas. Some Horses will enjoy attending interest-related events. For the sporting and music enthusiast in particular, the Rooster year can give rise to a good mix of occasions. Any Horses who have let their interests fall away should aim to rectify this during the year and consider taking up something new. Personal interests can be akin to a tonic and should not be ignored.

Horses should also make the most of the year's social opportunities. With friends to meet and various activities to participate in, they will often have things to look forward to. However, while much will go well, problems can still arise. A difference of opinion or petty jealousy or the attitude of another person could cause concern. At such times, Horses should proceed carefully, address the situation and talk matters through, as well as keep everything in perspective. And if some friendships fall away, new ones will surely take their place. However, while Rooster years can bring their awkward moments, there will be much to appreciate.

With the Rooster year favouring planning, Horses could also find it helpful to give some thought to domestic plans for the year. Whether these are personal or family goals or projects for the home, by talking their thoughts over with those around them, they will find courses of action can be agreed upon and worked towards. With combined effort, a lot can go ahead this year and everyone enjoy the benefits. Shared interests, individual successes and travel can also bring special times, but throughout this busy year, good communication between family members is so very important.

Horses like to be active and set about their undertakings with commendable determination. But in Rooster years they need to be mindful of others and prepared to adapt to situations *as they are*. They also need to show patience, as not all their plans will proceed as quickly as they would like or, indeed, in the way they had hoped. However, while the year will have its vexations, by focusing on the things they *can* do and developing their skills, Horses can prepare themselves for the more substantial opportunities that lie ahead. This is also a good time for travel, for pursuing personal interests and for enjoying quality time with loved ones. It may not be the easiest of years, but Horses can get much value from it and gain skills and insights that they can take forward.

Tips for the Year
Be patient. Situations may sometimes exasperate you, but they can be worked through and important lessons can be learned. Spend time on your interests and seize any chances to improve your skills. The experience you can gain now can have both present and (particularly) future value.

Horse Fortunes in the Year of the Dog

Good times await, with Horses set to reap some often substantial rewards for their efforts. This is a year for progress. However, to make the most of it, Horses will need to watch their independent tendencies. Dog years favour joint action.

Work prospects are particularly promising and Horses will find their experience and specialist knowledge placing them in a strong position to advance their career. By being active, becoming involved in initiatives and working well with their colleagues, they can impress others and help their prospects. As so many Horses have found, putting in that little bit of extra effort can make a lot of difference, and this will be the case again in the Dog year. This is a time to make strengths count. Over the year quite a few Horses will benefit from promotion opportunities and take on positions they have been working towards for some time.

For Horses who feel their situation could be helped by a move elsewhere, as well as those seeking work, the aspects are again encouraging. Not only should these Horses remain alert for openings, but also seek the advice of contacts and professional experts. The input of others can be an important factor in how they fare this year. Support backed by action can be an effective combination.

This is also an excellent year for personal development and Horses studying for qualifications are set to do well. Also, if any Horses feel an additional skill could help their prospects, they should see what can be arranged. Positive action will be an investment in themselves and their future.

Personal interests, too, can be beneficial and there will be a good mix of occasions and events to look forward to, often related to the outdoors.

With a strong sense of altruism existing in Dog years, some Horses may also give time to causes they support or help their community in some way. Those involved in local interest groups could see their involvement increase. Dog years encourage participation, and the enthusiasm and contribution of Horses are appreciated by many.

Financially, this can be an improved year, with many Horses benefiting from an increase in income and some able to supplement their means with additional work or an enterprising idea. However, to make most of this upturn, Horses should remain disciplined and set funds aside for specific requirements. If they are careful, they can make some pleasing acquisitions and realize some ambitious plans, including some related to travel.

Many Horses will also spend money on their home this year, perhaps freshening the décor or carrying out alterations. Some may decide to relocate. This is very much a year for action and Horses, with their eager nature, can drive a lot forward.

With a lot happening over the year, it is, however, important that they are forthcoming and talk over their thoughts and concerns with those around them. Sometimes just the process of talking can help clarify their own preferences as well as lead to helpful input from others. Dog years favour a coming together, and domestically, with individual successes to mark and various activities and plans underway, this can be a busy and memorable time.

Horses will also welcome the social opportunities of the year. Their interests will often have a good social element.

For the unattached and those who would welcome new friendships and perhaps romance, the Dog year can see quite a transformation in their situation, with the chance to meet someone who is destined to become significant. Events can move in exciting ways this year and romance add sparkle to the lives of many Horses.

In general, the aspects are very encouraging for Horses in Dog years and their efforts, strong work ethic and skills can reward them well. Much is possible and if they follow through their ideas, a lot can go in their favour. They do need to liaise well with those around them and watch their independent tendencies. But overall this can be a successful and often personally special time.

Tips for the Year

Believe in yourself and look to move forward. You can enjoy both personal and career success this year. But do draw on support and advice rather than rely on individual efforts. Also, use any chances to further your knowledge and skills. What you learn now can be useful in many different ways.

HORSE FORTUNES IN THE YEAR OF THE PIG

A variable year, with Horses sometimes struggling to make headway. However, frustrating though some of the year may be, Horses are resourceful and can still take much from it.

Something which can be of particular benefit to Horses this year is making a determined effort to achieve a better lifestyle balance. The Pig year encourages reappraisal and reconnecting with yourself, and during it Horses who lead busy existences will often look at introducing positive changes, including ways of using their time more effectively.

Personal interests can be of particular value, as often these will be an outlet for talents as well as offer Horses the chance to relax, unwind and spend time in ways they enjoy. In addition, Horses who are sedentary for much of the day or feel they are lacking in exercise would do well to seek advice on changes that could be of benefit to them.

Pig years also have an element of fun and there will be a lot to take pleasure in. Films, shows, concerts, sporting fixtures and other forms of entertainment may all be appealing to Horses, and some lively times can be had this year.

Travel, too, can be tempting, and Horses should take advantage of any chances to go away. Over the year they can visit some impressive places.

Another valuable aspect of the year will be the way that interests and activities can bring Horses into contact with other people. There will be good chances for them to add to their social circle this year, and romantic possibilities too. However, in matters of the heart, Horses need to be open and attentive and let any new relationship develop in its own way. Many relationships will build steadily during the course of the year.

In their home life, Horses will often be central to activities as they help and advise their loved ones and attend to a lot in the home. They will often be keen to make improvements as well as finish projects that have been requiring attention for some time. However, while keen, they should concentrate their efforts and focus on one task at a time. Also, if attempting anything ambitious or strenuous, they should follow the recommended procedures. This is not a year for risks.

At work, this will be a demanding year, with Horses often feeling they are putting in a lot of effort for little return. In addition, some of their activities could be affected by delays and factors outside their control. However, while this may sometimes be an exasperating time, rather than feel frustrated by the things they cannot do, Horses should concentrate on the things they *can* do. By showing flexibility and working their way through difficulties, they can do their reputation a lot of good. Progress may not be easy this year, but when it comes it will be truly deserved.

Horses who are seeking work or a change will also find that

effort will be required. There could be disappointments in store and some unfathomable delays in their quest, but with self-belief and persistence, they can find the opportunities they seek. The Pig year is a hard taskmaster and results will need to be worked for, but Horses are tenacious and many will triumph despite the sometimes problematic conditions of the year. The second half of the year will be generally better and more productive than the first.

Although progress at work may be muted this year, many Horses can nevertheless look forward to an improvement in their financial situation. Earnings could increase and some Horses could receive funds from another source, including a possible gift, bonus or maturing policy. To make good use of any upturn, they should manage their resources carefully and set funds aside for specific purposes. If they consider their plans and acquisitions carefully, they can make fine choices. If able, they should also consider making provision for the longer term, including making savings or adding to a pension policy. With careful management, many can improve their current situation this year and help their future too.

Horses like to get on and do, but could find progress difficult in the Pig year. Pressures and situations will not always help and great effort will be needed. But by adapting and doing their best, Horses can demonstrate their skills and enhance their reputation. Finances can show improvement, and personal interests, travel and time with others can bring pleasure. This is also an excellent year for Horses to balance their lifestyle and appreciate the rewards of their efforts.

Tips for the Year

Focus on tasks and adapt as required. This is no year to dissipate your energies. Time spent with others and furthering your interests will be of particular value. Also, ensure there is a balance to the year and it is not all work and no play.

Thoughts and Words of Horses

Experience is not what happens to a man. It is what a man does with what happens to him.

ALDOUS HUXLEY

I think luck is the sense to recognize an opportunity and the ability to take advantage of it. Everyone has bad breaks, but everyone also has opportunities. The man who can smile at his breaks and grabs his chances gets on.

SAMUEL GOLDWYN

If you do things well, do them better. Be daring, be different, be just.

ANITA RODDICK

The three great essentials to achieve anything worthwhile are, first, hard work; second, stick-to-itiveness; third, common sense.

THOMAS ALVA EDISON

Many of life's failures are people who did not realize how close they were to success when they gave up.

THOMAS ALVA EDISON

If we did all the things we are capable of doing, we would literally astonish ourselves.

THOMAS ALVA EDISON

Do what you can, with what you have, where you are.

THEODORE ROOSEVELT

No man needs sympathy because he has to work ... Far and away the best prize that life offers is the chance to work hard at work worth doing.

THEODORE ROOSEVELT

These three things – work, will, success – fill human existence. Will opens the door to success ... work passes these doors, and at the end of the journey success comes in to crown one's efforts.

LOUIS PASTEUR

5 February 1943–24 January 1944 — *Water Goat*

24 January 1955–11 February 1956 — *Wood Goat*

9 February 1967–29 January 1968 — *Fire Goat*

28 January 1979–15 February 1980 — *Earth Goat*

15 February 1991–3 February 1992 — *Metal Goat*

1 February 2003–21 January 2004 — *Water Goat*

19 February 2015–7 February 2016 — *Wood Goat*

6 February 2027–25 January 2028 — *Fire Goat*

24 January 2039–11 February 2040 — *Earth Goat*

The Goat

The Personality of the Goat

Whether clambering over mountain rocks, foraging in forests or grazing in lush fields, Goats have a talent for blending in and making the most of their surroundings. They like to be in groups and are sociable and peace-loving, and this holds true for so many born under the Goat sign. They, too, are friendly, companionable and enjoy being with others. Whether in a family unit, the workplace or some other situation, Goats like to be a part of things. They relate well, have a fine sense of fun, empathize, listen and join in. In their endeavours, they like to have the reassurance and approval of others and to know that they have support behind them. Without this, they are apt to prevaricate and can be notoriously fickle.

Goats are born under the sign of art and possess good imagination. Often adept with their hands, they may excel in crafts as well as enjoy expressing themselves in an imaginative capacity, including on canvas or paper or in the performing arts. Goats have style and flair, but they do like to have the backing of others. Indeed, it is when they are with others and feeling comfortable and secure that they give of their best.

Being imaginative, Goats also think a lot, including about the situations in which they may find themselves. Sometimes this can lead them to worrying and thinking the worst. As a result, they can be prone to mood swings and some tend to view things pessimistically. But here again, with support, plus their wide-ranging abilities, often they can find their doubts and fears misplaced. Rather than brood, worry alone or assume others are aware of their feelings, Goats can often help themselves by being more forthcoming.

Goats have much to offer. They are kindly, considerate and like to get things right. They often tend to the smallest detail and can be pernickety (or, as some may say, fussy). But this is the hallmark of Goats – they care. They care about the things they do as well as the opinions of those around them. And should things go wrong, they can be very sensitive to criticism and take any setback personally.

For a choice of vocation, Goats can do well in professions favouring creativity and interaction with others. They have great style and visual awareness, and some have enjoyed notable success as designers, creators and arrangers. The art world could also appeal, as will architecture, the fashion industry, show business or one of the caring professions. And, if they can have a mentor or an encouraging team behind them, so much the better. In their work Goats do, though, like freedom of expression and are not ones for structured routine, having their talents stifled or working in a hotly competitive commercial environment.

It has often been said that the more people you know, the luckier you can be, and this holds true for Goats. They know many people and can be assisted in many things. It is rare to find a Goat in need.

This also applies financially. Goats like to live well and, thanks to their own efforts, the support of a partner or their background, generally do. However, they do like to spend, and they have expensive tastes and appreciate quality, so there will be times when greater discipline and more control would not come amiss. Goats may enjoy their moments of luck, including welcome windfalls, but should not overreach themselves or overspend!

Being caring and loving, Goats welcome a partner and yearn for someone loyal, dependable and supportive. And while their quest for true love may not always be smooth (and thinking about it could cause much personal anguish), once they have found a soulmate, they can be truly content. And being a part of family life is something they especially value.

Although their home may not be the tidiest, it will certainly be kept clean and be embellished with all sorts of objects, artwork and mementos (particularly of their early years, for Goats can be nostalgic). Many a Goat home will be stamped with their personality and will be a relaxed and often carefree place with a charm of its own.

Both male and female Goats are very fond of home life and seek a peaceful and untroubled existence. Although the female may sometimes come across as shy and reserved, when she is comfortable in her situation, her true qualities will be very evident. Warm-hearted, friendly and often very talented in a special way, she may underplay her many strengths when she actually has much to offer and be proud about. Being attentive, she also devotes much time to her family and is very skilled in using her creative abilities around the home. She takes pride in her appearance and, with her sense of style, colour and fashion, she knows what looks good.

If a parent, Goats will be loving and very encouraging, and while their easy-going manner makes them no disciplinarians, they will often enjoy a close rapport with their children. Family bonds are important to Goats.

The Goat sign very much embodies the essence of the Yin principle in Chinese philosophy, with Goats being agreeable and kindly and having an appreciation of beauty and the finer things in life. And with their genial nature and ability to fit in well and engage with what is going on around them, they play a valued part in many a situation. William Makepeace Thackeray, born under the Goat sign, once declared, 'The world deals good-naturedly with good-natured people.' And Goats are certainly blessed with a good nature.

Top Tips for Goats

- Though you are caring and sensitive, if you think outcomes are uncertain or you are concerned about the reaction of others, you tend to hold back. To realize your potential, be bolder and more willing to take the initiative. As the proverb reminds us, 'Nothing ventured, nothing gained.' Venture more! It will be worth it.
- You like to do things well, but sometimes undermine your effectiveness by prevaricating or switching from one approach to another. You will achieve better results by being better organized and persisting. Take note, for planning and purposeful effort can reward you far more.
- If you are nurturing talents or aspirations, why not benefit from a helping hand? With the support and input of others, so much more can happen for you. Seek advice and then you can move forward.
- You think a lot and may be inclined to think the worst. At such times, talk to those you trust and share your concerns. Sometimes just the process of talking can help ease burdens. Also, rather than think of the negative, think of the positive, of successful outcomes, of former triumphs. As Charles Dickens, born under the sign of the Goat, once wrote, 'Reflect upon your present blessings, of which every man has many; not on your past misfortune, of which all men have some.' You have many blessings, and talents too.

Relations with Others

With a Rat

These two know how to have a good time, but their different temperaments do not always make for easy relations.

In work, the Goat could feel ill at ease with the Rat's bold and assertive style and working relations will be poor.

In love, there will be passion and a lively lifestyle to enjoy, but the sensitive Goat could feel unnerved by the Rat's candour and thrifty attitude towards money. A challenging match.

With an Ox

The different personalities and styles of Goat and Ox make understanding difficult. Relations will often be poor.

In work, the Goat may admire the Ox's redoubtable nature, but the Ox may have little appreciation of the Goat's inventiveness and style. There will be little agreement or accord.

In love, both desire a secure and settled home life, but the Goat delights in a carefree, easy-going existence while the Ox likes structure and order. Also, the Ox's forthright manner will cause the Goat some disquiet. A difficult match.

With the Tiger

The Goat likes and admires the lively and often positive and enthusiastic Tiger and relations between them will be good.

In work, both are creative, and with ideas aplenty and the Goat finding the Tiger an enterprising colleague, these two can do well. They do, however, need to remain disciplined in matters of finance.

In love, their lively, sociable natures and shared interests make for a close and meaningful match. The Goat will especially value having such a confident and supportive partner. These two can be good for each other.

With a Rabbit

The Goat enjoys the calm, good-natured ways of the Rabbit and relations between these two are often excellent.

In work, they will respect and encourage each other's strengths and the Goat will value the Rabbit's judgement and business acumen.

In love, both seek a secure and harmonious lifestyle and they will have excellent understanding and rapport. The Goat will especially value the loving and supportive nature of the Rabbit. They can find much happiness together.

With a Dragon

The Goat finds the Dragon fascinating company and for a time these two sociable signs can get on well, but their restless natures could lead to an eventual cooling in relations.

In work, the Goat could be enthused by a confident and enterprising Dragon colleague, and by combining skills and working towards a common aim, they can fare well.

In love, these two lively and spirited signs can have so much to share. The Goat will especially appreciate the Dragon's zest and buoyant nature, but both are restless and the Goat will find the Dragon's independent tendencies and impulsive nature disquieting. For the relationship to succeed, a great deal of understanding will be needed.

With a Snake

The Goat likes the calm, quiet and thoughtful ways of the Snake and relations between them will be good.

In work, these two can combine their creative energies to good effect and the Goat will particularly value the Snake's resolve and disciplined approach. With good respect and understanding, they could enjoy considerable success.

In love, there may be a strong attraction. Both seek a stable and harmonious lifestyle and have a fond appreciation for the finer things in life. The Goat will particularly delight in the Snake's quiet, affectionate yet confident manner. A good match.

With a Horse

The Goat likes the lively and spirited Horse and there will be excellent rapport and understanding between the two.

In work, their strengths are often complementary, with the Goat admiring the enterprise and drive of the Horse. With a good level of trust, these two can make a successful team.

In love, both will gain much from their relationship. The Goat will find the Horse inspiring and value their steadfast and confident ways. With many shared interests and outlooks, these two are well suited.

With another Goat

Easy-going, creative and with a liking for the finer things in life, two Goats get on well together.

In work, their creative skills and innovative approach can lead to great things, but Goats can sometimes be lax in money matters and need to remain focused, disciplined and financially savvy in any venture.

In love, both seek a harmonious and hassle-free existence and their shared interests, sociable natures and penchant for ideas, creativity and things artistic make them well suited. However, given their tendency to spend, these two will need to exercise control over the domestic budget.

With a Monkey

These two signs like each other's company and get on well.

In work, the Goat will often be enthused by the enterprising and determined Monkey and they can make an effective combination.

In love, these two have a great capacity for fun. Each will be supportive of the other and the Goat will often be lifted by their breezy and versatile partner. A close and meaningful match.

With a Rooster

With their different temperaments and outlooks, relations between Goat and Rooster are often poor.

In work, the Goat will not be comfortable with the Rooster's regimented style, or their candid nature, and they will not work well together.

In love, the Goat likes a relaxed and easy-going lifestyle while the Rooster is given to planning and organization. For a relationship to work, major adjustments will be called for. A challenging match.

With a Dog

Personality differences, together with a lack of common interests, do not make for easy relations.

In work, these two are both keen to do right, but both are worriers. They are not on each other's wavelengths and working relations will be poor.

In love, the Goat may value the Dog's affectionate and loyal ways, but with the Goat being creative and whimsical and the Dog practical and matter of fact, understanding and rapport could be difficult. A challenging match.

With a Pig

Lively, sociable and good-natured, these two signs will enjoy good relations.

In work, their skills and strengths will complement each other and the Goat will be encouraged by the drive and good sense of the enthusiastic Pig. With so much trust and respect, they will make an effective team.

In love, these two sociable, fun-loving and easy-going signs have much in common. Both like the good life and seek a settled and harmonious existence. With such similar outlooks and principles, they make an excellent match.

Horoscopes for Each of the Chinese Years

GOAT FORTUNES IN THE YEAR OF THE RAT

The Rat year is one of considerable possibility for Goats, but they do need to set about their activities in an organized and determined way. Rat years require purposeful action and to waver or just wait for something to turn up could lead to disappointment. This is a time for showing initiative and going after key objectives.

At work, this can be an important year. For Goats already established in a career there will often be the opportunity to progress to new levels. For many this will be in their existing place of work and their in-house knowledge and reputation will assist their progress. When openings occur, these Goats should be quick to indicate interest. Rat years move fast and Goats need to be nimble-footed lest chances slip away.

For Goats who consider their prospects could be improved by a move elsewhere, as well as those seeking work, the Rat year can open up interesting possibilities. But again these need to be actively pursued. By making enquiries and talking to contacts and experts, however, many Goats could find an ideal opening. Initiative can open important doors, and with the skills they offer, backed with determination, Goats can make impressive headway.

The dynamic nature of the Rat year also encourages Goats to make more of their personal interests. Creative activities could be particularly inspiring. Goats could enjoy the way their ideas develop and meet with some encouraging responses. Rat years nurture their talents. Outdoor activities can also find favour, and for Goats who like gardening, sport or being out of doors, the Rat year can provide some special moments.

As always, Goats will set much store by their relations with others. Often their personal interests will have a strong social element and they could also be attracted by events happening in their local area. There will be a good mix of things to do this year and many Goats will find their social diary filling nicely.

Prospects are also good for unattached Goats, as well as those who would like to add to their social circle. By remaining active, pursuing their interests and taking up their chances to go out, they can make some good connections and friends. For some, new love can blossom, often in fortuitous ways. A chance meeting may seem as if it was destined to be.

Domestically, this can be a busy year and Goats need to remain organized and plan ahead. With objectives in mind and the support of family members, a lot can happen. This is very much a time for combined effort and working towards desired outcomes. These can include home (and garden) projects, travel and shared interests.

In addition to the often considerable practical activity, there will also be individual successes to mark and key family events to look forward to. During the year many Goats will have good reason to feel proud, although if anything concerns them or they feel under pressure at any time, they do need to be open and share what is on their mind. The more forthcoming they are, the better others will be able to understand and assist.

In money matters, many Goats can look forward to some moments of good fortune. In addition to an increase in income, funds could come from another, often unexpected source. However, with all the activity of the year, outgoings will be high and Goats will need to keep track of spending and be wary of acting in haste. The cost of unplanned purchases could soon mount up. Goats, take note.

Rat years have great energy and Goats can benefit from their opportunities. But they do need to act with resolve and make things happen. With purpose, objectives in mind and the support of others, they can, however, enjoy encouraging results. Personal interests and relations with others can bring them particular pleasure and there will be some gratifying and often special moments to share.

Tips for the Year

Act with determination. Much is possible this year, but it requires focused effort. Also, look to develop your ideas and interests. Again, a lot can follow on, but you do need to engage and make the most of your often special abilities. It will be worth your while.

GOAT FORTUNES IN THE YEAR OF THE OX

Goats are highly perceptive and keenly aware of situations around them. During the Ox year, many could feel ill at ease with the uncertainties they detect. They will do best to keep expectations modest and draw on the support of others.

The Ox can be a hard taskmaster and in addition to an often considerable workload, many Goats will be grappling with new objectives and changing conditions. To do well in Ox years it is very much a case of knuckling down and focusing on what needs to be done. Also, while some years encourage creative approaches, Ox years favour practicalities, and the Goat's strengths will not always be appreciated. However, while this may be a demanding year, it will have its values. Dealing with often diverse workloads will not only give Goats the chance to gain new skills but also to discover aptitudes they can take forward. And by working closely with their colleagues, they can not only benefit from their support and camaraderie, but also build some potentially useful connections.

Opportunities for progress may be limited this year, and for Goats looking to make a change or find work, there could be disappointments in store. Results do not come easily in Ox years and these Goats will need to put a lot of effort into their applications if they are to succeed. In particular, they should find out more about the duties involved and stress their skills, experience and suitability. Giving that little bit extra can make an important difference.

Also, all Goats should make the most of training opportunities during the year. By keeping their skills up to date and learning new ones, they will not only be helping their present situation but also increasing the range of possibilities open to them in the future. Work-wise, this may be a demanding year, but it can be an instructive one.

Another area which requires care is finance. With ideas in mind, including purchases for themselves and their home, there is a risk that Goats could overspend. To avoid problems, they need to remain disciplined and avoid succumbing to too many impulse buys. This is a year to keep tight control over the purse-strings. Also, if taking on a new commitment or dealing with important paperwork, they need to check the details carefully. This is no year to be lax.

With the pressures of the year, many Goats will take much pleasure in their personal interests, as these will allow them to relax, unwind and enjoy something different. Whether their interests take them out of doors, give them the chance of additional exercise or offer an outlet for their creativity, it is important that Goats give themselves some 'me time'. Some may delight in setting themselves a personal goal and so give themselves something purposeful to aim for.

In addition, they should take advantage of any travel opportunities, as a rest and a change of scene will do them a lot of good.

With their genial nature, Goats get on well with many people and their relations with others will be of continuing value in the Ox year. However, they do need to recognize that not everyone is as perceptive as they are, and rather than assume that others know how they feel, they do need to be forthcoming and talk over any anxieties or concerns. There are many who are willing to lend a listening ear or advise in some way and Goats should speak out, remembering, 'A worry shared *is* a worry halved.'

Goats often regard their home as a welcome sanctuary from outside pressures and once again this year they will content themselves with domestic projects as well as enjoy following family developments. Ample time does, though, need to be allowed for practical undertakings, and costs need to be watched. Ox years require attention to detail. However, Goats' home life can bring them much pleasure this year, and just as they will be grateful for advice and input concerning their own situation, they will be glad to offer others help with several keynote decisions.

They will also appreciate their social life and the variety of events they attend over the year. They will particularly value their circle of friends. For any Goats who are feeling lonely, perhaps as a result of a recent change in circumstances, it could be worth finding out about social and interest groups in their area. With action and a willingness to participate, they can soon see benefits following on.

Overall, the Year of the Ox will be demanding and Goats may feel ill at ease with the pressures it brings, especially work-wise. However, by drawing on support of others, remaining organized and concentrating on their priorities, they can still make headway and add to their skills and experience. And throughout the year they should remember there are those around them who believe in them and are ready to advise when asked.

Tips for the Year
Focus on what needs to be done. With concerted effort and a willingness to develop your skills, you can learn a lot that can be important to your subsequent progress. Also, preserve time for your personal interests and for sharing with others. Both can be of great value in this often exacting year.

GOAT FORTUNES IN THE YEAR OF THE TIGER

Tiger years bristle with speed and activity. And while Goats may sometimes feel unsettled by the fast-moving developments, important opportunities can emerge. This is a year which can hold considerable significance for them, particularly with the following Rabbit year being so auspicious.

During the Tiger year Goats will need to keep alert and be prepared to adapt as required. This is no time to close their mind to unfolding situations or remain wedded to just one course of action. Instead, this is a year to participate, learn and, uncomfortable though it may sometimes be, venture out of their comfort zone. It can be an instructive *and* illuminating time.

At work, this can be a busy and eventful year. Whether through staff movements or developments in the workplace, many Goats will experience change and see new possibilities opening up. Their experience and in-house knowledge will stand them in excellent stead and many will take their work to a new level. However, with progress will come new responsibilities, and some Goats will face a steep learning curve. This will, though, give them an excellent chance to further their expertise and become more established in a certain sector or niche. In addition, those who work in creative environments can often benefit from Tiger years, which are abuzz with new ideas and approaches.

For Goats who are unfulfilled in their present position, as well as those seeking work, the Tiger year can offer interesting possibilities. By not being too narrow in what they are considering and looking at other ways in which they can develop their skills, these Goats can uncover some new opportunities. For some this could take their career in a new direction. By being adaptable and willing, these Goats can make progress and enhance their skills. Tiger years are vibrant, challenging *and instructive*.

With their personable nature, Goats should also use any chances to network and raise their profile. This way some useful (and sometimes influential) connections can be made.

Tiger years can also see many social opportunities and again Goats should make the most of the chances that come their way. Conversations and contact with others can be of value, and some of the people Goats meet now will become firm friends. Goats have the gift of relating well to others.

This can be an encouraging year for their personal interests. Tiger years favour originality and some Goats will find their talents meeting with a good response. They should have belief in themselves and develop what they do. Any Goats who have let their interests lapse and would welcome a fresh challenge should look to take up something new. Tiger years offer great scope, but Goats need to be proactive.

With the busy nature of the year, they will have many expenses and do need to keep tabs on outgoings and not be rushed into important decisions. Without care, spending could be greater than anticipated and if certain purchasing decisions are given more time, better choices can often be made. This is a year for careful control and being wary of risk.

Tiger years will also see much domestic activity. With Goats themselves and their family members likely to be experiencing changing routines and commitments, there will need to be flexibility and good cooperation. In view of the general level of activity, some plans and projects should be kept fluid and fitted in when time allows. Tiger years are no respecters of rigid timetables. Goats will be pleased, however, with the benefits their plans, purchases and changes bring. In addition, there can be much spontaneity to the year and sometimes surprise family occasions and trips out can be appreciated by everyone concerned. Domestically, a lively, rewarding and often very full year.

Overall, the Year of the Tiger will be a busy one. It will bring interesting possibilities, but to benefit, Goats will need to adapt and make the most of developments. This is no year to be resistant to change. If Goats engage, however, and seize their opportunities, they can help both their present and future situation.

Tips for the Year
Enjoy and develop your interests. These are a good outlet for your talents and ideas as well as of personal benefit. Also, look to build on your work position. Skills gained now can increase your options later.

GOAT FORTUNES IN THE YEAR OF THE RABBIT

Good times ahead. With conditions being encouraging, Goats will be feeling inspired and can make substantial progress this year as well as enjoy pleasing developments in their personal life. This is a fine year and for any Goats who have felt buffeted by recent events, now is the time to get back in the driving seat and *make things happen.*

To help get the year off to a good start, Goats would do well to decide on their aims for the next 12 months. That way they will be able to direct their energies well and be more aware of the things they need to do. They will enjoy good support and throughout the year would find it helpful to discuss their ideas with others, especially those who have relevant experience. With good input, their hopes and plans can often come to successful fruition.

During the year their personable nature can serve them well, and to benefit they should make the most of their chances to meet others and get themselves better known. Some good friends and work contacts can now be made. Goats who would welcome company or new friends should aim to go out more, take part in local activities and perhaps join a social group. By taking positive action, they could enjoy quite a transformation in their social life.

For the unattached, romantic prospects are excellent, while for those newly in love, this can be a blissful time, with many settling down together or marrying. For relations with others, Rabbit years can be very special.

Goats can also look forward to some pleasing developments in their home life, particularly with individual and family successes to mark. They will often be on inspired form, suggesting family activities that can lead to some fine occasions. They will also delight in the home improvements they initiate and their deft touches will add some pleasing embellishments. However, home projects could mushroom and become more extensive (and costly) than envisaged. Goats, be warned.

While Goats will busy themselves with many activities this year, they should not ignore their well-being. To keep on good form, they should give some attention to their diet and level of exercise. Also, if they experience a succession of busy days and late nights, they should allow themselves time to catch up. Driving themselves too hard could leave them prone to minor ailments. In addition, if involved in any strenuous or hazardous activities, they should follow the correct procedures. Where their well-being is concerned, this is a year for care and attention.

At work, prospects are encouraging. For Goats who are established in a career, the Rabbit year can open up important opportunities. However, to fully benefit (and sometimes secure significant promotion), these Goats do need to act quickly, lest the chances slip away. This is no year for delay.

For Goats who are unfulfilled in their present position or seeking work, again the Rabbit year can be significant. However, in their quest, these Goats should not act alone. By seeking advice, they could be alerted to vacancies or options they may not have considered before. The helpfulness and encouragement of others can be an important factor this year. Also, the positions some of these Goats now take on can be a welcome contrast to what they have done before and give them new incentive.

Progress made at work can lead to an increase in income and many Goats will also enjoy a bonus or generous gift. This improvement will lead to many going ahead with purchases they have been considering, and their eye for quality, taste and value can serve them well. However, while many plans and purchases will be gratifying, Goats do need to keep tabs on their spending and, if entering into an agreement, check the terms and obligations. The financial aspects may be favourable this year, but it is still no time to be lax.

In general, Rabbit years can be times of great opportunity for Goats. However, to make the most of them, Goats need to act and, if necessary, emerge from their comfort zone. Their efforts, skills and initiative can deliver substantial rewards, but so much rests with them. They will, however, be assisted by others, and socially and domestically, Rabbit years can bring many special times, especially as romance is favourably aspected. Goats have much in their favour this year and would do well to remember the words of Virgil, 'Fortune favours the bold.' In Rabbit years, fortune very much favours bold and purposeful Goats.

Tips for the Year
Seize the initiative. So much can happen for you this year, but you do need to be willing to venture forward. Also, value the support and goodwill of others. The times you share can be a very important part of this active and often personally special year.

Goat Fortunes in the Year of the Dragon

Dragon years are dynamic. They bring grandiose schemes, new ideas and fast-moving situations. And although Goats may sometimes feel uncomfortable with the pace and pressure of them, there will be good opportunities to pursue and special occasions to enjoy.

At work, the Dragon year will bring times of change. Few will be unaffected. Accordingly, many Goats will find themselves having to adapt to new procedures and routines. Some of the year will be hectic, but by doing their best and adjusting as required, Goats will have the chance to develop their skills. And with this being a time of innovation, their ideas could meet with a favourable response. Dragon years encourage input and Goats in creative environments or whose work involves communication can fare particularly well.

Many Goats will have the chance to build on their present position over the year, but for those who are uncomfortable with the developments and would welcome change, or are seeking work, there will be some good possibilities. To benefit, these Goats should widen the scope of the positions they are considering. In this year of change, many could secure a role that is different from what they have been doing but can provide an important platform for later growth.

However, to make the most of their opportunities, all Goats will need to remain focused and resist getting diverted into less helpful or productive matters. In Dragon years, time, energy and chances all need to be used effectively.

Progress at work can help financially, but with their existing commitments, plans they will be keen to fulfil and an often busy social life, Goats could find their spending considerable. While they may make allowance for certain requirements, actual outlay could still be higher than anticipated. Many Goats could also face some additional expenses in the first half of the year. Accordingly, throughout the year all Goats will need to keep a close watch on outgoings and be wary about succumbing to impulse buys. Financially, this is a year for discipline.

Many Goats will find the Dragon year inspiring, however, and their personal interests can be a good outlet for their ideas and talents. Some Goats could be particularly enthused by activities they start now or projects they set themselves. Also, with the Dragon year being a time of possibility, for those keen to do something different, there could be interesting chances to explore. This is a year favouring a game attitude.

Similarly, if interest-related events appeal to Goats or they see other tempting chances to go out, they should take them up. By being involved and making the most of the social possibilities the Dragon year offers, they can enjoy some good and often lively times. During the year some positive new friendships can be made, and for the unattached, romance can add sparkle to the year.

Home life too promises to be active, although with Goats and others affected by changing routines and commitments, there will need to be a good level of cooperation and some flexibility. At times of change and pressure it is important that implications are talked through, as this is a year for openness and collective input. In addition, with some developments causing uncertainty, Goats should not always assume the worst. Again helpful discussion can ease concerns and suggest ways forward. Many of the niggling matters of the year will often be short-lived in any event.

Busy though the year will be, Goats will enjoy many special times in the company of their loved ones, and with the spontaneity of some of what occurs, including trips and special occasions out, adding a buzz and joy to the year.

In general, Dragon years will see a lot of activity, also pressures, anxieties and adjustments to routine. As a result, Goats will need to keep their wits about them. However, there can be some good possibilities too. Goats will be encouraged to develop their skills and further their career and may make what could be potentially important advances. Throughout the year they will be well supported by those around them and by drawing on this and building positive relations with those they meet, they will enjoy much of what this year offers. Overall, a busy time, but with good possibilities, and personal relations likely to be especially rewarding.

Tips for the Year
Be receptive to what happens this year. You can make useful advances and enhance your skills. Also, what you learn now can be built on in the future. Personal interests can be of especial value. Enjoy times with your loved ones and look to extend your social circle.

GOAT FORTUNES IN THE YEAR OF THE SNAKE

This will be an encouraging year for Goats, with a lot going in their favour. Not only will they sense that the conditions are right for action, but they can also benefit from some moments of good fortune.

One of the most encouraging aspects of the year concerns their relations with others. As they face decisions and explore possibilities, often they will know someone who has the expertise to help and advise. In some instances, another person could assist in advancing their cause too. Over the year, Goats can benefit greatly from the goodwill and support of others.

Also, on a personal level the Snake year can give rise to many convivial occasions. In particular, there will often be much to talk about with friends, with news and fun to share. In addition, changing situations and mutual acquaintances can lead to Goats meeting new people and seeing their social circle widen quite considerably. Goats are popular company and will once more find their genial manner winning them new friends this year, including some potentially influential contacts.

For the unattached, affairs of the heart can also make this a special time. Goats enjoying romance could find their relationship becoming more permanent, while those seeking love could feel the effects of Cupid's arrow! These can be exciting and passionate times.

Home life is also favourably aspected. During the year Goats will again value the support of their loved ones, although they will need to be forthcoming and also listen carefully to others. Discussion can sometimes give rise to new ideas, especially when decisions have to be taken, and the helpfulness of others can be instrumental in some of the successes that Goats will enjoy this year.

In addition to personal support, they can also look forward to some fine family occasions. Whether marking their own progress or sharing in the good news of others, they can enjoy some meaningful and special times.

Travel, too, is well aspected and Goats should try to go away during the year if possible. A rest and change of routine could be very welcome. Many may be able to combine their travelling with an interest or event or sight they are keen to see. Here careful planning could lead to some exciting plans taking shape.

Born under the sign of art, many Goats enjoy cultural and creative pursuits, and their personal interests can be another source of pleasure this year. Their ideas could particularly enthuse them and they could become absorbed in what they do. Encouraging responses could also open up additional possibilities. Snake years are very much ones in which Goats can reap the rewards of certain talents.

Similarly, for Goats whose work involves creative input, this can be a successful year. By using their strengths to advantage and being active in their workplace, many can enjoy some notable triumphs. Even though some Goats may be shy and not always promote themselves as much they should, this year they should really have faith in their abilities and make the most of their opportunities.

Also, no matter what type of work they are in, Snake years encourage Goats to advance their career, and if an appealing vacancy or promotion opportunity opens up, they should put themselves forward. This is no year for standing still. During it, many Goats will move to a greater and often more fulfilling role.

For those seeking work, the Snake year can again see encouraging developments. Although the job-seeking process can be wearying, by making enquiries and exploring possibilities, they will find doors opening. In some cases, what is offered will mark a change from what they have been doing but give them the chance to use their skills in new ways. For some, this could reveal a new forte, one they can take forward.

Progress made at work will often help financially, and many Goats will enjoy a rise in income. However, to get the best from this, they should manage their situation well. By setting funds aside for specific purposes, including possible travel, they can see many of their plans coming to fruition and their purchases bringing them pleasure – and sometimes additional comfort too!

Snake years can help bring out the best in Goats. On a personal level, Goats can look forward to great support from others and their qualities being admired and respected. Not only can valuable backing be given, but special times can be shared. Family, friends and, for some, new love will be very important this year. Also, in their work and interests, Goats can see their creative talents making a real difference. They can make good headway this year. However, to make the most of it, they do need to have some self-belief and put themselves forward. If they do, they can make this a special and rewarding year.

Tips for the Year
This is a year of great possibility. Embrace it and look to move forward. Also, enjoy spending time with others and adding to your social circle. New friends, contacts and possible new love can underline how special this year can be.

GOAT FORTUNES IN THE YEAR OF THE HORSE

Goats will have seen a lot happen in recent years and the Horse year will be an excellent one in which to build on accomplishments as well as enjoy some personal and family developments. This is a time of considerable scope and potential.

At work, Goats will find Horse years hard but fair taskmasters, and with commitment, they can do their reputation a lot of good. However, they do need to immerse themselves in their place of work and, if relatively new to their current duties, aim to become more established. By building connections and being an active member of any team, they can impress and be encouraged to make more of their position. This is a year for building on recent gains and moving forward.

For Goats who feel their prospects could be bettered by a move elsewhere or are seeking work, the Horse year can again open up interesting possibilities. However, to benefit, they should consider different ways in which they could develop their strengths and follow up any openings and ideas that appeal to them. Over the year the earnestness of many of these Goats can lead to them obtaining a new position, and often one with the potential for growth.

One of the benefits of the Horse year is the way Goats can add to their knowledge and skills, and not just work-wise. Over the year they should look to further their personal interests too. Being naturally curious, Goats are rarely short of ideas and the Horse year will give them plenty more. Some Goats could be tempted by a new activity, enrol on a course or decide to contribute to their community in some way. Whatever they do, their actions can often make this a gratifying time. For Goats with busy lifestyles, time set aside for recreation can also give them the chance to relax, unwind and sometimes benefit from additional exercise.

Goats can fare reasonably well in financial matters in the Horse year, although they should avoid risk or being lax. Without adequate attention, mistakes could occur and some purchases may not meet expectations. This is a year for care and vigilance.

With their genial nature, Goats know many people and can look forward to a busy social life, as the Horse year offers a good mix of things to do. Any Goats who feel lonely or would welcome new interests may find it worth joining a local social group.

Affairs of the heart can also add excitement to the year. While there could be issues to reconcile, relationships can often grow in strength and significance over the course of the year. Here again, Goats can be on good personal form.

Domestically, the Horse year can see a flurry of activity, especially as Goats and their family members see routines and commitments change as well as have practical matters to address. Sometimes it will seem as if everything is happening at once, including some inconvenient equipment breakages. To cope with the extra activity, Goats (and others) need to focus on what needs to be done and use their time and resources effectively. Also, with practical undertakings, Goats should resist the temptation of involving themselves in too many tasks at any one time. Concentrated effort will deliver better results, and often with less pressure too.

While a lot will go well, should differences of opinion arise or interests clash, Goats need to talk matters through and find an acceptable solution. If not, sometimes niggling matters can escalate. Goats, take note, liaise well and be alert to potentially awkward situations.

They should also pay some heed to their own well-being this year. With such a busy lifestyle, sometimes they may not pay sufficient attention to their diet or level of exercise. To keep on good form, they do need to watch this, and if anything concerns them or they feel changes may help, they should seek advice. While this is an auspicious year, it is not one to drive themselves on regardless.

By the end of the Horse year, Goats will often be amazed by all they have fitted into it. It can be a busy and fruitful time. During it, many Goats will advance their career, sometimes in a new direction. Personal interests are likely to develop in encouraging ways too. Many Goats will enjoy an active social life and a busy domestic one. With so much happening, good time management will be needed, but this can be a full and productive year.

Tips for the Year
Much can be accomplished this year, but do be proactive. Follow through your ideas and look to build on your present situation. With support, experience and the opportunities that will come your way, this is a time for action. Believe in yourself and go forth.

GOAT FORTUNES IN THE YEAR OF THE GOAT

The fact that this is their own year will give Goats even more reason to make it special. And it can be. But while Goats may start the year full of hope and determined to do a great many things, they will need to pace themselves. Much is possible for them in their own year, but not everything can be achieved at once.

To help get the year off to a good start, Goats could find it helpful to plan ahead. Having some aims in mind and talking them through with those who are close to them will not only help give the year more direction, but possibly set some important wheels in motion.

A factor in their favour will be the support they enjoy. Goats have a talent for getting on well with many people, and during their own year they should raise their profile and make the most of social and networking opportunities.

At work the year can see important developments. For Goats who are established where they are, excellent opportunities can arise to take their career to a new level. Whether through staff changes, an increasing workload or internal reorganization, there will be scope to advance, and the experience and in-house knowledge of these Goats can be an important asset. Unlike some years, when Goats may feel weighed down and stifled, their own year can re-energize their situation and prospects.

For Goats who would welcome change or are seeking work, important chances can also arise. Not only should these Goats actively pursue any openings that interest them, but they could find it of value to talk to professionals and other contacts. This way they could be alerted to new possibilities. With assistance, advice and their own resolve, many could obtain a significant opportunity and have the chance to prove themselves in a different capacity. What happens this year can have far-reaching consequences, including shaping the future career pattern of some of these Goats.

Headway made at work can lead to a rise in income. However, with commitments and a busy lifestyle, this will be an expensive year for most Goats, and to do all they want (and more), they will need to watch their spending and to be wary about making too many impulse buys. Without watchfulness, their outgoings could become higher than they have allowed for. Goats, take note and be disciplined.

With their enquiring nature, Goats enjoy a myriad of activities and should put their knowledge to good use in their own year, whether by setting themselves a fresh challenge or a new project or following up their ideas in other ways. Some could be attracted by new pursuits, too. With this being an encouraging year, Goats should make the most of their talents and creativity. In addition, if they can join with others, this can give some of their pursuits added impetus.

They will also delight in the year's social opportunities. Others will often seek their company, and whether partying, meeting for chats or just enjoying things happening, Goats can have a special year. Existing friends may also introduce them to others and many Goats will see their social circle widening. Any who are alone and feel something is missing from their current lifestyle will find that by taking advantage of activities available in their area, they can help bring about a real improvement in their situation.

The Goat year can also be a special one for affairs of the heart. Some Goats newly in love will settle down together or marry, while quite a few who start the year unattached will meet someone, often in chance circumstances, who will quickly become important.

Home life will also be busy this year, with many Goat households having cause to celebrate. Whether this is due to a wedding, an addition to their family, a graduation or some other success, these can be special and meaningful occasions. Also, just as Goats will benefit from the support given to them, they too will dispense useful advice to others. This is very much a time for cooperative effort. It can offer some surprises too, perhaps an unexpected chance to travel, a special event or a family treat, which Goats will enjoy sharing with others in this favourable year.

Goats will have high expectations for their own year. However, while enthusiastic, they need to remain realistic. Rather than rush or overcommit themselves, they should work steadily towards their objectives and build on their position. This is a year which favours persistent effort. Also, they should use their ideas and experience well. Their strengths can lead to some pleasing results and particularly help advance their work position. Their relations with others can also make the year special, and there will be a lot to do, share and enjoy.

Tips for the Year
Use your time well and work steadily towards your objectives. Pace yourself and avoid rush. What you achieve now can have long-term value. Also, enjoy sharing your activities and plans with those who are close to you and look to extend your social circle. The year will encourage you to shine.

GOAT FORTUNES IN THE YEAR OF THE MONKEY

A reasonable year, although Goats will need to be on their guard. Monkey years can spring traps for the unwary and this is no year for Goats to push their luck, or the goodwill of others, too far. Also, they will need to show some flexibility during the year, as situations may change and plans alter.

One area which requires particular care is relations with others. Although usually expert in this area, during the year Goats do need to remain forthcoming and attentive if they are to avoid difficulties. If, at busy times, they come across as preoccupied or give scant attention to what is happening, this can undermine rapport and lead to possible disagreements. Also, Goats should not automatically assume that others are aware of their views and feelings. In the Monkey year it is important that they are open *and* communicative. If not, there is a risk of misunderstandings and subsequent disappointment. Goats, take note.

In their home life, good liaison will be especially important. With Goats and other family members likely to be involved in changing routines and commitments, implications need to be talked through and adjustments agreed. Also, while Goats may have specific hopes for the year, including modifications they are keen to carry out and purchases for the home, sometimes requirements will change or new options arise, and these need to be fully considered. In Monkey years, original plans should not be set in stone but altered as required.

However, while there needs to be a certain flexibility in the Goat household, there will also be many pleasures, including personal achievements and shared interests. In addition, Monkey years can bring surprises and some last-minute suggestions may lead to some special family occasions which are often made all the more so because of their unexpectedness.

The Monkey year can also give rise to some good social opportunities. Here again, more spontaneous gatherings can be pleasing. However, when in company, Goats do need to be attentive and wary of unguarded remarks. An uncharacteristic slip or *faux pas* could cause some awkwardness. Similarly, for those enjoying romance, extra attention is advised. In Monkey years, Goats need to keep their wits about them.

At work, the Monkey year can also bring surprises. Although many Goats will be content to focus on their role, sudden developments could have an impact on them. There could be staff movements, reorganization or other changes, and Goats will need to adapt accordingly. Some will be faced with a considerable change in workload. Monkey years are rarely straightforward. However, while Goats may not welcome the uncertainty and additional pressure, there will be opportunities to pursue, and many Goats will make good headway with their present employer.

For those who are keen to move elsewhere, as well as those seeking work, again the Monkey year can hold important developments. Although their quest for a new position may seem protracted, events can move in curious ways. Sometimes an opening could be discovered by chance and at other times Goats could secure a position even though they did not rate their chances too highly. With determination and willingness to adapt, they will find that deserved progress can be made.

Also, Monkey years are excellent for broadening skills and all Goats should take advantage of training courses and other ways to further their knowledge. This will be an investment in themselves and their future.

With Monkey years favouring originality and creative thought, Goats can also develop their own interests, and will often delight in the way ideas take shape and possibilities open up. For the creatively inclined, this can be an inspiring time, with some talents developing (and expanding) in sometimes surprising ways. Again it is a case of being receptive to what the year offers.

The busy nature of the year will make it an expensive one, however, and Goats will need to keep a close watch on spending levels. If taking on new commitments, they should check the terms carefully, and should keep paperwork, including guarantees, receipts and policies, safely. Risk, haste or assumptions (always a danger for Goats in Monkey years) could be to their disadvantage.

In general, the Monkey year promises to be a full one, and by making the most of its developments, Goats can gain a great deal. They do, though, need to adapt as situations require. This is also a time to be alert and mindful in their relations with others. However, with awareness and flexibility, Goats can emerge from the year with much to their credit, having done a surprising amount.

Tips for the Year
Enjoy the dynamism of the Monkey year, but be especially mindful in your relations with others. Also, be receptive and flexible, then you can see your ideas developing in encouraging ways and be able to turn some of the year's surprises to your advantage.

Goat Fortunes in the Year of the Rooster

Planning, efficiency and commitment are all hallmarks of the Rooster year that Goats would do well to note. Goats cannot afford to slack this year or give less than their best. Rooster years are action-driven and will bring interesting possibilities.

As the year starts, Goats should think ahead and work out what they would like to see happen. With purpose, they can achieve a great deal. Any Goats who start the year feeling discontented should be determined to make an improvement in their situation. This is a year which can offer positive change, but it rests with Goats to seize the moment and *act with resolve*.

At work, Rooster years can be hard taskmasters and many Goats will face a heavier workload and some challenging objectives. While sometimes concerned about the additional pressure, by knuckling down and using their skills to advantage, they could enjoy some impressive results. In addition, their ability to communicate and think laterally (Goats are great ones for thinking out of the box) will be appreciated and they will often play an increased role in their workplace. For those who are keen to advance their career, the Rooster year can offer some attractive opportunities.

Many Goats will remain in their current place of work this year, but for those who are hoping for a change or seeking work, the Rooster year can be significant. By considering ways in which they could advance their skills and taking advice from employment officials, they could see some interesting possibilities emerging. With persistence, new positions can be found, and while the early days in any new role could be daunting, many Goats will soon realize they now have a platform they can build upon.

Another important feature of the year is the way it encourages personal development. For creative Goats, their ideas and projects could be particularly satisfying this year. Input and advice from those around them will also spur many on.

Progress at work will increase the income of many Goats and some could also benefit from a generous gift or welcome bonus. However, while there is an element of good fortune to the year, with many outgoings and expensive plans, Goats need to manage their situation well. Too many unplanned purchases could eat into resources, and some impulse buys could be regretted. Rooster years favour a disciplined approach.

On a personal level, Goats will find themselves in demand. There will often be a varied mix of things to do and share and many Goats will have opportunity to add to their social circle and make some potentially important friends and acquaintances.

For the unattached, a chance meeting can add romance to the year too. Affairs of the heart are capable of surprising and delighting Goats this year.

However, while relations with others will often go well, Goats are good-natured and generally easy-going and they must not allow themselves to be put upon. If they have any reservations or concerns, they should let their views be known. This is no time to remain silent.

Domestically, with Goats and other family members facing work choices and mulling over ideas, it is important there is good liaison and communication between everyone concerned. That way decisions can often be made easier and plans usefully advanced. Whether helping with a problem or arranging joint activities, Goats will often play their part, and their ability to listen and empathize will be much appreciated in this full and satisfying year. For a few, a move is possible, and for any considering relocation, this is an excellent year to explore options.

By the end of the year, Goats will often be astonished by all that has happened. It is a year to be open to possibility and seize opportunities. However, Rooster years do require effort, and for those who slack or hold back, there could be disappointments. This is a time to move forward and build. At work especially, what is accomplished now can often be a platform for future growth. Also, throughout the year, Goats will benefit from the support of others and it is important that they are forthcoming in return. They have much in their favour this year, but much hinges on their resolve. To do well and reap the rewards, they need to *act*.

Tips for the Year
Be, believe, become. This is a year for having self-belief and venturing forward. Make the most of your abilities and engage in what is happening around you. Commitment, effort and a lot of application will be required, but with a positive 'can do' approach you can go far.

Goat Fortunes in the Year of the Dog

Goats are perceptive and this makes them aware of and some-times susceptible to influences around them. During the Dog year, they could feel ill at ease with certain situations and the attitudes of some people. It could be to their advantage to adopt a tougher stance and not take certain situations too personally. Sometimes the events that happen are outside their control and they should accept this rather than feel they are personal slights. Dog years can be difficult for Goats, but they are not without their more positive aspects.

At work this is a year for care and thoroughness and for Goats to concentrate on areas in which they have most expertise. To venture into the unfamiliar or take on duties without the necessary training could bring problems. In addition, they should be attentive in their relations with colleagues, taking note of their viewpoints and liaising well. This is no year to act in isolation. Parts of the Dog year could see some awkward moments, and rather than be overhasty and risk exacerbating these, Goats should think their responses through as well as exercise patience. Problems and tensions can blow over, but Goats need to be careful not to cause themselves problems or undermine the good working relations they normally enjoy with those around them. At times, adopting a low profile could be a wise course.

However, while the year will bring its challenges, difficulties can be valuable learning opportunities, and Goats will be adding to their professional knowledge as well as gaining greater insight into their capabilities. These can be illuminating times and some Goats could be alerted to future career possibilities.

For those who decide to move on from their present position as well as those seeking work, again the Dog year can be challenging. Sometimes these Goats will find themselves competing against many people for a particular vacancy and at other times their experience and suitability may seem to be ignored. Dog years can have their frustrations, but by remaining patient and persevering, many will have the chance to re-establish themselves with a new employer. Results *will* need to be worked for this year, but success, when it comes, will be well deserved.

In money matters, Goats also need to remain vigilant. During the year they should keep a close watch on spending and remain within their budget. To succumb to too many temptations or impulse buys could lead to possible economies later. Also, when dealing with forms, tax and bureaucratic matters, they should check the details and be prompt and thorough in their response. Again, without care, problems can arise. Goats, take note.

More positively, this can be an encouraging time for personal interests and these can be a good way for Goats to escape some of the year's vexations. Creative pursuits could be especially fulfilling and many Goats will be encouraged by the feedback they receive. Some could get particular joy from new projects too.

With the pressures of the year, Goats will also value their home life. Here shared activities and projects can be especially appreciated. In this busy year it is important other activities (and concerns) do not make too many incursions into home life. Also, Goats should be forthcoming and talk through any problems they may have. The more open they are, the more helpfully others can respond.

They will also value their social life. Their personal interests can bring them into contact with others and some will join local groups and/or decide to help with activities or charities in their area (Dog years have a strong altruistic element.)

However, while the year will see many happy occasions, Goats will need to be mindful of the feelings of those around them. A careless comment could mar an occasion or undermine a friendship. Goats, take note. Similarly, if concerned by a particular response or situation, they should aim to keep it in perspective. Dog years can sometimes trouble the sensitivities of Goats. Remember this, Goats, and try to have a thicker skin.

Overall, this is very much a year for treading carefully. Conditions could be challenging and progress difficult. However, Goats will have the chance to learn more about their capabilities and gain skills for the future. Their personal interests can develop in an encouraging manner and their family life can be of particular value in this sometimes vexing year.

Tips for the Year
Be vigilant and avoid acting without thinking through the consequences. Lapses, rush and risks could all lead to problems this year. 'It is better to be safe than sorry.' Be mindful of those around

you, liaise well and talk over any matters of concern. Dog years may not be easy, but their lessons can have important future value.

GOAT FORTUNES IN THE YEAR OF THE PIG

Goats can make much of the Pig year and enjoy some notable achievements. Many will feel more motivated than of late and be keen to pursue ideas and progress in the ways *they* want. Pig years can be inspiring and Goats are set to benefit.

At work this can be a productive year. There will be the chance for many Goats to take their career to new levels. With the experience they have behind them, they will often find themselves prime candidates when promotion opportunities arise or suitable vacancies occur elsewhere. This is very much a year to move forward. Goats can make their strengths count now – and should.

Many will make important progress in their present place of work, with some securing positions they have been working towards for some time. However, if they feel they could develop their talents better elsewhere, they should keep alert for openings as well as talk to friends and contacts. In Pig years the connections Goats have can prove very helpful in alerting them to possible vacancies or suggesting ways forward.

Prospects are also encouraging for Goats seeking work. By actively following up vacancies that appeal to them and drawing on the advice of those able to help, they can find some potentially important openings and sometimes set their career off on a more satisfying track. Such are the aspects that some Goats who take on a new role early on in the year could find other responsibilities being offered to them before the year's end.

Financial prospects are also favourably aspected and progress at work will often lead to a welcome increase in income. In addition, some Goats could benefit from a bonus, gift or funds from another source. However, to make most of any upturn, they should manage their outgoings carefully and take their time when considering costly plans and purchases. Too much haste could lead to more outlay than is necessary and not always the best decision being made. They should also be wary of risk. If tempted by anything speculative, they should check the facts and implications and seek appropriate advice. This may be a favourable year financially, but Goats should not become careless or lax, including with their personal possessions.

Their interests and recreational pursuits can bring them a lot of pleasure this year. Many Goats will be feeling inspired and will enjoy developing their ideas and using their talents in satisfying ways. Those with aspirations to take an interest or skill further should promote what they do. This is a year to be proactive. Any Goats who start it feeling unfulfilled or discontented should give some thought to what they would like to do. Taking up a new recreational pursuit could be just the tonic they need. Pig years can be inspiring, although to fully benefit Goats do need to make the most of what is offered.

The Pig year can also bring an increase in social activity and many Goats will see their social circle widening considerably as a result.

For the unattached, there will also be excellent romantic possibilities. Some Goats will find that someone they meet now quickly becomes an important part of their life, while those already enjoying romance could settle down with someone over the year, or get engaged or married. On a personal level, these can be exciting times.

Any Goats who start the Pig year at a low personal ebb should take heart and consider ways in which they could improve their situation. Taking up a new interest, joining a local group or just going out more can mark the beginning of an encouraging new phase. For so many Goats, the Pig year can be one of positive change, but they do need to *take action* if they are to benefit.

Domestically, it can be both an active and pleasurable time. In many a Goat home there will be some proud moments as a wedding, addition to the family, academic or career success or family milestone is celebrated. With much needing to be planned, Goats will often play a pivotal role, and their ideas, creativity and thoughtfulness will be valued. However, while keen, Goats also need to be realistic about what is doable at any one time and, when possible, spread activities out as well as draw on the support of others. With exciting plans and an abundance of ideas, good planning and support can make an important difference.

Overall, the Pig year can be a special one for Goats and there will be celebrations in store for many. However, to fully benefit, Goats need to seize the moment and make the most of their talents. With a sense of purpose, backed by the support and goodwill of others, they can enjoy some notable achievements.

Tips for the Year
Take the initiative and act. Good opportunities can open up for you this year. Also, enjoy spending time with others. Those who are special to you can help make this year special as well.

Thoughts and Words of Goats

The world is a looking glass and gives back to every man the reflection of his own face. Frown at it and it will in turn look sourly upon you; laugh at it and with it, and it is a jolly, kind companion.

WILLIAM MAKEPEACE THACKERAY

Diligence is the mother of good fortune.

MIGUEL DE CERVANTES

The real voyage of discovery consists not in seeking new landscapes, but in having new eyes.

MARCEL PROUST

Always do right; this will gratify some people and astonish the rest.

MARK TWAIN

Keep away from people who try to belittle your ambitions. Small people always do that. But the really great make you feel that you too can become great.

MARK TWAIN

Twenty years from now you will be more disappointed by the things that you didn't do than by the ones you did do. So throw off the bowlines. Sail away from the safe harbour. Catch the trade winds in your sails. Explore. Dream. Discover.

MARK TWAIN

25 January 1944–12 February 1945 — *Wood Monkey*

12 February 1956–30 January 1957 — *Fire Monkey*

30 January 1968–16 February 1969 — *Earth Monkey*

16 February 1980–4 February 1981 — *Metal Monkey*

4 February 1992–22 January 1993 — *Water Monkey*

22 January 2004–8 February 2005 — *Wood Monkey*

8 February 2016–27 January 2017 — *Fire Monkey*

26 January 2028–12 February 2029 — *Earth Monkey*

12 February 2040–31 January 2041 — *Metal Monkey*

The Monkey

The Personality of the Monkey

Whether swinging from branch to branch, playing chase or sitting ruminating, there is a sense of fun about Monkeys. Lively and curious, they can be fascinating. And those born under the Monkey sign are equally compelling and have a multitude of talents to offer.

Born under the sign of fantasy, Monkeys possess a creative and inventive mind. They are resourceful, quick-witted and, should they ever find themselves in an awkward situation, have a happy knack of extricating themselves. They can be cunning and sometimes devious. And they are not averse to bending the rules, should they need to do so to get their own way.

Monkeys are also observant and well informed. They can be widely read – indeed, Monkeys tend to read anything – and many have an aptitude for foreign languages. They also have remarkably good memories, which they use to advantage. In company, they can dazzle with their swift recall. Their good humour and personable nature make them fun to be with and they are also very able to offer advice. However, behind the charm, they can be up to tricks, perhaps bringing others round to their point of view or discovering useful information. Monkeys are opportunists.

However, while they may seem breezy on the surface, some Monkeys do not always have the confidence they project. They may feel insecure, lack self-belief or be seeking attention. They can have their vulnerabilities. But they will conceal them well.

In addition, while curious about others, Monkeys themselves can be secretive and only impart the information they want to. Sometimes their tendency to cover up and be evasive can tell against them. In some relationships, if another feels they are not being sufficiently open and upfront, a barrier could form.

This also applies to matters of the heart. While wanting love and to be loved, Monkeys can anguish over their situation, over the commitment needed and over letting another person into their world. For some, it will not be an easy process. But, when settled, Monkeys often have a large family. They relate especially well to children, often seeming to rekindle the joys of their own early years. They will also encourage their children to use their imagination and have an enquiring mind.

Monkeys make stimulating company. They enjoy widespread interests and, being ever curious, are always thirsting for new experiences and ready to try something different. They have a great capacity to learn. But because they engage in so much, they can be dabblers rather than experts. In some cases, were they to focus more on a particular activity or hone a certain skill, they could achieve a greater level of success.

This also applies to work matters. Monkeys are versatile and can be drawn to all manner of industries, but they need to build up expertise and give themselves time to get established. With discipline, together with their enterprise and intellect, they are certainly capable of going far in their chosen vocation. As to what that vocation should be, Monkeys need variety and challenge and could get bored if stuck in a routine. Marketing, sales, science, politics, education, finance and show business could all appeal, but Monkeys are resourceful and can use their talents in many different ways.

They also have good money-making skills and a good head for figures. They enjoy their money too, being generous to family and friends and living in style. They also like to keep tabs on their situation and control their budget well, although there can be times when wishful thinking or a certain temptation lures them into a mistake. Monkeys like to push their luck, but need to be careful not to push it too far.

Both male and female Monkeys have great zeal as well as wide-ranging interests. The female has an especially engaging manner and a wide social circle. She is a shrewd judge of character and her opinions and advice are regularly sought. Being so observant, appearance is particularly important to her and not only does she take particular care with her clothes but also her hairstyle. Always well presented, often fashionable, she is practical, skilled and adept in so many ways.

With their outgoing nature and joy in participating, Monkeys invariably have an active life. There will always be peaks and troughs in that life too, with the troughs sometimes caused by their lack of application or decision to take an unwise risk. But Monkeys are quick learners, and optimists too, and their energy and enterprise will often ensure they get good results. Eleanor Roosevelt was a Monkey and she wrote, 'The future belongs to those who believe in the beauty of their dreams.' And the imaginative Monkey certainly dreams – and will strive hard to turn many a dream into reality.

Top Tips for Monkeys
- You are blessed with great people skills. With your engaging manner, good way with words and ability to empathize, you know how to ingratiate yourself! But while charming company, you can be secretive, too, and this can lead others into thinking that you have something to hide or are trying to distance yourself. Open up more! Communication needs to be a two-way process and less caginess on your part can lead to much more fruitful relations with those around you.
- You have an insatiable curiosity and zest for life. But you can also jump from one activity to another without reaping the full benefits. Curb your restless energy from time to time and concentrate on building up your experience in certain areas.

With greater focus, the rewards and satisfaction can be greater too.

- Although you are certainly quick-witted and like to be self-reliant, sometimes you can let your enthusiasm run away with you (Monkeys are born under the sign of fantasy) and take risks or cut corners, and this can rebound and sometimes cost you dear. Do try to remain grounded and realistic. Setting objectives and timescales will help, as will being willing to seek advice. Not even you can do everything all the time.
- You may like to be spontaneous and throw yourself into the present moment, but to realize your full potential, some long-term planning is required. Whether acquiring a particular qualification, gaining a skill or keeping alert for developments in your industry or sphere of interest, by looking ahead and preparing well, you will be better placed to take advantage of opportunities (and you are certainly adept at taking advantage of opportunities).

Relations with Others

With a Rat

Enjoying active lifestyles and having a sense of fun and adventure, these two signs get on well.

In work, supremely resourceful and enterprising, they have the ideas, ambitions and talents to go far. Provided they do not try to outwit each other and they channel their efforts well, they can enjoy considerable success.

In love, these two sociable and outgoing signs can find much happiness together. The Monkey particularly appreciates the

Rat's kind and encouraging nature and skills as a homemaker. They are well suited.

With an Ox

Although these two have very different personalities, there is often good liking and respect between them.

In work, the Monkey will value and gain from the Ox's tenacious and practical approach. With their different strengths working well together and good respect and accord, they make an effective team.

In love, each will appreciate qualities found in the other. The Monkey will especially value the caring, dependable and redoubtable nature of the Ox. A good and mutually beneficial match.

With a Tiger

Lively and outgoing these two may be, but they do not always enjoy that strong an accord.

In work, they will have ideas aplenty, but, with each wanting to prevail, agreement could be lacking. They will prefer to stick to their own ways and methods.

In love, their fun-loving natures could bring them together, but, with both being strong-willed and sometimes restless, they will sooner or later clash. A challenging match.

With a Rabbit

The Monkey has great respect for the quiet and companionable Rabbit and relations between them are often good.

In work, though, their different styles could bring problems, with the action-orientated Monkey feeling inhibited by the more cautious Rabbit, who, in any case, may not be at ease with the Monkey's style and approach.

In love, relations can be considerably better. With a mutual liking of the finer things in life and many shared interests, they are well suited, and the Monkey will value the love, loyalty and serenity of the Rabbit. A good and often enduring match.

With a Dragon

With their energy, enthusiasm and many shared interests, relations between Monkey and Dragon are invariably excellent.

In work, their ideas, zest and enthusiasm can make them an effective combination and each will inspire and motivate the other. Their penchant for risks may need watching, though.

In love, they are good for each other. The Monkey will value the bold, assured and thoughtful Dragon. These two can look forward to a full and lively lifestyle and find much happiness together.

With a Snake

The Monkey is fascinated by the quiet and thoughtful ways of the Snake and relations between the two are often good.

In work, differences in outlook could lead to problems, with the Monkey geared up for action and the Snake preferring a more measured and cautious tone. Both are guarded in their approach, which can also prevent them from working well together.

In love, they complement each other well. The Monkey especially appreciates the Snake's calm, thoughtful manner. With good rapport and understanding, they can make a good match.

With a Horse

With both being spirited individuals with minds (and wills) of their own, relations could be tricky.

In work, these two may be hard-working and resourceful, but each will be keen for their own ideas and approach to prevail and their mutual wariness may prevent them from realizing their full potential.

In love, they share many interests and are active and outgoing, but their different outlooks could cause problems. The Monkey could feel uneasy about the Horse's restless and sometimes volatile nature as well as their forthright tendencies. A challenging match.

With a Goat

These two relate well together and relations between them are good.

In work, the Monkey will appreciate and encourage the Goat's creative talents and they can combine their ideas and strengths well. With good respect between them, they make an effective team.

In love, these two outgoing, sociable and fun-loving signs can form a close and meaningful relationship. The Monkey will especially value the Goat's homemaking skills as well as their kindly and good-natured ways. They are good for each other.

With another Monkey

With so much to do and share, who better to do it with than another Monkey? Relations between the two can be excellent.

In work, their combined enterprise, guile and inventiveness are certainly capable of delivering, but these two need to remain focused and disciplined. If not, they could find themselves going off on different tangents and spreading their energies too widely.

In love, they can enjoy a happy and harmonious relationship, many laughs and a multitude of interests and activities. They will support and encourage each other and have a talent for bringing out the best in each other. A splendid match.

With a Rooster

With such different styles and personalities, relations between these two could be poor.

In work, the Monkey will be keen to get results and will find the Rooster's assiduous planning and caution inhibiting. There will be little accord between them.

In love, the Monkey may admire the self-assuredness and attentiveness of the Rooster, but prefers a spontaneous lifestyle and could find their orderly and candid ways irksome. A difficult match.

With a Dog

Both these signs take time to feel at ease with another person, but as they get to know each other better, they can form a good and mutually beneficial bond.

In work, they can combine their strengths to good effect, with the Monkey gaining from the Dog's disciplined and persistent approach. When united in a goal, they are capable of accomplishing a great deal.

In love, the Monkey places much trust in the stalwart and dependable Dog and values their loyalty and judgement. Their different personalities complement each other well and together they can find much happiness.

With a Pig

Relations between these two active and fun-loving signs can be excellent.

In work, there is good cooperation and respect, with the Monkey valuing the Pig's work ethic and commercial acumen. With both being enterprising, they can make a highly successful combination.

In love, these two understand each other well and the Monkey will appreciate the Pig's homemaking skills as well as their loving and supportive nature. With many shared interests and a fondness for the good life, they can find much happiness together.

Horoscopes for Each of the Chinese Years

MONKEY FORTUNES IN THE YEAR OF THE RAT

This is the start of a new cycle of animal years and what a start for Monkeys! Not only are Rats and Monkeys highly compatible signs, but Monkeys can come into their own in Rat years. This is a time of growth and opportunity and many Monkeys will thrive in the favourable conditions. Particularly for any feel they have been languishing of late, this is a year to seize the initiative and *make things happen.*

As the year starts, Monkeys could find it helpful to set themselves a plan. By deciding on some objectives and working towards them, they can set important developments in motion. Indeed, serendipity can be a good friend this year, with Monkeys often lucky with their timing and in the right place at the right time.

At work, important progress can be made, and for Monkeys on a career path, there will often be the opportunity to take on greater responsibilities and secure promotion. Rat years encourage Monkeys' special talents, and Monkeys whose work involves communication and/or has an element of creativity can enjoy some notable successes. This is very much a time for Monkeys to be active and promote their strengths.

For Monkeys who are feeling unfulfilled or consider their prospects are limited where they are, this is also a time to take the initiative. By keeping alert for openings and considering ways in which they could develop their career, these Monkeys can identify and secure some important chances. Similarly, those seeking work will find that by emphasizing their skills and acting quickly when they see openings, they may be offered what can be an excellent opportunity. For some, the Rat year can mark the start of a more satisfying chapter in their working life.

Monkeys are by nature resourceful, and not only can this benefit them in a professional capacity this year, but in their interests too. During the year they should set time aside for these. Some could develop in an encouraging fashion, particularly if they have a creative element. Some Monkeys could be tempted by something new and enjoy the challenge this offers. Keen and inspired, whatever they do, Monkeys can get a lot of pleasure from their own pursuits this year.

Financial matters are also favourably indicated and progress at work will increase the income of many Monkeys. Some could also benefit from the receipt of additional sums or putting an interest or skill to profitable use. The active and enterprising can fare well this year. However, to make the most of any upturn, Monkeys should manage their outgoings with care, considering and costing purchases rather than rushing to buy and, if able, making provision for the longer term. With care, many can improve their overall situation and enjoy the benefits of their good work.

With their outgoing nature, Monkeys will once again welcome the social opportunities that come their way, and Rat years can provide a lively mix of things to do. Some important friendships and connections can be made, and for the unattached, Rat years can surprise and delight, with a chance meeting often leading to significant romance. These can be special times for many Monkeys.

Their home life, too, will see much activity and there may be some personal and family achievements to mark, including, for some, an addition to the family. Also, if there are ideas or home improvements that Monkeys have been considering for a while, this is a good year to make a start. When plans are set in motion, a lot can be accomplished, and new comforts and enhancements will be appreciated in many a Monkey home.

Throughout the year Monkeys will also give valued support to loved ones, including offering advice and helping when decisions need to be taken. Family members will often marvel at just how much they seem to be able to do, but Monkeys enjoy being the driving force behind events. They are both active and caring.

The Rat year is one of the best for Monkeys and they can make it a very successful time. If they follow through their ideas, they will often find that fortuitous developments and the support of those around them can lead to a lot being achieved. Monkeys have a lot in their favour this year and should use their time well.

Tips for the Year
This is a new cycle of animal years – look on this as a year to make more of yourself and push forward. With purpose, action and often helpful opportunities, you can accomplish a great deal. Also, value your good relations with others in this auspicious year. And enjoy yourself.

Monkey Fortunes in the Year of the Ox

For Monkeys, who like to get on and do, the Ox year can be frustrating. Results can take time to filter through and Monkeys may find their progress modest. However, while the year can see a slowdown in activity, it can, nevertheless, be a valuable one. Ox years are excellent for taking stock and reappraising situations. They are also good for enjoying the present rather than being forever in a hurry or looking ahead.

For Monkeys, one of the Ox year's most valuable aspects will be their relations with others. Quality time with loved ones can lead to many fine occasions, while shared interests and projects can be particularly satisfying and there can be some good travel opportunities too.

As with any year, there will be decisions that need taking and situations that may be concerning. But if matters are talked through, much can be satisfactorily addressed and agreed upon. Indeed, some collective decisions can prove important, especially when family members are facing decisions or some purchases need to be made for the home. This is very much a year for the Monkey household to join together and appreciate one another's contribution.

Monkeys will also welcome the year's social opportunities, including the chance to meet up with their friends. In some instances, when they are considering ideas or mulling over possibilities, they could know someone who could prove to be of particular help. Their relations with others can again be of especial value this year.

Given the favourable aspects, any Monkeys who may be lonely or feel their life is lacking sparkle would do well to consider joining in with activities and social groups in their area. By making enquiries and taking part, many can add a beneficial element to their lifestyle. Ox years are excellent for taking stock and looking to improve areas which Monkeys may feel are in some way lacking.

This can also be an interesting year for affairs of the heart. However, new relationships should be allowed to develop steadily and in their own time. If there is no pressure in the early stages, they will often have a better chance of becoming more established. Ox years are not ones to hurry.

Personal interests too can bring much satisfaction. Monkeys who have been involved in longer-term projects could now see them reach a successful conclusion. Any Monkeys who have let their interests lapse should look to rectify this over the year. Spending time on activities they enjoy can do them a lot of good.

Monkeys would also do well to give some consideration to their well-being and lifestyle and, should they feel below par, seek medical advice. This is not a year for ignoring ailments or concerns.

Work-wise, the Ox year can also be constructive. In view of recent changes, many Monkeys will be content to remain in their present place of work and improve their skills. By concentrating on their objectives and focusing on areas they know, these Monkeys will not only enjoy a more settled period but also become more established in their sector. It is making the most of the now that is so important in the Ox year. As the year develops, however, a few Monkeys could benefit from developments that allow them to focus on more specific tasks.

For Monkeys who are interested in making a change or are seeking work, the Ox year can be challenging. Not only could there be a limited number of suitable vacancies but many Monkeys could become frustrated by the length of time it takes for some applications to be processed. Wheels move slowly in Ox years and Monkeys will need to be patient and to persevere. Rather than looking to switch to a different type of work, they will find their best chances will come in areas where they already have proven experience. Effort will be required this year, but results will be all the more deserved when they do come.

In money matters, Ox years can be expensive, especially as Monkeys will be keen to travel and also to buy certain pieces of equipment. In view of this, they should plan ahead and be wary of succumbing to too many impulse buys. This is a year for good budgeting. Similarly, they need to be attentive when dealing with financial correspondence. Rush, assumptions or delays could be to their disadvantage. Monkeys, take note.

Ox years may lack the pace of some, but they can be good for Monkeys. Although they may feel frustrated at times, they will have the chance to enjoy what is around them and put their lifestyle into better balance. This is a time to take stock and enjoy the present. Home life, personal interests and travel can be especially satisfying, and in work, too, there will be the chance to use and improve skills. Ox years can offer Monkeys both personal and lifestyle benefits.

Tips for the Year
Be realistic in your aims. This is not a year to go off on tangents or spread your energies too widely. Focus on the present and make the most of it. Also, seize any chances to add to your skills. This can pay dividends later.

MONKEY FORTUNES IN THE YEAR OF THE TIGER

Tiger years have vitality and energy, but they also hold traps for the unwary. And Monkeys will need to exercise care. Pressures and problems could be a feature of the year and sometimes the wisest course could be to keep a low profile. Difficulties can *and will* blow over and volatile situations settle down, but in the meantime Monkeys need to proceed carefully and be on their guard.

Almost as soon as the Tiger year starts, Monkeys will get a taste of what it can bring. In work, new practices and procedures could be introduced, staff movements occur and delays add to the pressure and workload. Both at the start of the year and during it there will be uncomfortable moments, with Monkeys having to adapt accordingly.

In addition, while Monkeys usually have excellent people skills, they need to pay particular attention to their relations with their colleagues. Failure to do so could leave them isolated, criticized and/or undermined. In this exacting year, Monkeys need to keep their wits about them as well as be careful not to exacerbate any awkward situation. Monkeys, take careful note and tread carefully.

Some of the changes that occur can, however, give rise to opportunities, and, if tempted, Monkeys should put themselves forward.

Those who are looking for a change or seeking work should also remain active and alert. Chances can arise quickly and if Monkeys are swift in showing interest, their enthusiasm and skills could lead to success. Their best prospects will, though, be in areas where they have proven expertise rather than in anything very different.

For work matters, the second half of the year will often be easier and more productive than the first.

The need for care also applies to money matters. Throughout the year Monkeys will need to remain disciplined and give careful thought to spending decisions. If not, outgoings could all too easily creep up and be greater than budgeted for. Monkeys also need to be wary of risk and carefully check the terms and implications of any large transactions. Haste or assumptions could lead to possible loss. Monkeys, take note and be vigilant.

Although Monkeys lead active lifestyles, they could also find it to their advantage to give some thought to their well-being. With the pressures of the year and, for some, long hours at work, it is important that they take regular and appropriate exercise as well as have a balanced diet. If they have any concerns or decide to make changes, they should seek guidance.

In addition, they should try to go away at some point during the year. A break and change of scene can do them good.

The Tiger year's high level of activity will also be seen in domestic life, and while usually adept at keeping tabs on a great many activities, even Monkeys could be bewildered by all that is requiring attention. Accordingly, they should ensure that all in the household play their part and assist at busy times as well as talk through any matters of concern. Also, plans will need to be kept flexible and adjusted accordingly. Tiger years are not ones to plough on regardless.

However, amid the considerable activity, there will be special times to appreciate. For some, there could be a family event or milestone to celebrate and a personal achievement to mark. In addition, Monkeys will find their talent for coming up with ideas appreciated by those around them, with suggestions for joint activities (and treats) leading to some fun times together.

With the pressures of the year, Monkeys should also ensure their personal life does not get sidelined. Regular contact with their friends can be helpful and if they receive invitations or hear of events that appeal to them, they should follow these up. Their social life can help their overall lifestyle balance. However, with aspects as they are, if they find themselves in a delicate, difficult or inflammatory situation, they should be wary and discreet.

They need to keep their wits about them in Tiger years and be considered in their responses.

They should also allow time for their personal interests, as these can not only help them relax and unwind but also inspire them. Over the year many Monkeys could particularly delight in trying something new and pleasingly different.

Monkeys set about their activities with considerable verve, but in the Tiger year some of their plans and actions could be problematic. Pressures, changes and unhelpful situations could all make progress difficult. However, while this is not an easy time for them, Monkeys are resourceful, and by keeping alert, adapting and, when necessary, keeping a low profile, they can emerge from the year with skills and experience they can build on. In many ways, Tiger years prepare Monkeys for better times to come.

Tips for the Year

Talk to others, liaise with them, give them your time, be aware of their views. Your relations with those around you need careful and adroit handling this year. Also, be careful in money matters, particularly with spending levels. At work, watch developments closely and look to further your knowledge and skills. By making the most of the present, you can learn important lessons.

MONKEY FORTUNES IN THE YEAR OF THE RABBIT

Rabbit years are favourable for Monkeys and encourage them to make more of their ideas and strengths. As a result, many can look forward to making good progress as well as seeing the fruition of certain plans. For Monkeys who have felt hampered or frustrated in the previous Tiger year, this is a time to move ahead rather than feel hindered by what has gone before.

One of the strengths of Monkeys is their resourceful nature. They are keen and generate many ideas, and it is these talents, together with their ability to think ahead, that can serve them particularly well this year.

At work, some will already have detected patterns in their industry which could have potential for the future, and by finding out more, they can position themselves to benefit. Similarly, experience they have built up in their workplace can prove useful as promotion opportunities arise or staff are required for more specialist duties. The skills of many Monkeys can be recognized and rewarded this year.

For Monkeys who work in a creative environment, this is an excellent time to promote their ideas. Their input and initiative will often meet with a pleasing response. As the saying reminds us, 'Nothing ventured, nothing gained,' and in Rabbit years, Monkeys should venture.

Many Monkeys can make considerable progress in their current place of work this year, but for those who feel their prospects could be bettered by a move elsewhere or are seeking work, the Rabbit year can open up important possibilities. By considering the type of position they would like to take on, many of these Monkeys could have ideas or receive advice that will indicate the best way forward. Securing a position will involve much effort, but their approach, ideas and personable nature will help. By showing initiative in their application and a willingness to take on new challenges, many will be rewarded with a new and fulfilling role.

The encouraging aspects also apply to personal interests. Again creative pursuits are especially well aspected and ideas put forward now could be well received. Rabbit years nurture Monkeys' strengths. Projects started too can often be absorbing and open the way to other possibilities. Rabbit years have both present and long-term value.

Both in their interests and their work, Monkeys can also benefit from the support of those around them. Some influential people can be particularly encouraging. Throughout the year, Monkeys should seize any chances to get to know others and, in professional situations, network. Their efforts to engage and raise their profile can help in many of their activities.

Similarly, they should make the most of the year's social opportunities. Rabbit years can offer a pleasing mix of things to do, including some surprising and nicely different ones. Monkeys who would welcome the chance to meet more people will find that pursuing their interests can often lead to meeting like-minded people. And for some, romance can make this already promising year even more special.

Often on inspired form, Monkeys will also be keen to make changes to their home. They will derive a lot of pleasure from considering possibilities, discussing ideas and appreciating the improvements. Some may even decide to relocate. Rabbit years are very much ones for forging ahead with plans and bringing about positive change.

Although domestically, the year will see some especially busy and intense periods, there will also be some very special times. Monkeys will often be appreciative of the support of their loved ones and the Rabbit year favours togetherness.

This can also be a positive year financially. Progress made at work can improve the income of many Monkeys. However, with the possibility of some moving and many spending additional amounts on their home, as well as all their existing commitments, they need to proceed carefully and take the time to ensure their decisions are right. Where large purchases are concerned, by waiting, some could benefit from favourable buying opportunities as well as be fortunate in some purchases. Indeed, their talent for spotting items in the most unusual places can lead to some ideal buys.

Overall, the Rabbit year is a favourable one for Monkeys. During it they can use their strengths to good effect and profit from their opportunities. They will also be helped by their good relations with others. They have much in their favour and can gain some pleasing rewards.

Tips for the Year
Enjoy spending time with your family and friends and seize any chances to meet new people. Domestically and romantically, this can be a special and active year. Also, make the most of your ideas and creative talents. These can develop in often encouraging ways.

Monkey Fortunes in the Year of the Dragon

Exciting times ahead. This is a year which can deliver change, especially for Monkeys who start it nurturing a particular ambition or keen to see an improvement in their situation. For some, it can mark a turning point. Dragon years are supportive of Monkeys and the year's vitality and the Monkey's resourcefulness are a powerful combination.

This will be especially evident in work situations. In view of the experience many Monkeys have built up, they will often be in an excellent position to advance their career. For some, promotion will beckon or, if openings are limited where they are, they could successfully make a move elsewhere. This is no year to stand still. Particularly for those on a career path or keen to progress in a certain way, some excellent (and sometimes timely) chances can arise, but they do need to be acted on quickly.

Throughout the year Monkeys can find that their initiative is also capable of bringing rewards. Whether putting forward ideas or enquiring about possibilities, their proactive approach will often impress and lead to developments in their favour. In Dragon years, Monkeys can make their talents and presence very much felt.

For those who are currently unfulfilled and desire change, as well as those seeking work, there are interesting prospects in store. By keeping alert for openings, these Monkeys can succeed in securing a position with the potential for development and growth. Also, those who take on new duties early on in the year could have the chance to expand their role in the later months. Work-wise, the skills, efforts and resourcefulness of Monkeys can come into their own this year.

Progress at work can also bring a welcome rise in income. However, any increase could tempt Monkeys to spend and, without care, outgoings could start to mount up. Ideally, Monkeys should plan key purchases as well as consider setting funds aside for future requirements. Good management can be to their advantage both now and later.

With their enquiring mind, Monkeys enjoy wide interests and over the year these can bring them considerable pleasure. New ideas and pursuits can capture the imagination of many Monkeys and they will enjoy the chance to try something different. Dragon years reward a game and enthusiastic approach. Some Monkeys could also benefit by seeking instruction in a subject which intrigues them. By doing something definite, they can not only find their activities satisfying but also leading on to other possibilities.

They will also enjoy sharing their activities. Monkeys who are members of groups or are active in their community could find their involvement growing over the year and their skills and enthusiasm being valued. For many, Dragon years can see an increase in social activity. These can be active and often fun times.

For unattached Monkeys, a chance meeting could seem as if it was meant to be, and it may be the start of a long and meaningful relationship.

Monkeys can also look forward to an active home life, although, with a lot happening and commitments changing, there will need to be good cooperation as well as some flexibility over arrangements. However, Monkeys are adept at organizing and they will be the driving force behind some of the projects that are carried out, in addition to suggesting and making plans for activities (including for a possible holiday) that everyone can enjoy. A lot revolves around Monkeys this year and those close to them will have good reason to value their organizational skills.

In general, the Dragon year offers great scope for Monkeys and, by making the most of themselves, their skills and their chances, they can accomplish a great deal. This is a year to seize the initiative and move forward. For Monkeys who are nurturing particular ambitions or hopes, *now* is the time to act. This can be one of the best years for Monkeys, but it does require application on their part.

Tips for the Year
Act. Once wheels are set in motion, you can go far. Also, embrace the new, whether new duties, new interests or new opportunities. Value the support of others as well, and enjoy spending time with those who are close to you.

Monkey Fortunes in the Year of the Snake

A reasonable year ahead, although during it Monkeys would do well to adopt a more measured approach. Monkeys do like to spread their energies and involve themselves in a great many activities, but this year the best results will come from focused and concentrated effort. To dabble or jump from one activity to another will limit effectiveness as well as sometimes undermine prospects. In Snake years Monkeys need to channel their energies wisely.

At work, in particular, they should focus on priorities and avoid being drawn into less productive or petty matters. Snake years require discipline. Also, Monkeys should work closely with their colleagues and be active in their team or unit. By contributing and using their skills to advantage, they will not only accomplish more now but be helping their prospects for the future. In addition, they should avail themselves of any training opportunities as well as keep themselves informed of trends within their industry. With involvement and participation, their efforts will, in time, be well rewarded.

For Monkeys who decide to move from where they are or are seeking work, this can be an important year. Although the job-seeking process will be challenging and they may experience disappointments in their quest, their commitment will often prevail. It will take considerable effort, but by making enquiries and investigating possibilities, they can uncover opportunities and be rewarded with the offer of a new position. In many instances, it will come with a steep learning curve and require adjustment, including to routine, but it will give many Monkeys the chance to establish themselves in a new capacity.

In money matters, although many Monkeys will enjoy a rise in income and could also benefit from an additional sum, they will need to control their budget. To make purchases or enter into agreements too hurriedly could lead to problems and regret. As with so much this year, Monkeys need to be vigilant *and* take their time.

An important feature of Snake years is the way that Monkeys can further their knowledge and skills, not only in a professional capacity but with personal interests too. By setting time aside for activities they favour and looking to develop their ideas, they can make this a satisfying time. Some could especially benefit from going on study courses or investing in equipment which would further their capabilities. In addition, with the Snake year's emphasis on culture, if they see events or exhibitions which appeal to them, they should aim to go. Snake years encourage self-development and a broadening of the mind.

They also provide an interesting mix of things to do. As always, Monkeys will appreciate their chances to go out. However, while a lot will go well, they need to be on their guard. An ill-timed comment or oversight could prove embarrassing.

Similarly, where romance is concerned, Monkeys need to be attentive, mindful and true. This is no year for personal lapses or to take the feelings of another person for granted. Monkeys, take note.

This need for awareness also applies to home life. Sometimes, with the pressures of work or concern over certain situations, Monkeys may become preoccupied or lack their usual patience. At such times, it is important they are forthcoming about their concerns and talk openly to others. This way not only can those around them better understand, but they may also be able to assist more with certain tasks and chores. This year in particular, Monkeys should not regard some activities as just their preserve but draw readily on the assistance that is available to them. Also, while Monkeys and their family members will have various commitments, preserving some quality time to share can be good for all. Time and awareness will be important factors this year.

With their keen and eager nature, Monkeys like to make the most of their situation. However, in the Snake year they will need to concentrate on the things they *can* do rather than those they *would like* to do. In their relations with others, they need to be attentive and thoughtful, as this is a year to tread carefully, liaise, listen and be aware. It may not be the best or smoothest of years, but with care, and the Monkey's usual consummate skill, it will not necessarily be a bad one either. And by making the most of it, Monkeys can do much to prepare themselves for the chances that lie ahead.

Tips for the Year

Be mindful of others. Distraction, preoccupation or even an uncharacteristic *faux pas* could cause difficulty. Be careful and attentive. Also, seize any chances to further your knowledge and skills, both professionally and personally. What you learn now can be to your present and future advantage.

MONKEY FORTUNES IN THE YEAR OF THE HORSE

Monkeys are quick to spot opportunities and also adept at making the most of their situation. And the Horse year *will* contain good possibilities, but there is a 'but'. In this busy and fast-moving year, Monkeys need to be careful not to overreach themselves or push their luck too far. To be careless, over-zealous or try to do just too much could lead to difficulty and disappointment. Throughout the year Monkeys need to be vigilant *and* realistic.

At work, prospects are encouraging. With Horse years often seeing change, Monkeys will be keen to take advantage. Whether through staff movements, new initiatives or changing workloads, there will be opportunities they can pursue. Some of what arises could mean a shift in responsibility and require training, but by being adaptable and willing, many Monkeys can make useful headway.

For those who are feeling staid or unfulfilled or would like a new challenge, the Horse year could offer just the chance they need. In some cases, the responsibilities they take on now can mark a new juncture in their working life.

There could be interesting opportunities for Monkeys seeking work as well. By not being too restrictive in their search, many could secure a new position which offers the chance to re-establish themselves. Again there could be considerable readjustment involved, but what is obtained now can re-energize their career and prospects. Horse years reward effort and commitment and many Monkeys are set to do well.

However, while the aspects are generally promising, a warning does need to be sounded. Although game, Monkeys need to be realistic in what they take on. To overcommit themselves, be lax or rush could leave them vulnerable and prone to error. Horse years can be exacting taskmasters and have high expectations.

Financial prospects are good, however, with some Monkeys benefiting from a gift, bonus or the fruition of a policy. However, while additional money may flow their way, they need to be careful not to let it flow away again. Extravagance could lead to regret. Horse years require Monkeys to be vigilant and on their mettle.

With the active nature of the Horse year, Monkeys will welcome the travel opportunities that come their way and by planning a holiday in advance can look forward to visiting some impressive attractions as well as enjoying some new experiences. Over the year some exciting ideas can take shape and there may also be the chance of some short and often surprise breaks.

Monkeys should also make sure they set aside some time for their own interests. These can add valuable balance to their lifestyle as well as provide opportunities to go out and meet others. Monkeys who lead particularly busy lifestyles, do give yourself the chance to relax and unwind now and then.

Their social life can also add valuable balance and they will welcome the many and varied social opportunities of the year.

During it, many Monkeys can considerably extend their social circle as well as meet some people with very different lifestyles from their own. Again their ability to converse and engage can make them popular company. However, while having great social skills, Monkeys can at times be secretive and in some cases this could lead to misinterpretation and resentment. Monkeys, take note. Greater openness this year will not go amiss.

This also applies to their home life. With a lot happening at an often fast pace, Monkeys do need to regularly consult others and talk through their plans and hopes. This way they can not only benefit from the advice they are given and find some plans quickly advancing, but also, importantly, prevent misunderstandings. This is a time favouring shared and considered approaches. Should any disagreement arise, often caused by pressure and tiredness, it is important this is addressed and a solution found rather than matters be left to fester. Greater care and attention could help in a lot this year.

Horse years can see high levels of activity, and to do well, Monkeys need to channel their energies and efforts. With commitment, they can gain skills and experience that can be important stepping stones to later success. However, to benefit, they do need to act quickly when they see opportunities and be prepared to adapt. They also need to pay careful attention to their relations with others as well as maintain a good lifestyle balance. Overall, a constructive year, but one requiring a disciplined approach.

Tips for the Year
Prioritize and concentrate your efforts. With application, you can enjoy some good results and gain experience that can be of later benefit. Also, enjoy your personal interests, travel and time spent with others, but do remain organized and balance out all your activities.

Monkey Fortunes in the Year of the Goat

Inventive, resourceful and ambitious, Monkeys are adept at making the most of situations and can again do so in the Goat year. Goat years favour creativity and thinking outside the box, and when Monkeys have ideas or can use their skills to advantage, they should act. With initiative and drive, they can make useful advances.

At work in particular, prospects are encouraging and many Monkeys will have the chance to make more of specific strengths. Often this will be in their present place of work and their in-house knowledge will be a valuable asset. For those who work in communication or the media and whose role has an element of creativity, this can be an especially rewarding time.

For Monkeys who feel their prospects could be bettered by a move elsewhere, as well as those seeking work, the Goat year can open up interesting possibilities. When making applications, the initiative and interest these Monkeys can show, together with emphasizing their relevant skills, can lead to many securing a new position. It will take time and some will have to revise their initial career intentions, but what many take on now can give them experience in a new area and a base to build on in the future.

Working closely with colleagues and using any chances to network and raise their profile will also help all Monkeys. By being active and contributing, they will allow those around them to better appreciate their skills and potential. However, there is a 'but'. If at any time Monkeys experience a clash of personalities or find themselves in a fraught situation, they should proceed carefully, using their people skills to defuse any tension. Some of the Goat year will require deft handling and Monkeys need to be alert and mindful throughout.

Another area requiring care is finance. Over the year many Monkeys could face additional expenses, including repair costs and replacing equipment. With these, along with their existing commitments, their outgoings will be high, and they will need to keep a close watch on spending. Also, if entering into any new agreement, they need to check the terms carefully. This is no year for risks or assumptions. Also, when out, Monkeys should look after their personal possessions. A loss could be upsetting. Monkeys, take note.

Many Monkeys will, however, have the opportunity to travel this year and they should try to make provision for a holiday. A change of scene can do them a lot of good. In addition, some will enjoy visiting friends and relations some distance away as well as have the chance to see some impressive attractions.

With the year's emphasis on creativity, Monkeys can also find their personal interests satisfying. New ideas could be exciting and some Monkeys will find projects they start broadening out in scope over the year.

Monkeys should also give some attention to their own well-being, including the quality of their diet and their level of exercise. If either is deficient, they should take advice on ways to improve. The changes they make could have a noticeable difference on how they feel. They should also seek advice if feeling below par at any time. In the Goat year, some self-care is important.

With their genial nature, Monkeys enjoy company and can once more look forward to an interesting mix of social occasions. However, while many agreeable times can be had, the Goat year does call for care. The attitude of another person could be annoying, a remark could be misconstrued and/or someone could let the Monkey down. Throughout the year all Monkeys need to be on their guard and diplomatic in their responses. Over the year, the patience of many will be tested. Monkeys, take note and do to be aware of the year's more difficult elements.

Home life is set to be busy, but here too there may be awkward matters to deal with. In some instances, a problem facing a loved one could cause anxiety or a clash of interests could arise. Again the fortitude and resourcefulness of many Monkeys will be valued, and if difficulties are talked through and a consensus reached, many issues can be satisfactorily resolved.

However, while the Goat year will have its busy and sometimes stressful times domestically, with everything seeming to happen at once, there will also be pleasing occasions to look forward to. Shared projects and interests can be especially satisfying, as will a holiday or more local trips. Goat years may have their awkward aspects, but they also offer many interesting things to do.

Overall, however, Monkeys will need to keep their wits about them and be especially mindful in their relations with others. Minor issues or disagreements could be a concern and need to be addressed and handled diplomatically. However, Monkeys are skilled at handling people, and by working well with others and making the most of chances that come their way, they can make useful headway. Ideas and creative activities are particularly well aspected and the good Monkeys do this year will help pave the way for their own year, which follows.

Tips for the Year
Be mindful and alert to potentially difficult situations. Your skills and patience will be tested this year, but at the same time your qualities will be highlighted. Also, advance your ideas and build connections.

MONKEY FORTUNES IN THE YEAR OF THE MONKEY

Aware that this is their own year, Monkeys will be keen to make it special. And their actions, backed by the auspicious aspects, can make this a full and personally successful one for them. However, to get the most from it, they would do well to decide on their objectives for the next 12 months and have something definite to work towards. With some aims in mind, they will be able to achieve more. They will also be assisted by the support and goodwill of those around them. This again will help much go forward.

At work this is a year of considerable opportunity. Monkeys who are established where they are will often have the chance to benefit from promotion opportunities and take their career to a new level. Those in large organizations may also have the chance to relocate and/or transfer to another area. By keeping alert for developments and acting quickly when opportunities present themselves, many Monkeys will be well placed to advance. This is a year rich in possibility.

For Monkeys who are unfulfilled in their present position, as well as those seeking work, the Monkey year can also have significant developments in store. By considering different ways in which they could use their skills and keeping alert for vacancies, many could secure the type of position they have had in mind for some time. In many instances, there could be considerable adjustment involved, but by showing commitment, these Monkeys can soon re-establish themselves and be encouraged (quite quickly) to take on additional responsibilities. Their enthusiasm, initiative and personable manner can be an effective and winning combination.

There will also be some Monkeys who, in the view of their experience, will be keen to set up their own business. By taking professional advice and getting the appropriate support, many will be able to set their hopes and plans in motion.

Progress made at work will also help financially and this will persuade many Monkeys to go ahead with plans and purchases they have been considering for some time. Here their canny nature can stand them in excellent stead and they may secure some great buys on attractive terms. There is an element of good fortune to the year. Also, if they are able, Monkeys should consider making provision for the longer term, including possibly adding to a savings or pension policy. In years to come, they could be grateful for it.

Monkey years also offer considerable scope and Monkeys themselves will enjoy developing their interests. Both existing and new pursuits can bring much pleasure and develop in encouraging ways. For sporting and outdoor enthusiasts, the year can have exciting highlights.

In addition, with this being their own year, some Monkeys will regard it as an opportune time to make lifestyle changes. Some will start an exercise programme, while others will make dietary improvements or set time aside for study. By following through their ideas, these Monkeys could reap some fine benefits.

Travel, too, can figure prominently, and if a destination or event appeals to them, Monkeys should see what can be arranged. Some interesting plans could take shape.

The Monkey year can also see much social activity. Personal interests and local events can provide chances to go out and friends will often seek the company of Monkeys and sometimes share confidences. Here their empathy can be of particular value. However, just as Monkeys will help others, they too should avail themselves of the support and expertise others can offer. In this important year, they should not rely on just their own efforts, but benefit from the input and backing of those they know.

For the unattached, a chance meeting could quickly become special, and for those who have had recent personal difficulty, new activities and new people could put some meaning (and sparkle) back into their lives. Here again this can be a year of encouraging developments.

Home life can be busy, especially as many Monkeys will be keen to go ahead with improvements. However, while much can be accomplished, Monkeys do need to plan and cost projects carefully and discuss choices and implications with loved ones. This is a year for collective effort. There will be some celebrations too, including the possible marking of a personal or family milestone as well as individual successes. Domestically, this can be a full and exciting year.

There is a Chinese proverb which reminds us, 'He who comprehends the times is great,' and by making the most of their own year, Monkeys can enjoy many favourable results. It is a time to seize the initiative and set their plans in motion. Monkeys have much in their favour now. Overall, a year to savour.

Tips for the Year
Take action and make things happen. With purpose, the backing of others and the opportunities now emerging, you can see interesting possibilities opening up for you. Also, enjoy developing your ideas and interests and sharing many of your activities with your loved ones.

Monkey Fortunes in the Year of the Rooster

A satisfying year ahead, and while Monkeys may sometimes feel the structured nature of the Rooster year cramps their style, there will still be good gains to be had. Their personal life will see much activity and this is also an excellent time for personal development.

At work, Monkeys can fare well, but throughout the year they need to remember that the Rooster year calls for planning and sticking to the rulebook. This is no time for short cuts or lax approaches. However, while the Rooster year may not always allow the latitude Monkeys favour, its structure and discipline can be to their advantage. By focusing on their current objectives, they can not only develop greater expertise in their area of work, but also become a more integral part of their workplace.

Many Monkeys will build on their present position over the year, but for those seeking change, as well as those looking for work, the Rooster year requires a disciplined approach. When making an application, these Monkeys should find out more about the duties involved so they can highlight their suitability. By showing initiative and preparing well for interview, they can find their extra effort making a difference. Rooster years favour attention to detail. Also, when taking on a new position, by immersing themselves in their duties and adapting as required, these Monkeys can impress and be encouraged further. What is accomplished now can prepare the way for subsequent advances.

While the income of many Monkeys will increase during the year, spending levels do need to be watched, however. In addition to the appeal of certain purchases, Monkeys could face repair costs as well as increased outgoings. As a result, they need to keep track of their situation and exert sensible control over the purse-strings. They should also be careful in their dealings with others too, as there is a risk that some may fall victim to a scam, suffer as a result of unscrupulous dealings or be let down by someone. If involved in speculation or having any uncertainties over a situation, it is important that they check it out and take further advice. In money matters, this is a year to be careful and thorough.

If possible, however, Monkeys should consider making provision for travel. It is favourably aspected this year and if they plan a holiday and/or some short breaks in advance, they can not only look forward to them but profit from some useful offers. Monkeys have an adventurous nature and this can be well satisfied this year.

Personal interests can also be gratifying, and with the Rooster year's emphasis on personal development, Monkeys should consider ways in which they can develop certain talents. Some may decide to enrol on courses, seek personal instruction or set themselves a goal. They can enjoy some pleasing results.

As a result of their activities, they will find their social circle widening over the year and some people they meet could be especially helpful in certain plans or projects.

For unattached Monkeys, the Rooster year has good romantic possibilities as well, although rather than rush into a commitment, Monkeys should proceed steadily, enjoy the present and let any romance develop over time.

Also, during the year all Monkeys will face many commitments and it is important these do not make too many incursions into home life. To prevent this, Monkeys should ensure quality time is set aside to be with their loved ones and encourage shared pursuits and mutual interests. Here their thoughtfulness and input can make an important difference.

They will often be keen to carry out some home improvements over the year, and while the end result may be pleasing, the actual doing could be time-consuming. Monkeys, take note, and plan, prepare and cost your undertakings carefully. This is not a year that favours hurry and it will already be busy enough. Be careful not to overcommit yourselves.

Overall, the Rooster year can be a useful and productive one, but Monkeys need to remain watchful and disciplined. By putting in the effort and making the most of their current situation, they can enjoy some solid results and considerably enhance their prospects. Personal interests and travel can bring particular pleasure, although with many commitments, Monkeys do need to balance out all they do. Quality time with loved ones can be particularly important and meaningful and should not be overlooked.

Tips for the Year

Use your time effectively. Focus on your priorities and seize any chances to add to your knowledge and skills. Also, strive for a good lifestyle balance, including giving time to your loved ones. Extra attention can make an important difference.

MONKEY FORTUNES IN THE YEAR OF THE DOG

Monkeys set about their activities with commendable energy, but while good results can be enjoyed in the Dog year, this is a time when they should avoid risk or haste. The Dog year can trip the unwary and Monkeys need to be on their guard.

At work, good opportunities can arise and many Monkeys can further their position. Especially for those who have been in their existing role for some time, this is a year to explore fresh possibilities. Often Monkeys will find their experience and reputation standing them in excellent stead and quite a few will enjoy well-deserved (and sometimes overdue) promotion. In addition, several workplaces will see the launch of new initiatives and these will offer Monkeys the chance to have greater involvement. Their expertise will often be valued.

However, while the aspects are encouraging, Monkeys need to work closely with others and watch their independent tendencies. This is a year for participating. In addition, they should use any opportunities to network and raise their profile. Contacts and support can be important factors this year.

The Dog year will also contain fine opportunities for Monkeys who are eager to move elsewhere or are seeking work. Rather than be too narrow in what they are considering, these Monkeys should look at different types of work and other ways in which they could use their skills. By being open to possibility, many will secure a position which offers change and future potential. Work-wise, Dog years encourage Monkeys to make considerable advances and put their strengths to greater use.

Income is set to increase too, but considerable care is needed in money matters this year. If entering into any agreement, Monkeys should check the terms carefully, including the details. This is no year for risk. In addition they should be wary of speculation and take particular care if lending to another person. Misjudgements and unexpected expenses can be unwelcome features of Dog years. Monkeys, take note and do remain disciplined and vigilant in financial matters.

With the busy lifestyle Monkeys lead, it is also important that their personal interests do not get sidelined. These can be a valuable part of their lifestyle. Existing pursuits can bring particular pleasure this year and new ideas or ways of broadening skills open up fresh possibilities. While spending needs to be watched, some Monkeys may acquire equipment which will extend their capabilities. In the Dog year, interests and recreational pursuits can be satisfying and a good outlet for Monkey talents.

This will also be a rewarding year for domestic activities, with Monkeys helped (and buoyed up) by the support they are given. Throughout the year they should be open about their thoughts and listen carefully to the advice of family members. Even though some of it may be cautionary, it will be said with their best interests at heart. Monkeys, do take heed.

With Monkeys and other family members making advances at work, the Dog year will have a progressive feel to it, and there may be news and a surprising family development to celebrate too. Where practical activities are concerned, however, timescales need to be kept fluid. Delays and interruptions could impede progress and a certain amount of patience be needed.

Socially, the Dog year can bring an interesting mix of things to do, and Monkeys who are tempted by particular events or receive invitations would do well to follow them up. The social occasions of the year can add value and balance to their lifestyle. There will be some lively times to enjoy, and when they are facing changes or decisions, Monkeys will appreciate being able to draw on the expertise of their friends.

For Monkeys enjoying romance, this can become more significant as the year develops, while those who are unattached could find a chance meeting leading to new love. Dog years have the capacity to surprise.

Monkeys can fare well in Dog years, but need to keep their wits about them. This is a time for care and caution, especially in money matters. Throughout the year, Monkeys should liaise well with those around them and watch their independent tendencies. Monkeys like to be their own master, but with support, consultation and listening to advice, they will fare that much better. In their home and social life there will be good times and news to share, and overall this can be a busy and often pleasing year, but Monkeys do need to watch developments and respond positively to them.

Tips for the Year
Make the most of unfolding situations. Pleasing headway can be made both at work and with your personal interests. Also, be mindful of others and draw on the support and advice of those around you. And take care with money matters.

MONKEY FORTUNES IN THE YEAR OF THE PIG

Monkeys are resourceful and quick-witted and have a talent for making the most of situations. However, in the Pig year they will need to exercise care. This is a year to proceed cautiously and be thorough. Additional pressures may arise and activities may not always go as smoothly as Monkeys would like. Pig years have their awkward elements, but by being alert and careful, Monkeys can do much to minimize their effects.

Many Monkeys will face an increased workload this year, as additional duties are added to what they already do. Some tasks could be daunting and objectives challenging. However, while this can be an exacting time, by focusing on what needs to be done, Monkeys can still achieve some notable successes and in the process gain what can be valuable experience. In their work, though, they need to be careful not to let standards slip or to bend the rules. To do so could leave them open to censure and undermine the good work they have done. Monkeys, take note.

The majority of Monkeys will continue to build on their present position, but for those seeking change or looking for work, the Pig year can have important developments in store. Obtaining a new position will not be easy, but by putting in for vacancies that appeal to them and stressing their skills and experience, many of these Monkeys will find their persistence rewarded. Again, though, what they take on will ask a lot of them, especially as there will be new routines to adjust to and often a lot learn. Pig years expect a lot of Monkeys and it rests with them to deliver and be thorough in what they do. However, by rising to the challenge, many Monkeys will soon establish themselves.

The year's need for care also applies to financial matters. With a busy lifestyle and plans in mind, Monkeys need to watch their spending and set themselves a budget for specific activities. The better their control, the better the outcomes will be. They also need to be wary of taking risks or entering into commitments without fully checking the terms and details. Carelessness or haste could be to their disadvantage. Monkeys, take note.

With their lively nature, Monkeys will appreciate the increase in social activity that the Pig year will bring and will attend a variety of events. For the music, sport and entertainment enthusiast, the Pig year can serve up some veritable delights. Certain interests can also have a pleasing social element and give rise to some memorable times, and, as always, Monkeys will also enjoy meeting up with their friends.

Romance, too, can add joy to the year, with many relationships developing well. However, while Pig years can bring their pleasures, Monkeys do need to remain mindful of those around them and tread carefully in any delicate or awkward situation. Lapses could risk undermining their position.

In their home life there will be much to occupy them. Loved ones could face key decisions this year and the support and advice Monkeys give could be of particular value. In addition, with changes likely to be happening and much else besides, their ability to keep tabs on (as well as remember) so much will prove a real asset. Monkeys will be a mainstay of many a household this year and will enjoy all the activity. The Pig year will see quite a few domestic changes and improvements.

Although Monkeys will already be kept occupied, their personal interests can also develop in interesting fashion. Some Monkeys may become intrigued by a new pursuit, join a local society or spend time on an idea. Whatever they do, they can enjoy the way their interests develop this year.

Some positive lifestyle changes can be made too. Monkeys lacking regular exercise could benefit from taking advice on activities that may be suitable and then trying them out.

Overall, the Pig year has its pressures and Monkeys will need to put in a lot of effort to secure results. This is no time to be half-hearted or lax. Risk, rush or carelessness can all undermine the good that has already been done. However, while the year can be demanding, it can be instructive too, and the challenges it brings will give Monkeys the chance to extend their experience. This can be a valuable legacy of the Pig year, especially as prospects are so very much improved in the following Rat year.

Tips for the Year
Proceed with care. Avoid rush. Think responses through. Be thorough. Check facts, details and implications. Also, use your skills. The experience you gain now can have much future benefit.

Thoughts and Words of Monkeys

Man needs, for his happiness, not only the enjoyment of this or that, but hope and enterprise and change.

BERTRAND RUSSELL

Anything you're good at contributes to happiness.

BERTRAND RUSSELL

'Where there is a will there is a way' is an old and true saying. He who resolves upon doing a thing, by that very resolution often scales the barriers to it, and secures its achievements.

SAMUEL SMILES

Those who are the most persistent, and work in the true spirit, will invariably be the most successful.

SAMUEL SMILES

Great results cannot be achieved at once, and we must be satisfied to advance in life as we walk – step by step.

SAMUEL SMILES

Life will always be to a large extent what we ourselves make it.

SAMUEL SMILES

Life was meant to be lived, and curiosity must be kept alive. One must never, for whatever reason, turn one's back on life.

ELEANOR ROOSEVELT

26 January 1933–13 February 1934 — *Water Rooster*

13 February 1945–1 February 1946 — *Wood Rooster*

31 January 1957–17 February 1958 — *Fire Rooster*

17 February 1969–5 February 1970 — *Earth Rooster*

5 February 1981–24 January 1982 — *Metal Rooster*

23 January 1993–9 February 1994 — *Water Rooster*

9 February 2005–28 January 2006 — *Wood Rooster*

28 January 2017–15 February 2018 — *Fire Rooster*

13 February 2029–1 February 2030 — *Earth Rooster*

The Rooster

The Personality of the Rooster

In China the Rooster is associated with the five virtues. Its crown symbolizes authority; its spurs represent the military; it displays courage in standing up for itself and benevolence in sharing grain; and its early morning crowing shows reliability and trustworthiness. Those born under the Rooster sign are similarly blessed with many qualities.

Born under the sign of candour, Roosters are direct and no-nonsense sort of people. They stand their ground and say what they think. And while their frank manner may sometimes offend, they are well meaning and honourable and their opinions are respected. With the Rooster you know exactly where you stand.

Roosters are also colourful and engaging. Often smartly dressed, they care about their image and conduct themselves with dignity. To garner attention, some may be flamboyant in their manner or dress, and Roosters are not averse to being in the limelight. They enjoy company, are adept at conversation and enjoy a wide variety of activities. Roosters like to live life to the full.

As they fit so much into their days, they are also organized and good at using their time. Roosters like to prepare themselves, whether for the day, week or longer term, so they can best use their energy and opportunities. They are efficient and meticulous planners. However, in their eagerness to take action, they can sometimes be guilty of taking on more than they can sensibly handle, and at times they could find it helpful to be more discerning with commitments.

Roosters are, though, hard-working and conscientious. They care about what they do and set themselves (and others) high standards. And should they feel another person is slacking or not pulling their weight, they will be sure to let them know. Roosters can be critical, and sometimes over-analytical, but they are attentive and can be relied upon.

With their outgoing manner, the confidence they project and their willingness to take the lead, Roosters often do well in their chosen vocation. They can enjoy particular success in positions which harness their managerial skills and mastery of detail. They are skilled presenters, and marketing, commerce, PR, politics and the financial sector appeal to many. With their liking of the outdoors, farming could be another favoured occupation and some Roosters will also be attracted to uniformed professions, including the military and the police. In such roles, Roosters can look particularly distinguished as well as carry themselves with authority.

With their methodical nature, Roosters like to keep their finances in order and manage their budget carefully. They can be shrewd investors, with their analytical mind helping their decision-making. However, where money is concerned, Roosters fall into two camps. Some are disciplined in spending, while others are notoriously spendthrift and self-indulgent. And when they are out and about, particularly socializing, Roosters like to impress and tend to spend generously. They also like to live in fine style and, if they can, build up assets. With their many capabilities, that will be possible, but it will be down to how disciplined they are.

Enjoying wide interests and keeping themselves well informed, Roosters make stimulating company and enjoy an active lifestyle. Some particularly enjoy being members of clubs and social groups. They will be keen to play their part.

They also have no shortage of friends and admirers, and very much delight in the pleasures and passions of love. But to secure lasting affection, Roosters need to watch their sometimes forthright tendencies (which could cause some disquiet) as well as be more effusive in expressing their innermost feelings – not something all find easy. Once committed, however, they will be attentive, loyal and dependable, as is their nature. And they will also make sure their home is orderly and efficient and everyone is provided for. Roosters are conscientious *and care*.

If a parent, Roosters will be supportive and loving, but also strong on discipline. They like to lead by example.

The female Rooster is, like her male counterpart, outgoing and sociable. She presents herself well and with considerable aplomb. She is also perceptive and many of those around her value her thoughts and advice. She makes a good and dependable friend. She also has a good sense of fun and is particularly skilled in the art of conversation, both in expressing her thoughts and listening. Highly efficient, she applies herself to the tasks and objectives she sets herself and can enjoy considerable success in her vocation as well as in certain of her interests. She uses her talents well.

It is said that Roosters born between the hours of five and seven, both at dawn and sundown, tend to be the most extrovert of their sign, but all Roosters enjoy going out and socializing, including attending parties and big functions. With their caring nature, they could also have an interest in humanitarian issues, the welfare of others and environmental concerns. Roosters enjoy the outdoors and some have a particular fondness for gardening.

Principled, diligent and alert, Roosters have style and presence. And they do not hold back. They are bold, colourful and hard-working. With their ambition and belief, and carefully laid plans, they certainly have the ability to achieve a great deal, although on their life's journey their candour, bluster and sometimes over-zealous nature could result in some painful lessons.

But the Rooster's resilience and sterling qualities will invariably shine through and they will lead a rich, varied and often very fulfilling life.

Top Tips for Roosters

- One of your hallmarks is your ability to plan ahead. But sometimes circumstances change and flexibility is required. 'There are many routes to the top', as the saying goes, by being open to what arises and adapting accordingly, you can often achieve that much more.
- You may be born under the sign of candour, but do need to be mindful of the views and sensitivities of others. To speak hurriedly or bluntly can sometimes undermine relations. As a Chinese proverb states, 'Once you have spoken, even the swiftest horses cannot retract your words.' Take note!
- You throw yourself into your activities, drive yourself hard and enjoy socializing, but it could be good for you to pause every now and again to collect your thoughts and to be at one with yourself. Balance your lifestyle – factor some 'me time' into your busy schedule.
- While it is good that you are thorough and like to get everything right, sometimes you can get embroiled in the intricacies of detail and waste time over the inconsequential. Always try to keep the broader picture in mind and consider setting time limits for the completion of certain tasks. This will help you keep focused and moving forward.

Relations with Others

With a Rat

These two enjoy conversation and share many interests, but both speak their minds – and will.

In work, Roosters like to organize and plan and will not feel easy with the Rat's haste and style. A difficult combination.

In love, both enjoy active lifestyles, but the Rat's more spontaneous nature will not fit in with the Rooster's orderly ways. With both being strong-minded (and willed) as well as outspoken, a match could be tricky and volatile.

With an Ox

These two signs like and respect each other and relations between them are good.

In work, both are orderly, efficient and methodical, and together they will harness their strengths well. An effective and often productive team.

In love, with similar outlooks and values, these two are well suited. The Rooster will especially admire the Ox's loyal and redoubtable nature, and with both having a fondness for the outdoors and many other shared interests, they can make a successful match.

With a Tiger

Sociable and active these two signs may be, but with both being candid and upfront, relations could become tricky.

In work, their different strengths could be complementary,

with the Rooster gaining from the Tiger's enterprise, ideas and zeal, but with each keen to prevail and both forthright, lasting accord could be difficult. If they can settle their differences and be more accommodating, however, their combined abilities can take them far.

In love, each has qualities the other likes and the Rooster will admire the Tiger's open manner and sincerity. However the Tiger's restlessness and impulsive nature will not fit comfortably with the Rooster, and as both are dominant personalities, relations could become challenging.

With a Rabbit

Although each has qualities the other admires, their different personalities do not gel.

In work, the Rooster has preferred methods which do not fit in with those of the quieter, more reserved and cautious Rabbit. They do not tend to work well together.

In love, the Rooster may be attracted by the Rabbit's kindly nature and finesse, but prefers a busier lifestyle. These two live their lives at different speeds. A difficult match.

With a Dragon

The Rooster admires the zest and style of the Dragon and relations between them are good.

In work, these two are ambitious and keen and the Rooster will be enthused by the Dragon's determination and enterprise. By combining their strengths, these two could enjoy success. They certainly have the talents.

In love, they have a great understanding and each will be supportive of the other. The Rooster especially appreciates the

Dragon's confident, self-assured manner. With both liking active lifestyles, they are well suited. A good match.

With a Snake

Roosters and Snakes have a great regard for each other and relations between them are very good.

In work, these two methodical signs like to follow carefully laid plans and the Rooster will appreciate the Snake's business acumen and calm, determined nature. An effective team.

In love, they are ideally suited and enjoy excellent rapport. The Rooster values the Snake's calm, thoughtful nature and keen intellect. These two are good for each other and can find much happiness together.

With a Horse

With both being active, sociable and great conversationalists, relations for a time can be good, but their strong wills and forthright natures could make things awkward.

In work, these two are hard-working and ambitious and the Rooster will admire the Horse's determination and focus. They make an effective team, although when success comes, each will want to take the other's share of the credit!

In love, these two have style and presence. They both enjoy an active lifestyle and will have many interests to share. The Rooster will particularly value the Horse's practical and spirited nature, but with both being forthright and strong-willed, there will be difficult moments. A lively but sometimes challenging match.

With a Goat

With the Rooster being methodical and organized and the Goat more laid-back, relations between these signs are not always easy.

In work, the Rooster favours method, order and discipline, and could despair over the Goat's more easy-going approach. Neither will they be comfortable with their more innovative notions. With little empathy, working relations could be difficult.

In love, these two operate on different wavelengths. The Rooster likes an ordered lifestyle, the Goat a more relaxed one. The Rooster could find the Goat's capriciousness and mood swings difficult. A tricky match.

With a Monkey

The Rooster does not always feel at ease with the Monkey's style, manner or indeed motives. Relations do not tend to be good.

In work, the Rooster likes method and working to a plan, while the Monkey is more opportunistic and relies on wits, chances and guile. With little empathy, these two will prefer to work in their separate ways.

In love, the Rooster may find the Monkey fascinating company. Both are sociable, but as both are also independent-minded and the Monkey does have secretive tendencies, the way ahead could be tricky.

With another Rooster

Roosters are proud, indomitable, candid and like to be in charge. Two Roosters will be sure to clash.

In work, they have great capabilities, but both will want to dominate. Working relations will be fraught.

In love, these two will mean well and have so much to give, but their candid natures will be their undoing. And with both being strong-willed too, a challenging and testing match is inevitable.

With a Dog

The Rooster and Dog are both firm in their convictions, but with differing outlooks, relations between them do not tend to be good.

In work, their strong-willed natures and different styles mean there is a lack of accord between them. They will not usually work well together.

In love, both Roosters and Dogs are loyal, caring and protective, and they mean so well, but with both being dominant and direct, relations could be challenging.

With a Pig

The Rooster has great respect for the Pig's genial, good-natured ways and relations between them are good and mutually beneficial.

In work, these two will harness their different abilities to good effect, with the Rooster valuing the Pig's business skills and enterprise. They can be highly effective together.

In love, with their love of home life and the outdoors and many shared interests, these two make a great match. Each can be good for the other and the Rooster will draw strength from the Pig's positive, ebullient and affectionate nature.

Horoscopes for Each of the Chinese Years

Rooster Fortunes in the Year of the Rat

Rat years are busy and active and Roosters may be ill at ease with some of the fast-paced developments. However, while the aspects are mixed, Roosters are vigilant by nature and can do much to negate or minimize the problems the Rat year can bring.

One of the year's most awkward areas is finance. Over the year many Roosters could face increased demands on their resources as repair costs arise, equipment needs replacing and/or plans involve additional expense. This can be a costly year and Roosters need to watch outgoings and, if possible, make early provision for known expenses. In addition, when conducting any kind of transactions, they need to check the terms and implications and compare the options. A good maxim for the year is: 'If in doubt, check it out.' Money matters require careful attention this year. If Roosters are lax, problems and shortfalls could occur. Roosters, take note.

Roosters are well known for their candour and many of those around them do admire their honest and straight-talking ways. However, in the Rat year they need to be on their guard. In some cases, if they are too blunt or candid, there is a risk they could undermine rapport. This is very much a year for tact and discretion, especially in volatile or fraught situations. In some instances, keeping a low profile could be politic.

For Roosters who are enjoying romance or who would like to meet someone special, this is a year to remain particularly attentive and let any new relationship develop in its own way and time. Roosters should not hurry this year.

However, while Roosters need to be alert and careful, the Rat year also has its pleasures. In many cases there will be much happening in their locality, and if they are tempted by any of the events, they should aim to attend. By making the most of what is available, they can enjoy some good times.

Personal interests can also benefit them. Not only can these be a satisfying outlet for their talents and ideas, but some will have a pleasing social element too.

In their home life, there will be a lot to consider and deal with. A loved one could be affected by changing routines and there could also be the inconveniences of equipment breaking or delays impacting on plans. However, while Rat years can have their frustrations, by showing patience, being prepared to talk matters through and adapting as required, Rooster will find that many problems can be resolved and benefits eventually result. This is a year to pool together and be mindful. Also, while Roosters and others will have many competing commitments, preserving time for shared interests and activities can make an important difference to family life. Rat years require care, attention and thoughtfulness, but if Roosters offer this, a lot can be gained from the present time.

At work this is a year requiring focus. Roosters will do best by concentrating their efforts in areas where they have most experience. Accordingly, many will decide to remain where they are. While progress is possible, these Roosters need to be aware of the year's trickier undercurrents. Office politics or the attitude of another person could concern them and bureaucracy could complicate certain tasks. They will need to stay focused, as this is no time to get distracted or diverted into less helpful matters. In any volatile situation, they should watch their words and proceed cautiously.

For Roosters who decide to change their position or are seeking work, the Rat year can again prove challenging. There could be a lack of suitable vacancies and competition could be fierce.

However, it is at such times that the fortitude of Roosters can come into its own. By taking particular care with their applications, stressing their skills and preparing well for interview, many can see their extra effort pay off. Progress will need to be worked for this year, but when it comes, it will be all the more deserved.

Overall, the Rat year will be demanding and Roosters will need to be careful and vigilant. Particularly in money matters, this is a year requiring good management and the avoidance of risk. Also, with the many pressures of the year, Roosters need to be careful not to exacerbate situations with hasty or ill-judged responses. However, difficult though the aspects may be, time spent on personal interests, sharing activities with loved ones and enjoying the social opportunities of the year can do Roosters good as well as provide valuable balance to their often busy lifestyle.

The Rat year may be testing, but its lessons are manifold and it can prepare Roosters for the opportunities that lie ahead.

Tips for the Year

Be attentive and vigilant. Extra care can make a difference to your relationships, money matters and work situation. Also, be wary of risk or haste.

ROOSTER FORTUNES IN THE YEAR OF THE OX

Like the Ox, Roosters like method and order and are very hard-working. And they are set to do well this year, both making good progress and benefiting from timely developments. 'He who comprehends the times is great', as the Chinese proverb reminds us, and, for Roosters, this is a time to understand that they have a lot in their favour and should *seize the moment*. With purpose, belief and a positive 'can do' attitude, they can gain a great deal.

In work, prospects are especially encouraging, and in the light of their recent experience many Roosters will be well placed to take their career to a new level. When openings arise, they should be quick to show interest, whether these are in their current place of work or elsewhere. This is no year to stand still. Fate could also play a part, with some Roosters alerted to an ideal opening by chance or being offered a better position in the wake of a rejection. Things tend to happen for a reason this year and Roosters are set to benefit.

For those seeking work, their characteristic resolve will often lead to them securing a new position. While it could be in a different capacity and involve adjustment, what they take on now can often set them off on a new and successful track. With effort, commitment and initiative, Roosters can show their true strengths and reap considerable rewards.

Progress made at work can lead to rise in income and some Roosters will also benefit from a bonus, gift or sum from another source. Financially, this can be a much-improved year and this will persuade many Roosters to go ahead with various plans and purchases. However, these should not be rushed – time spent comparing choices and costs will lead to better decisions. Also, if Roosters can use any financial upturn to reduce borrowings or add to savings, this could be of advantage to them in the future.

Travel is well aspected this year and Roosters should try to make provision for a holiday and/or break. By planning this in advance, they may be able to link their travels to an interest or special event, as well as visit some impressive attractions while away. Ox years can open up some interesting possibilities and Roosters may see their ideas developing in encouraging fashion.

Although they will be busy this year, they should also make sure their personal interests do not get ignored. These can not only bring them pleasure and help them relax, but also open up new possibilities. Furthering their knowledge and skills can reinforce the positive nature of the year.

This will also be a pleasing time domestically, with many plans and activities going forward. Roosters will be behind many of these and their input can be of particular value. In addition, the Ox year can be marked by some memorable times, with individual successes and a possible family milestone to celebrate, as well as travel possibilities to enjoy. Any Roosters who have had strains in their home life of late will find that talking, listening and giving more time to others can make an appreciable difference. Ox years encourage positive input and interaction.

Similarly, for any Roosters who start the year lonely or feeling that something is lacking from their current lifestyle, the Ox year offers opportunities of improvement. However, to benefit, these Roosters need to be active and make the most of what is happening. Joining a local society or going to events that appeal to them can help brighten their situation. The Ox year does have good social possibilities and many Roosters will see their social circle widening as the year progresses.

For the unattached, affairs of the heart can also make the year special, with a chance meeting being potentially significant. However, although this is a favourable year, Roosters do need to remain mindful of others. Sometimes their strong personality can lead to them dominating certain situations and greater consideration of the views of others can be an important factor in the success of their relationships.

Overall, however, Roosters can do themselves a lot of good this year. By looking to further their position and seizing their opportunities, they can make significant progress. Also, once action is taken, helpful influences can often help the process along. Roosters have a lot in their favour this year and their skills, resolve and sense of purpose can be a winning combination.

Tips for the Year
Take action and make the most of your strengths and ideas. Also, enjoy your relations with others. New friendships, romance and joint activities can all add joy and meaning to the year.

ROOSTER FORTUNES IN THE YEAR OF THE TIGER

In Tiger years a lot can happen at a bewildering pace and Roosters will need to keep their wits about them. While they may like to plan and be prepared – Roosters do not like to leave things to chance – certain developments will require quick responses. The Rooster's orderly ways can be thrown into turmoil this year, but despite the trickier aspects there will still be many good times – and accomplishments – to appreciate.

With events happening fast, Roosters will benefit from drawing on the support and advice available to them. By talking to others, including those with expertise, they can be helped in important ways as well as often reassured. Roosters should not feel alone this year.

In addition, they should be prepared to adapt. By making the most of situations *as they are*, rather than remaining set in their ways, they can make gains that can be to their longer-term advantage.

At work, Roosters need to be careful and alert. Over the year situations can suddenly develop which require prompt action. And although some developments may be disconcerting, by doing what they can, Roosters will not only have the chance to demonstrate their skills but will also be able to add to their experience. Whether they find themselves covering for absent colleagues, adapting to new working practices or contending with challenging situations, they can learn a lot from these pressured but instructive times. For some, there will be the opportunity to take on to a greater role, although in Tiger years it could be best to keep expectations modest.

For Roosters who decide to move away from their present employer or are seeking work, these can be fast-moving and frequently surprising times. These Roosters should keep alert and also widen the scope of their search. By being prepared to use their skills in new ways, many could secure a position in a different capacity with potential for the future. Some new roles may not be what the Roosters were originally envisaging at all, but nevertheless they will be to their longer-term benefit.

Although the income of many Roosters will increase this year, there are quite a few who enjoy spending and like to indulge themselves. And while many of their activities and purchases will be pleasing, these Roosters do need to watch outgoings. Without care, their spending could become greater than anticipated and lead to economies (or additional interest costs) later. This is a year for good control over the purse-strings. Also, if taking on a new agreement, Roosters should check the terms and clarify the implications if necessary.

With all their commitments, it is also important that they allow time for their own interests. Relaxing pursuits can often be the tonic they need. Over the Tiger year, some may become intrigued by a new and, for them, very different activity. Again, they need to be receptive to what is available.

As they will be contending with a lot this year, they also need to be receptive to others and be open and communicative. Particularly in their home life, consultation and cooperation can make a big difference. Ideally, all in the Rooster household should pool together, help one another at busy times and talk through developments. That way many matters can be satisfactorily addressed, and in times of uncertainty Roosters will find much truth in the saying, 'A worry shared is a worry halved.' Joint activities and interests will also not only be good for rapport but lead to more happening.

The Tiger year can also see an increase in social activity, although the pace of some weeks could be frenetic, with everything seeming to occur at once. However, amid all the activity there will be occasions that Roosters will very much enjoy and that will offer the chance to catch up with friends not often seen.

In matters of the heart, relationships can develop encouragingly, although Roosters do need to remain attentive. An ill-timed remark or *faux pas* could prove awkward. Roosters, be mindful and exercise care.

Roosters may not like the pace and volatility of Tiger years, but they can be instructive and move Roosters forward in new and potentially beneficial ways. In particular, developments at work and in personal interests will open up new possibilities. And importantly, much that happens now can be successfully built upon in the future.

Tips for the Year

Be prepared to adapt. These are fast-moving times – do not get left behind. Liaise with those around you and draw on their support. Also, enjoy sharing time with your loved ones, although when in company, remain mindful and watch your sometimes candid tendencies.

ROOSTER FORTUNES IN THE YEAR OF THE RABBIT

Roosters will welcome the steadier nature of the Rabbit year and the way certain plans and hopes can now be advanced. However, developments can be slow and patience may be required.

At work, this is a year favouring steady growth. For the many Roosters who have experienced recent change and are relatively new in their present position, this will give them the chance to become more conversant with various aspects of their role. Here their ability to organize, master detail and present themselves well can prove a real asset. The reputation of many Roosters will increase substantially during the year. All Roosters can help their current situation – and future options – by taking advantage of any training that is available and, if relevant, joining a professional organization.

For Roosters seeking work, the Rabbit year calls for patience. It may take time to find a suitable opening and even longer for the application to be processed. For quite a few Roosters, some of the year will be frustrating, but by remaining persistent as well as considering other ways in which they can use their skills, many will secure the chance they have been seeking. Success, when it comes, will be all the sweeter, given the time and effort involved.

One of the main benefits of the Rabbit year will be the way Roosters can add to their knowledge. Whether professionally or in their personal interests, they should make the most of the chances available to them. In some instances, if there is a specific skill that could be helpful, or an additional qualification, they should look at ways of obtaining this, including courses and self-study options. Similarly, if a subject or new interest appeals to them, they should follow it up. With their inquisitive mind, Roosters can derive much personal satisfaction from the activities they pursue, or start, this year.

Many too will be keen to introduce some positive lifestyle changes, including improving their exercise levels and the quality of their diet. By seeking advice and following through their ideas, they will be pleased to have done something definite.

Socially, the year will be quieter than some, with Roosters being more selective in the events they attend. However, by choosing these carefully, they will appreciate them all the more.

In addition, they will particularly value their contact with their friends, including sharing mutual interests and talking over current situations. And where work and personal interests are concerned, some new people met during the year could prove to be highly useful connections.

Domestically, this can also be a satisfying year, although with Roosters and other family members contending with different commitments, there needs to be good communication. Here the Rooster's ability to ensure the smooth running of home life can be a much-appreciated asset.

During the year it is, however, important that Roosters listen carefully to the words of their loved ones. They do speak with their interests at heart and some of the thoughts expressed this year could potentially be significant. In Rabbit years, Roosters need to be receptive. However, there will also be the chance for them to reciprocate, perhaps bolstering a family member's confidence or helping solve a problem. Mutual support can be an important factor this year.

Roosters will be pleased with the way certain home projects are advanced, although timetables should be kept elastic. Rabbit years do not favour haste and Roosters need to show patience, especially where practical undertakings are concerned. This is a time for adapting to the rhythm of the year and for family members to work together as a unit.

One area which will require particular attention will be finance. Not only will many Roosters face additional outgoings, but spending needs to be watched. Too many unplanned purchases could mount up, and for the more spendthrift Roosters, problems could ensue. Also, if tempted by anything risky or speculative, all Roosters need to consider the implications. Similarly, while usually meticulous with paperwork, Roosters need to deal with forms and financial correspondence promptly and keep important documents safe. Roosters, take note and be thorough and cautious in your financial dealings.

Much in the Rabbit year will proceed at a steady pace. This may not be a time for amazing successes or sweeping progress, but gradually and slowly results *will* filter through and effort be rewarded. Working closely with others will be of benefit and Roosters will need to watch their independent tendencies. This year there is strength in numbers. Of particular value will be the way Roosters can further their knowledge and skills. These can be to their present and longer-term benefit.

Tips for the Year
Be vigilant in money matters. Good control over your outgoings is advised. Also, rather than look too far ahead, concentrate on what can be done now, especially in improving skills and making positive lifestyle changes. Enjoy time with those around you and look to build connections. Much can follow on as a result.

ROOSTER FORTUNES IN THE YEAR OF THE DRAGON

Roosters will be quick to detect the energy and potential that exist in Dragon years and keen make the most of this time of exciting possibility.

As the Dragon year starts, Roosters would do well to give some thought to their key aims for the next 12 months. With objectives in mind, they will be more aware of the actions they need to take. These are significant times and ones not to waste.

Also, while Roosters do like to take charge, they should not feel they have to act alone. By talking over their hopes and ideas, they could find themselves helped in unexpected ways. Roosters invariably do much for others and many close to them will be glad to reciprocate.

Work prospects are especially favourable. Roosters on a particular career path may have the opportunity to secure promotion and/or take on responsibilities they have been working towards for some time. In many cases their in-house knowledge and reputation will be important factors in the progress they make and employers will be keen to encourage their often special strengths.

For Roosters who feel they have languished in recent years, this is a time to seize the initiative and look for change. By making enquiries, talking to contacts and pursuing openings, many will be successful in securing a different and more satisfying role.

Similarly, many currently seeking work will enjoy good fortune, often obtaining what can be an ideal new role. Roosters are very much in the driving seat this year, and once actions are taken and enquiries made, encouraging developments can quickly (and often fortuitously) follow on.

There will also be some Roosters who decide to become self-employed. Again much can become possible this year, although these Roosters should draw on the advice available to them. With professional input, many a business plan can be strengthened and improved.

Progress at work can also make a difference financially, and this will persuade many Roosters to go ahead with plans they have in mind as well as make purchases for themselves and their home. By considering these carefully and taking advice over the suitability of their choices, they will often delight in what they acquire over the year. Also, if possible, they should make provision for a holiday and give careful thought to possible destinations. The more they can plan and make appropriate provision, the better. In addition, if they can use any financial improvement to reduce borrowings or add to savings, this too could be to their advantage.

Roosters will be kept busy this year, but to be at their best, they do need to make sure they have a good lifestyle balance and allow themselves time to relax and unwind. Personal interests can be of particular benefit and all Roosters should allow themselves regular 'me time' over the year. In addition, if any special events related to their interests appeal to them, they would do well see what can be arranged. Over the year it is important they enjoy the rewards they work so hard for.

Roosters will also value the social opportunities that arise and, enjoying conversation as they do, will attend many convivial occasions. Often their interests can have a good social element too, and work changes can introduce them to some people with whom they will get on particularly well.

Affairs of the heart are also favourably aspected. Existing romances will often become more meaningful, with marriage possible for some Roosters, while quite a few who start the year unattached will meet someone who is destined to become significant.

Home life, too, will see much activity and there will need to be good liaison between all and flexibility over plans and arrangements. However, mixed in with the high levels of activity will be special and meaningful times. Some Rooster households will see a wedding, a birth in the family, a graduation or another personal achievement. There can be proud moments for many Roosters this year, and if a special occasion needs organizing, they will enjoy doing it.

With Roosters often buoyed up by developments this year, many will also be keen to set about home improvements. However, a word of caution: these could be more disruptive than anticipated, with one project leading to another.

Overall, however, the Dragon year can be an especially rewarding one for Roosters, giving them the opportunity to advance and to use their strengths to advantage. To benefit fully, they need to be prepared to put themselves forward and act with determination. But they will be encouraged not only by timely developments but also by the support of those around them. Roosters have much in their favour this year and their talents and qualities can reward them well. And for many, a personal celebration can make the year all the more special.

Tips for the Year
Take the initiative and make things happen. Look to build on your present position or, if unfulfilled, seek change. Also, value your relations with those around you, for the year can have special times to share. Wonderful indeed are the possibilities of the Dragon year. Enjoy it and use it well.

Rooster Fortunes in the Year of the Snake

An encouraging year. During it, Roosters can derive much satisfaction from the way ideas and plans develop. Snake years encourage Roosters and they are set to impress on both a personal and professional level.

At work, many will be able to build on their present position and make more of their skills and specialisms. For some, this could include the chance to focus more on specific aspects of their work or take on new projects which allow them to make greater use of their strengths. Whatever happens, by making the most of any offers or openings, many Roosters will not only make important advances but also enjoy greater levels of work satisfaction. Snake years also encourage creative input, and for Roosters in positions which allow for creativity and communication, this can be an inspiring and often successful time.

For Roosters who are dissatisfied in their present position, as well as those seeking work, the Snake year offers good possibilities. By widening the scope of their search and indicating their willingness to adapt and learn, many will secure a position that offers the change, challenge and incentive they need.

During the year it will be important, however, that Roosters pay attention to their relations with their colleagues and, if new to a position, establish themselves in their place of work. By being active in any team and using any chances to network, they will enable their qualities to be better appreciated. However, at more pressured times, they do need to tread carefully and keep their candid nature in check.

Being conscientious, Roosters drive themselves hard and throughout the year they need to keep their lifestyle in balance as well as give themselves the chance to relax and unwind. To push themselves relentlessly could lead to stress and undermine effectiveness. Here time given to personal interests can be beneficial. Creative activities could be particularly satisfying.

In money matters, Roosters will be pleased with the way they are able to proceed with various plans and purchases. However, in view of the costs involved, they should make early provision for more sizeable outlays and budget accordingly. Financially, this is a year for good management.

Travel will appeal to many Roosters, and by making allowance for this, they can plan ahead and look forward to visiting some interesting destinations.

They will also welcome the many and varied social opportunities of the Snake year. With their wide interests and liking of conversation, they will enjoy talking to many people as well as attending a lively mix of occasions, some celebratory. Over the year, many Roosters will give valued help to a close friend on what could be a delicate matter. Here their thoughtful input can be both telling and appreciated.

Affairs of the heart can also bring them considerable happiness, although new relationships should be nurtured carefully and time allowed for each person to get to know the other better. That way, many a romance can be built on a more solid foundation.

In their home life, Roosters will again busy themselves in many activities and, thanks to their skills, ensure much goes smoothly, including the changes caused by new routines. However, while they will arrange a lot themselves, they do need to make sure there is agreement over plans, activities and home purchases.

With cooperation and good family input, a lot can happen this year and some pleasing times (including travel) be enjoyed. As with any year, though, the Snake year will have its difficult moments. Whether caused by work pressures, domestic worries or social situations, Roosters will be keen to resolve the issue, but need to proceed carefully. To speak out or act prematurely could lead to problems. Snake years favour a more measured and patient approach. Roosters, take note. In Snake years, it is worth allowing time for thoughts and situations to become clear before you try to address them.

In general, however, the Snake year can be a constructive time for Roosters. Some good opportunities can arise and their ideas and creativity can lead to some successful outcomes. This is a time when their talents can reward them well. Throughout the year, they will also be encouraged by the support of others, although in any pressured situation they should think their responses through and keep their candid nature in check. In Snake years, tact, discretion and patience are key requisites. Overall, though, this can be a satisfying time for Roosters, with their efforts reaping some fine and deserved rewards.

Tips for the Year
With so much to do, maintain a good lifestyle balance. Enjoy spending time with others and look to further your personal

interests. Also, adopt a more measured and patient approach than usual. That way your results can be even more satisfying.

Rooster Fortunes in the Year of the Horse

Roosters like to plan and be prepared, and as the year starts they would do well to give some thought to what they would like to do over the next 12 months. With purpose and clear aims, they can see a lot happen, although there is a 'but'. Horse years can see high levels of activity and Roosters need to be realistic. This is not a year to be overambitious or overcommit, but to focus on key priorities.

For many Roosters, their aims will revolve around their work position. Here the Horse year will offer some good possibilities. Roosters established in a particular career will often feel ready in themselves to move forward. Accordingly, they should keep alert for openings and be swift to apply. In some instances, the new roles they take on could involve much adjustment and learning, but these Roosters will be pleased to be making more of their potential.

Many Roosters will make important headway in their existing place of work, but for those keen to move elsewhere or seeking a position, the Horse year can again have encouraging prospects. Effort will be required, but by emphasizing to prospective employers their experience, qualities and achievements, many of these Roosters will be successful in their quest. Initiative and commitment will be important factors this year.

However, while work prospects are encouraging, throughout the year Roosters need to pay close attention to their relations with colleagues. Roosters do have a dominant personality and not being sufficiently mindful or aware of the views of others could cause problems. Roosters, take note.

This need for awareness also applies to financial matters. Over the year quite a few Roosters could be tempted by impulse buys or take on what could be costly commitments. These do need to be factored into their budget. Roosters need to keep a tight rein on outgoings this year. This is no time to be lax or take risks. The terms of any new agreements need to be checked and professional advice taken if required.

This can be an inspiring year for personal interests, however. Some Roosters will set themselves a specific goal and enjoy the challenge of reaching it. Others could be tempted by a new activity or take a talent in a new direction. Horse years encourage self-development.

Some of their interests will also bring Roosters into contact with other people, and they will once again enjoy the social opportunities of the year. However, while much will go well, Horse years may not be entirely problem-free. Jealousy, a disagreement or a clash of personality could all surface and cause anxiety. Roosters do need to be careful in their handling of personal relationships and make sure that minor matters do not escalate. Similarly, romances need careful nurturing if they are to develop and strengthen.

Domestically, there will be a lot happening, often at a fast pace. Not only could the schedules of some members of the household alter, but some matters could require prompt attention, including failing equipment. Roosters should avoid trying to deal with too much single-handed and overburdening themselves. In this busy year, household tasks and decisions need to be shared by everyone.

In addition, it is important that quality time together does not suffer due to general busyness. There needs to be a good balance to family life this year. If not, there is a risk that tensions could arise, which, with more time and consideration, could have been avoided. In the Horse year, Roosters need to be alert to signs of possible discord. Thanks to their perceptive nature, most will be.

In general, the Horse year will encourage Roosters to make greater use of their strengths and build on their present position. Both professionally and personally, it offers scope and encourages development. However, Roosters do need to use their time effectively and be careful not to overcommit themselves. In addition, they need to liaise well with those around them. Personal relationships require careful handling this year and some situations may be troubling. But by remaining aware and talking matters through, Roosters can successfully overcome many of the year's more awkward aspects. Overall an active and generally progressive year, but also one for awareness and care.

Tips for the Year
Keep your lifestyle in balance and preserve quality time to share with others. Be aware of the views of those around you. Also, focus on key plans and priorities. The year will require effort, commitment and care, but it is one of possibility.

Rooster Fortunes in the Year of the Goat

A pleasing year ahead. Rather than feel buffeted by events or diverse pressures, Roosters will be able to enjoy a better lifestyle balance and see their personal life and activities progressing well. Goat years can do Roosters good, although to make the most of them they need to allow themselves some slack. Rather than sticking rigidly to plans, they should embrace the spirit and spontaneity of the time.

In view of recent changes at work, many Roosters will welcome the opportunity to concentrate on their present role and use their skills to advantage. Here their ideas, presentational talents and ability to respond to developments can impress and lead to some notable successes. Working well with others and being active in any team will also help their standing and lead to them being involved in more. In Goat years many Roosters will enjoy a good level of work satisfaction.

While many Roosters will concentrate on their present area of work, for those keen to develop in other ways or seeking work, the Goat year can see encouraging developments. However, to benefit, these Roosters would do well to consider the type of position they would like and actively make enquiries. Their style, verve, enthusiasm and initiative can lead to some interesting possibilities. Also, as many will find, events in Goat years can take a surprising course. Some Roosters will take on a position that is different from what they have done before and will revel in the chance to develop their skills in new ways. Goat years offer scope and possibility.

This also applies to personal interests. Roosters will enjoy making fuller use of their ideas and talents, and creative activities can be especially satisfying this year. Many Roosters will be on inspired form and any who have let their personal interests fall away due to recent commitments or would welcome a fresh challenge should consider what they would like to do and make a start. Goat years encourage a better lifestyle balance.

In addition, if Roosters are lacking regular exercise or feel their diet is not sufficiently balanced, some modifications could be helpful.

Over the year they should also try to take a holiday at some point. Many could successfully combine their time away with pursuing an interest or attending a special attraction or event.

With the possibility of travel, plus other interests and commitments, Roosters will need to remain disciplined in money matters, however, and make early provision for larger outlays. With good budgeting, they will be able to go ahead with many of their plans, but the Goat year does require sensible control over the purse-strings. More spendthrift Roosters, take note.

Home life can bring much pleasure this year, and by carrying out plans and activities with their loved ones, Roosters may find that much can be completed, including some pleasing home (and garden) improvements. However, over the year, Roosters should show some flexibility. In some instances, original thoughts and plans will need to be modified as other considerations arise. Roosters may like to plan, but this year plans should not be set in stone, especially when alternatives offer certain advantages.

In addition, Roosters will do much to assist their loved ones, particularly during times of change. Here their good counsel can make an important difference. They will also delight in the well-deserved success of someone close.

The Goat year will provide a good mix of things to do and Roosters will enjoy many special occasions and see their social circle widen appreciably. For the unattached, including those who may have had recent personal difficulties to overcome, the year can see a great improvement, with romance and new friend-ships set to blossom. In some instances, a chance meeting will seem as if it was meant to be. The Goat year has the capacity to surprise and delight.

Overall, Goat years can be good for Roosters. Rather than continually drive themselves on, they will have the chance to relax and appreciate the present. At work, many will find a greater level of fulfilment and have the chance to develop their strengths. Personal interests can also be enjoyable, as well as help lifestyle balance. The Goat year can be rich in social possibilities, and romantic prospects are good. Domestically, much can be accomplished, to the delight of everyone. Roosters have much in their favour and they should make the most of the possibilities this interesting and encouraging year offers.

Tips for the Year

Be flexible and enjoy the opportunities that come your way. Personal interests in particular can develop in an interesting manner. Also, enjoy spending time with those around you. Goat years can be good for lifestyle balance.

ROOSTER FORTUNES IN THE YEAR OF THE MONKEY

Roosters like to plan ahead, but during the Monkey year they could face interruptions, distractions and delays. Some parts of the year will be frustrating and Roosters will have to make the best of situations *as they are* rather than as they would like them to be. But they should not necessarily assume the worst. True, there will be problems and disappointments (as there are in all years), but these will be surmountable and in many cases will leave Roosters wiser and more experienced. Monkey years can, in spite of their vexations, be illuminating as well as highlight Rooster resilience. Also, with next year being their own year, what Roosters can accomplish now can often pave the way for the opportunities that lie ahead.

At work, this can be a year of swift-moving developments. Whether through reorganization, changes in personnel or the introduction of new practices, there can be periods of intense activity and volatility. And for Roosters, who pride themselves on efficiency, some of the year's developments will seem muddled. But, disquieting though some situations may be, Roosters should remain focused on their role and adapt as required. Out of seeming chaos there will be chances for them to add to their skills and benefit from opportunities. In addition, they should take advantage of any training that is available and follow up any new possibilities. Work-wise, Monkey years will be challenging, but what happens now will prepare many Roosters for future success.

For Roosters seeking work, Monkey years can also have far-reaching developments. By keeping alert for vacancies and widening the scope of their search, many could secure a position in a different type of work that has the potential for growth. A lot that happens in Monkey years has longer-term value.

In money matters, Roosters need to keep their wits about them. When entering into agreements, they should check the terms carefully, and when considering major purchases, they should think through whether their requirements are being met. This is no year for rush or hurried decisions. Outgoings need to be managed carefully.

Domestically, Roosters need to be aware and attentive. With the pressures of the year, their minds will be on many things, and they need to be careful their general busyness does not make incursions into their home life. In addition, while they like a certain independence, they do need to be forthcoming and talk over concerns or uncertainties. In the Monkey year a worry shared can be very much a worry eased, and Roosters should draw on support and advice available to them.

It is also important that more pleasurable aspects of family life do not suffer due to high levels of activity. Shared interests, special occasions and trips out can do everyone good.

Unfortunately, though, Monkey years do have their inconveniences, and equipment may break or practical activities be affected by delay. At times, Monkey years can be exasperating, although once repairs or replacements have been made and solutions found, often benefits will have been gained. Indeed, some problems can be blessings in disguise, prompting actions or purchases which would not otherwise have been taken.

In this sometimes challenging year, Roosters will value talking to their friends and seeking their advice, and should aim to take advantage of the social opportunities the Monkey year will bring.

For the unattached, Monkey years can have fine and potentially significant romantic possibilities too.

With their busy lifestyles, it is also important Roosters give themselves the chance to relax and unwind over the year. Interests, recreational pursuits and, for some, a fitness discipline can all be beneficial as well as good for lifestyle balance. In this active year, Roosters should not ignore their own well-being.

Overall, Monkey years will ask a lot of Roosters and they will sometimes be troubled by the fast-moving developments and additional pressure. For those who like method and structure, these can be exasperating times. But by being prepared to adapt and make the best of their situation, they can usefully add to their experience and prepare themselves for the better times ahead. The year will be demanding, but instructive. A good lifestyle balance and sharing time with others will add pleasure and joy to it.

Tips for the Year
Make the most of the present but also give some thought to the future. Skills gained, activities undertaken, connections built – all can be of subsequent value. Also, enjoy quality time with your loved ones. Together, more can be accomplished and satisfactorily dealt with.

ROOSTER FORTUNES IN THE YEAR OF THE ROOSTER

Excited and encouraged that this is their own year, Roosters will be keen to make it special. And it can be. This is a year when their strengths and qualities prevail and they can enjoy success. For any who have been disappointed with recent progress, it is a time to seize the initiative and start a new chapter in their life. With resolve, belief and the favourable aspects, there is much to be gained.

At work, this can be a year of significant developments. Many Roosters can now benefit from promotion opportunities and make what can be substantial advances. Now is the time when honours can flow their way and commitment and loyalty be rewarded. For those on a particular career path, this can be a year of growth and success.

For Roosters who are unfulfilled in their present role, now is the time to consider other possibilities. Roosters are in the driving seat this year, and by taking action to change an unsatisfactory situation, they can see their initiative rewarded with the opportunity to set their career on a positive new track.

Those seeking work should also be active in following up possibilities. Determination can lead to many securing a new role and the chance to re-establish themselves. What some take on could be a considerable change from what they have been doing before but give them the opportunity and incentive they need. Quite a few Roosters will have felt they have not made the most of their potential in recent times and their own year will encourage them to give of their best.

Progress made at work will also increase the income of many Roosters. However, while this will be welcome, Roosters need to remain disciplined. Over the year there could be many temptations to spend, and outgoings should be monitored, otherwise spending levels could become greater than budgeted for. Also, with Roosters liking to look ahead, if there are able to start or add to a savings plan or pension policy, they could be glad of it in years to come.

Roosters like to keep themselves informed of new developments and their own year will encourage this. Often new work and/or duties will lead to new knowledge, but if Roosters feel an additional qualification or skill could help their prospects, they should see what can be arranged. They will not only be reinforcing the encouraging nature of the year but also investing in themselves and their future.

This also applies to their personal interests. Some Roosters may decide on a new personal challenge, start a project or take up an activity they have been considering for a while. Any Roosters who start the year feeling dispirited will find that new interests can re-energize them and give them purpose.

The Rooster's own year will also see much social activity. In addition to sharing times and news with friends, there will be a good mix of occasions to enjoy and places to go. Many Roosters will find themselves in demand this year and will have the chance to extend their social circle. Again, any who start the year despondent should take advantage of what it offers. If they make the most of their chances to go out, including to social groups and activities in their area, they could see a considerable brightening of their situation.

For the unattached, existing romances can often gain in significance this year, while new romances should be nurtured steadily.

There will also be enjoyable times in many a Rooster home, with special occasions, successes and sometimes milestones to mark. There could also be family news that will delight everyone. Whenever arrangements need making, Roosters will find their organizational skills in demand and they will revel in the opportunity. They will also be pleased with the way various ideas and plans develop, including home improvements and travel arrangements. The year will contain many gratifying moments.

Overall, Roosters have a lot in their favour this year and should seize the moment. This is a time when their efforts can reward them handsomely. At work they should look to advance their career as well as explore how they can best use their skills. Throughout the year they will be encouraged by their good relations with many around them and their social and home life will be active and pleasing. Their own year is rich in possibility and their many sterling qualities will help them make the most of it.

Tips for the Year

Act! Purposeful action can bring you success this year. Also, make the most of your strengths and look to build on your knowledge. By investing in yourself, you can not only benefit now but also in the future.

ROOSTER FORTUNES IN THE YEAR OF THE DOG

Roosters can make steady progress during the Dog year, but need to be careful. Dog years can throw up their problems, which can cause delays and rethinks. This year Roosters cannot expect to have things all their own way and should adapt accordingly.

At work, in view of the changes many Roosters will have recently experienced, this is a year for them to concentrate on their current position. By immersing themselves in their role and working well with their colleagues, their involvement is set to grow over the year. However, while usually so meticulous, they should not let standards slip. Roosters, take note and be aware, attentive and thorough. Dog years can be exacting, but will help you to hone and strengthen your skills.

While many Roosters will remain in their existing place of work this year, for those who decide to make a change or are seeking work, their quest will not be easy. However, in addition to keeping alert for openings and widening the range of positions they are considering, if they talk to experts and contacts, they could be alerted to other possibilities. Roosters should not act too much on their own this year but draw on the advice and support available. Importantly, the positions many take on now will have the potential to develop, but will require commitment and a willingness to adapt and learn.

In money matters, Roosters need to be vigilant. When making sizeable purchases or entering into agreements, they should check the terms carefully. Time also needs to be allowed to assess the suitability of what they are considering. In some instances, by being prepared to wait, Roosters could not only benefit from more favourable buying opportunities but also make more appropriate choices. They should also be thorough when dealing with paperwork. Lapses or delays could be to their disadvantage. Bureaucratic matters could be problematic this year. Roosters, take note.

There could, though, be some good travel opportunities and Roosters should aim to make provision for a holiday as well as find out more about events and destinations that appeal to them. Some exciting plans can take shape. Some travel possibilities may arise at short notice this year.

Personal interests can also be satisfying and be good ways for Roosters to relax. If keen to develop ideas or become more proficient in a certain skill, they should talk to other enthusiasts and seek advice. Some may enrol on courses. Over the year, Roosters can see their interests developing in encouraging ways.

In view of their many activities, Roosters will also have some good social opportunities this year. Some could arise at short notice and Roosters may have to juggle various commitments in order to enjoy them. Good times can be had, but Roosters still need to remain on their guard. An inadvertent comment or uncharacteristic *faux pas* could cause problems. Similarly, they should not act in ways that could leave them open to censure. The Dog year can be hard on personal errors or lapses. However, provided Roosters remain mindful, from a social point of view this can be a full and pleasing year.

In their home life, they will also find this a busy time. Not only will they have their own commitments, but their loved ones may be involved in taking keynote decisions. Here Roosters' empathy and ability to consider the broader picture can be of especial value. In turn, should they be concerned about a particular matter, they should be forthcoming and discuss it with those around them. Good communication will be to the advantage of all.

Also, while Roosters like to plan and organize, they will need to show flexibility over certain arrangements this year. Delays, unexpected developments and changing circumstances can all be features of Dog years and require Roosters to adjust accordingly. In addition, with the year already being busy enough, Roosters should make sure they do not overcommit themselves. Ideally, they should allow time just to sit back and enjoy themselves rather than be continually occupied. They will deserve it.

Overall, the Dog year will place many demands on Roosters. At work, much will be expected of them and there will be increasing pressures to deal with. However, many can emerge from it with their reputation enhanced. Throughout the year, though, they need to remain vigilant. Lapses can trip up the unwary, for the Dog year has high standards. Rush and risk should also be avoided. While not the easiest of years, this will not be without its high points, though, including the pleasures shared activities bring and the way some ideas develop.

Tips for the Year
Liaise well with those around you and be mindful of their views. With support, you can accomplish much more. Also, adapt to changing situations. Dog years require flexibility, awareness and effort. In addition, enjoy quality time with your loved ones. You can benefit from their support this year.

ROOSTER FORTUNES IN THE YEAR OF THE PIG

A satisfying year, with Roosters benefiting from some interesting and sometimes surprising developments. This is a year of progress with much to do and enjoy.

Pig years encourage activity and going forward, and for Roosters who feel they have been languishing of late, are discontented in their present position and/or would welcome a fresh challenge, this can be a significant time. It is one full of possibility, but to benefit, Roosters need to be proactive and make things happen.

Work prospects are encouraging and Roosters who are established in their present position could benefit from some unexpected developments. Sudden changes in staff or new initiatives could open up promotion opportunities, or Roosters could learn of an opening elsewhere that offers the chance to advance their career or develop in new ways. Tempting possibilities can suddenly arise this year.

For Roosters who are seeking a change from their present role, as well as those looking for work, the Pig year also offers encouraging developments. By keeping alert and making enquiries, these Roosters can uncover some good opportunities. Pig years can develop in curious ways and some may be alerted to an ideal position by chance or secure a position in the wake of disappointment. Pig years are ones of possibility.

With the progress enjoyed at work, many Roosters will benefit from a rise in income. This will often persuade them to go ahead with plans and purchases they have been considering for some time. However, where more substantial outlay is involved, they would do well to make early provision for this as well as check the terms and obligations of any agreement they enter into. This is no year to be lax or make assumptions. Also, with a busy lifestyle, they will need to keep a watch on spending and be wary of too many impulse buys. Spending levels can easily creep up and resources need to be managed well.

The year's developments will also give Roosters a good chance to further their skills, and this need not be restricted to work. Pig years have a fun element and Roosters should make sure their personal interests do not get sidelined. This is an excellent time for enjoying favourite pastimes or setting new personal challenges. There are many possibilities this year and Roosters should allow themselves some slack from time to time and enjoy the rewards of their efforts.

Home life, too, can be a source of great pleasure. Not only could there be family occasions to celebrate but individual achievements as well. The Pig year can bring some memorable and proud moments. In addition, shared activities and interests can give rise to some lively times as well as be good for relationships and rapport. Pig years favour a coming together.

During the year many Roosters will also be keen to proceed with some domestic changes, including altering routines and updating equipment. There are considerable gains to be had, although Roosters do need to talk their plans through with those around them and be mindful of their viewpoints. Again, however, good discussion and cooperative effort can lead to a lot going ahead.

There will also be some good travel opportunities, including spur of the moment chances to go away. Whenever possible, Roosters should take advantage of these. Holidays and short breaks can do them good.

An increase in social activity is also likely and Roosters may find a range of local events appealing. During the year, they will get to meet many new faces, and for the unattached, the Pig year has exciting romantic possibilities. Such are the aspects that some

Roosters will get engaged or married or settle down with another person. Pig years are often lively *and* personally significant.

Overall, Pig years do Roosters good, particularly as they encourage them to enjoy a better lifestyle balance. By joining with others, giving time to personal interests and following through ideas and opportunities, Roosters can make this a gratifying time. The year can bring some special occasions in their home and social life, while at work many will be able to make good headway as well as have the chance to further their knowledge and skills. Pig years are encouraging, and by responding to developments and taking their opportunities, Roosters can do well.

Tips for the Year
Value your relationships and give time to others. Also, rather than feel continually driven, allow yourself time to enjoy the rewards of your efforts. And be flexible, so that you can benefit from what this favourable year makes possible.

Thoughts and Words of Roosters

Perhaps the most valuable result of all education is
the ability to make yourself do the thing you have to
do, when it ought to be done, whether you like it or
not. It is the first lesson that ought to be learned.

THOMAS H. HUXLEY

When schemes are laid in advance, it is surprising
how often circumstances will fit in with them.

SIR WILLIAM OSLER

Do not squander time, for that is the stuff life is made of.

BENJAMIN FRANKLIN

Never put off until tomorrow what you can do today.

BENJAMIN FRANKLIN

If I were to wish for anything, I should not wish for wealth and power, but for the passionate sense of the potential, for the eye which, ever young and ardent, sees the possible … what wine is so sparkling, so fragrant, so intoxicating, as possibility!

SØREN KIERKEGAARD

Take calculated risks. That is different from being rash.

GEORGE PATTON

A wise man will make more opportunities than he finds.

FRANCIS BACON

If you create an act, you create a habit. If you create a habit, you create a character. If you create a character, you create destiny.

ANDRÉ MAUROIS

14 February 1934–3 February 1935 — *Wood Dog*

2 February 1946–21 January 1947 — *Fire Dog*

18 February 1958–7 February 1959 — *Earth Dog*

6 February 1970–26 January 1971 — *Metal Dog*

25 January 1982–12 February 1983 — *Water Dog*

10 February 1994–30 January 1995 — *Wood Dog*

29 January 2006–17 February 2007 — *Fire Dog*

16 February 2018–4 February 2019 — *Earth Dog*

2 February 2030–22 January 2031 — *Metal Dog*

The Dog

The Personality of the Dog

It has often been said that the Dog is man's best friend. Dogs are loyal, faithful and protective, and these are just some of the qualities that are also found in so many born under the Dog sign.

Dogs are reliable and trustworthy. They take their duties seriously and their word is their bond. They are also selfless and are prepared to put others, or causes, before themselves. Of all the Chinese signs, the Dog is the most altruistic.

Dogs loathe injustice and are prepared to speak out against wrongs. Quite a few champion humanitarian causes as well as support those in need. If something riles them, they are sure to speak out. They are defenders, crusaders and very principled.

With their firm beliefs and desire to do right, they also worry a lot. In essence, they do not want to let others down. So they think, they dwell and at times they can be anxious and given to pessimism. At such times, it would be to their advantage to talk more readily to those around them. Sometimes just the process of talking can do much to help unburden the anxious Dog.

Dogs are also cautious. They do not like risks and are conservative in their outlook. They prefer sticking to the tried and tested and proven ways. In addition, they like to be sure of themselves, and this is seen in their approach. Rather than having a great many interests, they prefer to have a favoured few and concentrate on the areas in which they can build up expertise. They are not ones to chop and change. Similarly, in their work, once they have chosen their vocation, they will remain with it, building skills and progressing steadily. And the successes they enjoy – and there can be many – can be put down to their dedication and commitment.

At work, Dogs like to feel that what they do has value and purpose. When inspired, they are capable of rising to great heights. They have desire, passion and great integrity. As well as being an inspiration to others, they have considerable leadership qualities. In addition, they have a desire to serve, and whether in politics, the law, medicine, education, the caring professions or religion, their capabilities and competence make them compelling figures. But should they ever find themselves in an unfulfilling role, there is a tendency they could drift and the more pessimistic side of their nature could surface. Dogs have to believe what they are doing is worthwhile.

While Dogs have good earning abilities, they are not especially interested in money. Provided their needs are covered and their loved ones are provided for, they will be content. Indeed, some get more pleasure in spending on their loved ones than on themselves. Material possessions are not overly important to them.

Dogs also tend not to be the greatest of socializers and may be uncomfortable with large gatherings or big events. They prefer to spend time with friends they trust and have got to know over many years.

This also applies to love and courtship. Rather than rush into a relationship, Dogs like to take their time and be sure both in heart and mind that they are making the right decision. When they do commit themselves, though, they will be a very loyal, loving friend and partner. As with so much, Dogs take commitment seriously.

Similarly, as a parent, they will be attentive and keen to set an example, but they are also apt to worry over concerns or problems their children may have. Dogs are selfless and care so very deeply.

The female Dog is, like her male counterpart, direct in manner and prepared to speak her mind as well as defend the people and principles she holds dear. She is also efficient and uses her time and energies well. Indeed, some female Dogs are veritable multi-taskers, juggling home and work commitments supremely well. The female Dog can also be ambitious and certainly has the ability to go far. She presents herself well. Many female Dogs are renowned for their natural beauty.

Many Dogs take care of themselves and strive for a good life-style balance. And, with a liking for the outdoors, there are many who enjoy following or taking part in sport or some other outdoor activity.

Dogs are strong-willed and can be stubborn. But they are reliable and prepared to devote themselves to their loved ones and to the causes in which they believe. They are indeed redoubtable figures – caring, thoughtful and born under the sign of loyalty. They are inclined to worry and think the worst, and they really should have more faith in themselves, the skills they have built up and their sense of purpose. With commitment, they are indeed capable of achieving great things. As Robert Louis Stevenson, born under the sign of the Dog, wrote, 'To be what we are, and to become what we are capable of becoming, is the only end of life.' And Dogs, with their great capacity to give and serve, can so often make a difference and, in the process, win the admiration and gratitude of many.

Top Tips for Dogs
- You are conscientious and caring – and often worried. Share your concerns with others. This can often help defuse them, put them into perspective or bring a resolution to the situation. Spending time on satisfying interests can also be akin to a tonic for you. 'One joy scatters a thousand griefs', as the Chinese proverb says.
- You may favour tradition and not like change, but remember that advances are always being made and by being willing to embrace these, you will be better able to benefit from them.

- Although, with your practical nature and expertise, you are capable of coming up with some very fine ideas, you do not always have the confidence to put them forward. Rather than let them come to nothing, advance them when appropriate and see what results. You may be pleasantly surprised.
- You like to specialize, master what you do and be sure of your ground, but it could be to your advantage to broaden your horizons from time to time. By doing something different, you will be adding a new and potentially beneficial element to your lifestyle. Fresh challenges and activities every now and again can do you a lot of good.

Relations with Others

With a Rat

The Dog will admire the Rat's outgoing and personable ways and these two will enjoy each other's company.

In work, their outlooks and approaches tend to differ, however, with the Dog not being as commercially minded as the Rat. Not the best combination.

In love, relations will be far better and often mutually beneficial. The Dog will especially value the Rat's confident, supportive and enthusiastic nature. With home life important to both, together they can find much happiness.

With an Ox

These signs may both be loyal and dutiful, but also redoubtable and stubborn. Relations can be tricky.

In work, these two may be entrenched in their ways and neither be disposed to change. True, they will work hard, but ideally will choose to do so apart.

In love, both are cautious and take their time in building a relationship. While the Dog will recognize the Ox's thoughtful and dependable manner, their stubborn natures and tendency to speak their minds could cause difficulties. If their relationship is to work, patience and considerable understanding will be needed.

With a Tiger

Their different natures can help bring out the best in both and relations between them are good.

In work, there will be a good level of trust and respect and the Dog will be inspired and encouraged by their Tiger colleague. An effective and successful combination.

In love, their shared values (both are loyal, trusting and honourable) will help bond these two together and their different qualities will be complementary. The Dog will especially value the Tiger's optimistic disposition and wide-ranging talents. A close, loving and mutually beneficial match.

With a Rabbit

Loyal, caring and with many interests in common, these two signs value each other's company.

In work, their combined skills make for a rewarding partner-ship, although when problems arise, both can be prone to anxiety. They need good times in order to flourish. But then there will be no stopping them!

In love, both value security and stability and the Dog will be encouraged by having such a reliable, supportive and good-natured partner. A successful match.

With a Dragon

The Dog is not comfortable with the energy and flamboyant ways of the Dragon and there will be little accord between them.

In work, their different styles will cause difficulties, with the cautious Dog being wary of the Dragon's more impulsive and risky notions.

In love, these two live life at different speeds and finding common ground can be difficult. The Dog may find the Dragon a lively companion, but overall their relationship could prove challenging.

With a Snake

Both these signs take their time in forming friendships, but as they slowly get to know one another, they can often form a good bond.

In work, these two respect each other, but their ways of working and motivating factors can often be different. While the Dog will recognize the Snake's expertise, neither will tend to bring the best out in the other.

In love, the Dog will particularly value the Snake's calm, quiet and thoughtful ways, and although there will be some differences to reconcile, with care and understanding, these two can make a loving and meaningful match.

With a Horse

Their personalities are different, but these two like and understand each other.

In work, the Dog finds the Horse an enthusiastic and inspiring colleague. There will be a good level of trust between them and they can combine their talents well, often with success.

In love, they are well suited. The Dog will value the Horse's zest and energy and find them uplifting to be with. A highly compatible and mutually beneficial match.

With a Goat

Dogs and Goats have many qualities, but their different outlooks and personalities do not gel.

In work, there tends to be lack of accord. Neither is particularly commercially minded and the Dog will find the Goat's often laid-back manner and creative approach at odds with their own.

In love, the Dog may recognize the Goat's genial and good-natured ways, but the Goat's capricious temperament could exasperate them. Both can be prone to worry as well. A challenging match.

With a Monkey

On the surface there are many personality differences between these two, but when they get to know each other well, they will value each other's qualities.

In work, their different strengths can combine well and the Dog can be enthused by the Monkey's enterprise and zeal. When focused on a specific goal, they can achieve a lot.

In love, both are supportive and encouraging. The Dog feels

reassured by the Monkey's lively and often upbeat manner. A meaningful and mutually beneficial match.

With a Rooster

Both Dog and Rooster hold strong opinions and speak their minds. Relations between the two will not be comfortable.

In work, the Dog could bristle at the Rooster's stringent, organized and commanding ways. Relations will be fraught.

In love, their different outlooks and styles, as well as forthright natures, will not make for easy relations. In addition, the Dog could find the Rooster's structured routine inhibiting. A challenging match.

With another Dog

There is great camaraderie between two Dogs. They understand each other well and relations between them are good.

In work, there will be trust and respect, but Dogs tend not to be the most commercially minded of signs and two Dogs may not be the most effective combination.

In love, these two will be supportive and loving. With similar values and a fondness for home life, they can enjoy a strong and enduring relationship. A successful match.

With a Pig

The Dog admires the genial and good-natured Pig and there is good understanding between them.

In work, both are hard-working as well as open and honourable in their business dealings. They can enjoy a good and beneficial working relationship.

In love, these two share many interests, including the outdoors and their humanitarian leanings. The Dog will appreciate the Pig's buoyant and optimistic nature. Together, they can find much happiness and be good for each other.

Horoscopes for Each of the Chinese Years

DOG FORTUNES IN THE YEAR OF THE RAT

The Rat year tends to bristle with activity and Dogs are often wary of the fast-moving developments it brings. But despite their misgivings, the Rat year has considerable potential. This is not a time to hold back or resist change. By embracing it and going with the flow, Dogs can do well.

During the year, many workplaces will experience change – and many Dogs will be well placed to benefit. For those who have been with their employer for some time, their loyalty, commitment and in-house experience will be valuable assets and there will be good opportunities to move ahead. Over the year, many Dogs will secure well-deserved promotion and their role and responsibilities will become more wide-ranging.

Another factor in their favour will be the good working relations they have with those around them. Over the year they should also aim to meet others in their line of work. By networking and raising their profile, they will be helping both their present situation and future prospects.

For Dogs who feel their situation could be improved by a move elsewhere, as well as those seeking work, again the Rat year holds good opportunities. By giving careful thought to the type of position they would like and exploring possibilities (including talking to experts), they can see their initiative paying off. This could take time and there may be some disappointments along the way, but Dogs are purposeful and determined and they can win through this year. Many will revel in the chance to re-energize their career and prospects.

Progress made at work can also help financially and many Dogs will increase their income over the year. However, they do need to manage their situation well. With their active lifestyle and often growing number of commitments, they may find spending creeping up. This needs to be watched. In addition, they could find it helpful to make early provision for forthcoming plans and other outgoings. With good control over their budget, they will not only be able to do more but could also improve their overall position.

With the year's emphasis on moving forward, they should also look to develop their interests and recreational pursuits. Taking up something new could also be an enjoyable personal challenge. In some cases, what they do can have a good social element or allow them to use their talents in new ways. Rat years encourage Dogs to make more of themselves.

The year can also see an increase in social activity, with Dogs again enjoying spending time with their friends and attending local events. Rat years are vibrant, and if Dogs take up their invitations and make the most of their chances to go out, they can enjoy some good times. With their sincere and genial nature, they will be popular company and can forge some important new friendships.

For unattached Dogs, the Rat year has good romantic possibilities too. In some cases, a meeting could come about by chance, almost as if fate were playing a special part. Rat years can surprise and delight.

Domestically, the Rat year will also see considerable activity, especially as many Dogs and their loved ones will experience changing routines and commitments. As a result, there needs to be good cooperation as well as some flexibility over arrangements. Similarly, when problems raise their head (as they will in any year), often as a result of pressure or tiredness, they should be talked through. Openness and good communication will be so very important throughout the year.

With their practical nature, many Dogs will also set about home improvement projects in earnest this year. However, while they may be keen, they do need to plan these out carefully and allow plenty of time for them as well as be careful not to have too many happening all at once. Rat years will be busy enough without trying to cram in even more activities. Dogs, take note and aim to spread your projects out as well as draw readily on the assistance of those around you.

Overall, Dogs will see a lot happen this year and the speed of some of the developments will be unsettling. However, by looking to develop their skills and ideas, they can gain a great deal. This is a year to move with the times rather than resist them. Also, Rat years have their enjoyable elements. Dogs will find their home and social life both active and rewarding, and for the unattached, romantic prospects are good. Dogs may be busy in the Rat year, but their achievements may be many and far-reaching.

Tips for the Year
Seize your opportunities. This is a year to move forward. With so much happening, use your time well and liaise with those around you. Good communication is so very important in these busy and often special times.

Dog Fortunes in the Year of the Ox

Despite their efforts and noble intentions, Dogs can find Ox years challenging. Progress can be difficult and delays and obstacles can hinder plans. This is a year to exercise care and keep expectations modest. However, challenging though the aspects may be, Ox years can be instructive and Dogs can learn a lot about themselves and their capabilities as well as lay the foundations for future growth.

One of the features of the Ox year is that it favours tradition, and for those who tend to be outspoken and/or delight in championing causes, difficulties could lie ahead. More idealistic notions could get short shrift in Ox years and these are times for Dogs to tread warily. In some instances, it could be politic for them to keep a low profile rather than risk antagonizing others.

At work, in view of recent changes, many Dogs will decide to remain in their present role and concentrate on the areas they know best. However, over the year many could find their workload increasing and their tasks hampered by bureaucracy or factors outside their control. In addition, office politics or changing personnel may be of concern. Dogs will need to proceed carefully and do their best in not always easy conditions.

However, tricky though some of the year may be, taking on additional responsibilities and dealing with problems can provide good experience, and Dogs can build on this in the future. In addition, if they are offered further training or are able to vary their role in some way, again they can benefit from it later. And in view of the ambitions some Dogs will have, if they feel another skill or qualification could help their prospects, they should find out more.

For Dogs who decide to move on from where they are or are seeking work, the Ox year can again be challenging. Despite their experience and the effort they may put into their applications, obtaining a new position will take time and there will be disappointments along the way. However, Dogs are tenacious and many will eventually succeed in their quest. Results *will* need to be worked for, but will be all the more welcome (and deserved) when they do come.

In addition, Dogs should give some time to their personal interests this year. These can not only bring them pleasure but be a valuable respite from some of the year's pressures. As the year develops, some Dogs could be tempted by a new activity or set themselves a project. This can again help to open up interesting avenues for the future.

In money matters, Dogs will need to be careful, however. Over the year, they could find it helpful to make early provision for more expensive plans. Their discipline will enable more to go ahead. They will also need to deal with forms and financial paperwork promptly and thoroughly. To delay, make assumptions or take risks could be to their detriment. Dogs, take note.

In view of the year's pressures, Dogs will often regard their home as a private sanctuary and they will delight in family developments and domestic activities. Being open and sharing their thoughts, including any concerns, with those around them will help others to understand and assist. And they will do much to help their loved ones too, including offering advice on what could be special and personal matters. Here their understanding and input can be telling. Also, by contributing to family life, Dogs will appreciate many of the activities that take place all the more. In this mixed year, relations with their loved ones can be valuable and often special.

Their social life, too, can be of benefit. By going out, they can not only enjoy some good times but also achieve a better lifestyle balance. And while some Dogs may prefer smaller events, some of the bigger occasions they go to will often turn out to be better than they thought. The Ox year may have some unexpected highlights.

Overall, though, it will be a demanding one. It will be difficult for Dogs to make headway, but by treading a careful course and remaining mindful of those around them, they can learn a lot from the year. Experience gained now can be of particular value, as prospects are greatly improved in the following Tiger year. Spending time with others can also help to put some of the year's vexations into perspective. Dogs need not feel alone this year. And while situations may not always be easy, the experience and insights gained can often be of considerable future value.

Tips for the Year
Be thorough in money matters and wary of risk. Also, proceed carefully at work, watching developments and adapting as need be. And enjoy spending time on your interests and with those who are close to you. These can both benefit you in this sometimes vexing year.

Dog Fortunes in the Year of the Tiger

Dogs are very observant and also susceptible to conditions around them. And when they feel times are right, they come into their own. This will be such a year. With chances aplenty and good support, many Dogs will be able to move ahead with ease and enjoy some personal triumphs. For Dogs who start the year dissatisfied or who would welcome change, this is a time to focus on the *now* rather than feel hindered by what has gone before. By taking action, they can help bring about the improvement they desire.

Throughout the year Dogs will be helped by the support of those around them, including some who have influence or can assist in telling ways. However, to fully benefit, they do need to be forthcoming and talk over their plans and ideas. This is no year for them to keep their thoughts to themselves.

This need for openness also applies to social situations. When first meeting people, Dogs can sometimes come across as reserved. They do not always show their personality to best advantage. In the vibrant Tiger year, it really is worth them making the effort to overcome this and allow others to appreciate their true nature.

During the year many Dogs will see an increase in social activity and will have a variety of interesting occasions to attend. As a result, their circle of acquaintances is set to grow and they may make some valuable new friends. For any Dogs who are feeling lonely or that their social life has lacked sparkle of late, it would be well worth joining a local activity group this year.

There are also good romantic possibilities and some Dogs are destined to meet their soulmate. In so many ways, Tiger years can be significant and sometimes transforming.

Dogs can also look forward to special times in their home life. As always, they will give a lot of time to their loved ones and be proud of their achievements. Family members will be keen to reciprocate, and may help a lot with decision-making this year, especially as they may raise some additional considerations. With all helping one another and enjoying marking milestones and successes, domestic life can be particularly pleasing.

Tiger years can also open up interesting possibilities, including some related to personal interests. Some Dogs may decide to improve their fitness levels and seek guidance on taking up a new activity or discipline, while others may be intrigued by other recreational pursuits, hobbies or interests. Tiger years are times to be receptive to what is available and starting something new could be just the tonic some Dogs need.

The Tiger year also holds considerable potential work-wise. Particularly for Dogs who are unhappy in their current position or feel they have been languishing in recent times, this is a year to seize the initiative and look to make changes. By making enquiries, talking to contacts and keeping alert for openings, many Dogs will secure a position that gives them a new chance. Dogs, take note. This is no year to stand still.

This also applies to Dogs seeking work. While some may feel disillusioned, this is a year for them to have self-belief and put themselves forward. By being quick in following up openings and emphasizing their experience, many will be given the chance they are hoping for. For some, the year can set their career on a new but potentially significant track.

For Dogs who are established in a particular career, the aspects are also encouraging. There may be the chance of promotion in their present place of work, and for those in large organizations, an attachment or transfer could be tempting. Many Dogs will see their career progressing to new levels in the Tiger year.

Progress at work can also bring an increase in income, and some Dogs will also benefit from a bonus or gift. However, to make the most of this, Dogs need to remain disciplined, otherwise anything extra could quickly be spent. Also, if entering into a new agreement, they should carefully check the terms and obligations. While this is a good year, this is not one to be lax, especially in matters with long-term implications.

Overall, however, Dogs can do well this year and make good progress. At work, their potential could be recognized and encouraged and there could be opportunities to move ahead. Personal interests too can develop in satisfying ways, while domestically and socially there will be special times to enjoy. Romantic prospects are good as well. A rewarding and often special year!

Tips for the Year
Draw on the support of those around you. With additional input, so much more can become possible for you. Also, take action. Great are the possibilities of the Tiger year. Act well to do well.

DOG FORTUNES IN THE YEAR OF THE RABBIT

When Dogs look back at the Rabbit year, they could well be surprised by all they have accomplished in it. This promises to be a very full 12 months, both personally and professionally.

Their personal life can bring them especial joy. Dogs currently enjoying romance will often see it grow in significance and many will settle down with their partner or marry. For the unattached, someone they meet can quickly become special, and although Dogs like to take their time in forming relationships, some could be swept off their feet this year by the wonders and excitement of new love.

They should also make the most of their social opportunities. Not only will they enjoy many convivial times with others, but they will find that some of the people they meet will be able to help with their current aims or interests. It has often been said that the more people you know, the more opportunities open up for you, and this will be true for Dogs this year. Their growing numbers of acquaintances can assist and encourage them in many ways. This year Dogs should do all they can to raise their profile, engage with others and enjoy what happens.

The auspicious aspects also extend to their domestic life. There will be celebrations in many Dog households this year – perhaps a marriage, an addition to the family or an individual success or milestone. And for Dogs who have thoughts of moving, this is a year to set plans in motion. A lot can be accomplished.

However, while Dogs will instigate many of the plans and activities that are carried out this year, family members do need to join together and pool energy, talents and resources. The greater the collective effort, the more extensive the gains and improvements will be.

Work prospects are also favourably aspected and this is a year for Dogs to take action. Those who are considering self-employment or setting up a business should explore this more fully and seek appropriate advice. Many plans can be set in motion now.

Dogs following a particular career path can also make substantial progress. They will often be well placed to benefit from a sudden opportunity, whether through the departure of a colleague or the need for staff for a more specialist role. The changes that occur this year may not be what these Dogs were envisaging, but they will nevertheless enable many to advance their position and enjoy greater success and recognition.

For Dogs who are looking for a new challenge elsewhere, as well as those seeking work, the Rabbit year can again open up exciting possibilities. By considering ways in which they can adapt their skills and exploring openings, these Dogs may be rewarded with a position that is very different from what they have been doing but gives them the opportunity and incentive they need. Some of what occurs can mark a considerable change in these Dogs' working life, including in location, industry and skills, but by being receptive and willing, they can make important headway.

Progress at work will help financially and some Dogs could also profit from an interest or enterprising idea. However, in view of some of the plans and purchases they have in mind, they should keep a careful eye on their budget. For those who move in particular, costs and obligations need to be closely monitored. With good control, many plans can successfully go ahead, but this is a year for discipline, good planning and good management.

If possible, Dogs should, however, make provision for a holiday. A break and a change of scene can be of benefit and many will delight in the places they get to visit.

All Dogs can also derive much satisfaction from their personal interests and this is an excellent year to enjoy their talents. Whether they prefer practical activities, outdoor pursuits or more creative ones, by spending time on them and using their skills, they can be very pleased with the way they develop.

Overall, Dogs should be alert for opportunities in the Rabbit year. Even though some may be surprising, what happens often happens for a reason, and this year it will be to their advantage. This is a time to set plans in motion, and Dogs should explore possibilities, particularly if they want to move house. They can accomplish a great deal in Rabbit years. Their personal life can also be special, and, for some, engagement, marriage and an addition to the family can beckon. Dogs can see a lot happen this year and realize some cherished hopes.

Tips for the Year
Take your plans forward. Draw on the support of those around you and be receptive to what opens up for you, as helpful (and sometimes surprising) developments can often assist the process. Also, enjoy your personal relations, especially as there may be significant developments to share.

Dog Fortunes in the Year of the Dragon

Dragon years are dynamic and Dogs may be ill at ease with some of the fast-moving developments. They are not ones for acting on impulse or embracing sudden change, but this is the way of the

Dragon year. It can be a challenging time, but Dogs can gain both experience and fresh insights into their skills and capabilities.

A key feature of Dogs is their conscientious nature. They care and take their responsibilities seriously. It is because of this that they worry so – and the Dragon year can certainly bring its worries. However, by sharing their concerns with those around them, Dogs can not only be helped but also reassured. Sometimes just the process of talking can put matters into perspective or bring forth solutions. Dogs should not feel they are on their own. They do much for others and this year they should let others reciprocate.

At work, this can be a demanding time. Changes could suddenly occur, including staff movements and alterations to working practices, and Dogs could face increased pressures. Some of the year will be tricky, but by focusing on what needs to be done and avoiding distractions, they can make the best of the situation, and their steadfastness and reliability will be noticed and much appreciated.

Also, while Dogs may have misgivings about the changes taking place, these can give rise to opportunities. New positions could be created or staff could be required to work in different capacities. If Dogs are tempted by a particular possibility, they should follow it up. This is no year to be resistant to change but to make the most of it.

For Dogs who decide to move on from where they are, as well as those seeking work, the Dragon year can again be challenging. There may be limited vacancies as well as fierce competition. However, Dogs are tenacious, and by putting extra effort into their applications and stressing their experience and suitability, many will ultimately prevail. Some could chance upon a position which could set their career off on an interesting new track. Dragon years may be challenging, but they are not without potentially significant opportunities.

In money matters, however, Dogs need to be careful. If considering a major purchase, they need to check that their requirements are being met and be aware of all the implications and costs. They should keep track of spending, too, and give prompt and thorough attention to financial paperwork. Delay and carelessness could be to their disadvantage. This is very much a year for careful financial management.

In view of the year's pressures, Dogs should make sure they set aside time for themselves. Personal interests can be of especial value and there will be the chance for many Dogs to further what they do this year or to try something different.

A further pleasure could come from travel, and if possible, Dogs should aim to take a holiday as well as enjoy some unexpected windows of opportunity to go away. A break and the chance to visit some famed attractions could be delightful and beneficial.

In addition, to keep on good form, Dogs would do well to give some thought to their well-being. If they are lacking regular exercise or feel dietary modifications could be of benefit, they should seek medical advice on actions they could take.

Throughout the year Dogs will value the company and support of their often close band of friends, and again they should avail themselves of the help and expertise they offer, as well as take up other social opportunities. This is no year for them to draw into themselves or miss out on things happening.

In matters of the heart, they will, though, need to proceed mindfully. New relationships should be nurtured and allowed to build in their own time.

Domestically, this promises to be a busy year, with Dogs assisting loved ones and attending to a great many things. Again it is important they do not shoulder too much on their own, but consult others and share responsibility. Also, while liking to plan, they will need to show flexibility over arrangements, as circumstances may change. Amid all the activity, however, there will be family times and individual accomplishments to savour.

Dragon years have great energy and move along at a heady pace. And for Dogs, who prefer order and consistency, they can be challenging times. However, by being prepared to adapt and make the most of situations, Dogs can learn a great deal, develop their skills and discover strengths and opportunities they can build on. And they should also share fully in the activities this lively year presents.

Tips for the Year
Do not feel alone. Support and advice are there for you. Also, set time aside for yourself and for recreation. Personal interests, travel and quality time with your loved ones can be of consider-able value in this busy and fast-moving year.

Dog Fortunes in the Year of the Snake

A pleasing and productive year. Rather than feel buffeted by events or have to cope with diverse pressures, Dogs will be able to reassert themselves and set their own plans in motion. This will be a much more satisfying year for them. Not only can they make good headway, but they will also enjoy a certain amount of luck.

Like Snakes, Dogs like to plan, and as the year begins, they should give some thought to their plans for it. Having some objectives in mind will not only help them channel their energies more effectively, but also make them aware of the actions they need to take. And those who start the Snake year nursing hurt or feeling they have not been making the most of their potential should take heart. This is a year that can bring the positive change they need.

Work aspects are encouraging and there will be good opportunities to take on greater and often more rewarding responsibilities. Over the year many Dogs will reap the rewards of recent good work.

For those who feel there is a lack of opportunity where they are or who are seeking work, again the Snake year can open up good possibilities. By remaining active in the job-seeking process, swift in following up opportunities and not too restrictive in the type of positions they seek, many of these Dogs could take on a position with potential for development and growth. In many cases there will be considerable learning involved, but this will give them the incentive they need.

All Dogs will benefit from the way their work brings them into contact with others. They can impress this year, and by networking and raising their profile, their commitment and capabilities can again help their prospects.

Progress made at work will help financially and many Dogs will enjoy an increase in income over the year. Some could benefit from a bonus or gift as well, or find an interest remunerative. However, while Dogs may find this a financially improved year, they will need to remain disciplined. Spending should be carefully controlled and early provision made for more expensive outgoings. This is a year rewarding good financial management.

Personal interests can be satisfying and also good ways to meet others. Snake years particularly favour creative endeavour and any Dogs who would welcome a new challenge or who become intrigued by a certain interest should follow this up and be open to possibility.

Although Dogs are often selective in their socializing, their work, interests and contacts can all lead to them meeting people this year and winning new friends. Dogs who feel their social life has been lacking sparkle recently will find that getting involved in local activities can bring the improvement they want.

For the unattached, the Snake year also has romantic possibilities and a chance meeting is capable of growing in significance.

The Snake year can also bring some special domestic occasions. Not only will Dogs find their loved ones keen to share in their progress, but there could also be a personal occasion or family milestone to mark. Whether celebrating a birth, wedding, graduation or other achievement, quite a few Dogs can enjoy some gratifying times.

Over the year, Dogs will also give sterling advice and support to their loved ones as well as instigate some ambitious home improvements. However, practical activities should not be rushed, but undertaken as and when time allows. Also, any projects and other improvements do need to be carefully costed, as some may prove more expensive than envisaged. Dogs, take note.

In general, the Snake year is an encouraging one for Dogs. In their work, this will often be a more fulfilling time and they can look forward to making good headway and enjoying some impressive results. Throughout the year they will be encouraged by the support of those around them and there will be good times and successes to share. Dogs have much in their favour this year and if they act with purpose they can make some well-deserved progress.

Tips for the Year
Henry Ford declared, 'Whether you think you can or you think you can't, you're right.' This year, think you can! Have some aims in mind and work towards them. Also, value your relations with others. Colleagues, friends, loved ones and new contacts can all help you make the most of the year.

Dog Fortunes in the Year of the Horse

A constructive year which will allow Dogs to build on their present position and enjoy many positive developments. It will be a busy time and Dogs will need to use their energies effectively and focus on their key aims. For any nurturing a particular ambition, though, this is an excellent time to take this further. With purpose and self-belief, they can see possibilities unfolding.

At work, the experience and reputation many Dogs have built up will place them in a good position to advance their career. Those following a particular career path may find themselves making especially good headway this year.

Any Dogs who have felt held back in recent times (maybe through lack of opportunity) or would welcome fresh challenges should keep alert for openings and put themselves forward. By making applications and indicating their desire to better themselves, many will now secure the chance they need. This is no year to stand still.

Dogs seeking work could find friends and contacts helpful in alerting them to possibilities. By widening the scope of their search, many can secure a position they can build on. However, it should be noted that the Horse is a hard taskmaster and with progress will come new challenges. This is very much a year for Dogs to show the stuff they are made of – which many will successfully do.

Progress at work can lead to rise in income too and many Dogs will be keen to proceed with more substantial purchases. By giving careful thought to these, they will be able to make some good decisions, and often secure them on favourable terms. They could also find it helpful to review their financial situation at some point during the year. In some cases, modifications can lead to savings and improvements. Making provision for their future requirements and the longer term could also be of advantage. Good financial management can make an important difference this year.

Also, Dogs should not be lax with personal security or looking after valuables. A loss could be upsetting.

Many Dogs will enjoy the way they can extend their knowledge in the Horse year, and this need not be restricted to work matters. Over the year they should give some thought to ways in which they could further their personal interests. If they have a certain talent, extra practice, study and instruction may help them to delight in what they do. For those who enjoy creative pursuits, this can be a particularly gratifying and productive time.

Another pleasure of the year will be travel. If possible, Dogs should make provision for a holiday, and if certain attractions or events are tempting, they should see what can be arranged. Sometimes their interests and work will give rise to travel opportunities as well. Many Dogs will be travelling more than usual this year.

They can also look forward to an increase in social activity and there can often be an interesting mix of things to do. For Dogs who are lonely or have had recent upset to overcome, the Horse year can see improvement in their situation. Both new and existing friends can be supportive, and shared interests and activities can help restore some sparkle to their life.

For the unattached, the Horse year can see a flurry of romantic activity. Cupid's arrow will be aimed in the direction of many Dogs, and for quite a few this can be a fun, lively and exciting year.

In their home life, they can also expect much activity. Over the year some key plans can be realized, perhaps concerning interests, travel, projects or individual achievements. There will be some surprises too. However, being so caring, Dogs could be concerned about the situation of another person. At such times, they should keep things in perspective, encourage communication and, if appropriate, seek advice. All years have their problems and this one will be no exception, but in the main, home life will proceed well.

Horse years are busy and productive, and by acting with resolve, Dogs can make good progress and benefit from some timely opportunities. This is a time to look to advance, and Dogs will be pleased with the way many of their plans progress as well as how their skills develop. Their domestic and social life will be active, there will be travel opportunities, and for the unattached, the year holds exciting possibilities. Overall, a pleasing and rewarding year.

Tips for the Year
Take action. Have self-belief and make the most of your opportunities. Enjoy travel and your personal interests, though take care with your personal possessions. Value your relations with those around you and enjoy spending time with them.

Dog Fortunes in the Year of the Goat

A mixed year. Dogs like structure and are both methodical and conscientious. The volatility of the Goat year could worry them. Progress will be more difficult and parts of the year will be trying, although to compensate, on a personal level the Goat year can give rise to some special times.

In view of the prevailing aspects, Dogs will need to show flexibility this year. This is no time to be wedded to a single approach or regard plans as set in stone. New developments can arise at any moment, and opportunities too. To benefit, Dogs should adapt accordingly.

This is especially the case in their work. Over the year a plethora of new ideas, schemes and working practices will be suggested, and Dogs, who favour tradition, will often be filled with misgivings. However, rather than act or speak out too hastily, they should show patience, watch developments and wait for situations to settle. This is no time to jeopardize their position by appearing too set in their ways. They may not be happy about the situation, but during times of change, keeping a low profile and concentrating on what needs to be done could be the best option.

For Dogs who are keen to move on from where they are, as well as those seeking work, the Goat year can be tricky but significant. To help their chances, these Dogs should not be too restrictive in the type of positions they are seeking. By widening the scope of their search and considering other ways in which they could use their skills, they may be able to secure an interesting (and often different) position. Again flexibility is key – Dogs who are prepared to adapt will be the ones benefiting from unexpected opportunities.

For some Dogs, the Goat year can also be considered a time of reappraisal, and for those who want a career change, now could be the time to explore options.

All Dogs can also help their position by working well with others. By being a part of what is going on, rather than isolated and removed, they will not only keep themselves better informed, but also be able to adjust accordingly. In the Goat year, Dogs need to keep their wits about them.

Many Dogs will enjoy a rise in income over the year and some will benefit from a bonus payment or gift as well. Again the Goat year, despite its vexations, has the capacity to surprise. However, while anything extra will be welcome, this will be an expensive year, especially as some Dogs will move or face repair costs. All Dogs will need to manage their finances carefully and check the details, paperwork and obligations of any large transactions. This is not a year to be lax or make assumptions. Delays and snags may also slow down certain transactions and care and patience be required.

Home life will, though, be especially busy and see considerable change. Some Dogs will decide to relocate and the moving process will take up much of their time and energy. Others could embark on ambitious home improvements as well as have to deal with the annoyance of failing equipment. Domestically, a lot will require attention this year, although when plans have been realized, problems resolved and purchases made, the benefits could be many and far-reaching.

In addition to all the practical activity, the Goat year will bring some family highlights. Whether celebrating an addition to the family, an academic achievement, a personal success or a house-warming, the Dog could enjoy some pleasurable occasions. Goat years may have their troublesome aspects, but can be domestically gratifying.

They can also give rise to some good social opportunities. Despite the pressures of the year, Dogs should not deny themselves the chance to go out, especially if tempted by certain activities and events. Some of the people they meet this year could become firm friends.

For Dogs enjoying romance, their relationship could develop in meaningful ways this year, while for those who start the year unattached or have had a recent personal upset, a special person could now enter their life.

With the busy nature of the year, it is also important that Dogs allow time for rest and relaxation. Driving themselves relentlessly could take its toll. Here personal interests can add valuable balance to their lifestyle. Creative activities in particular could broaden out in interesting ways this year.

Overall, the Goat year will be demanding and Dogs will be concerned about its uncertainties and pressures. However, at times of change, Dogs can not only gain useful experience but also have the chance to prove themselves in new ways. Family and accommodation matters can be highlights of the year, as many plans can now be realized. Throughout the year Dogs will be encouraged by the support and goodwill of their loved ones and the year will give rise to some special personal and family times.

Tips for the Year
Problems have been said to be opportunities in disguise, so view the changes of the year as chances to learn, further your experience and (sometimes) try the new. Be willing to adapt and to draw on the support of others. And enjoy your relations with those who are special to you.

Dog Fortunes in the Year of the Monkey

The Monkey year can be a fine one for Dogs, with much to do and enjoy. However, to get the best from it, Dogs will need to act with purpose. With resolve and persistence, they can see a lot more happen.

Also, Dogs rely a lot on instinct, and as the Monkey year begins, many will sense an improvement in fortunes and will set about their activities with greater resolve. This, in itself, will give impetus and direction to the year as well as set important wheels in motion.

Work prospects are encouraging and many Dogs will feel ready in themselves to progress. As a result, they will not only keep alert for openings in their present place of work but also start to look elsewhere. And very early on, interesting possibilities could arise. The Monkey year can provide Dogs with some very good opportunities, whether they are building on their present position or moving elsewhere. Their reputation and commitment will be important factors in their quest, and senior personnel (or contacts) will often be supportive too.

For Dogs pursuing a particular career, promotion can beckon, and they will enjoy the chance to take their work to new levels. Dogs who take on a new role in the early months of the year could have the opportunity to make further progress before the year's end.

For Dogs who are unfulfilled in their present role, this is a year to seek change. By taking advice from employment experts as well as considering what they would like to do, many could secure the improvement they have been hankering for. Similarly, those seeking work should widen their search. Many of these Dogs will also have the chance to take on a new role over the year. Admittedly, any new position could initially be daunting and there could be much to learn, but these Dogs will be glad of a new platform on which to build.

Progress made at work will help financially, but Monkey years are active and expensive. Much spending on the home is indicated, and for those who have considered relocation, a move is possible. In addition, many Dogs will decide to update equipment and install new comforts. Quite a few Dog homes will benefit from improvements this year. However, with much outlay likely, costs do need to be monitored and budgets adapted accordingly.

In addition, travel is well aspected and Dogs would do well to make provision for a possible holiday and/or short break.

With the activity and demands of the year, it is also important that they take good care of themselves. If neglectful of their own well-being or driving themselves hard without sufficient rest, exercise or suitable food, they may find themselves susceptible to colds and other niggling ailments. Extra self-care would not come amiss this year, and if they have any concerns, they should get these checked out.

Socially, they will find themselves in demand and the Monkey year can provide a varied mix of things to do. Over the year Dogs will enjoy spending time with their friends as well as renewing some earlier acquaintances. Also, in view of certain hopes and decisions, they could know of someone with the right knowledge to help. For any Dogs who are feeling lonely or have had some personal difficulty of late, someone they meet now could put some sparkle back into their life. Socially, these can be pleasing and rewarding times.

Home life can also be special this year, with personal achievements and the fulfilment of plans often being celebrated in style. Dogs will appreciate the many shared activities of the year. However, to prevent undue pressure, it would be advisable to spread activities and projects out rather than having everything happening at once.

The Monkey year holds good prospects for Dogs, although to make the most of it they need to be the drivers of change. By looking to advance and setting their plans in motion, they can achieve a great deal. At work, there will be opportunities to make greater use of their strengths, while at home they will delight in the realization of some key aims. And throughout the year they will benefit from the support of others. With a busy lifestyle, they do need to give some consideration to their well-being, but overall, a pleasing and rewarding year.

Tips for the Year
Look to move forward in this year of great possibility. Take action! Also, look to raise your profile. By engaging in what is going on around you and getting to know others, you can benefit

in many ways. And in this busy year, balance your lifestyle as much as you can.

Dog Fortunes in the Year of the Rooster

The Rooster year can be an exacting one. Dogs will find much being asked – demanded – of them. Also, the structure of Rooster years mean that Dogs need to conform and go with the flow. This is no time for them to dig their heels in or be too independent-minded. However, while they will be tested, they can nevertheless get much value from the year. Developments now will often prepare them for the opportunities that await in their own year, which follows.

At work, many Dogs will not only face an increased workload but also find some duties made difficult by bureaucracy, failing systems and delay. Being conscientious, they will be keen not to let anyone down and will find parts of the year frustrating. However, it is often in more challenging situations that skills can be honed, experience gained and attributes discovered, and so it will be for many Dogs this year. Rooster years can not only highlight their strengths, but also bring some to the fore, enhancing their reputation in the process and sowing important seeds for the future.

Many Dogs will remain with their present employer this year and build on their experience. However, for those who decide on change or are seeking work, the Rooster year can have significant developments. Obtaining a new position will require time and effort and Dogs should not be too restrictive in what they consider. This is a year to make the most of situations *as they are* rather than as they would like them to be. However, the positions many Dogs do secure will often give them the chance to gain experience in another capacity and will not only add to their skills and employability but also open up possibilities for the future. Rooster years, despite their pressures, can have far-reaching value.

Dogs will, however, need to give careful attention to their finances this year. With their busy lifestyle and many commitments, their outgoings could be greater than anticipated. This is a year for discipline and good control over the purse-strings. Also, if involved in a large transaction, they will find that taking the time to compare prices, terms and implications could lead to more appropriate decisions.

With the busy nature of the year, it is important that Dogs do not allow their personal interests and recreational pursuits to become side-lined. These can not only help them rest and unwind but also give rise to many pleasurable moments. Looking ahead, if there are skills they feel could be helpful or a particular subject that appeals to them, they should find out more. Positive action can be to both their present and future advantage.

In their relations with others, care is advised. An issue with another person could be worrying or someone could let them down. Such instances will disappoint and sometimes hurt the faithful Dog. The Rooster year can bring some hard lessons. But these will pass, and even if a friendship flounders, another could quickly take its place. Dogs relate well to others, and despite some awkward moments (and all years have their share), they will enjoy the social opportunities that arise this year.

Their home life will also keep them busy and may not always prove straightforward. Not only could there be failing equipment to deal with but practical activities could be more disruptive than anticipated. Rooster years can have their frustrations, but by drawing on the support of those around them, Dogs will be able to overcome these and out of problems can come improvements that everyone can appreciate.

Throughout the year, Dogs do need to be forthcoming, however, and discuss any concerns and anxieties with their loved ones. If not, their preoccupation could lead to awkward moments. Dogs, take note and do be open and communicative. However, while the Rooster year will bring its pressures, there will also be family successes that will delight all concerned, as will shared occasions, some of which will be appreciated all the more for their spontaneity.

In general, the Rooster year will be a demanding one and Dogs will need to exercise care and make the best of situations. Some plans and activities will be problematic. Also, while enjoying good relations with many of those around them, Dogs need to be aware of any awkward undercurrents. But while certain situations will test them, they will also highlight their qualities and give them further experience. And, with their own year following, the lessons of the Rooster year can be far-reaching. Dogs can take comfort in the knowledge that the good they do now can be the catalyst for better times ahead.

Tips for the Year
Use any chances to add to your experience and skills. Also, join with others and share plans and activities, although do be alert and tactful in pressured or awkward situations.

DOG FORTUNES IN THE YEAR OF THE DOG

'Every dog has its day', as the saying has it, and it could also be said that every Dog has its year. This is it. It is a year offering great prospects for Dogs themselves. However, it is also one requiring effort. Dogs will need to take purposeful action. Once they do, helpful influences – and some serendipity – will often come into play. Dogs who start the year unfulfilled or disappointed with recent developments should focus their attention on the *now* rather than what has gone before. For some, this year can be the start of a much brighter chapter.

At work, the experience, reputation and ambition of many Dogs can lead to good headway being made. With changes often occurring this year, they may be well placed to benefit. In some cases, training they have recently had, together with their current responsibilities, will have prepared them well for the opportunities that now become available.

For Dogs who feel there are limited prospects where they are or are seeking work, again the Dog year can bring some excellent opportunities. By keeping informed of developments in their area and making enquiries, many of these Dogs will find their initiative rewarded with a position with good prospects for growth. Some of what occurs may happen in curious ways this year. Also, Dogs who are considering a career change or have been looking for work for some time should take advantage of any refresher or training courses that are available. With help and guidance, new possibilities can open up.

Throughout the year, Dogs should also make the most of their often unique strengths. In their work, their input can lead to some notable achievements, but in their interests too, their talents and ideas could develop in encouraging ways. No matter whether they prefer creative, practical or outdoor pursuits, they should enjoy them this year and, if appropriate, promote what they do. The feedback they receive could encourage them as well as lead on to other possibilities.

In addition, if a new interest or skill is tempting, or Dogs feel another qualification could help, they should follow it up. Investing in themselves can have both present and future value.

Progress made at work can also help financially, and many Dogs will enjoy a rise in income over the year. Some may also be able to supplement their means through an enterprising idea or some extra work. The earning abilities of many will be on good form. As a result, they may decide to proceed with ideas and purchases they have long been considering. Some will also use an upturn to reduce borrowings or make savings for the future. With good management, Dogs will be pleased with the decisions they take.

If possible, they should make provision for a holiday with their loved ones. It could be among the year's many highlights.

They may also be pleased with improvements they carry out in the home, including refreshing décor and reorganizing and tidying certain rooms. Over the year quite a few Dog homes will enjoy a makeover.

With Dogs' own successes and the achievements of their loved ones, there can also be celebrations in many a household, and Dogs will enjoy being involved in them. Family life means a lot to Dogs.

They will also appreciate the social opportunities that come their way. Their work, interests and friends can all introduce them to new people this year and they can make some useful connections. Any Dogs who are feeling lonely or have had recent problems to overcome should take advantage of the events and activities in their area. Positive action can brighten their situation. And for the unattached, serious romance can beckon.

Overall, the Dog year has considerable potential for Dogs themselves, and during it they would do well to remember the saying, 'Nothing ventured, nothing gained.' This is a year to venture. At work, considerable progress can be made and their strengths and initiative help bring success. Personal interests and plans can also develop in encouraging manner, while on a personal level, they will enjoy sharing activities with others and be encouraged by the support and love shown to them. A great year and one to very much enjoy.

Tips for the Year
Look to move ahead. With resolve and self-belief, you can accomplish a lot in your own year. Also, appreciate the support of those around you. And enjoy your well-deserved success!

Dog Fortunes in the Year of the Pig

Unlike some years, when Dogs feel buffeted by events, the general pace and nature of the Pig year will be to their liking. As a result, many will be able to make good headway as well as enjoy some personally pleasing developments.

In many of their activities, Dogs will be well supported by those around them. However, to fully benefit, they need to be forthcoming and willing to share their hopes and thoughts. Support and input can make an important difference and lead to more going ahead. Also, Dogs will get to meet many people during the Pig year and should seize any opportunities to build connections and add to their social circle. By doing so, they are set to impress many.

The Pig year can also give rise to an increased number of social opportunities. There will be a good mix of things to do, and for any Dogs who are feeling lonely or would like to add something new to their lifestyle, joining a local group could be worth considering.

Those newly in love or who find love this year – and the aspects are encouraging – will often see the relationship developing in significance. Quite a few Dogs will settle down with another person or marry this year. On a personal level, the Pig year can be special.

Dogs will also derive much contentment from their home life. Here again, if they are open and communicate well with those around them, useful support can be given and plans advanced. During the year there will also be family successes that will be particularly pleasing and Dogs will feel justifiably proud of their loved ones.

However, while much will go well, problems may still arise. When they do, Dogs should address the situation. Their empathy and support may be of particular value.

Pig years offer variety, and if Dogs become attracted by a new interest this year or are keen to develop an existing one in a new way, they should follow up their ideas. These are times of scope and possibility and Dogs should be receptive to what opens up for them.

If possible, they should also try to fit some travel into the year. A rest and a change of scene can do them a lot of good. However, they do need to check their connections and make sure their documentation is in order. A mistake or error could be inconvenient. Travel arrangements need close attention this year.

Work-wise, Pig years are encouraging and will give many Dogs greater chance to focus on their area of expertise. As a result, this can be a fulfilling time and, feeling inspired, Dogs can look forward to achieving some impressive results. Some may play a greater role as the year progresses, while others will be offered the chance to take on more specific tasks.

While many will make good headway with their present employer, for those who feel their prospects could be bettered by a move elsewhere or are seeking work, the Pig year can develop in encouraging ways. By keeping alert, talking to contacts (who could prove particularly helpful) and considering other ways in which they could use their strengths, these Dogs could uncover some interesting opportunities. For some, what opens up now could mark a considerable change in their working life but give them the chance to prove themselves in a different capacity. Pig years have much potential and will leave many Dogs enjoying a greater level of fulfilment in their work environment.

Financial prospects are also encouraging, with many Dogs increasing their income over the year. However, to get the most from any upturn, they should manage their finances with care and make early provision for large purchases rather than proceeding on an ad hoc basis. Discipline and careful planning will lead to more going ahead. Also, if able to do so, setting funds aside for the longer term could be something they are grateful for in years to come. In this favourable year, good financial management can help the overall position of many Dogs.

Generally, the Pig year can be a pleasing one and Dogs will be able to use their strengths to good advantage. Particularly at work, some notable successes can be enjoyed. Ideas and personal interests can also develop well, although Dogs do need to be open to the possibilities of the year and respond well to what happens. They will, however, be encouraged by the support and goodwill of others. In the Pig year, Dogs have much in their favour and much to gain and enjoy.

Tips for the Year
Take purposeful action. Follow up your ideas. Seize your chances. Much can be achieved this year. Also, enjoy sharing the good times with those who are special to you.

Thoughts and Words of Dogs

Whatever is worth doing at all is worth doing well.

THE EARL OF CHESTERFIELD

Each player must accept the cards life deals him or her. But once they are in hand, he or she alone must decide how to play the cards in order to win the game.

VOLTAIRE

All experience is an arch to build upon.

HENRY BROOK ADAMS

There is one thing which gives radiance to everything. It is the idea of something around the corner.

G. K. CHESTERTON

You are never too old to set another goal or to dream a new dream.

C. S. LEWIS

I am not the smartest or most talented person in the world, but I succeeded because I kept going, and going, and going.

SYLVESTER STALLONE

Don't be afraid to take a big step if one is indicated. You can't cross a chasm in two small jumps.

DAVID LLOYD GEORGE

The price of greatness is responsibility.

SIR WINSTON CHURCHILL

We make a living by what we get, we make a life by what we give.

SIR WINSTON CHURCHILL

It is no use saying, 'We are doing our best.' You have to succeed in doing what is necessary.

SIR WINSTON CHURCHILL

Above all things, never think that you're not good enough yourself. A man should never think that. My belief is that in life people will take you very much at your own reckoning.

ANTHONY TROLLOPE

If you think you can win, you can win. Faith is necessary to victory.

WILLIAM HAZLITT

4 February 1935–23 January 1936 — *Wood Pig*

22 January 1947–9 February 1948 — *Fire Pig*

8 February 1959–27 January 1960 — *Earth Pig*

27 January 1971–14 February 1972 — *Metal Pig*

13 February 1983–1 February 1984 — *Water Pig*

31 January 1995–18 February 1996 — *Wood Pig*

18 February 2007–6 February 2008 — *Fire Pig*

5 February 2019–24 January 2020 — *Earth Pig*

23 January 2031–10 February 2032 — *Metal Pig*

The Pig

The Personality of the Pig

According to the legend in which the Buddha invited all the animals in the kingdom to a party, the Pig was the last to show and so the last to have a year named in their honour. And, in China, being born under the sign of the Pig is both a compliment and an honour.

Pigs are born under the sign of honesty and are good-natured and fun-loving. They work hard but also play hard and lead full and often contented lives.

Pigs are also very sociable and like meeting others. And they relate well. They listen, notice and empathize. Thanks to their kindly nature, they are also thoughtful, and if someone has suffered adversity or sadness, they know how to respond. Also, with their dislike of unpleasantness and confrontation (they often wonder why everyone can't just get on), they do their best to defuse awkward situations and bring calm. They are skilled diplomats and arbiters of disputes. If they feel it can make life easier, sometimes they even turn a blind eye or ignore certain factors to preserve the peace.

Pigs are also trusting and scrupulous in their dealings. Unfortunately, though, there are times when their trust is misplaced and they fall victim to those less principled. They can sometimes be naive and in some situations learn the hard way.

Although Pigs have an easy-going manner, they think a lot. And when they have made their mind up, they are not ones to change it. At times Pigs can be stubborn and obstinate. They also take their obligations seriously and see their commitments through. Pigs do not like unfinished business. Indeed, rather than abandoning undertakings, or giving up on them halfway through, Pigs are great finishers and enjoy the satisfaction of seeing a job well done.

That is partly why Pigs are so successful in business. They not only work hard and apply themselves to the task in hand, but they are reliable and persistent. They also have good business sense and are certainly enterprising. Another asset is their ability to forge good working relations with many people. Their competent yet personable nature helps get others on their side and brings valuable support. In their choice of vocation, Pigs often do well when their work brings them into contact with others, whether in commerce, education, counselling, social work or some other capacity. They can enjoy success in the performing arts and (with their love of food) the culinary arts. Pigs make fine chefs and caterers. And whatever they choose to do, their skills and dependability ensure that many go far.

Pigs are also adept in money matters and enjoy living well. They can be indulgent and have expensive tastes and an eye for quality. They can also be generous and some are keen to support charitable causes. Money for Pigs is to be used, and used well. But although they can be big spenders, they are also canny and financially astute. They can be shrewd investors and their enterprising nature is capable of rewarding them well. If they ever suffer misfortune, they will learn their lessons well. Indeed, some Pigs have gone on to enjoy great success after an initial setback. In later life, many can be financially secure.

Pigs set great store by their relations with others and, with their capacity to give and their good humour, make friends with ease. They like socializing, partying and being with others.

They also very much enjoy the pleasures of love. Sensual, passionate and companionable, Pigs are certainly capable of winning hearts and minds. As they are easy-going, loyal and devoted to harmony, out of all the Chinese signs it is Pigs who tend to find domestic bliss most often. And, with their fondness of comfort and the good life, they will also make sure they and their loved ones live in style.

Many Pigs also revel in parenthood and, as a parent, will be caring and attentive as well as guide and inspire their children.

The female Pig has a warm, personable nature. She is very family-orientated and devotes much time and attention to her loved ones. She is also highly practical and able to turn her skills to many different uses. She is perceptive, too, and can rely on her intuition. Enjoying wide-ranging interests, she is adept and versatile. Although she may not be as career-driven as some, her hard work, team spirit and integrity ensure she makes a success of whatever she sets out to do. In appearance, she has good dress sense and presents herself well.

Active, genial and hard-working, Pigs often enjoy great success. They may have their weaknesses – they are, after all, stubborn and can be naïve – but their capacity to act, give and persist often ensures successful results. They may come across as easy-going, and they do like their pleasures and to indulge themselves, but they have a good and wise head on their shoulders. And this, combined with their skills, zest and personality, ensures a full and so often very rewarding life.

Top Tips for Pigs
- Often giving that little bit extra makes a huge amount of difference – be prepared to try it now and then. You can come across as laid-back and must be careful not to lose out because of it. By presenting yourself well and giving that little bit more, you can enjoy those extra rewards.
- Although you like to make the most of the moment, it could be to your advantage to think longer term. In particular, if pursuing a particular career or wanting to make more of a certain skill or interest, by building up skills and taking

advantage of training and guidance, you can be better equipped to advance.

- You are financially adept, but at times greater discipline would not come amiss. Rather than give way to whims or impulse buys, consider saving towards specific items (or indeed a good holiday), as well as the longer term. It can be to your advantage.
- With a busy and often demanding lifestyle, you would do well to give some thought to your well-being. If sedentary for long periods, it could be worth considering forms of exercise that would help. Also, aim for a healthy and balanced diet. To do well, you need to keep on good form and pay attention to self.

Relations with Others

With a Rat

With interests in common and a fondness for the good things in life, these two get on well.

In work, both are canny in business and together they have the talents to go far. The Pig in particular will value the Rat's resourcefulness and ability to identify opportunities.

In love, with a strong physical attraction and many shared values and interests, including a love of their home, these two are well suited. The Pig will delight in the companionship and support of the attentive Rat. A successful match.

With an Ox

While their personalities are different in so many ways, these two have great respect for each other and relations between them are good.

In work, both are persistent and diligent and they can harness each other's strengths. The Pig will particularly value the Ox's methodical, no-nonsense ways. An effective combination.

In love, there will be a close bond based on trust as well as many shared interests and values. The Pig will especially value the caring and dependable ways of the Ox, and with both taking their responsibilities seriously, they are well suited.

With a Tiger

Active, sociable and vivacious, these two enjoy each other's company and get on well.

In work, they may respect each other, but may not be the most effective combination. While the Pig may recognize the Tiger's enthusiasm and inventive streak, they will need to remain disciplined and channel their efforts towards specific objectives.

In love, there will not only be a strong physical attraction but also a special empathy. Each will value qualities found in the other and the Pig will find the Tiger encouraging and inspiring. A close and happy match.

With a Rabbit

Genial, peace-loving and sociable, these two get on well.

In work, there is good understanding and respect between them, with the Pig valuing and benefiting from the Rabbit's efficient and orderly ways. They work well together.

In love, both like their comforts and strive for an ordered and harmonious existence. The Pig will delight in the Rabbit's affection and good-natured ways. A successful match.

With a Dragon

Lively, sociable and sharing many interests, these two like and respect each other.

In work, their combined energy and different strengths go well together, with the Pig especially valuing the Dragon's dynamism, enterprise and business acumen.

In love, their passionate, sensual natures and sheer love of life make for a strong and enduring match. The Pig will delight in the Dragon's confident and caring ways.

With a Snake

With the Pig open and upfront and the Snake reserved, relations can prove difficult.

In work, the Snake likes to plan and think, while the Pig is more action-orientated and could find the Snake an inhibiting influence. Their different outlooks could prove awkward.

In love, their different personalities may for a time intrigue each other, but the Pig enjoys a more active lifestyle and will struggle to understand the Snake's more guarded and secretive ways. The portents are not good.

With a Horse

Sociable, lively and enjoying active lifestyles, these two share a great rapport.

In work, both are hard-working and adept and the Pig will value the Horse's enthusiasm and work ethic. When committed to an objective, and with each clear of the other's responsibilities, these two work effectively together.

In love, their energy, passion and strong understanding make for a close and loving match. Each will be inspired and supported by the other and the Pig will especially like the Horse's zest, style and positive outlook.

With a Goat

Genial, easy-going and good-natured, these two signs like one another and get on well.

In work, each will be appreciative of the other's strengths, with the Pig recognizing the Goat's creative and innovative flair. A good team.

In love, the Pig will value the kindly and loving ways of the Goat and also their home-making abilities. With both seeking a harmonious and (ideally) stress-free existence, these two can make an often excellent match.

With a Monkey

Outgoing, active and fun-loving, these two have a great understanding.

In work, their energies, skills and acumen fit well together and the Pig will draw strength from the energy and inventiveness of the Monkey.

In love, there can be great attraction between them, as well as much love and good humour. The Pig will value the Monkey's zest, enthusiasm and general encouragement. A mutually beneficial match.

With a Rooster

The Pig may initially be wary of the Rooster's matter-of-fact manner, but once these two get to know each other, relations between them can be generally good.

In work, the Pig will value the Rooster's good work ethic, but may find their exacting nature inhibiting. However, there is good respect between them.

In love their relationship can be mutually beneficial. The Pig can become more efficient and organized with a Rooster partner and possibly more successful too. A fine and meaningful match.

With a Dog

The Pig has much admiration for the loyal and dependable Dog and relations between them are good.

In work, their mutual respect makes for a good working relationship. Their skills are often complementary and the Pig will have a high regard for the Dog's judgement.

In love, these two can make a close and happy match. With often similar interests and outlooks, they enjoy a good rapport and the Pig will value the Dog's thoughtful and dependable ways.

With another Pig

With good rapport and similar tastes and outlooks, two Pigs get on very well together.

In work, they make an effective combination. Both are hard-working and enterprising and have a good head for business. Together, they can achieve great success.

In love, two Pigs will certainly know how to enjoy themselves. Fun-loving, home-loving and loving each other – what more could you ask? An excellent match.

Horoscopes for Each of the Chinese Years

PIG FORTUNES IN THE YEAR OF THE RAT

A variable year. While it will not be without its possibilities, Pigs could feel ill at ease with some of the change and volatility seen in the Rat year. They will need to keep their wits about them and adjust as situations require. However, while some of the year's developments may not be of their choosing, they can have important implications for the longer term.

At work, this can be a busy and demanding year. While many Pigs would prefer to just get on with their duties, they could find their workload affected by the slow workings of bureaucracy and matters outside their control. In addition, they could have misgivings about changes taking place and the additional pressure caused. Some situations could be particularly frustrating. However, Pigs are enterprising and will still be able to use their strengths to advantage and add to their working knowledge. This is not a year to close their mind to developments, but to observe, show patience and be prepared to learn. With their friendly nature, by networking and using their chances to get to know others, they can also form some useful connections and become an integral part of where they are. This may not be an easy year, but it can bear later fruit.

For Pigs who decide to seek change or are looking for work, the Rat year can have significant developments. Obtaining a new position will require time and considerable effort and these Pigs should not be too restrictive in their search but cast their net wide. That way, many will be able to secure a position that will give them the opportunity to develop their skills in new ways. This can be important in view of the encouraging aspects in the following Ox year.

In the Rat year, Pigs will need to exercise care in money matters. Outgoings will often be high and Pigs will need to watch spending levels. This is no year to be lax or take risks. Financial paperwork too needs prompt and thorough attention. Bureaucratic matters could be troublesome this year. Extra care is advised.

A more positive area concerns personal interests. Pigs will often delight in the way their ideas develop and new possibilities follow on. Whether they are inspired by a project they set themselves, new equipment or activities in their area, they can enjoy some fun and pleasing times. Also, they may discover talents they can take further. They should be receptive to what opens up for them this year.

With a busy lifestyle, they should also give some attention to their own well-being and consider their diet and level of exercise. If they feel either is deficient (or both), they should take advice on the best way to correct this.

The Rat year can see much social activity, with Pigs enjoying their chances to meet up with their friends. Their personal interests can also have a good social element and many Pigs will build some helpful connections over the year.

Where matters of the heart are concerned, Pigs enjoying romance will often find this deepening in significance as the year progresses, while for those currently unattached, someone met by chance could quickly become important. Rat years can, despite their vexations, be personally special.

Similarly, the Rat year will bring both domestic pleasures and demands. With Pigs and family members often experiencing changes in working patterns, there will need to be some adjustment and good cooperation between all. In addition, any problems and pressures should be talked through. Good-hearted discussion and quality time together will be of benefit. Busy though parts of the year will be, shared projects and interests will also be much appreciated, as will travel and some of the more spontaneous occasions that just seem to happen. Rat years are full, varied and sometimes surprising.

Although Pigs may not welcome the pressures and volatility of the year (especially in the workplace), by being prepared to adapt and make the most of what arises, they can still gain much from it. In particular, experience gained now can be built upon in the future. Contacts, friendships and, for some, new love can also be potentially significant. Personal interests and attention to their well-being can also be to Pigs' benefit. This may not be the easiest of years for them, but they can pack an amazing amount into its 12 months and prepare the way for further progress.

Tips for the Year
Be flexible and make the most of situations. This is not a year to be resistant to change but to gain valuable experience. Also, seize any chances to meet others as well as enjoy what this year offers. Good times can be had and important connections formed.

PIG FORTUNES IN THE YEAR OF THE OX

A constructive year ahead. Ox years reward effort and commitment and Pigs are naturally tenacious. They could also benefit from a certain amount of luck and some timely developments. However, in order to make most of the year, they do need to focus on priorities. If they use their time and skills well, they can achieve a lot.

Work prospects are encouraging and in view of the experience many Pigs have recently gained, they may have the chance to take their work to new levels. In some cases, staff movements or new initiatives will create new openings and they will be well placed to benefit. For those on a particular career path, this is a highly favourable year.

Many Pigs will make important progress in their present place of work, but for those who feel there is a lack of opportunity where they are and would welcome change, as well as those seeking work, the Ox year can bring encouraging developments. If they give careful thought to the type of position they would like and take advice, their efforts and commitment will be noticed and lead to many securing what can be an ideal new role.

Another valuable feature of the year will be the way many Pigs will have the chance to develop their skills in new ways. Pigs are enterprising, and by adapting and being willing to learn, they will not only have the opportunity to do more but also help their present standing and future prospects. The solid work ethic of the Ox year suits the Pig's psyche.

Headway made at work will increase the income of many Pigs over the year and some could supplement their earnings through an interest or enterprising idea. However, to make the most of any upturn, Pigs need to remain disciplined. Rather than spend too readily or overindulge, they would do better to plan more major purchases. With careful control, they will often delight in what they acquire, including items for their home, and the way they are able to carry out their plans. In addition, if they are able to add to their savings or pension policy, they could be grateful for this in years to come.

With travel well aspected, Pigs should also consider making provision for a holiday. By giving careful thought to places they would like to visit, they can see some exciting plans taking shape and realize some long-held hopes. And in true Pig style, they will very much enjoy their time away.

Pigs enjoy wide interests and should make the most of their ideas once again this year. Whether setting themselves new challenges, starting projects or just enjoying their favourite pursuits, they can benefit personally as well as reinforce the constructive nature of the year. Some activities will have a good social element too.

Throughout the year, Pigs will have good reason to value their close circle of friends. Not only will they benefit from the encouragement and goodwill they are shown, but whenever they are facing decisions or pondering an idea, they will often be able to call on someone with the expertise to help.

Where matters of the heart are concerned, they do, though, need to be attentive and let any new relationship build up steadily. To rush into a commitment may lead to disappointment. In the Ox year it is better to allow relationships to evolve in their own time and way.

Domestically, this can be a busy and eventful year. Quite a few Pigs will see their family increasing in numbers, whether through birth or marriage, and there could also be some other family news or milestone to commemorate. A few Pigs may decide to relocate and be excited and enthused by the possibilities this opens up. A lot is set to happen and everyone in the Pig household will need to pull together. It is collective effort that will enable much to go forward this year.

Overall, the Ox year is an encouraging one, but Pigs do need to take the initiative and act. This is no year to be half-hearted or let chances slip. Ox years require commitment and solid effort. But Pigs are skilled and redoubtable, and with objectives (and benefits) in mind, they can make the most of the year, making progress in their work, furthering their personal interests and enjoying some special domestic achievements. And the rewards (and pleasures) of the year can be substantial.

Tips for the Year
Ralph Waldo Emerson, born under the Pig sign, once declared, 'Be an opener of doors.' Take action and open some doors! Have some aims in mind and put the effort in. Also, look to develop your skills and interests. They can help both your present and future situation.

PIG FORTUNES IN THE YEAR OF THE TIGER

Change and volatility are features of the Tiger year and Pigs will often be concerned about the fast-moving developments and feel that they are putting in a lot of effort for little in return. Tiger years can be frustrating, but on the positive side, they can also be instructive and bring changes that Pigs can subsequently profit from. In many ways Tiger years can prepare Pigs for future success.

One area which will require particular care is finance. Tiger years can be expensive. In addition to assisting family members, Pigs could also face repair and home maintenance costs. There will be many demands on their resources and they should keep a close watch on spending and, at times, consider reining in certain outgoings. They should also be wary of risky undertakings and exercise care if lending to another person. The terms of any new agreements also need to be checked carefully and financial correspondence dealt with promptly and with Pigs taking advice if required.

The Tiger year's vexations can also apply to work matters. Some Pigs could find their duties and workload affected by bureaucracy or by changes taking place. Also, while Pigs enjoy good working relations with many of those around them, the attitude of a colleague could concern them. In view of this, they need to proceed carefully and avoid distractions. There could also be times when they feel their efforts are going unnoticed or they are not making the headway they feel is their due. But they can take heart. All years have their challenges and these *will* pass and the volatility of the Tiger year *will* eventually settle. Patience can help, and the year will give Pigs the chance to add to their experience and gain greater insights into their capabilities.

For Pigs who are keen to change their position or seeking work, the Tiger year can be challenging. Not only could there be limited vacancies in the type of work they favour, but competition could be fierce. In such cases, these Pigs should widen the scope of what they are prepared to consider as well as think of other ways in which they could use their skills. With resolve, time and effort, they can be rewarded with a position that has potential for the future. For all its difficulties, the Tiger year can be constructive and important for the longer term.

With their genial manner, Pigs enjoy good relations with many of those around them, but in Tiger years they need to be on their guard. A lapse, *faux pas* or inadvertent comment could cause difficulty. In addition, Pigs should remember the saying, 'Walls have ears' and be wary about speaking too freely or passing on information in confidence. Another person could let them down or take advantage of their trusting nature. Pigs, take note.

However, while care is needed, the Tiger year can contain a good mix of things to do, and if any events related to their interests appeal to them, including concerts, sporting fixtures or other gatherings, Pigs should take advantage of them. Tiger years favour activity and some lively social occasions can be enjoyed.

Domestically, these can also be busy times for Pigs. Not only will they be coping with their own commitments but also dealing with family matters. Whether they are assisting loved ones or dealing with the annoyance of failing equipment, there will be many calls on their time and attention. However, while the Tiger year will bring its demands, with cooperation and collective effort, many difficulties can be overcome. In some instances, problems can even be blessings in disguise as equipment is replaced with something better or tasks that have been put off are finally tackled.

There will be a certain spontaneity to some of what happens too. Whether enjoying a trip or treat or unexpected chance to go away, Pigs will find the Tiger year has a capacity to surprise.

Here again, though, it is important that Pigs remain aware and attentive. With much on their mind, there is a risk they could be preoccupied or tetchy. This needs to be watched.

It is also important that with the pressures of the year, Pigs preserve time for recreational pursuits and allow themselves the chance to rest and unwind. With much to do this year, they do need to pay attention to lifestyle balance.

Overall, Tiger years will be challenging ones and Pigs need to be careful and cautious. In money matters in particular, this is a time to be vigilant and thorough. In work situations, Pigs will also face pressures, but by adapting and doing their best, they can demonstrate their skills and extend their experience. In their relations with others, they should be attentive and mindful, as lapses, preoccupation or a possible disagreement could bring difficulties. But by being aware of the year's trickier aspects, Pigs can often steer their way around problems and emerge from the year wiser, more experienced and with skills and ideas to take further, especially in the promising Rabbit year that follows.

Tips for the Year
Be aware and wary. This is no year for risk or personal lapses. Also, be patient and wait for situations to settle and become clear. And preserve some time for your own interests as well as to spend with your loved ones.

PIG FORTUNES IN THE YEAR OF THE RABBIT

Great prospects ahead. With conditions more conducive, Pigs will be better able to focus on their aims and progress in the direction *they* want. This is a year to move forward and enjoy some pleasing results. Rabbit years are encouraging and Pigs will be able to give of their best.

As the Rabbit year begins, Pigs could find it helpful to give some thought to what they would like to achieve over the next 12 months. With some plans in mind, they will not only be able to channel their energies more effectively, but also be more aware of the right opportunities to pursue. Indeed, there is an element of good fortune to the year and Pigs are set to do well. Any who start the year dissatisfied or discontented should very much focus on the now and work towards the improvement they want. With purpose, they can make a lot happen.

At work, the skills and expertise many Pigs have built up can lead to significant opportunities coming their way. Whether in their present place of work or elsewhere, there will be chances to take on a greater and more specialist role. With their often ambitious nature, they will relish reaping the rewards of recent endeavours and moving their career to a new level. However, whenever an opportunity presents itself, they need to act quickly. Speed is of the essence this year and developments can move swiftly.

For Pigs who feel unfulfilled and would welcome a new challenge, as well as those seeking work, the Rabbit year can again bring encouraging developments. Again, chances should be acted on quickly, but by making enquiries, considering various possibilities and taking advantage of the guidance available to them, many of these Pigs will be rewarded with a position which brings the change (and chance) they need. In some cases, considerable adjustment could be involved but, enthused and motivated, many of these Pigs will quickly establish themselves and re-energize their career.

Progress made at work will increase income levels and this can be a financially improved year. However, with no shortage of ideas and plans in mind, Pigs need to remain disciplined in their spending and spend time considering their major purchases and outlays. To rush could lead to less satisfactory choices and, in some cases, incur additional expense. Pigs may also find it to their advantage to review their present situation. If they are able to reduce borrowings, or take advantage of tax incentives to save, or supplement a pension policy, they should do so. With good management, they can help both their present and future situation. However, while they can fare well, if they find themselves in a complex situation or having doubts about a financial matter, it could be worth seeking professional advice. With important implications sometimes being involved, expert guidance could ensure the best decisions are made.

Pigs are keen socializers and this certainly promises to be an active and pleasurable year in that respect. Rabbit years offer fun, variety and plenty to do. Personal interests and work changes can also lead to Pigs meeting new people and forming some good friendships. For any Pigs who start the year in low spirits, the Rabbit year can see a brightening of their situation. New activities, interests and friendships can all bring new joy into their life. This is a year for participation and for making the most of opportunities. For some Pigs, a chance meeting could blossom into a glorious romance. Rabbit years are favourable for Pigs.

Domestically, the year can also be marked by some special times, including, for some, an addition to their family or a wedding. Pigs will be central to much of the activity and their thoughtfulness and ability to drive plans forward can lead to many successful outcomes. However, while enthusiastic, Pigs need to be realistic about what is doable at any one time and spread their activities and commitments out over the year.

Also, if able, they should aim to take a holiday with family members, as everyone will benefit from the rest and the chance to see places new.

Overall, the Rabbit year is an encouraging one for Pigs and they can make good progress. At work, many will take on a greater role and use their strengths to good advantage. Finances can see improvement, although important matters require careful attention, and relations with others can bring much joy in this active and personally rewarding year.

Tips for the Year
Take action and seize your opportunities. This is no year to delay, prevaricate or let chances slip away. Enjoy spending time with others, especially on shared activities. However, if any complex matter concerns you, especially related to finance, seek guidance.

Pig Fortunes in the Year of the Dragon

While some years are progressive and successful and others more challenging, the Dragon year sits in the middle. For Pigs, it can be a reasonable one. While they may not always like the brouhaha which tends to characterize Dragon years, they can often enjoy themselves and make steady progress.

A particularly pleasing aspect of the year that Pigs can look forward to a great many convivial occasions. Whether meeting friends, going to events – and the lively Dragon year will see many – or sharing interests, this is a time when Pigs will find themselves in demand and with a good mix of things to do and enjoy. Pigs have a great capacity for fun and Dragon years will not disappoint them.

As a result of all the activity, Pigs will find their social circle growing quite considerably. With their genial nature, they should make the most of their opportunities to build connections, network and raise their profile. Some of the people they meet this year will not only be taken with their qualities but also have knowledge, expertise or influence which could be useful in the future.

For the unattached, the activities of the year could lead to meeting someone who is destined to become special, while for Pigs currently enjoying romance, the relationship can often deepen in a meaningful way as the year develops.

Home life too can bring much satisfaction, with Pigs often regarding their home as a welcome sanctuary from some of the year's pressures. As a result, they will often be happy to spend time carrying out home improvements, including smartening décor and adding embellishments. Those with gardens could derive a lot of pleasure from spending time out of doors.

However, with Pigs and other family members being involved in decisions and changes over the year, it is important that everyone is prepared to be open and discuss implications and choices and, at times of pressure, rally round. Home life will mean a lot to Pigs this year and there will be special developments to share.

With this being an active year, they should also make sure their personal interests do not get sidelined. These can bring them pleasure, but do need to be scheduled in!

Pigs should also give some thought to their well-being, as this is no year to neglect themselves. Without sufficient care (and a nutritious diet), some Pigs could find themselves susceptible to colds and niggling ailments. If they have any concerns, they should get these checked out.

At work, Dragon years will see much activity, with the Pig's workload often affected by changes. And while they may look askance at some developments (and, to their mind, unnecessary changes), they will need to adjust accordingly. This is no year to close their mind to developments, but to make the best of situations as they are. Some of what occurs could also give rise to training or the chance to gain experience in a different capacity, and Dragon years encourage Pigs both to use and develop their skills and knowledge.

Many Pigs will make steady progress in their present place of work, but for those who decide on change or are seeking work, there can be some interesting possibilities. Dragon years have a capacity to surprise, and openings may be discovered by chance or Pigs may apply for a position on the off-chance and unexpectedly triumph. In the Dragon year, a certain boldness can pay off.

Pigs can also do well financially. Many will enjoy a rise in income and some will also benefit from a bonus or profitable idea. For the more enterprising, this can be a successful time. However, while money may flow into their accounts, with a busy lifestyle and purchases for themselves and their home, outgoings could creep up too. Spending levels should be watched. Also, Pigs should be wary about too many impulse purchases. More time and discipline could lead to better decisions.

Dragon years are active and fast-paced ones and Pigs need to work hard and adjust to keep up. There will be challenges and pressures in their work and many calls upon their time. However, from all the activity will flow developments (some surprising) that they can turn to their advantage. Their personable nature will serve them well, leading to a busy social life and many chances to extend their network of friends and acquaintances. Pigs may not always welcome the pace and pressures of the Dragon year, but there will be good times to be had.

Tips for the Year
Watch developments closely and adapt as required. Keep tabs on your spending and also preserve time for yourself and your interests. In addition, make the most of your social and networking opportunities.

Pig Fortunes in the Year of the Snake

As Chinese signs, Pigs find Snakes mysterious creatures. While they themselves are open and upfront, Snakes are guarded and inclined to secrecy. And in Snake years, Pigs could feel bemused by the twists and turns that take place. They will need to keep their wits about them.

One of the trickier aspects concerns their relations with others. Although Pigs pride themselves on their ability to get on well with many people, the Snake year can bring its problems. At times Pigs could find themselves in a disagreement or be concerned by someone's pettiness or jealousy. There is a risk of minor differences escalating and causing anxiety, and Pigs need to exercise care, especially if they sense any impending difficulty or discord.

Where affairs of the heart are concerned, lapses in personal conduct or differences in outlook could also bring problems and sometimes heartache. In Snake years, Pigs need to be their honourable selves as well as wary of intrigue and possible mischief-making on the part of others. Luckily, they have an excellent understanding of human nature and can often successfully steer their way round the complexities of the year, but the more aware and tactful they can be, the better.

On a social level, they will welcome their chances to go out, especially to events happening locally. Good times can be had, but again, when in company Pigs need to be aware of the viewpoints and sensitivities of others.

In their home life it is important they spend quality time with their loved ones as well as encourage shared activities. This will not only be good for rapport but can also lead to plans going forward and some enjoyable occasions. When differences of opinion do arise (as they will in any year), these need to be addressed rather than left to linger or escalate. This is very much a year for increased mindfulness. Extra effort and input can make a telling difference.

Snake years can also bring their snags, and when tackling practical activities, plenty of time needs to be allowed. In some instances, delays can occur, other matters interrupt proceedings or some undertakings become more wide-ranging than anticipated. With patience and shared effort, however, much can be accomplished.

The Snake year can also bring some good travel opportunities, however, and Pigs should aim to take a holiday with their loved ones. A break from routine can do everyone good. In addition, there could be unexpected windows of opportunity to go away. When able, Pigs and their loved ones should take advantage of them.

Pigs also have an inquisitive nature and enjoy broad interests, and over the year they could become enthused by a new activity or decide to carry out research into an area of interest. By following their ideas through, they will often be pleased with what this opens up. Snake years encourage learning and personal growth.

At work, this can be a busy time, with Pigs facing an often growing workload and having challenging objectives to meet. Snake years can be exacting in this respect, but by knuckling down and focusing on what is required, Pigs will not only demonstrate their skills but also their competence and integrity. It is in difficult times that reputations can be made.

Many Pigs will build on their present position this year, but for those who decide on change or are seeking work, the Snake year can have important developments in store. Here these Pigs' versatility can be used to good advantage. By looking at other ways of using their skills, they may be able to establish themselves in a different capacity. The Snake year encourages personal development, and for quite a few Pigs, the seeds of their future success can be sown now.

In money matters, however, all Pigs need to exercise care. Rush, risk or assumptions about important matters could all lead to problems. In addition, with many outgoings and large outlays likely, Pigs should keep watch on their spending levels and make early provision for forthcoming expenses. This is a year for vigilance and good management.

Snake years can bring their difficult moments and Pigs need to be on their guard. Lapses and risks can lead to problems, which, if not properly handled, could escalate. But Snake years will also encourage Pigs to build on their knowledge and expertise in both their work and their personal interests, and what is learned now can often be successfully built upon in the future. During the year, Pigs' qualities and adroit handling of some matters (and workload) can impress others and the experience they gain will help their prospects. Overall, a challenging year, but not one without benefits *and* future value.

Tips for the Year

Be aware and cautious and tend to matters as they arise. Although you may wish problems and pressures would just go away, they do need to be dealt with rather than left to linger or escalate. Focus on what needs to be done. Also, liaise well with others.

PIG FORTUNES IN THE YEAR OF THE HORSE

Prospects for Pigs are on the up. After the pressures and tribulations of the Snake year, they can look forward to some improved times as well as reap some overdue rewards for previous efforts.

To help get the year off to a positive start, they should give some thought to their aims and objectives for the next 12 months. Having something to work towards will not only help give the year some direction but also underline its constructive nature. This is a time for moving ahead. Any Pigs who have felt held back recently or start the year in low spirits should take action to bring the improvement they desire. With their skills and personable qualities, Pigs have much to offer and their efforts will bear fruit this year.

This can be particularly the case in work matters. With the skills they have acquired and reputation they have built up, Pigs will often find themselves well placed to advance their career. Whether in their existing place of work or elsewhere, they should keep alert for openings and act quickly on any that appeal to them. If they show initiative and highlight their suitability, they can often be offered the chance to take on greater responsibilities over the course of the year. Especially for those on a particular career path, this is a year to progress to the next level. And senior colleagues will often encourage their advance.

For Pigs who feel unfulfilled in their present position, this is also a year for change. By keeping alert for openings and talking to experts and contacts, many can be rewarded with a different position that can re-energize their career.

Similarly, for those seeking work, their resolve, self-belief and persistence can open doors this year and give them chances to build on.

However, while the aspects are favourable, Pigs will need to exert themselves and give their best. To slack or coast could deny them the headway that is possible this year. Pigs, take note and put in the effort. The rewards can be substantial.

Progress made at work can also lead to an increase in income, but Pigs do need to remain disciplined. While anything extra will be welcome, it could quickly be spent, and not always in the best way. To help, Pigs should plan – and save for – key purchases and resist too many impulse buys. They should also be wary of risk or making informal agreements with others. Without care, they could find themselves at a disadvantage or ruing what could be hasty and ill-considered actions. This is a year for careful control and good management of resources.

With work and other activities, Pigs will be kept busy, but it is also important they allow themselves time to enjoy the rewards of their endeavours. Personal interests can not only do them good but also allow them to relax and unwind. Particularly for sport and music enthusiasts, there will be several special occasions to enjoy over the year. Pigs do need to make sure their lifestyle stays balanced.

Also, with an often demanding schedule, they should give some thought to their well-being, including the quality of their diet. To ignore this, or perhaps overindulge, could leave them susceptible to minor or niggling ailments. Pigs, take note.

The Horse year can give rise to a good mix of social occasions and Pigs will once again be popular company. The activities and changes of the year can also lead to meeting others and forming some good friendships.

For the unattached, romantic prospects are good. For some, a chance encounter could quickly become special, while for those who feel a certain relationship was not meant to be, developments could move on swiftly and someone new could enter their life. Horse years can be very eventful for affairs of the heart and many unattached Pigs will revel in the opportunities that come their way.

Domestically, there will also be much activity, especially as Pigs and other family members have work and routine changes to attend to as well as much else besides. To help, it is important everyone pulls together, including in sharing tasks and household activities. Also, plans, especially involving practical activity, need to be kept fluid over the year and fitted in when it is convenient. However, very full though the year may be, there will be successes to enjoy and fine family occasions to look forward to, some of which Pigs themselves will instigate.

In general, the Horse year can be a fine one for Pigs, particularly in encouraging them to make more of their skills and potential. Although an often busy year work-wise, there will be opportunities to move forward. Personal relationships can be special and Pigs will once again be helped by the support and goodwill of those around them. For the unattached, romantic prospects are also good. In this busy year, it is important that Pigs keep their lifestyle in balance and enjoy the rewards of their efforts.

Tips for the Year
Act with determination and make the most of your opportunities. Put in the effort and work hard. Also, seize any chances to meet others and raise your profile. The extra effort can pay off.

PIG FORTUNES IN THE YEAR OF THE GOAT

A pleasing and often special year ahead. Not only will Pigs be pleased with the way many of their plans and activities can be advanced, but their personal life is well aspected.

One of the great abilities of Pigs is their talent for relating to others. They empathize and converse well, but also listen and take note, and this is what many appreciate. Pigs make good friends, and this year they will find themselves in demand.

Their social life can see an increase in activity over the year, with parties, celebrations and times spent with friends all giving rise to many pleasing occasions. Pigs will be on impressive form and their social circle is set to grow. Particularly for those who are keen to meet others, perhaps having moved to a new area or seen a recent change in circumstances, this is a year to go out and engage in what is happening. Local groups could be worth considering, especially with the social opportunities they offer.

For the unattached, the Goat year can have good romantic opportunities. Many Pigs will be enjoying newfound love and those in the early stages of a relationship could see this strengthening over the year. Some Pigs will settle down with their partner or marry. For personal relationships, the Goat year can be very special.

Pigs will also get much contentment from their home life, with individual successes, family news and possible milestones to commemorate. There could be some fun gatherings and special occasions in many a Pig home and their significance will make Pigs proud and happy.

Amid all the activity, Pigs will also give sterling help to those around them and their judgement and empathy will be valued assets. In addition, they will be pleased with the way certain projects develop and with the benefits and additional comforts these bring. Some plans which have been considered for some time could now come to successful fruition.

Pigs will also enjoy shared activities and if particular events or local activities appeal to them (Goat years are strong on arts and culture), they and their family members should aim to go. Not only can these times be fun, but also be good for rapport and strengthening bonds.

Goat years have a strong creative element to them and Pigs will often be enthused by ideas related to their personal interests. By giving time to these and enjoying their talents, they can derive much pleasure from them.

At work this is more a year of consolidation than major advance. Pigs may have been involved in recent change and they should aim to become more established where they are this year and learn about the different aspects of their work. Also, as the inevitable problems and pressures occur, they will have the chance to be more involved and their ideas and resourcefulness will impress many. They should take advantage of any training that is available to them as well as make the most of networking opportunities. With effort and commitment, they can make this a constructive time.

While many Pigs will concentrate on their current role, for those keen to make a change or seeking work, the Goat year can have interesting possibilities in store. By taking note of developments in their industry, these Pigs may uncover chances to develop their skills in new ways. Goat years are encouraging and even if progress is not necessarily substantial, at least initially, what opens up now can nurture the abilities of many Pigs.

Financially, while Pigs could enjoy a modest rise in income, their commitments and active lifestyle will often keep their spending levels high. And although they will enjoy themselves (Pigs have a great capacity for pleasure), they do need to be careful not to make too many impulse buys or be lax with spending. Outgoings could easily creep up during the year and result in economies later. Pigs, take note and remain disciplined.

Overall, though, the Goat year can be a good one for Pigs, especially on a personal level. There will be moments of fun, much to do and share, and for the unattached, romantic prospects are excellent. All Pigs will delight in their good relations with many of those around them and in developing their strengths and putting them to greater use. This is a year of steady and rewarding progress and Pigs will appreciate it.

Tips for the Year
Add to your skills and develop your talents and ideas. Also, value the time you spend with others and be active and engaged.

PIG FORTUNES IN THE YEAR OF THE MONKEY

A reasonable year. While progress can be made, it will require considerable effort. Over the year, Pigs could run into snags and delays. Also, in Monkey years there are many influences in play. Pigs will find that the attitude of other people, their current obligations and factors outside their control can all have a bearing on what they get to do. Monkey years can, in part, be frustrating, but by being watchful and prepared to adapt, Pigs can successfully steer their way round the more awkward aspects and emerge with some important gains to their credit.

This is particularly the case with their work. Although Pigs would prefer to concentrate on their duties, over the year complications can arise and these will need to be dealt with. At times, relations with a colleague may be difficult or routines and long-established practices altered. Some Pigs could find themselves affected by problematic equipment or the slow workings of bureaucracy. This may all be frustrating, but by doing their best and adapting as required, Pigs can find their tenacity leading to some impressive results. Some of the problems and pressures of the year may prove to be opportunities in disguise. The year can certainly highlight the strengths and enterprise of many Pigs.

For Pigs who are looking for work or who decide to move on from their present employer, the year can again hold interesting possibilities. However, with vacancies often attracting many applicants, to be successful these Pigs need to show initiative. Finding out more about the duties involved and emphasizing their experience and suitability can do much to strengthen their chances. In addition, professional organizations and experts could suggest possible ways forward. By putting in the effort, Pigs can make useful headway.

They will, though, need to be careful in money matters. As well as their existing commitments, many could face repair costs or have to replace failing equipment. The Monkey year can bring inconveniences and additional costs. Also, Pigs need to be thorough when involved in any major purchase. The terms and obligations of any agreement should be checked and risks avoided. Over the year Pigs need to be vigilant and budget carefully.

More positively, personal interests can be a source of great pleasure and new ideas and projects particularly inspiring. Creative Pigs could be especially satisfied by what they do. All Pigs will find that by exploring their ideas and talents more fully, they can enjoy some pleasing times *and* results.

They will also delight in the social opportunities of the year. Sometimes their personal interests can have a pleasing social aspect and they may enjoy meeting (and befriending) other enthusiasts. In addition, they will welcome the mix of other activities taking place. The Monkey year can give rise to some lively times.

For the unattached, romantic prospects are good and existing relationships will often develop well, while, for some, new love can be found in fortuitous ways. And when in love, life can be so wonderfully different!

Domestically, the Monkey year can see much activity and there could be the inconvenience of repairs, the rearranging of plans and other niggling problems to contend with. With good co-operation, though, difficulties can be overcome and solutions (including new equipment) found. However, Pigs and other family members will be grappling with many commitments and it is important that these do not impact adversely on home life. To be preoccupied or too involved in other matters could cause difficult moments. With so much happening, it is important there is good communication. Here the Pig's thoughtfulness and inclusive nature can be an asset.

Overall, the Monkey year will have its challenges. Many different influences will be at work and much will need to be considered. Plans and situations will not always be straightforward, but Pigs are redoubtable, and if they proceed carefully, they can enjoy some well-deserved success. In particular, their ideas, creative abilities and enterprising streak can be used to telling effect. Romantic prospects and relations with others can be good, but Pigs do need to ensure that quality time with others does not suffer due to disruption and other pressures. A sometimes tricky year, but it can be a reasonable one.

Tips for the Year
Use and enjoy your creative talents. However, do take note of developing situations and the attitudes of those around you. This is a year to be aware and adapt accordingly. Also, ensure that quality time with your loved ones does not suffer due to the year's busy nature. Join together when dealing with problems, pressures and changing situations.

PIG FORTUNES IN THE YEAR OF THE ROOSTER

This year Pigs have much in their favour, and if they act with determination, they can see many of their plans come to fruition.

With their enquiring and ambitious nature, Pigs attach great importance to self-development and should look to further their knowledge and skills this year. If they feel it could help their prospects, enrolling on a course, setting time aside for study or working towards another qualification could reinforce the positive nature of the year. This is a time for Pigs to invest in themselves.

Work prospects are particularly encouraging and many Pigs will have the chance to take on positions of greater responsibility. Here their reputation and in-house knowledge can often help their progress. Many will benefit from the support of influential colleagues too. Having proved so much in recent times, they can now reap the rewards.

For Pigs who feel prospects are limited where they are, as well as those seeking work, the Rooster year can again hold significant developments. In addition to keeping alert for openings, these Pigs should consider how they themselves would like to develop. By exploring possibilities, they may be able to use their skills in a new way and this will give them the challenge and fresh incentive they need.

However, while the aspects are encouraging, Rooster years are hard taskmasters and not only will much effort and high standards be expected, but Pigs should be wary of distractions. At times office politics or the pettiness of another person could be a cause for concern. This is a year to stay focused on the tasks in hand. By remaining professional, Pigs will be demonstrating their competence and enhancing their reputation.

Progress made at work will increase the income of many Pigs, but again, discipline is required. A busy lifestyle will lead to many outgoings and Pigs will often be tempted by expensive purchases for themselves and their home. Over the year they should watch their spending and ideally keep within their budget. They should also be wary of risk, and if tempted by anything speculative, be aware of the implications. Money can be made this year, but it can also go easily. Pigs, take note and do monitor spending.

Pigs will also take much delight in their home life this year. In addition to their own achievements, other family members could have good news to share, and this could give rise to some pleasing and proud times. Shared interests, domestic projects and trips out can all offer fun too, as well as be good for relationships and rapport. This is a year for joining together.

However, while a lot will go well, when problems and pressures occur (as they do in any year), these need to be talked through and defused. In some cases, flexibility and a more accommodating approach will help. Similarly, when anybody is under stress or tired, additional support and understanding can make an important difference. Home life means much to Pigs and over the year their helpfulness and empathy will often be a valued asset.

The Rooster year will bring social opportunities too. Cultural activities will be highlighted, but there will be a lot happening and Pigs will find themselves in demand. Over the year their social circle can widen appreciably.

For unattached Pigs, a personal interest could lead to meeting someone new, while many of the Pigs currently enjoying romance could decide to settle down together or marry over the year. On a personal level, these can be special times.

Generally, the Rooster year is an encouraging one for Pigs. As the Chinese proverb reminds us, 'You must invest a little to gain a lot,' and in the Rooster year Pigs will be investing in themselves and will stand to gain a lot. Socially, they will enjoy the active nature of the year and their genial nature can make them popular company. However, while this is a generally favourable year, they need to remain disciplined in money matters and aim to address and defuse any difficulties rather than ignore them. If they bear this in mind and take positive action, they can emerge from the year with some well-deserved gains to their credit.

Tips for the Year
Concentrate on your strengths and develop your skills and knowledge. With commitment, you can see a lot following on from what you do. Also, enjoy the social opportunities of the year as well as the chance to develop your interests. If you remain active and engaged, there are many benefits to be had.

PIG FORTUNES IN THE YEAR OF THE DOG

One of the best-known Chinese sayings is, 'A journey of a thousand miles begins with a single step.' In the Dog year, Pigs will take some particularly important steps on their journey. Next year is their own year and what they do now will prepare them for the success they are soon to enjoy. Dog years are constructive ones for them and have important long-term value.

One of the most encouraging features of the year will be the way that Pigs can expand their skills. At work, the training they may be offered or additional responsibilities they may take on will not only give them the chance to do more now, but also open up possibilities for the future. In some instances there could be the chance to fill in for an absent colleague or become involved in new initiatives. By being active and contributing to their workplace, many Pigs can considerably enhance their reputation this year and help both their present and future situation.

Many Pigs will enjoy a considerable widening of their duties in their current place of work, but for those who feel they have accomplished all they can where they are or are seeking work, the Dog year can have important developments in store. Not only should these Pigs actively pursue any openings that appeal to them, but also make contact with professional organizations and employment experts. With additional advice, they will find new doors can open and they may be offered some interesting opportunities. Whether these Pigs choose to remain in the industry and sector they know or to make a change, progress made now – steps taken on the journey – can have great relevance later on. Also, as many will find, things tend to happen for a reason, and even if some applications do not go their way, eventually the chance that is right for them will be given to them.

Also, Pigs enjoy good relations with many people and over the year all Pigs should get themselves even better known, as their personable and enthusiastic nature will often impress.

In addition, the Dog year can bring some fine social opportunities. Not only will Pigs enjoy regular contact with their friends, but their interests can also bring them into contact with others. Any Pigs who are feeling lonely or would like to add something extra to their lifestyle would find joining a local activity group worth considering. In addition, there is a strong sense of altruism in Dog years and some Pigs will give time to causes in which they believe, help other people or assist in their community in some way. Pigs have a generous spirit and their kindness will be appreciated.

For the unattached, the Dog year can also bring exciting times and new romances have the potential to develop in significant ways.

Pigs can also derive much pleasure from their personal interests. Any Pigs who are keen to make more of a particular talent should look to take this further during the year. Study, instruction or a new objective could all inspire them and underline the constructive nature of the present time.

In their home life, Pigs will see high levels of activity, especially as routines and commitments change. At times there will be additional pressures to deal with too, and Pigs will find their ability to keep tabs on so much (and remain calm) of particular value. Their advice and guidance will also be appreciated – more than many may realize. However, while Pigs do much for others, they need to let those around them reciprocate, and when considering possibilities or having concerns, they should speak out. That way, they can benefit from the insights and suggestions of those who know them well.

Financially, Pigs can fare well this year. In addition to an improved income, some could receive some additional funds from another source. This upturn will persuade many to proceed with plans they have been considering for some time. Travel can bring some memorable times this year, although where home projects are concerned, these can have a tendency to mushroom and become more extensive and costly than envisaged. However, by managing their outgoings well, Pigs will be pleased with what they are able to accomplish.

Overall, the Dog year can be a pleasant and constructive one for Pigs. Although progress may be more modest than substantial, what is set in motion now can bear significant fruit. It is an excellent time to build on capabilities as well as give some thought to the future. Plans made, ideas nurtured, skills gained, people met – all can have a bearing on what happens both now and in the near future, with exciting times awaiting in the Pig's own year, which follows.

Tips for the Year
This is a year to invest in yourself. Take any chances to develop your skills and add to your experience. This can not only make the present more interesting and fruitful, but open up possibilities for later on. Also, liaise well with those around you. Not only can there be a lot to enjoy this year, but new friendships and contacts could have future value.

PIG FORTUNES IN THE YEAR OF THE PIG

Pigs play hard and work hard and will do both this year. This is a splendid year for them and will see the realization of some long-held hopes. To make most of it, Pigs do need to act with purpose. However, the aspects are firmly on their side.

Any Pigs who start the year in low spirits should view their own year as the start of a brighter chapter. By concentrating on the now and looking to move forward, they can help initiate the change they desire. Pigs are in the driving seat this year and should act with purpose.

In their personal life, they can look forward to some exciting times. For the unattached and those enjoying romance, Pig years can be very special, with some meeting their soulmate and others settling down together, marrying and/or starting a family. Pig years are often personally significant for Pigs themselves.

The Pig year can also be abuzz with social activity. However, while fun times can be had, Pigs do need to be careful about overindulging. Without care, waistlines could suffer and a succession of long days and late nights might leave Pigs not at their best. In their own year, they should strive for a sensible lifestyle balance.

Home life will also see much activity this year, as well as celebrations. Some Pigs could see an addition to their family, mark a special anniversary and/or relocate. Many hopes can be realized this year. However, Pigs need to be realistic about what is doable at any one time. Enthused and buoyed up, some could overcommit themselves. They should aim to spread their activities out over the year. Also, they need to liaise well with their loved ones, draw on offers of support and listen to suggestions. By working with others, they can achieve far more, and often at a more measured pace too.

Pigs can derive considerable pleasure from their personal interests this year and, if appropriate, should promote any special skills or work they produce. They could meet with an encouraging response. For any Pigs who have let their interests lapse, this is an excellent year to consider starting something new. Their own year offers much possibility.

In recent years Pigs will have seen a lot happen in their work. They will have added to their skills and adjusted to changes in their workplace. In the Pig year, their experience can now pay off and lead to them making substantial advances. Whether benefiting from promotion opportunities where they are or securing a different (and more remunerative) position elsewhere, many Pigs will relish the chance to take their career to a new level. Pigs have many skills to offer and their enthusiasm and expertise are important factors in their progress.

While many Pigs will enjoy success in their existing area of work, for those who desire change or are seeking work, their own year can offer important chances. By actively pursuing any opportunities that appeal to them, they could find their determination and talents rewarded with the chance they have been seeking. There could be considerable adjustments to make and much learning involved, but what opens up now can re-energize the career and prospects of many Pigs. This year, their skills and ambitions can lead to some exciting (and in some cases overdue) rewards.

Progress made at work can also lead to a welcome rise in income. However, to benefit, Pigs will need to manage their money carefully and budget for major outgoings, including accommodation expenses. Also, while keen to go ahead with their plans, they do need to allow time to think them through. Too much haste could lead to misjudgements or unnecessary outlay. Patience would not come amiss and would result in better decisions.

This Pig year marks the end of the cycle of 12 animal years, and for Pigs, it can be a significant one, bringing both personal and career success. If they look back to where they were 12 years ago, they will be amazed (and proud) at all they have achieved. But their own year also offers the chance to look ahead and to give some thought to what they would like to accomplish in the future. The successes of this year are there to be built upon and the Pig year can be a springboard to exciting possibilities ahead.

Tips for the Year

Act with purpose. This is a year to make your strengths and talents count. Also, enjoy it. You have earned the rewards and good times and personal celebrations that are now coming your way. Make the most of what your own year offers.

Thoughts and Words of Pigs

Life is a series of experiences, each one of which makes us bigger, even though sometimes it is hard to realize this.

HENRY FORD

If there is any great secret to success in life, it lies in the ability to put yourself in the other person's place and to see things from his point of view – as well as your own.

HENRY FORD

What's important is that one strives to achieve a goal.

RONALD REAGAN

Sow a thought and you reap an act;
Sow an act and you reap a habit;
Sow a habit and you reap a character;
Sow a character and you reap a destiny.

RALPH WALDO EMERSON

For the resolute and determined there is time and opportunity.

RALPH WALDO EMERSON

All life is an experiment. The more experiments you make, the better.

RALPH WALDO EMERSON

The world makes way for the man who knows where he is going.

RALPH WALDO EMERSON

Appendix

In addition to the key traits of each animal sign, there are also several other factors which influence the make-up and nature of a sign. These include the element (ruling the year of birth) and the ascendant (based on the time of birth), and by considering these you can gain further insights into your own sign and being.

Elements

The five elements, according to Chinese belief, rule the cycles of the universe. Wood burns, producing fire. Fire creates earth, and from earth, metal is mined. And metal melts, like water, which feeds growing wood. From here the cycle begins again.

Each Chinese year is associated with one of these elements. To discover the element influencing your year of birth, check the table of Chinese years at the start of the chapter on your animal sign. Once you have identified your element, you can read what it signifies.

Wood

As a tree grows and reaches out, so those born with the wood element are similarly expansive. Cooperative, with high principles, they are good team members. They are also creative and possess a fine imagination. Reliable, determined and confident, they are good at organizing and like to see projects and commitments through. Many have faith in their abilities, and with good reason.

Fire

Just as flames are intense, so those born with the fire element possess great energy. Dynamic, purposeful and passionate, they are strong-willed and have considerable leadership qualities. They are also good decision-makers and, being keen and active, like to make the most of the moment. They are risk-takers and always heading for new challenges and objectives.

Earth

So much issues from the Earth, and those born with the earth element are known for their stability and practical qualities. They are reliable, can be depended upon and are noted for their common sense. Good organizers, they are also patient and work steadily towards their goals. They think and plan well and their methodical, careful nature leads to many successful outcomes.

Metal

Metal is strong and those born with the metal element are strong-willed and redoubtable. They have a great sense of purpose and focus on aims and objectives. They can be stubborn and independent-minded and rely a lot on their own abilities, but are passionate and firm in their convictions. Forceful, determined and sometimes blunt, they set about their activities with considerable might and faith.

Water

As water flows and adapts its course, those born with the water element are similarly adaptable and responsive. Creative, observant and aware, they tune into people and situations around them. They are intuitive, have questioning minds and generally have a quiet and sedate nature. They empathize, are persuasive and are skilled communicators. Just as flowing water finds a way and wears down obstacles, so they are at getting their own way, slowly, patiently, but oh, so effectively.

Ascendants

As with your element, your ascendant can have a very strong influence on you and give you another insight into your true personality according to Chinese horoscopes.

The hours of the day are named after the 12 animal signs and the sign governing the time you were born is your ascendant. To find your ascendant, look up the time of your birth in the table below, bearing in mind any local time differences in the place you were born.

11 p.m.	to	1 a.m.	The hours of the Rat
1 a.m.	to	3 a.m.	The hours of the Ox
3 a.m.	to	5 a.m.	The hours of the Tiger
5 a.m.	to	7 a.m.	The hours of the Rabbit
7 a.m.	to	9 a.m.	The hours of the Dragon
9 a.m.	to	11 a.m.	The hours of the Snake
11 a.m.	to	1 p.m.	The hours of the Horse
1 p.m.	to	3 p.m.	The hours of the Goat
3 p.m.	to	5 p.m.	The hours of the Monkey
5 p.m.	to	7 p.m.	The hours of the Rooster
7 p.m.	to	9 p.m.	The hours of the Dog
9 p.m.	to	11 p.m.	The hours of the Pig

Rat

The Rat ascendant is likely to make the sign more outgoing, sociable and careful with money. A particularly beneficial influence for those born under the signs of the Rabbit, Horse, Monkey and Pig.

Ox

The Ox ascendant has a restraining, cautionary and steadying influence that many signs will benefit from. This ascendant also promotes self-confidence and willpower and is especially good for those born under the signs of the Tiger, Rabbit and Goat.

Tiger

The Tiger ascendant is a dynamic and stirring influence that makes the sign more outgoing, action-orientated and impulsive. A generally favourable ascendant for the Ox, Tiger, Snake and Horse.

Rabbit

The Rabbit ascendant has a moderating influence, making the sign more reflective, serene and discreet. A particularly beneficial influence for the Rat, Dragon, Monkey and Rooster.

Dragon

The Dragon ascendant gives strength, determination and ambition to the sign. A favourable influence for those born under the signs of the Rabbit, Goat, Monkey and Dog.

Snake

The Snake ascendant can make the sign more reflective, intuitive and self-reliant. A good influence for the Tiger, Goat and Pig.

APPENDIX

Horse

The Horse ascendant will make the sign more adventurous, daring and on some occasions fickle. Generally a beneficial influence for the Rabbit, Snake, Dog and Pig.

Goat

The Goat ascendant will make the sign more tolerant, easy-going and receptive. It could also impart some creative and artistic qualities. An especially good influence for the Ox, Dragon, Snake and Rooster.

Monkey

The Monkey ascendant is likely to impart a delicious sense of humour and fun to the sign. It will make the sign more enterprising and outgoing – a particularly good influence for the Rat, Ox, Snake and Goat.

Rooster

The Rooster ascendant helps to give the sign a lively, outgoing and very methodical manner. Its influence will increase efficiency and is good for the Ox, Tiger, Rabbit and Horse.

Dog

The Dog ascendant makes the sign more reasonable and fair-minded and gives an added sense of loyalty. A very good ascendant for the Tiger, Dragon and Goat.

Pig

The Pig ascendant can make the sign more sociable and self-indulgent. It is also a caring influence and one that can make the sign want to help others. A good ascendant for the Dragon and Monkey.

A Final Word

I hope that having read about your sign and prospects you will have been alerted to the many possibilities available to you, whatever the year.

Whether you are making more of your qualities and skills or taking advantage of the chances that await you in the various years, as you venture forward, believe in the power and potential that lie within you.

You are indeed special and have a valuable part to play in the world.

Good luck and good fortune.

Neil Somerville